GENEROSITY AND JEALOUSY

GENEROSITY
AND JEALOUSY

The Swat Pukhtun of
Northern Pakistan

CHARLES LINDHOLM

This book has been published with the assistance of a
grant from the National Endowment for the Humanities.

Columbia University Press
New York   1982

Library of Congress Cataloging in Publication Data

Lindholm, Charles, 1946–
   Generosity and jealousy.

   Includes bibliographical references and
index.
   1. Pushtuns—Social life and customs.
2. Swāt Kohistan (Pakistan)—Social life and
customs. I. Title.
DS380.P8L56   954.9'12   82-1120
ISBN 0-231-05398-3 (cloth)   AACR2
      0-231-05399-1 (paper)

Columbia University Press
New York   Guildford, Surrey

Clothbound editions of Columbia University Press books are Smyth-
sewn and printed on permanent and durable acid-free paper.

Book design by Kenneth Venezio.

To the children of Swat

Contents

Acknowledgments

THE writing of these acknowledgments is a great pleasure for me, since it calls to mind the many people whose kindness, interested attention, and hard work have helped to make this book possible.

The first people I would like to thank are Muhammad Zaman Khan and his wife, Qajira Khana, who were hosts, friends, and surrogate family for myself, my wife, and our daughter during our stay in Swat. They accepted us into their household with warmth and affection that can never be forgotten. They shared everything in their lives with us, and taught us a great deal. Zaman was also my researcher, and a marvelous and inquisitive investigator into his own culture. I often felt that he was the anthropologist, while I was a backward student. Zaman always joked that he wanted the "P" of my Ph.d. degree, and I am glad to publicly award it to him here.

Other people in Swat who were of invaluable assistance included Muhammad Qamar Khan, Zaman's father, a true gentleman, and my instructor both in Pukhto and in local history; Shad Muhammad Khan, Zaman's younger half-brother, a lawyer of note, and a wonderful singer and story-teller; Dr. Sher Muhammad Khan, Zaman's elder half-brother, who was able to bring his own considerable cross-cultural experience to bear on my research; Muhammad Qawi Khan, one of Zaman's patri-lateral cousins, a teacher and man of intelligence, sought after by his fellow villagers as a peacemaker; and, finally, Abdul Sattar Khan, Zaman's sister's son, whose conscientious work gave the village survey a high degree of reliability. There were many others who helped. The villagers, and the people of Swat in general, were always honest and straightforward in answering my many tedious questions. They were invariably patient, hospitable, and kind to me and my family, despite our strangeness and our status as non-Muslims. They accepted us with a tolerance that reflects their own justified pride in themselves and their culture. Their world is a hard one, and they live in it with a rough integrity I came to admire greatly. Sometimes, I was honored by being given the greatest of compliments, that I was "like a Pukhtun." I can think of no greater compliment to pay in return to the people of Swat. They are real Pukhtun.

But hospitality in Pakistan is not the sole property of Pukhtuns. Our American friends in Islamabad, Drs. Sherry Plunkett and Ruth Schmidt Plunkett, and Dr. Charles Boewe and his wife Mary, were always more than kind. The bureaucracy of Pakistan deserves credit as well for permitting me to do my work without interference.

In academia, I had the great advantage of experiencing the stimulating and open-minded atmosphere at Columbia University. My major advisor and influence has been Professor Abraham Rosman, whose generous encouragement of new ideas is combined with a scholarly attention to detail. His help in developing this work is inestimable. I would also like to thank Paula Rubel and Robert Murphy who, from their different viewpoints, added rigor to my argument. Harvey Pitkin gave me linguistic training and, as a result, a method of analysis. Richard Christie and Stephen Rittenberg helped me avoid egregious errors in either psychology or history, respectively. Thanks are due to Howard Wriggins, who took time from his duties as ambassador in Sri Lanka to press me to write, to Conrad Arensberg for his valuable suggestions on the Durkheimian viewpoint, and to Joan Vincent for her advice on social structure. Of course, only I am responsible for any mistakes.

All figures and maps in this book were drawn by Cherry Lindholm. She took all of the photographs as well. Stephen Senigo redrew the village map and reduced it photographically. I am very grateful for their work.

None of the research could have been done without funding. My original stay in Swat was sponsored by the Henry Evans Traveling Fellowship awarded by Columbia University. My later visit was funded by a Fulbright-Hayes Predoctoral Research Fellowship and a National Science Foundation award. I would like to express my appreciation to these institutions.

I would also like to express my appreciation to the staff at Columbia University Press, who worked hard to publish this book. I would especially like to thank Jennifer Crewe for her sympathetic editing, Kenneth Venezio for his help in design, and Charles Webel, whose suggestions greatly strengthened the book's conclusion.

Having acknowledged my debts to informants, to the scholarly world, to funding agencies and publishers, I am happy to acknowledge my deepest gratitude to my wife Cherry, and our daughter Michelle, for their help, their courage, and their forbearance. They followed me into a remote and potentially dangerous region, never complained, and entered into my work with spirit. Without them, I could never have had any insight into the private worlds of women, nor could my relations with men have been so intimate. They gave me a base and an identity. Besides the photos, which breathe life into the book, and besides drawing all the figures and maps, Cherry also contributed a great deal to many of the theoretical discussions, especially those concerned with child-raising, sex roles, and personality. If Zaman gets the "P" of my Ph.d., Cherry should get the "h."

Introduction

A scientific law is a statement (an assertion, a judgement, or a proposition) which possesses certain characteristics: (1) it is true only under specific conditions; (2) under these conditions it is true at all times and in all cases without any exceptions whatsoever (the exception which proves the rule is a dialectical nonsense); (3) the conditions under which such a statement is true are never fully realized in reality but only partly or approximately. So it cannot be asserted literally that scientific laws are detectable in the reality under study (discovered); they are thought up (invented) on the basis of the study of experimental data calculated in such a way that they can afterwards be used to derive new judgements from the given judgements about reality (including use for prediction) by the route of pure logic. The laws of science themselves can neither be refuted nor confirmed empirically. They can be justified or not depending on how well or how badly they fulfil the role indicated above. (Zinoviev 1979:38)

Man's behaviour is very variable, it is true, but not infinitely so; and, though cultural differences are great, certain commonalities can be discerned. (Bowlby 1969:39)

THIS book is based on my experiences as a guest, as a friend, and as a professional anthropologist in the village of "Shin Bagh" (the name is fictitious), among the Yusufzai Pukhtun of Swat in Pakistan's mountainous North-West Frontier Province.

The Yusufzai are considered famous by anthropologists because of Fredrik Barth's magnificent work with them three decades ago, work which culminated in the publication of his classic monograph *Political Leadership among Swat Pathans* (1965). But when I first went to Swat in 1969 I had never heard of Barth or of the Pukhtun (Pathan is the British term). I had recently received my B.A. degree from Columbia after the riots of 1968. My major subjects were English and Oriental studies, but my real interests were drawing pictures and writing fiction, and I had been lucky enough to win an award from Columbia University for achievement in the arts. This award, the Henry Evans Traveling Fellowship, was a grant of $4,000 to be used specifically, as its name suggests, for travel. So I traveled. I had failed my draft test, I was disgusted by America's involvement in Vietnam, and I was anxious to test myself and to see the world.

Thinking I would end up in Japan and study Japanese brush technique, I slowly meandered through Turkey, Iran, and Afghanistan. By the time I reached Swat, which was then an independent state within Pakistan, having its own king (the Wali) and its own laws, I was ready for a rest. Swat is a beautiful place, a green valley nestled in the mountains. The climate was invigorating, and the people were friendly, but not intrusive. I settled into a hotel in the capital of Saidu Sherif to do some drawings.

It was there that I happened to meet Muhammad Zaman Khan, who was to be my friend, my host and, later, my assistant. In his late twenties, slim and dark, Zaman looked forbidding when his face was in repose, but he loved to joke and laugh. His English was fairly good, he was extremely open and intelligent and, like me, he was away from home and looking for a friend. He and his young wife, Qajira Khana, had left his father's household in Northern Swat to seek their fortune in Saidu, but Zaman hated being an employee. He was, he told me, a real khan, or noble, and working as a servant was demeaning to him. Before long, he decided to return to his village to see if he could reestablish good relations with his father. I could come with him, he said, and stay in the men's house, called the *hujera*. I was ready for adventure, I liked Zaman, and so I went.

I stayed in the village, a densely packed cluster of 300 houses and 2,000 people, which I have called Shin Bagh (meaning, appropriately, Green Garden), for three months. I was enchanted by the village, though also somewhat frightened. I understood little of what I saw and heard, and relied on Zaman to tell me the proper way to behave. We became very close in a way I had never experienced before. The relationship was not sexual, but there was a romance about it, a strong feeling quite unlike male friendships in the West.

After my fellowship money ran out, I left the village and flew back to America, but I didn't want to stay in the United States. I was able to get some backers for a venture of importing antiquities from Pakistan. This enterprise was no great success—I was only able to repay my backers— but it did allow me to go back to Shin Bagh for five months. Zaman had managed to convince his father to give him land for a house of his own, and we hired some men to build what Zaman called a "bungalow" for me to live in. The bungalow consisted of a couple of concrete rooms gaily painted in pink, blue, and yellow. It was perched atop Zaman's own house and included a verandah overlooking his garden. His wife kept her privacy and did the cooking in the main courtyard which was just to the north of the bungalow and connected to it through steps and a side door. I never saw her during my first two stays in Swat except once, when I was delirious from a high fever, and she came up to see her husband's friend before he died. Luckily, I was able to get some antibiotics and survived the fever.

Although invisible, Qajira Khana was a strong presence in the compound. I often heard her talking, scolding, and giving orders in her powerful voice. Zaman told me that she was from a great family and that she was highly intelligent. In fact, she was one of the only women in the village who could read, though she could not write. Zaman respected her judgment and asked her advice on business matters, but he also feared her sharp tongue, and there were some tumultuous fights during my stay. They had two children, both beautiful girls.

I returned again to the United States in 1971 after five months in the village. I had learned from my business venture that I was no business-man, and I felt at a loose end. It was my wife Cherry who convinced me to go back to school, and in 1972 I entered the Graduate Department of Anthropology at Columbia. Through my studies, I hoped I might be able to return to Swat again to see Zaman and to do fieldwork. I also hoped that anthropology could help me understand Pukhtun culture, since much of what I had seen and experienced seemed chaotic and unintelligible.

For a time, it looked as if my dream of returning to Swat would not come true, since Pakistan was keeping researchers out of the volatile North-West Frontier Province. My requests were rejected several times, but finally permission was given, and in 1977 I set off with my wife and twelve-year-old daughter to Swat. Zaman had kept in constant touch with me through letters, and was anxiously awaiting us. The bungalow had been put in good repair, he wrote. He had purchased many chickens for feasting and had even installed what he called a "flush system" for our convenience.

There is an indefinable change in atmosphere when the traveler crosses the Indus River at the Attock Bridge and enters the North-West Frontier Province, home of the Pukhtun. Perhaps it is the romantic history of the region, or perhaps it is the proud bearing of the people by the wayside, but somehow the air lightens and there is a sense of freedom. Cherry and Michelle felt it as well. The excitement carried us through our trip into Swat over the Malakand Pass with our packed trunks rattling around in the back of the little taxi and vertigo threatening at every turn.

Zaman and his cousin Qawi Bacha met us in Saidu to escort us north to Shin Bagh. His face was more seamed and leathery than the last time I'd seen him, but otherwise Zaman looked exactly the same. Swat itself had also aged. Many trees were cut down and the hills were more denuded than ever, but otherwise almost everything was no different than it had been. The village had only changed a bit as well. Electrical lines, which often failed, provided light and heat to a fortunate few. New shops had opened and new compounds were being built. But the narrow winding lanes, the bulging grey stone walls, the smell of smoke and animals, the hubbub and the crowding—all were as they had been before. The new only served to direct my attention to the old. I felt as though I had returned home.

We set ourselves up in the bungalow, where the flush system proved to involve a hole in the floor and buckets of water brought from the well below. Cherry and Michelle immediately went down to meet Qajira and the other women. Qajira greeted them with open arms and affection. Cherry was now her sister, she said, as Zaman translated, and Michelle was her eldest daughter. The other women were also approving, though

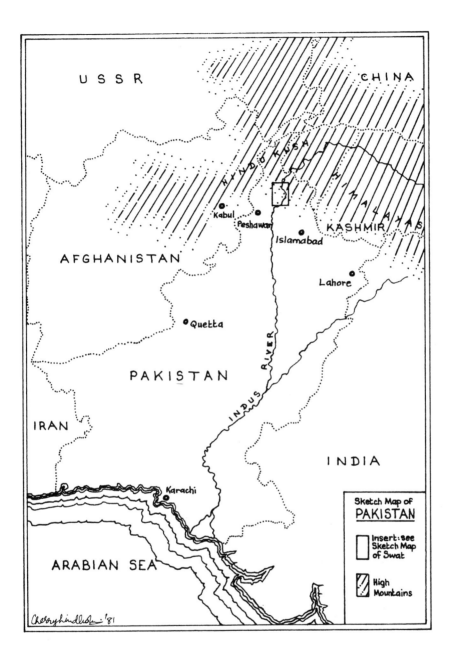

USSR

CHINA

HINDU KUSH

HIMALAYAS

Kabul

Peshawar

Islamabad

KASHMIR

AFGHANISTAN

Lahore

Quetta

INDUS RIVER

PAKISTAN

IRAN

INDIA

Karachi

ARABIAN SEA

Cherryhindlish '81

Sketch Map of
PAKISTAN

Insert: see
Sketch Map
of Swat

High
Mountains

Landscape in Lower Swat. (All photographs by Cherry Lindholm.)

they agreed that the American women had a poor jewelry collection. This did not stop one of the women from appropriating a bracelet of Michelle's and taking it home. Zaman had to send one of his daughters over to get it back.

Zaman now had five daughters, one an infant, and one son called Drun Bacha, or "heavy king." He also had two daughters by a second wife, but she and her children were not coresident. Frightened by Qajira's lashing tongue, she had fled back to her father's house, where she remained during our entire stay. We never met her or her children.

With the household set up, I was ready to begin my work. Zaman worked days as representative for a tobacco company, but he had plenty of free time to talk with me. He was what anthropologists always look for, that is, a gifted and intelligent informant. He had traveled in his early years, and had spent some time in Karachi. His education was good, and he had even taken a year of college in Peshawar (the major city of the Frontier). But he was, and is, very much a man of the village. His experience and his own quick curiosity made him an ideal research assistant, and we spent many long hours talking about everything under the sun, planning research strategies, interviewing village elders, collecting survey material, giving attitude tests to schoolchildren, discussing politics in the men's house, drawing maps, and generally following our ideas wherever they might lead. His creativity and energy were boundless and I must admit that toward the end of the fieldwork, when I was exhausted and weak from fever and malnutrition, I could no longer follow his lead.

We traveled about during the nine months we stayed in the village. We visited Qajira's home, a tiny and remote hamlet along the Arnwai River where even the veneer of modernity had not yet appeared. We sat in the men's houses of the great khans of Badera, who were Zaman's allies, and of Durushkhela, who were his traditional enemies. We went to Kohistan, further north, where we talked to the red-bearded men who were his great-grandmother's people. Zaman and I even went to the neighboring region of Dir, riding his tiny motorbike through a terrible hailstorm and flood. But primarily we remained in Shin Bagh, since I was hoping to get to know a small part of the society well rather than knowing a great deal of it superficially.

My situation was unique. No outsider, so far as I know, has ever lived inside a Pukhtun household; the rules of purdah, or female seclusion, are simply too strict. But having my own family along made a great difference in my relationship with Qajira Khana and Zaman. I had entrusted the women in my family to their care, and if Cherry was Qajira's sister, then I was her brother, and she need no longer hide from me. Besides Qajira, there were also the children, who were always underfoot and always ready to talk. And then there were the men who came by almost every night to sit, listen to the radio, perhaps smoke some *charas* (the local intoxicant, a form of hashish), and gossip. These were Zaman's allies, brothers, and dependents, who encompassed a spectrum of the village men, from laborer to carpenter to small farmer to khan. First among them was Shad Muhammad Khan, Zaman's younger half brother, who also spoke English and worked as a lawyer. Zaman's cousin and main ally, Muhammad Qawi Bacha, was feuding with Shad, and only appeared when Shad was absent, but we often visited him in his father's *hujera*. Qawi had an M.A. in economics and spoke excellent English.

These educated men were among my main informants, but if I wanted to talk to elders and to the ordinary people, who visited us and whom I saw on the street, I had to learn Pukhto. I had an extremely good grammar (Chavarria-Aguilar 1962) of the language, which sounds like a lovely cross between French and German without the disconcerting nasals of Urdu, but no English—Pukhto dictionary of any quality exists. So while Zaman was away working I spent hours trying out my Pukhto with the children, with Qajira, and with anyone who would listen. But my best teacher was Zaman's father, Muhammad Qamar Khan, a great man in the valley who came by almost daily to talk to me and to see Cherry. She gave him aspirin, dressed his minor wounds, and was charmed by his courtly manners. It was Qamar Khan's acceptance of us that really made us a part of the village, and it was his knowledge of the past which informs a great deal of my work.

In my own eyes, my role in Shin Bagh was as a researcher. But for the villagers, I was Zaman's friend; a friend who had proven his loyalty by returning twice from America, the land of gold, and by placing his own women under Zaman's care. These were all seen as tokens of friendship, as they are, but no other motive was attributed to me, although I tried to explain that my career as an anthropologist depended on my work in the village. As far as the villagers could see, however, my so-called work consisted mainly of lolling about and gossiping. But then, this is the proper activity for a khan, and I had naturally been assimilated into the khan group. My talk was certainly less astute than that of the other men, and my anthropological questions were tedious (though the older men seemed to relish my appearance, because they could then recount their days of glory), but generally I was not regarded as anyone very disruptive or strange. No one ever discussed the book I was to write, except to say in jest, "tell that we are a great people, the best people." Nor was any curiosity ever shown about us or our background, save for an occasional inquiry over Western burial practices or a question whether, in infidel America, the sun still rose in the east.

My role was therefore structured neither by my position as researcher, nor even by my origin in the wealthy and powerful West. The Pukhtun, totally convinced of the superiority of their own way of life, may admit that the British (and, by extension, the Americans) are very clever, and that the technical inventions of the West are desirable, but Pukhtun pride still comes first. Never subdued for long by any invader, the Yusufzai of Shin Bagh do not suffer from the obsequiousness cultivated by so many colonized peoples. They take the visitor as they find him, and offer respect or contempt according to the personal relationship that develops.

In my case, the friendship between myself and Zaman Khan was the main element in determining the attitudes of others toward me. It is the source of both the strengths and the weaknesses of my field data. Those who have done research in areas with more history of centralization, with recent past experiences of colonization, or with long-established peasant populations, may find my experience very different from theirs. Because I was Zaman's friend, I was under certain constraints in my work. I could not visit people on my own. This would be regarded by Zaman and by the village as an insult to the friendship. Nor could I visit with many people in the village who were Zaman's enemies. If I asked to visit with such a person, it was awkward for Zaman's honor. Furthermore, even with those I did visit, certain questions about property, profits, and so forth, beloved by data-hungry anthropologists, were considered in bad taste, and would not only receive evasive answers, but would also embarrass Zaman Khan who, as my host, was responsible for my good behavior. It was impossible to offset this reticence by the expedient of going through land records, since there are no records to go through. The tax collector and land surveyor, figures dear to the historian and to no one else, have not yet made their mark in Upper Swat.

Finally, among the Pukhtun it is simply not possible to sit passively and observe, counting, for example, the orders given by a mother to a child. Interaction is obligatory, and rude behavior, even for the sake of science, is considered quite intolerable. The Pukhtun demand that they be recognized and confronted as individuals; they affirm their humanity by respecting the personal integrity of others, and expect the same respect in return. In a very real sense, the outsider is not long allowed to retain his observer status; he must participate, follow the rules of etiquette, or else risk losing the regard of the people who are his only source of information.

Personally, the proud attitude of the Pukhtun has always greatly appealed to me. At the same time, I find the overtly instrumental attitude of some modern anthropologists toward their informants morally repugnant. Also, my friendship with Zaman was prior to and lay beneath the entire fieldwork enterprise. It was difficult enough to change our relation from one of elder—younger to the more coequal relation of main informant—researcher. I did not want to strain the friendship even more by flouting rules that I knew were important to Zaman. Because of these factors, I did not do many of the things often deemed necessary for good research. I did not conduct door-to-door census-taking; I did not interview all the village leaders; I did not measure fields or try to find out exactly how much grain is harvested; nor could I collect accurate data on rents or daily consumption. Statistics, in general, are in short supply in my work, and I am afraid that I do not have the ability to justify all my statements numerically. This is regrettable, no doubt, and will make my work suspect, though I would follow DuBois when she says "it seems sadly true that the most theoretically elegant and simultaneously verifiable problems are humanly the least meaningful" (1961:xxvi). Furthermore, it seems to me that statistics themselves, though concrete in aspect, are too often very malleable in content.

Nonetheless, I did make a strong effort to collect statistical information on the village, and to draw an accurate map of Shin Bagh as well (see appendix A for some of the results). This project had a very special methodology due to the problems of working among Pukhtun. It was obviously impossible for me to keep my position in the village and still have a census done by interviewing each family. Instead, I selected five reliable men who were Zaman's allies from every section of the village. These men supplied me with survey data and cooperated in drawing the map. Cross-checking was done between informants, and the survey material was also cross-checked with the map. It is, of course, impossible to say whether this method was accurate, but all cross-checking proved remarkably consistent in most areas. Each informant had lived in his section all his life and could casually check with others over any material he did not know. The survey, in my opinion, is closer to the truth than material collected by more conventional methods. It is axiomatic that anthropologists must always work within the context they are given, and the context of the Pukhtun demanded indirect techniques.

But if doing research in Shin Bagh had methodological disadvantages (disadvantages which, I admit, suited my own character), it also had great advantages. Because the kind of relationship I had with Zaman is highly valued in Pukhtun culture, people were receptive and forthcoming. Also, Zaman's own respected position rubbed off on me, and his allies and relatives were always most helpful. Even more important, the position of my family as adopted members of the household made us part of an ongoing set of intimate social relations. Disallowed the distancing usually permitted outsiders, we were instead obliged to participate in the often tedious, sometimes tumultuous, round of daily life. We mediated disputes and dispensed medicine. Cherry acted her role as Qajira's elder sister, and Michelle immersed herself (sometimes to excess) in the authority of eldest daughter. We became embroiled in schemes of various sorts and learned about political manipulation first hand. We saw and experienced the emotional life of the hidden world of the compound; we were with the actors when the dramas of power, violence, anger, love, and even death were played out. Emotionally, it was difficult for all of us, but the experience was deep and rewarding. The richness of the material, such as it is, derives from this intimate and demanding family relationship which we were privileged to share.

But, if the central data come from interaction with a small circle of people, does this make the book on which it is based valid? This is a reasonable question, and one which can only be answered conclusively by further fieldwork. Let me note, however, that the circle was not so small as it may seem. Certainly our most intense and personal experiences were within our own compound, but we had access to other households as well. The gossip of women, in particular, is always concerned with household happenings, and both Cherry and Michelle (who both spoke good Pukhto) were well informed by the women's network as to local goings-on. As non-Muslims, they did not have to keep purdah, while as women they were welcome to visit women's quarters, and thus were freer to move from house to house than I, since I could not penetrate purdah except in my own compound with Qajira. They therefore were able to verify that all households were much alike. Further validation came from the stories of the men, whose tales of family strife and political manipulation were woefully repetitious. From my experience, the proverb that "the Pukhtun are like rain-sown wheat; they all came up at the same time; they are all the same" appears to be fairly accurate. My experience also taught me that the correspondence between speech and act is exact among the Pukhtun, as Akbar Ahmed notes for the neighboring Mahmund: "A remarkable sociological characteristic is the almost poker-faced truthfulness of the tribesmen. Facts about sensitive issues that were difficult to accept at face value because of their startling frankness were repeatedly cross-checked and found to be accurate" (1980:21). Hearsay, then, could be accepted with more readiness than in other cultures, where a discrepancy between word and deed is often characteristic.

Because of the remarkable similarity of life for all the villagers, and because of the strong cultural pressure for truthfulness, I feel it is fair to generalize from the experiences my family and I had in the village. I know already that some elite westernized Pukhtun will disagree with the portrait to be given here. I can only say that they will have to live as anthropologists, not as rulers, in a village, with the people, to judge whether my work is accurate. Generalizing is also under a cloud in anthropology itself at the moment, in a quite understandable reaction against overly abstract formulations of earlier theorists. Conflict, deviance, and charting the course of individual networks are current topics of interest in anthropology now. But this is not the thrust of my work. Instead of looking at variation and at the manipulations of individuals, I have, in a rather old-fashioned way, concerned myself with norms and first principles of action. As a result, I have presented what some may see as an overly idealized normative view of Pukhtun society.

My reasons for proceeding in this manner are twofold. In the first place, as I have intimated, Pukhtun people adhere extremely closely to their social code, as Ahmed says, "young or old, rich or poor, the Pukhtun . . . upholds his social values by the prevalent Pukhtun ideology" (1980:17), and "it is remarkable . . . how similar the ideological model is to the actual immediate model of empirically observed social behavior and organization" (1980:89). Given a situation such as I will describe in Swat where social structure, genealogy, morality, political action, and economic life are all governed by the same set of rules, it is natural for me to focus on the norms which, in actual fact, govern the daily lives of Pukhtun men and women. Within this culture, variation is of far less importance than it might be in a less highly compacted social structure.

Second, I have a theoretical propensity for looking at structure and pattern. My study at Columbia centered around the theories of Lévi-Strauss, whose work may have many faults, but who at least has made an attempt to lift anthropology from the fascinating but sterile depths of pure description. The idea that social life does indeed have an underlying organization is at the root of anthropology, and I think the first job of the anthropologist is to outline that order and reveal the rules which give it form. Only then can an emphasis be placed on variation, and, more importantly, only then can comparisons be ventured and broader hypotheses essayed. Finally, only with an idea of the principles which underpin activity can contradiction be exposed.

This brings me to a discussion of the method I have employed, both in the collection of data and in the writing of this book. There are really two ways to do anthropological research. The first, greatly favored by funding agencies because of its concrete look, is to have a ready-made problem in mind before even beginning work. For example, it might be hypothesized that women's roles in a village will change in a certain way due to the introduction of irrigation technology. Two villages, one with irrigation and one without, would then be studied and compared. This style of research is valuable, but it is most valuable when the society being studied is already well understood and when there is a technical transformation in progress. In a little-known culture, however, a preselected problem poses the paradox of assuming what is to be discovered before research really begins. The fieldworker may end by ignoring complexities and subtleties of great interest because of dogged adherence to an increasingly irrelevant research plan.

The second method looks easier, but is actually more difficult. Instead of postulating a restrictive hypothesis (except for the benefit of funding agencies) the fieldworker learns the culture much as a linguist learns a language. Flexibility and responsiveness to the unexpected is all-important in this approach, which assumes that any and all data are potentially significant. In the first stages of work, the researcher is like a tape recorder which is always on, collecting an enormous mass of data which must be looked over, analyzed, and coded for coherence. Like the linguist, the anthropologist must keep an open and willing mind which allows his informants freedom and which allows the researcher the possibility of discovering that which he did not know existed. The relation between fieldworker and informant is not just a channel for eliciting raw data; their dialectic is creative, opening (sometimes) an unexpected avenue for discourse.

Like the linguist, who knows that the sounds, words, and sentences of any language must follow some basic rules, the anthropologist also seeks to formulate rules and patterns which account for his data and his own observances. As patterns begin to emerge, questioning can become more pointed, observation more particular. Like a scientist who is looking at a new phenomenon, the anthropologist does not assume that he knows a priori the general properties of the culture. Instead, he studies it in context and seeks to discover the pattern of relations which gives it form. The underlying assumption, of course, is that the data does have a coherent structure. The anthropologist, in his creative relation to the culture, uncovers the implicit form in the mass of information, much as a sculptor uncovers the form in a block of stone.

The test of the worth of a sculpture is in its aesthetic appeal, its ability to condense the artist's experience into a meaningful and evocative symbol. The test of anthropological research is also found in its capacity for condensation and revelation, but what is revealed is an abstract set of principles. These principles purport to explain parsimoniously and thus unite the myriad relations and exchanges, the attitudes and items, which make up the seeming disorder of daily life in any culture. The ambition of structural analysis, as stated by Lévi-Strauss, is nothing less than the comprehensive exposure of the hidden but fundamental rules of form which lie beneath the surface of society. Explicitly, such an effort strives to be all-encompassing, to bring the entire repertoire of a culture under the aegis of the postulated rules.

In Swat, the rules derive from a few basic principles. Like many Middle Eastern peoples, the Pukhtun are organized in what is technically termed an acephalous patrilineal segmentary system. What this shorthand designation means is very specific and very far-reaching. First, the system does not have centralization, developed hierarchies, or even any accepted leaders. It is indeed "headless." Second, descent is traced only through the father's line. Individuals have their property rights and gain their social identity through membership in a lineage traced through the father, the father's father, the father's father's father, and so on, back in theory to an original ancestor who is the mythical progenitor of all Pukhtun. All lineages merge at this ultimate level, but proliferate on the ground as subdivisions occur in every generation. The Swatis call lineages *khels,* and each person can name at least three or four ever more inclusive *khels* of which he or she is a member. For example, a whole region may be dominated by descendants of Ahmad. They are the Ahmad *khel.* Ahmad's sons divided the region between them, and descendants of each son rule a village. One son is Rahman, and his descendants are Rahman *Khel.* In the Rahman *Khel* village, further subdivisions have taken place, and each of Rahman's sons has founded his own smaller *khel.* When one asks a Pukhtun his name, he gives not only his own given name, but also the name of one or two of the *khels* to which he belongs. In Swat, all Pukhtun look back to their remote ancestor Yusuf, and call themselves Yusufzai (*zai* means "place" and is used instead of *khel* to designate descendants of very distant ancestors), and then further subdivide themselves into regions, villages, sections of villages, and subsections of villages.

These divisions are of more than purely genealogical interest. The next property of this system is that political and economic relations are structured by and through the genealogy. This is done through the principle of "complementary opposition" which is implicit in segmentation. Each lineage or *khel* stands in a relation of opposition to its closest neighbor of an equal level. Thus the different sections of a village are in opposition, but will unite should they be threatened by another village. The principle has been succinctly stated in the Arab proverb, "I against my brother, my brother and I against our [patrilineal] cousin, my brother, my [patrilineal] cousin and I against the world."

Science aims to generate abstractions, to seek simplicity and clarity, and to attempt generality. The formal principles of the segmentary system, modified in actual activity, allow for scientific statements. My effort in this book is to show that society in Swat expresses, in every aspect, the relations implied by the segmentary system. It will be demonstrated that this system not only structures political, economic, and social life, not only organizes people spatially, but also provides a worldview, pervades child raising, forms values, and permeates all possible spheres of human activity and thought.

Although most of the book seeks to reveal the centrality of segmentary principles in Swat, the main argument lies in quite another direction. To prepare for that argument, I would like to return to the methods of the linguist or the scientist. Each assumes that what he or she is studying has a certain coherence and is governed by a set of rules. These rules can be teased out through observation, experiment, and comparison. But what is exciting is the appearence of something unexpected, something which does not fit the apparent pattern, something which demands a new explanation. Contradiction is the real stuff of discovery.

My training was not only in Lévi-Straussian structuralism. I also had an interest in Marx and the French school of structural Marxism. Since I had read as well in Freud and in the critical theory of the Frankfurt School, I was prepared to look for contradiction in my analysis. Some contradictions, for instance the contradiction between an ideology of equality and the reality of class distinction, were expected, as was the contradiction between an intruding money economy and a traditional value structure. These offered problems for meaningful work, but I felt that I had nothing really new to say on these subjects, which have been worn to death in recent years.

For a long time, even after I had completed my fieldwork and was writing up the first draft of my results in a little house on the beach in Sri Lanka, no stimulating problem came to mind. Again and again I read over my reams of notes, again and again I recoded them, shifted them, tried to see some break which offered potential for creative analysis. Then I saw, or rather saw again, the opposition I could build upon. It was something I had noticed from the very beginning of my life in Swat, but which had become such an ordinary part of experience there that I had almost forgotten it. From the first I had been impressed by the depth and nature of the friendship which had quickly developed between myself and Zaman. The more I knew the society, the more I realized that this particular relation was a cultural ideal, often dreamt of but rarely, if ever, achieved. Hospitality, which is a prime value in Swati society, seemed to me to be a sort of ritual of friendship, and the warmth and generosity of the Swati host has often been commented upon by foreign guests.

But if friendship and its ritualized enactment in the offering of hospitality are of central importance in the worldview of the Pukhtun, how can this be reconciled with a social order which presses, in every instance, for competition, opposition, and mistrust? Here was the break in the pattern!

Others who had worked with the Pukhtun also saw the offering of hospitality as a problem, though no attention was paid to the ideal of friendship which lies behind hospitality. Elphinstone, the first European visitor to write about the Pukhtun, notes that "a man, who travelled over the whole country without money, would never be in want of a meal, unless perhaps in towns" (1815: 1:295), and concludes that "there is no point in the Afghaun character of which it is more difficult to get a clear idea, than the mixture of sympathy and indifference, of generosity and rapicity, which is observable in their conduct to strangers" (1815: 1:297).

Bellew, a later and much less empathetic observer, denied the generosity of Pukhtun hospitality, claiming it to be "a mere customary interchange of services or favors." Hospitality has a functional explanation. "Owing to the disturbed and barbarous state of their society, and the absence of public places of accommodation for travellers, such as sarais, it is the custom of the several tribes to lodge and feed each other when travelling. . . . Strangers and foreigners generally receive neither food nor shelter . . ." (1864:210). But Bellew's sour aspersions on Pukhtun generosity are given the lie by many accounts. Furthermore, he ignores the central place of hospitality in the Pukhtun value system, and assumes that the Pukhtun need to travel and therefore must rely on one another for food and shelter. This is untrue. The villages of Swat are quite self-sufficient and have been supplied with luxury goods by traders and armed caravans which did not rely on hospitality. Unlike the situation in nomadic societies, hospitality in Swat has no apparent overt economic function. Finally, contrary to Bellew's statement, the most valued guest is not a neighboring tribesman, but a stranger. Far more attention is lavished on an outsider than on an ally or relative, for reasons which I will discuss later.

Barth takes a different tack, seeing hospitality as a way of validating a leader's political position. The Pukhtun's "striking hospitality and reckless spending only seems intelligible if we recognize that the underlying motives are political rather than economic. It is a development in some ways analogous to the 'potlatch' institutions of many primitive, nonmonetary societies" (1965:12). Barth sees hospitality as a way of winning a dependent following.

Gift-giving and hospitality are potent means of controlling others, not because of the debts they create, but because of the recipient's dependence on their continuation. . . . The chief also establishes a reputation for lavishness, shows himself capable of profitable management of his estates, and in general gains prestige as a desirable leader. Followers flock to his men's house and his political influence increases. (1965:79–81)

But Barth's political explanation is contrary to the villagers' own view of hospitality. Offering the necessities of life in return for loyalty is thought to be like feeding one's servants; it is an obligation, not a pleasure. Those who accept such gifts are not guests, they are *kurimar,* eaters of the khan's curry, and they form the private army for politically ambitious men. Nor is feeding the needy in times of hunger considered hospitality; it is *zakat,* charity for religious merit, or *gherat,* charity for personal honor. Those who must accept such charity feel shame, whereas the guest is honored. Finally, once again, the best guest is a stranger, and proper etiquette for the host is not even to inquire as to the name of the guest. Entertaining an unknown visitor can hardly be seen as a political act as Barth has formulated it.

The last commentator supports a nonpolitical interpretation of hospitality. "If 'political support' alone is the reason for hospitality, then this argument cannot be sustained in explaining the 'striking hospitality' of the ordinary Pukhtun villager to any passing stranger or foreigner" (Ahmed 1976:58). But Ahmed's own explanation is no improvement. He first claims hospitality exists because it is enjoined by Islam, thus explaining a cultural phenomenon by exegesis from Scripture. This is no explanation at all, since many pronouncements of the Koran (for example, inheritance for women or the right of divorce) are stoutly denied by the tribesmen. The important question is why the Koranic injunction for hospitality fitted the social needs of the community so well. Second, Ahmed claims that hospitality is a way of maintaining Pukhtun identity. "Hospitality, whether individually or collectively expressed, is one of the major cognitive, tangible and coherent symbols to the Pathan . . . [it serves to] maintain cultural identity and ethnic boundaries" (1976:58–59). There are really two claims being made in this second argument. The first is simply that hospitality exists because it is part of Pukhtun behavior. This is explanation of a phenomenon by reference to itself. The second idea is that hospitality is practiced because it differentiates the Pukhtun from his neighbors. By this reasoning, any attribute of a people can be "explained" as such a differentiating mechanism.

It seems, then, that none of the attempts to understand Pukhtun hospitality have been particularly successful. It stands as a practice at right angles to the dominant pattern of the rest of Swati society, which, structured by the system of segmentary opposition, stresses relations of animosity and hostility. It was, therefore, exactly the sort of problem I wanted.

My effort to understand the contradiction offered by Pukhtun friendship and hospitality led me in a totally unexpected direction, but not before I had first made an exhaustive attempt to understand the problem within the structure I had postulated. Most of this book is a demonstration of the pervasive influence of the segmentary principles on the Swati social order; yet, though pervasive, these principles cannot include hospitality and the friendship ideal. At this point, with the demonstration that the structural approach is not able to explain several central aspects of Swati culture, I might have rested my case. But the empty space demanded some sort of postulate to fill it. The opportunity to invent a theoretical addendum which would complete the analysis led me toward a consideration of psychological universals.

Like many, if not most, younger anthropologists, I had paid little attention to psychological anthropology, the Culture and Personality school which had been so popular in the thirties and forties and so derided in later decades. I had accepted the widespread belief that psychological explanations in anthropology are inevitably reductionist, unprovable, and faintly ridiculous. It was with reluctance, then, that I began to consider a psychological explanation for the problem I had found in my data. In fact, I ended by proposing that human beings have an irreducible emotional structure which is certainly molded in its expression by culture, but which in turn molds culture as well. If the culture does not allow easy expression of certain inherent and necessary emotions, then they must be expressed in ritual or ideology. The whole structure of Swati society, it seems, presses against demonstrations of affection and attachment, and so these emotional relations find their release in hospitality and the dream of the friend. This is my argument in a nutshell.

In presenting this theoretical postulate, I have tried to avoid the errors of Mead and Benedict, who tended to view cultures as entities dominated by an idée fixe. Benedict (1934) has been rightly criticized for rigidly categorizing cultures into preconstructed molds, ignoring contradictory elements within them, such as the frenzy sometimes shown by the supposedly Apollonian Zuni, or the careful preplanning that went into ecstatic Dionysian rites of the Kwakiutl (see Barnouw 1973 for a review of the literature). The emphasis on cultural variability and a dominant ethos led Mead (1935), a meticulous fieldworker, simply to leave out the fact that the mild-mannered and "effeminate" Arapesh actually engaged in headhunting warfare caused by abduction of women (Fortune 1939). This sort of exaggeration was in large part responsible for the poor reputation of Culture and Personality studies in recent years.

Because Mead, Benedict, and their school spoke "as if human temperament were fairly constant in the world, as if in every society a roughly similar distribution were potentially available, and as if the culture selected from these according to its traditional patterns and moulded the vast majority of individuals into conformity" (Benedict 1939:233), they concentrated their work on what was selected, on difference, and not on what must be retained for man to remain human. My purpose is to redirect attention to this element, to the underlying and universal emotions which make us all kin.

Before beginning, one last caveat: I have made extensive use of quotations in this book, both from Westerners who have studied or lived with the Pukhtun and from Pukhtun sources. These quotes are not proof of anything, but fit so well with my own observations that I could not resist using them. The Pukhtun quotations have the characteristic straight-forward honesty which the Pukhtun themselves display, and they show, I think, a rather unique attitude toward life. Though I cannot read Pukhto, I made some of the translations myself from listening to recitations in the village and I hope that I have caught their original flavor. Some will argue that my selection is biased and unrepresentative. I will agree to the bias, since I selected quotes which would be illustrative, but the attitudes revealed are not unrepresentative. In fact, I think the quotes and proverbs show that the people themselves are quite self-aware, and that they would accept the picture I have drawn of them.

GENEROSITY AND JEALOUSY

1. The Valley and the Village

In climate it is glorious, lovelier far than Kabul,
Bleak is Kabul, Swat is mild and gentle,
Its air and verdure are like unto Kashmir,
Though it spreads out not so finely;
In every home there are cascades and fountains,
Fine cities there are, fine dwellings, and fair markets,
Such a country, with such a clime and such streams,
Wherein every place is by nature a garden of flowers,
Hath no homes, no garden, no fragrance or freshness,
For the Yusufzai have made of it a desert.
(Khattak 1963:242)

A BEAUTIFUL and fertile mountain valley, advertised by the Pakistani Tourist Board as "the Switzerland of the Himalayas," Swat remains difficult to reach, though its veil has been torn by a British-built road which twists through the tortuous curves of the Malakand Pass. Swat itself has good roads, built by the former ruler Miangul Abdul Wadud with the aid of his British supporters; roads which wind through the entire valley and up into the high mountains where a number of rest houses command gorgeous views and where trout from well-stocked streams can be netted by the well-heeled visitor. There is even a ski resort being planned, and an airport is under construction to accommodate a hoped-for influx of monied travelers. Swat, long the center of resistance to outside influence, home of warriors who successfully opposed not only the British, but also the Mughals and the Afghans, now looks thoroughly tame to the casual eye of the tourist.

On his way to the mountain resort areas, the visitor will drive through the heartland of Swat, where his impression will be one of wealth and plenty. Everywhere the rich black soil has produced luxuriant crops, and the lush fields are picturesquely framed by sparkling canals that crisscross the landscape. On every side there are the hills and mountains which put Swat itself into a frame: to the south the dry range of the Malakand, to the east and west the treeless hills, and to the north the huge snowy mass of Falakser, about 20,000 feet high. It all seems as open as a picture postcard; the sense of enclosure comes much later.

The people of Swat also look attractive and quaint as they plod along the road behind their bawling unruly herds, struggle behind a plow in the fields, or crowd around the car while the tourist rests and refreshes himself at a roadside teahouse, drinking milky sweet tea ladled out of huge kettles. The pace is slow, the scenery lovely, and the patched clothes and haggard, bearded faces of the men look rather biblical and charming. The people are unfailingly friendly, and always have time for a smile and a wave at the car as its speeds by, though some rowdy boys might spoil the idyllic impression a bit by slinging a few well-aimed rocks.

Most of the people of Swat live within the main watershed of the Swat River, which meanders down from the high mountains to the north, collecting the waters of numerous small streams along the way, and flows eventually into the Kabul River in the plains near Nowshera. In the north, the valley narrows considerably until it becomes almost a gorge, and

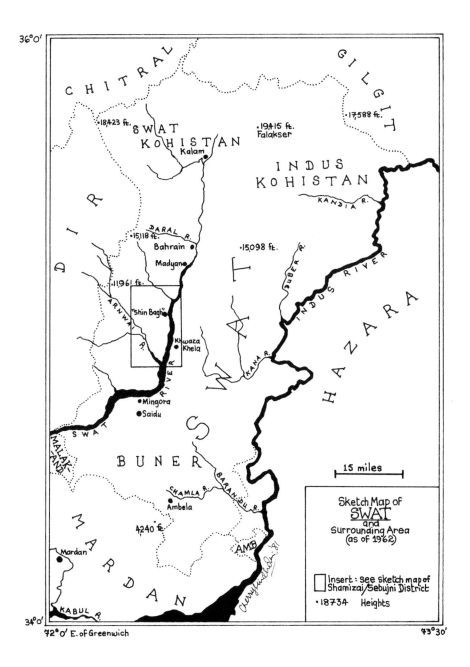

farmhouses cling precipitously to the valley walls. The same holds true of the many tributaries, so that extensive terracing is necessary for farming. The main part of the valley, though, is wide and flat, and its rich soil is easily worked.

The climate of Swat is often stimulating, especially in the spring and fall, when the air is crisp and clean. The Swatis themselves boast that the air of the valley increases the appetite, and there is a saying in the North-West Frontier Province that Swat is soft, while the rest of the region is hard. But "softness" is a relative thing, and the visitor might be surprised at the climatic extremes of the valley. The Swat region is on the edge of the monsoon, and its weather is notoriously unpredictable. It is common for one village to experience severe rainfall while its neighbor village, just a mile or two away, basks in sunlight.

Despite general variability, precipitation may be said to concentrate in the spring, reaching a peak in April, then dropping off to almost nothing in the heat of June and breaking again in late July or early August. Rain in the winter is quite light and snow in the valley bottom is rare, though hailstorms can occur at any season. Annual rainfall varies from thirty to fifty inches. Precipitation is greatest in the mountains, where it accumulates in winter snows. Temperatures are the hottest in June, when they may reach well over 100 degrees Fahrenheit in the lower parts of the valley, and coldest in January, when occasional frosts may even strike in the Swati capital of Saidu Sherif in the southern part of the watershed. The long winter, though a time of little work, is dreaded by most people because of the difficulty of finding fuel to heat their houses. The months before the break of rain in the summer are also disliked because of the high humidity and numerous fevers which strike during this unhealthy season.

The excesses of the climate have long been recognized as harmful. "The peculiar vernal and autumnal intermittents, frequently, from all accounts, assuming the remittent or continued forms of fevers, and prevailing as epidemics, are in their seasons the plague of the country, and attack both sexes and all ages alike. The effects of this generally prevalent disease are plainly visible in the physical condition of the people" (Bellew 1864:39). During the time of my fieldwork malaria, typhoid, recurring fevers of unknown origin, skin diseases (especially boils in the hot season), and all sorts of intestinal problems prevailed. According to local doctors, tuberculosis was common, and deadly cholera struck occasion-

Wheat fields being harvested.

ally. Some progress has been made since Bellew's time, however, and large-scale plagues no longer wipe out whole villages as they did only forty years ago. There has been an attempt to curb the mosquito population, but to no avail. Flies are also numerous, and contribute to the unhealthy conditions in the villages.

But if the visitor is lucky and does not contract one of the debilitating fevers endemic to Swat, he will retain his vision of it as a pleasant and even paradisiacal place, a sort of Shangri-la, a land of milk and honey. To an extent, the uninformed impression of the richness of the valley is quite accurate. Swat is indeed one of the most fertile regions of Pakistan, producing sizable crops of rice, wheat, fruit, wood, and opium. Cultivation is carried out on every possible bit of land. Even the tops of the enclosing hills, where the land is level, are farmed. In the wider part of the valley the climate and soil allow double cropping, with wheat and clover harvested in the spring and rice and maize being grown in the fall. On unirrigated land, wheat and maize alternate. Crops are rotated and clover planted once every two or three years to replenish the soil. Beans are also grown within the maize fields to replace nitrogen. Chemical fertilizers have come into wide usage in the last few years, greatly multiplying productivity.

Besides the staple crops, mustard is grown in the spring and lentils and soy beans in the fall. Much land is being given over to cash crops now that the market system has penetrated the region. Oranges are grown in the south, while apples are popular further north, and the spring is a riot of blossoms. Vegetable market gardening has recently come into vogue, and the newly introduced tomato and potato crops are thriving in the higher, colder regions. Tobacco is widely grown on the east bank of the river, and opium production has rapidly multiplied in recent years, despite government attempts at curtailment. Sugar beets are also grown, as is cane in the south. Eggplants, onions, chili peppers, okra, pumpkins, garlic, radishes, and other vegetables are grown as well, mainly for home use.

In addition to the variety of crops, the visitor will also see a number of different kinds of domestic animals. Huge water buffalo with their swept-back horns wallow in the canals by the roadside. Both cattle and buffalo are used for plowing, while in the hills herds of goats scavenge for food. Donkeys and mules are the beasts of burden, and innumerable scrawny chickens of every imaginable color run wild underfoot.

Yet, in spite of the apparent wealth of the region, the majority of its people are desperately poor. In 1970, the per capita income annually in Swat was reckoned at 133 rupees (a rupee is worth approximately ten American cents) as against the national average of 525 rupees and the North-West Frontier Province average of 360 rupees. A great many of the people had no income at all, but rather relied on largesse from their khans (landlords). Even in 1977, when much more liquid capital was flowing into Swat from migrant labor, some people had never touched a five rupee note.

A major part of the problem is overpopulation. The 1972 census claimed 935,444 people in the district; an increase of 49.7 percent in eleven years. The statistics of the 1971 *Integrated Resource Survey* of the Swat watershed quotes a population of 633,437 within the watershed area, giving a population density of 267 persons per square mile (F. M. Khan 1971:68). However, this figure must be viewed in relation to the amount of land which is actually available for farming. It is estimated that most of the region (52.23 percent) is deforested rangeland suitable only for grazing, while 21.26 percent is virgin forest and 10.06 percent unusable glacier or riverbed, leaving only 16.45 percent as farmland. The land available for agriculture is therefore only 249,963 acres out of a total of 1,519,811 (F. M. Khan 1971:126). Using the population figure of 633,437, less than four tenths of an acre of farmland is available per person. The population density in relation to farmland then becomes 1,622 persons per square mile: an extremely high density for an almost totally agrarian society. Furthermore, the population figures given by F. M. Khan were based on a hypothetical 25 percent population increase from 1961 whereas the 1972 census claims an increase of almost 50 percent. The population in the watershed might, therefore, be as much as 752,579, giving a population density of 1,927 per square mile.

These statistics must be viewed in the light of several other factors which render the figures even more stark. First, many of the people do not own any land at all, but rather are the direct dependents of the landowning class. In Shin Bagh,* for example, 180 of 312 households own some land, while the remainder are landless. Second, despite the fertility of the soil, the yield is not high. Given ideal conditions, a return of thirty kernels of corn for each one planted is considered excellent. To get such a yield, extensive use of expensive imported nitrogen fertilizer is necessary. Furthermore, all the land included as farmland is not prime land. Only on the well-irrigated valley bottom land (called səm) can such yields be expected. A good proportion of the land located on hills is not irrigated, but rather relies on sporadic rainfall. The soil here, on what is called kas land, is rocky and unproductive and gives a low yield of inferior quality. Ten kernels of corn for every one sown is considered excellent.

Soil productivity in general is also radically cut by the outmoded farming techniques and excessive fragmentation of holdings. Seeds are simply broadcast and the wooden, bullock-drawn plow cannot cut the earth very deeply. Weeding is not done, nor are the crops sprayed. Since individual holdings are scattered into many small, separate plots and since people are generally unwilling to act cooperatively, plowing by tractor is inefficient and expensive, though it is now undertaken on the larger plots.

The yield of farming is also reduced by the vicissitudes of climate for which the valley is famous. Whole crops are sometimes destroyed by rain, hail, or other inclement weather. Rice and wheat are particularly

* "Shin Bagh" (Green Garden) is the fictitious name I have given to the village I lived in during my fieldwork.

vulnerable to hailstorms near harvest time, and excessive moisture can ruin a crop. In 1976, the villagers of Shin Bagh ate bread which was black with mold due to unseasonable rains which fell and rotted the harvested wheat. In 1977, much of the rice in Swat was completely destroyed by hail and flooding, while the apple crop was depleted by hail damage. Farming in Swat has always been a risky business.

A final factor, more sociological than ecological, has to do with the recent transformation of the economy and an increased reliance on cash cropping. Formerly, the landowner gave shares of his crop to his dependents first, before he took his own share. These dependents supplied labor and service and the landlord, in return, supplied adequate food according to a traditional scale. However, the entrance of the mass market has made many services unnecessary. For instance, shoes and pots are easily purchased at low prices, rendering the shoemaker and potter superfluous. Furthermore, some of the new crops, such as apples, do not require much labor; or the labor has been replaced by mechanical devices such as tractors and harvesters. The dependents are also no longer needed to back up their patron in private wars. As a result of these factors and others the amount of food being redistributed has been radically reduced. Instead, food is being exported and the profits converted into luxury goods.

The result of these different pressures is that "food production is just sufficient in the valley" (F. M. Khan 1971:xxix). Even in 1962, the former ruler of Swat complained that "life has become so expensive that none but the rich can afford to have two square meals a day" (Wadud 1962:136). Census data shows that population is rising, while the survey of resources notes that "it is evident that per capita agricultural land is extremely scarce in the valley and this alarming situation is becoming worse day by day" (F. M. Khan 1971:79). Not only is population pressure increasing, but the amount of land potentially available for cultivation is shrinking due to the extensive sheet erosion which effects almost 90 percent of the total area. "This is because vegetative cover in the form of trees, bushes, and grasses is either being removed completely or tampered with ruthlessly. Also, agricultural practices being followed are outdated and damaging to the cultivated fields" (F. M. Khan 1971:72). As a result of deforestation, large tracts of arable land are washed away at every heavy rain, and some villages, such as Dagai in Sebujni District, are presently in danger of being completely inundated.

Under these circumstances, the major export of Swat is no longer rice, timber, or opium. Rather, it is men: unskilled labor for heavy construction, factory hands in textile mills, fieldworkers, and other badly paid menial labor flows from Swat in a steady stream. The stream began as a trickle in the 1930s when a few Pukhtun found work in India as watchmen, collectors for money-lenders, bootleggers, laborers and, occasionally, as criminals. After partition, with the development of Karachi and the increased market for unskilled labor, the trickle increased to a flood. Swat Pukhtun now make up a large percentage of the one million Pukhtun workers who have taken up residence in Karachi. Recently, demand for cheap, hardworking laborers in the Middle East has further increased the outflow of men. This siphoning off of some of the excess population has delayed the crisis of production and distribution which has threatened the social structure of the valley in the last few decades.

Some of the problems of Swat as a whole are evident in Shin Bagh, a moderately sized village (312 houses, nearly 2,000 inhabitants) located in the center of the rich Shamizai District in Upper Swat. The village is roughly eighteen miles north of the twin main towns of Mingora and Saidu Sherif and the same distance south of the resort town of Madyan. Until 1977, the village was on a major roadway, but in that year a bridge was washed away in a flood, and Shin Bagh became more isolated than ever. But isolation has not prevented the village from suffering the same difficulties as the rest of the valley. Many men have left the village to find work elsewhere (see appendix A, tables 5 and 6), the old ties between patron and client have been eroded by a money economy, and there is a vague sense of dissatisfaction in the air.

The migration of labor has led to changes in lifestyle. Those who return from Saudi Arabia with their pockets full of money have introduced luxury goods such as radios, digital watches, cassette tape recorders, synthetic cloth, and the like. They have used their hard-earned cash to build themselves fancy new houses of brick and to buy Suzuki three-wheel cars for use as taxis.

But, despite the new influx of money, the status differentiation remains relatively unchanged. The returnees, usually men of the landless class, find that land is still generally impossible to buy. Their proud new homes are built on the land of their khans, and they must pay an oppressive rent. Their attempts at business fail, their luxury goods break, and they remain in an impotent position. Some go again to work abroad, others reconcile themselves to the disappointment of failure.

The khans also feel dissatisfied. They hold the land and therefore hold power, but money is scarce, and they envy the ephemeral possessions of the returned migrants. Many talk of leaving and doing menial labor for the sake of wealth and the status items money can buy, but few can bring themselves to swallow their pride and self-respect and join the migrants. They remain in the security of the village, bemoaning their poverty.

The poverty may be becoming even greater, since out-migration has led to a labor shortage. The landowners are finding it ever more difficult to hire workers at harvest and planting seasons, and the available workers demand inflated salaries. The flow of cash into the village economy has disturbed the local equilibrium, raising prices for goods and services but not contributing to building a new economic base. Ownership of land continues to be the only steady source of income, but the rate of income appears less and less compared to the large salaries brought in from abroad. The sense of frustration is pervasive. The returned workers see their hard-won possessions slipping away, leaving nothing behind, while the elite landowners cannot escape the unrewarding grind of small-scale farming. "We have no opportunity here. We are trapped in the jail of this valley," they say.

But despite these threatening changes, the village does not feel itself to be on the verge of transformation. In fact, one of the things which depresses the younger men is a sense of inevitable continuity. The village will undoubtably go on as it always has. It is somehow timeless.

The village itself is a densely packed cluster of stone houses and mud streets. It sits in the middle of its fields, half a mile from the road and nearly a mile from the river. To the west, beyond the road, are low mountains. They rise 2,000 feet or so from the valley bottom, which is 4,000 feet above sea level. These mountains, which are about another half-mile from the road, are desolate and dry in their upper reaches, but are well-cultivated with some terracing on the lower elevations. The tops of the mountains are also cultivated, despite the snow which covers them in winter. All of the land from the river to the hilltops is controlled by the Pukhtun of the village, though some of the more remote fields are let out to sharecroppers who live on them.

Village rooftops.

The pathways which lead into the hills are well defined and dry, since the hills are uniformly unirrigated (*kas*) land. However, the paths leading to the river often double as tributaries to irrigation ditches, and footing is very precarious in the rice season. The river itself is not very impressive in the winter, as its main channel narrows to about 500 feet wide; but in the summer the volume of water increases ten- to twentyfold, and the river, with its numerous channels, broadens out to nearly a mile. Dikes of rounded river stones are built up in strategic locations to control the summer floods, which pose a serious erosion problem. Despite the dikes, land by the riverside is steadily being worn away, especially on the east bank. In the winter people sometimes get together in one of their few communal activites, the blocking up of a channel in order to scoop out the carp struggling in the shallows. In all seasons, men can be seen wading the river with nets, braving the freezing water and the current in the hopes of catching some fish. In the summer, young men and boys take buffalo-hide floats to the river and ride them downstream. Unfortunately, very few know how to swim, and drownings are common.

In order to reach the village, one must know the way, although the small dirt road which is the main pathway is usually marked by a cluster of men and boys waiting for a bus, a Suzuki taxi, or a horsecart (*tanga*), while a few women, looking like shy ghosts in their enveloping shawls, squat at a decorous distance. The path is marked by the enclosure which contains the village's only "factory," a small wood-cutting and rice-milling enterprise. Walking toward the village on the rutted roadway, the visitor will pass through the irrigated fields and see the work and the crops of the season. The most beautiful time of the year is probably April, when the bright green of the newly risen wheat contrasts with the shining yellow mustard. At all seasons, herdsmen use the road to take their animals to the hills for grazing. The visitor may have to make way for a flock of sheep, a few scrawny cows, or half a dozen enormous water buffalo, many with blind blue eyes rolling frighteningly as their tender, a boy of about six, enthusiastically applies his stick to keep them from wandering off the road and fatally gorging themselves in the fields. Or a muleteer may be seen herding his string of donkeys into the village, each one staggering under a weight of stones for a new house or a load of grain collected from the fields.

Entering the village itself, one finds oneself in a mazeway of narrow alleys which twist between the high walls of the houses. These walls, built of rounded river stones held together by mud and hope, often bulge

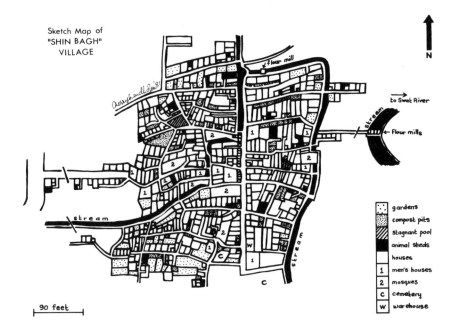

Sketch Map of
"SHIN BAGH"
VILLAGE

N

to Swat River

flour mill

flour mills

stream

stream

stream

90 feet

gardens
compost pits
stagnant pool
animal sheds
houses
1 men's houses
2 mosques
c cemetery
w warehouse

menacingly into the alley and, during rains, sometimes collapse completely. On one side of every path there is a stream. These streams flow into a larger canal which winds right through the village. The rivulets and the parent canal serve as places for bathing animals, dishwashing, cleaning clothes and children, drainage for the houses and, often, as a source of drinking water. In some of the wider portions of the canal, when it spreads to ten or twelve feet in width, a few ducks and geese paddle about contentedly.

The pathways wind between the houses, opening out only to accommodate a *deran,* or compost pit. Into these holes human and animal excrement, along with all other organic waste, is stored for later use as fertilizer. The same mixture of fecal matter, contributed by children and animals, adorns the path itself, making for slippery footing. Occasionally, a wall has fallen and exposed an abandoned house. Other openings are provided by the men's houses (*hujeras*), where a few elders recline on their string cots. The tedium of the grey stone walls is relieved sporadically by straggly green trees shooting up from the concealed courtyards. Most of the trees are trimmed ruthlessly every season for firewood, making them look like brooms or tormented bonsais. Here and there the grave of a forgotten holy man stands in the middle of the path, sprinkled with glittering shards of glass. One recently built mosque sends up a whitewashed spire, but the other six mosques are traditional wood and stone constructions, looking much like *hujeras* in layout. The doors that lead into the houses and the pillars of the men's houses are often heavily carved with rough but intricate geometric designs and spirals. A few houses, used for storing corn, have complex designs on their outer walls. Otherwise, the village streets are dreary and indistinguishable from one another.

A few poor women may be seen on the street, perhaps getting water from the stream, running an errand, or going for a visit. They are dressed in brighter colors than the men, but the style is the same: trousers up to five feet wide at the waist, tied at the top with a cord slotted through; this is topped with a loose shirt which comes down to the knees. All wear a shawl (*sadar*) over their heads. Men's shirts have Western-style collars, while those of the women have scallop patterns or some other decorative style. In winter, blankets are worn by both men and women. The ensemble produces an impression of volume which disguises the often emaciated frame it covers. Plastic shoes or sandals complete the

Village street with drainage ditch.

outfit, and the women wear bangles, earrings, and nose rings, preferably of gold. At special events, the women tie their hair in a braid and lengthen it with an artificial braid of wool. Most people have black hair, olive skin, and brown eyes; but some are light-skinned or ruddy, with blue or green eyes and blond or even red hair. Some of the men have biblical beards, others are clean-shaven, others have moustaches. The style of facial hair varies with the lineage, but all have short hair with a part, Western style. The men and women look strikingly alike with their generally slender builds, narrow, high-cheekboned faces, and hawk noses. Most of them are tall, and their height is emphasized by their erect posture. In other villages, the standard look may be different, but Shin Bagh is known for its tall and angular residents.

The most evident occupants of the village are the children, for the women are usually in the house and the men are in the fields. Children seem to be everywhere and in incredible numbers. One sees dozens of them sitting by the streams making mud pots or animals, pretending to make bread (a favorite game of the girls), running wildly over the roofs, or climbing trees. The air is full of the sounds of children—fighting, laughing, crying, shouting, and playing. Like their elders, the girls and boys are distinguished by dress. Girls wear garish synthetics in patterns while the boys wear plain cottons of a dark hue. At around the age of eight the girls begin to wear the *sadar* when they go out and to cover their hair in front of boys. The boys are generally much cleaner than the girls, since the mother or elder sister cares for them, while the girls are left to fend for themselves as they are able and inclined. Children of both sexes play together until the girl starts wearing the *sadar*. The boys then begin congregating in gangs and tormenting the girls when they see them. By the age of eleven or twelve girls of good families no longer leave their father's compound.

The boys, each with a slingshot around his neck, are the guardians of the village, along with the pye-dogs. An uninvited peddler or beggar may find himself pelted with rocks as he tries to fend off the attacks of the village curs. A stick to hit the dogs and a guide to frighten the boys are necessary props for a visit.

The depredations of the boys' gangs, their petty thieveries, destructive pranks, beatings of unpopular children, and other mischief are prime sources of women's raucous fights. Other causes may be refusal to give a loan to a neighbor, refusal to adequately repay a loan, family enmity, and so on. Whatever the causes, shrieking fights between women, which may escalate into rock-throwing contests, are a great source of entertainment in the village. Poor women may even venture out into the street to confront one another, while women of a better class stand on the roofs of their houses and pour insults toward the compound of their enemy.

Elite women stay within their compound and shout over the walls. Fights between husbands and wives also become public due to the volume of the women's complaints. Women prize volubility and lung power, since these are their greatest weapons against the physical strength of their husbands. The incessant fights, accompanied by the whines and screams of babies, the continuous yapping of the starving dogs, and the usual animal chorus of braying donkeys, bellowing buffalos, and crowing roosters soon dispel any of the visitor's romantic notions of a rural idyll. Only the men are silent, relying on physical force rather than argument to settle domestic disputes. The recent influx of radios and cassette recorders has added to the din, as has the installation of a loudspeaker system in the modern mosque. In using these new toys, it is considered de rigueur to test their full volume.

The hubbub in the villages arises mainly from the houses and courtyards, hidden behind their stone walls. The public places, such as the *hujera* and mosque, are generally hushed except, in the latter, for the murmur of prayers. Men together are silent and idle. "They seem to sit listlessly for the whole day, staring at each other" (Burnes 1834: 1:144).

The private space behind the decorated doors of the houses will never be seen by the visitor unless he is a close relative. Such a visitor will enter a courtyard, which is either large or small according to the means of the family. Within the courtyard a few stunted fruit trees may grow, and some of the more industrious families have planted a vegetable garden. Others simply use the yard as storage space or as a pen for their cattle or buffalo. In every courtyard, chickens are busily scratching through the garbage and offal that is strewn about.

The house itself is most often only one room (see appendix A, table 3). It is usually built of the same river stones as the outside wall. The furniture in the house is simple and spare. It consists of a few string beds scattered about outside in the summer and inside in the cold season. There will be a metal or wooden trunk and dilapidated suitcase or two lying on the dirt floor within the house. These contain the separate treasures of the husband and wife: clothes, shoes and, for the wife, jewelry. Every house, no matter how poor, has a cheap Chinese tea pot with matching cups and saucers. This important implement is central in displays of hospitality, and it is placed conspicuously on one of the few shelves in the house. Some cabinets will be set into the mud-covered walls, and these serve to store other breakables, such as dishes, eggs,

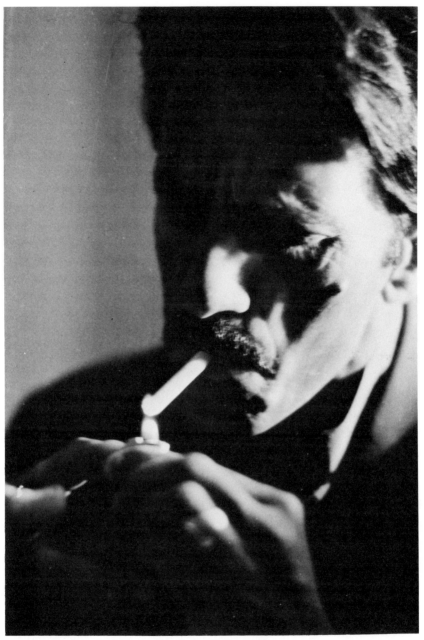

Our host, Zaman Khan.

A Pukhtun woman.

and so on. A big wooden box, sometimes elaborately carved, is used for storage of grain, and a standing cabinet, also covered with carvings, may substitute for the cabinets set in the walls. A few pegs serve in lieu of closets, though sometimes children's clothes are just dropped on the floor. There may be a slightly raised wooden platform, pointed at one end, which serves the woman of the house as a place to kneel for prayer. A cradle is usually suspended from the ceiling, filled with rags and a squalling bundle. A few Swati chairs, covered with carvings, with their high backs and seats just a few inches off the ground, and perhaps a wobbly table or two, complete the furniture collection. The beds are covered winter and summer with heavy quilts. The pillows are large cylinders stuffed with cotton. Special quilts and pillows for guests are stored away in a cabinet to keep them clean but, in ordinary life, dirt is not considered very disturbing. In the hot season, flies are thick during the day and mosquitoes abound at night, while in the cold season fleas are constant companions.

In the winter the kitchen is often simply a fire in the middle of the room. Before escaping through a smoke hole, the smoke blackens the mud walls and reddens the eyes of the family. In the summer, the kitchen is in the courtyard under the eaves of the flat-roofed house. Here the wife crouches nearly the whole day on her low stool. All her utensils are within easy reach as she squats surrounded by her blackened pots and pans. There may be a fireplace to channel the smoke, but usually it is left to disperse in the breeze. Cooking is a woman's main work, and most of the work goes into making the delicious flat breads of wheat, rice, or corn flour which constitute the family's main food source. The diet of Swat is simple, and spices are not much used, though some people season their rice by tamping a hot pepper into it. Generally, people eat plain bread or rice with perhaps a thin soup to sop up or spoon over the main dish.

Cooking is done over a clover-leaf shaped mud fireplace which can hold pots of all different sizes. Some women also build a special mud oven for the sake of the tasty bread which can be prepared in it. This oven is a dome with a hole at the top and a space at the bottom for coals. Bread is slapped against the extremely hot interior of the oven and peeled off when it is cooked, at the cost of burned fingers. Wood is the favored fuel as it gives a hot flame, but it is expensive, and most people rely on dried dung for cooking.

Children at the doorway of their compound.

Besides the kitchen area, most homes have a little room which is used as a toilet by the women. This enclosure has some pots in it that children or a servant carry to empty in the compost pit or the fields. The men and children have no need of a special room, but rather relieve themselves in the fields or, in the case of smaller children, anywhere at all.

The space in the house is generally cramped and there is a sense of claustrophobia implicit in the clutter, the noise, and the awareness that, for the women, the house compound is the total extent of their horizons.

The homes of the wealthier families usually have more than one room and some have five or six. They may differ from poorer houses in other aspects as well. Elite residences are sometimes built of concrete or brick, with a concrete floor. The plastered walls are painted yellow or blue. The shelves have glass fronts and more possessions are displayed in them; there may be a fireplace with a mantlepiece where colorful knickknacks are on show. Three houses even have televisions, none of them in working order. But the differences between the homes of the wealthy and the homes of the poor are superficial. The kitchens and toilet are the same in all houses. The size of the elite homes simply means that more nuclear families are accommodated within. Husband, wife, and children are still all in one room. For instance, the wealthiest lineage segment or *khel* in Shin Bagh is that of Zaman Khan, my friend. This segment, the Malik *khel*, averages 2.6 persons per room, and the average for the village as a whole is almost 4.3 per room (see appendix A, tables 1, 2, and 3 at the end of this book for more complete information). Only the very few have the privacy of separate rooms.

Zaman Khan's house was perhaps roomier than most, but its furnishings were far more spartan than those of his father's house next door. All of the luxuries were for what the Pukhtun call a "bungalow," a concrete building perched atop Zaman's own house where I and my family lived in relative splendor during my fieldwork. I've described this bungalow in my introduction, but should perhaps point out here that it was the only such structure in the village, though wealthy khans in neighboring villages had recently built similar imitations of British Colonial rest-houses. It was a more prestigious and up-to-date item than the *hujera*, and Zaman was immensely proud of it, despite the poverty of his own living space.

Twenty years ago, most of the men and all of the unmarried boys slept in the mens' houses, but this custom has almost died out. Some of the elders have moved in with their wives, and only senior men who are

Compound yard.

widowers and a few of their dependent servants and sons now live in the *hujeras* full time. As a replacement for the mens' house, and in imitation of North Indian usage, small guest rooms have been built onto the houses of men who can afford the expense. These *betǝks,* which usually have a separate entrance from the house proper, are the repositories of the best furniture in the family's possession. Even though the interior of his own home is mud and stone, a man will try his best to make the public portion as grand as possible. If financially able, a man will construct his *betǝk* of concrete and plaster; if the house owns an electric fan, it will be in the guest room along with the radio or, even more prestigious, the cassette deck. Pictures of Mecca may decorate the walls of the guest room, and gold and silver tinsel may be hanging in glittering shreds from the ceiling, giving the *betǝk* the appearance of a Muslim shrine during a festival.

However, the popularity of the *betǝk* has not meant that the *hujera* (men's house) has ceased to function. Families who own *hujeras* are the wealthiest and most respected of the village, and include men who were recognized by the government as village leaders and were awarded stipends. The families of these important khans use their guest houses for entertaining or holding dancing parties or political meetings. The younger men sometimes secretly use the unoccupied rooms for assignations with prostitutes.

The *hujera,* unlike the *betək,* has a separate grounds away from the main house. Along with the mosques, these are the largest and most elegant buildings of the village. This is appropriate since, like the mosques, they are centers of ceremonial life. The *hujera* consists of a line of rooms, each with a separate entrance, fronted by a long verandah which is shaded by the roof. Ornately carved columns support the roof, their capitals a florid imitation of the Ionic style. On this verandah, the boys used to sleep in their cots and the men met in the day to pay respects to their khan and perhaps eat with him or have tea. In 1977, the two, three, and four rooms of the *hujeras,* each formerly a sleeping place for a khan or an important guest, were bare and empty. Despite the decrease in usage, men's houses continue to have great symbolic power, to the extent that two young, aspiring leaders of the village have exerted themselves to construct new *hujeras* in the past few years.

Besides the men's houses, the mosques are the other major public buildings. Although they continue to fulfill their role as meeting places for prayer, there is an air of neglect about most of them. This is because of the disintegration of the small huts within them which were formerly used to house the *murids,* or disciples, of the village religious teachers. These mendicant students, who used to be numerous in Swat, now flock to better known centers of Islamic learning, such as Lahore. Swat retains a reputation of sanctity only for foreigners, and the sole seeker of wisdom to stay in Shin Bagh in the last decade was a French boy who impressed everyone with his sincerity, but did not remain for very long. One mosque in the village is new. Rather than following the traditional style, which apes the form of the men's house, this mosque has a minaret and, as mentioned previously, a loudspeaker. This modern mosque was the center of religious protest against the reforms of the ruling national party, the Pakistan People's Party (PPP), during the 1977 elections. The other mosques also may be centers of political discussion and sometimes for political dissension, despite their sacred character. There are also sporadic disputes over which parishioner has the right to oversee the mosque funds. These arguments can lead to a splitting of the congregation.

Another, less formal, gathering place for the village men is the shop (*dukan*). There are thirty-eight of these small stores in the village, most

Cooking area in compound yard.

of them in the village center. However, each neighborhood has its share of shops. Sometimes they are separate buildings, but more often they are simply annexes to a mosque or *hujera* or house. Most sell a very small variety of items: cigarettes, chewing tobacco (*nəswar*), a few eggs, candles, matches, thread, buttons, needles, peanuts, salt, sugar, flour, tea, perhaps a toy or two, and some battered tomatoes and potatoes complete the stock. Poorer men of the neighborhood often sit around the *dukan* exchanging gossip. They thus declare their independence from their khan by socializing in the neutral ground of the shop.

Some shops, especially those on the main street, are better stocked and more specialized. There are two shops which specialize in materials; two others are barbershops; two more stock bangles and shoes. Some shops do a wholesale business, buying flour and rice from the farmers and selling most of it to urban retailers. A few shopkeepers double as tailors. The biggest shop is a sort of general store, stocking everything the smaller *dukans* have, but more of it and of better quality. In addition, small-scale entrepreneurs set up stalls in the street to sell vegetables or the meat from a recently slaughtered animal.

These shops are a recent development in the village. Previously, the only shop was that of the goldsmith. All other services were supplied either in traditional shares or by itinerant tradesmen from Kabul. But the traditional division of the crop has gone into abeyance (except in a few special cases), and the shops have appeared instead. The Kabuli peddlers continue their ancient trade, but face more and more competition from local stores and greater legal restrictions on importing goods into Pakistan without paying customs. As a result, these colorful wanderers may also be on their way to becoming obsolete.

Another type of building found in the village is the animal pen (gojal). There are thirty-six of these pens, owned by the more affluent farmers. They are built in approximately the same style as the houses, but lack an enclosing wall. Some poorer men may rent space in a neighbor's gojal, but most follow the simple alternative of keeping their animals within their own house compound (see appendix A, table 10).

A final feature of the village is a large, low-lying, vacant area in the upper section. This open lot, which fills with water during the rainy season and serves as a breeding ground for mosquitoes, is a symbol of the lack of cooperation in the village. Although all agree that it is an inconvenience and an eyesore, it is owned by the village ward as a unit and the villagers are unable to reach any agreement on what to do about it.

On the outskirts of the village, to the south, are several silo-shaped structures. These buildings, owned by the community, serve as storage for the silage fed to the donkeys of the muleteers (parachas). In the village, grain is stored in the houses, and the storage place is marked by intricate designs. Just beyond these silos the main graveyard begins. Stretching nearly a quarter of a mile, it is full of the pointed, flat stones which mark the head and foot of each Pukhtun grave. A few great men have monuments of cement built in the shape of a casket. This graveyard is regarded as of special holiness, because it is here that the decisive battle of Mahmud of Ghazni's conquest of Swat is said to have been fought. Many martyrs for Islam are said to be buried among the flowers of the graveyard. When we first came to Shin Bagh this was the most beautiful place in the village, especially in the summer when huge purple crocus bloom on the graves. The canal widens here into a quiet pool, and enormous chinar trees provided welcome shade over the grassy graves. With land at a premium, the graveyards are the only places where grass is allowed to grow, and it used to be the only place where groves of trees were to

Men lounging in front of a *dukan*.

be found. Cutting trees in the graveyard was regarded as a desecration. However, during my fieldword, avarice and a scarcity of fuel led the khans who owned the trees to cut them down and sell them, leaving the graveyard with a desolate and dusty air of neglect.

Another beautiful place outside the village has remained unchanged: the row of flour mills which crosses a fast flowing canal east of the town on the way to the river. A second group of flour mills is located just north of the village. In each of the little huts of the mill a member of the carpenter specialist group crouches, following his traditional task of milling the grain of the village.

In the days of warfare, only recently ended, the village was strongly nucleated, but with the coming of peace it has spread out. This process was begun twenty years ago by a wealthy khan who built himself a second house on his property west of the main road, in the foothills. His son has kept up residence there. Other men, squeezed for space in the village, have started constructing houses on the village outskirts, and a number of such houses were being built in 1977.

There is also a small, dependent village of *sahibzada,* or descendants of a holy man, who live in the hills above the junction of the road. The parents of these men were given the land for their village and their fields by the landlords of Shin Bagh. Other dependents are the herdsmen (*gujars*) whom the khans have settled as sharecroppers on their hillside land, as well as other tenants scattered in the irrigated lands.

Shin Bagh is in the center of Shamizai District. Its fields are regarded as among the most fertile in the valley, although the actual quantity of land in the village holdings is relatively small. Durushkhela, about a mile north, and Badera, a mile south, are larger and wealthier than Shin Bagh. Shin Bagh's weakness is indicated by the size of its school, which reaches only to the sixth grade, while the Badera school goes to the ninth and Durshkhela's up to the twelfth. These schools were built in the era of the Wali, and indicate his favoritism. The buildings look modern; they are painted in yellow and white, surrounded by small flower gardens and situated along the main road.

Although Shin Bagh is at present weaker than its nearest neighbors, this was not always the case. In the recent past, the village was famed for its leaders, and the dominant lineage in Shin Bagh were called the Malik *khel,* or lineage of rulers, because of their illustrious history. Men of the

A *gojal* with dung patties drying on the wall.

Malik *khel* were heroic figures in Shamizai for over 200 years, and the modern Malik *khel* still dream of regaining their lost glory.

But even though the Malik *khel* no longer hold sway in the district at large, they do control Shin Bagh. They are the most numerous single *khel* (lineage segment) in the village, own the most houses, have the most rooms per house, and preponderate in the all-important area of landowning (see appendix A, tables 7, 8, and 9). They and their landed subordinates own almost all the cattle and buffalo in the village as well (see appendix A, table 10). Despite the disruptive influence of out-migration (180 of 1,148 men are presently migrant laborers working somewhere out of the village), the old distinction between landed and landless continues in force. Lack of clients at the men's house may be seen as the choice of the khan, who no longer wishes to feed useless dependents, as much as it can be seen as an assertion of independence by the poor. Even the newly rich returned migrants cannot break the old system. Some try to start businesses, but the possibilities are few and the competition great, as the proliferation of small stores attests.

Physically, the village has remained pretty much unchanged in the eight years I have known it. But to some extent, physical conditions

Design on the wall of a grain storage area. Making these designs is the job of old women, and is rapidly becoming a lost art.

appeared to be worsening. Wood had become very scarce in 1977, and those without cattle to supply dried dung for fuel were hard-pressed to do their cooking. The village's only open area, the graveyard, had been denuded of its ancient trees and stood, dusty and barren, as an ugly reminder of local poverty and avarice. Disease remained common, sanitation continued to be extremely bad, and the main effect of modern medicine seemed to have been to allow a decrease in infant mortality, a subsequent increase in population pressure, and a lowering of living standards.

The themes of overcrowding and the struggle for survival stand out in the discussion of the physical world of the Pukhtun. The tribesman may wear a pretty flower in his hat, and the poet may appreciate the exquisite beauty of the valley, but the ordinary villager, though he loves his homeland, generally has little time for aesthetics in the deprivation and hunger of his daily life. Given the physical reality, the best that can be expected of living is a drawn-out battle for the simplest of necessities. It is in this dreary and harsh crucible that the Pukhtun is formed.

2. History

Of course we are brave warriors;
Have we not sucked the milk of Pukhtun mothers?

The Pukhtun is never at peace
Except when he is at war.
(Pukhtun proverbs)

In the old days we were always at war. War was our
sport, our hobby.
(Yakub Khan, Mahmat *khel*)

THE valley of Swat has a long but shadowy history which was written, until recent times, by conquerors, would-be conquerors, and pious pilgrims. The fertility of Swat has always lured predators, and the chronicle of its past is one of victories, betrayals and intrigue, heroes and villains, saints and heretics; full of stories of bravery, mysticism, and revenge. Like the lives of the Pukhtun themselves, the history of Swat seems timeless, simply repeating again and again the same mythic images.

But change has occurred, especially in this century, and the changes have been far reaching. Since the late 1800s, Swat has evolved from a tribal society without a state to a prototype of despotism. Then, within the last generation, the ruler fell and Swat has been integrated into the modern nation-state of Pakistan.

Even in the modern era, however, certain themes repeat themselves. History is neither totally contingent, nor is it totally preordained; both accident and underlying patterns have their effect as the local social structure finds itself in a dialectic with the forces of modernization and transformation. By looking at history, and at the configurations which persist through time, we can begin to see the roots of Pukhtun culture; we can grasp its resilience and its uniqueness.

Swat first enters Western history with the invasion of Alexander the Great in 327 B.C. According to Stein (1929) and Caroe (1965) Alexander was unable to conquer Swat, and was in fact wounded in the seige of the fort of Massaga, proving, as Alexander himself is reported to have said, that the king of the Greeks is not a god. To pacify the tribesmen, Alexander resorted to a technique that has been followed by many hopeful politicians since; he took a local woman as his wife.

This ploy, however, proved as futile as it has in more recent history, and Swat soon returned to unrecorded "barbarism." Gandhara, or the kingdom of Paktuike, as described by Herodotus, included Swat in its compass. The inhabitants then were probably Zorastrian, and hints of the ancient religion remain in the local ritual of throwing fireballs prior to beginning the Muslim month of fasting and in the reluctance of the Swatis to ever extinguish a flame. Buddhism later came to prevail, and Gandhara, especially Swat, became the home of a beautifully achieved artistic style which combined the humanism of the Greeks with Eastern contemplation. It was here that the first figurative representations of the Buddha were sculpted. Some are still dug out of the ground and sold to antiquities dealers for smuggling out of the country. The sculpture was an expression of a great religious efflorescence in Swat. Many stupas were built, and the valley became known as a center of holiness and Buddhist learning. In A.D. 403 the pilgrim Fa Hien stopped in Swat on his way to India and described the monasteries as flourishing, but another Chinese pilgrim, Hiuen Tsiang, traveling 200 years later, was disgusted by the heresies and deceit of the Swatis (Stein 1929:15).

Buddhism faded away without leaving any traces other than its precious artifacts. In the hills west of Shin Bagh, for instance, the remnants of a stupa are still to be seen. It is probable that the inhabitants of the valley at this time were those now called Kohistani (mountain men), who at present live in the rocky defiles above Madyan, having been driven from the valley by Mahmud of Ghazni in 1004. Mahmud, though he reputedly converted the Swatis to Islam at swordpoint, had no interest in establishing a state or in ruling the people he defeated. He was a raider, not a conqueror. After looting as much as he could carry, he returned to Ghazni, leaving Swat and the whole Peshawar Valley depopulated and desolate. Into this vacuum the Dilazaks migrated. Caroe contends this extinct group were Karlani Pukhtun from the Khyber (1965:173), while Bellew claims they were Rajputs (1864:158). Whatever their background, they moved into a land which had perhaps once been well populated, but was now almost empty. A history of invasion and warfare, begun historically by Alexander, carried through into Muslim times.

The Dilazaks, however, did not rule for long. They were soon displaced and extinguished by the Yusufzai, who had themselves been exiled from their homeland in Afghanistan by the King Ulugh Beg (see Caroe 1965 for a detailed account). Led by Malik Ahmad, his son Khan Kajju, and aided by the presence of a man of holy lineage, the famous Shaikh Mali, the Yusufzai forced the Dilazaks out of the Peshawar plains. The Yusufzai then turned their attention to Swat. The frightened ruler of the valley, a Sultan Awes, tried to forestall invasion by arranging a marriage with Malik Ahmad's daughter, but the invasion took place anyway, and in 1515 the Yusufzai entered Swat through the Malakand Pass, forcing some of the Swatis into exile and turning others into their serfs.

After this conquest (which may have been mythical: see Caroe 1965:55–56), Shaikh Mali was called upon to divide the booty fairly among the tribesmen. What he put forward was one of the greatest land redistribution schemes in the world; a scheme in which land was allotted equally to each lineage according to the productivity of the soil, but reallotted every ten years or so to insure fairness. This redistribution, in its original form, supposedly moved lineages from Swat into the Peshawar Valley, while those from Peshawar trekked into Swat. Movement on this scale, however, was impractical, and *wesh*, as the land redistribution scheme was called, was soon confined to the regional level.

Whether the *wesh* actually began as the brainstorm of a holy man or represents a much older form, perhaps akin to the land redistribution programs of the Russian *mir* and other closed corporate communities, is irrelevant here. What is important is the fact that the Yusufzai maintained a system of land redistribution that forced them into a seminomadic life and a constant rebalancing of power relations. No single group was allowed to retain a permanent land base, and the continual reshuffling of lineages and dependents, coupled with a lack of easily monopolized resources, limited any tendencies toward centralization. Although it has been claimed by Ahmed that the *wesh* system was "a mechanism to preserve the mythology of territorial rights. . . . [that] ceased to function as a viable land tenure system universally sometime early last century" (1976:38), the fact is that local men remember the movement of whole villages occurring in Upper Swat until stopped by the ruler some fifty years ago. Plots were redistributed within the villages until very recently, and *wesh* is reportedly still practiced in some villages east of the Swat River, where it equalizes land losses caused by flooding.

Another area of controversy is who actually moved when the *wesh* took place. Meeker (1980) argues that only the Pukhtun moved, leaving their helots on the land to serve their next masters. But the people themselves say that almost everyone moved, excluding a few of the very poor and landed members of holy lineages, who stayed on to act as mediators. They held a special sort of land, called *tseri,* which was not included in the tribal land and did not circulate at redistribution. This land, which was donated to the holy lineages by the Pukhtun owners, generally lay between two villages, and represented the duty of these stationary lineages to mediate in intervillage disputes. (A great deal has been written on the role of these sedentery "holy" lineages as mediators. See Barth 1965; Ahmed 1976; Lindholm 1979, 1981a).

From the beginning of the Yusufzai occupation several aspects of social structure were evident. The system relied on conquest and the labor of the conquered local people, who were regarded as inferior to the victorious Yusufzai. But tendencies toward the evolution of caste-like ranks implicit in this situation of conquest were minimized by a periodic land redistribution. Finally, the role of the holy lineage as administrators (Shaikh Mali) and as mediators in disputes was established. The sedentary life of these holy lineages gave them a certain advantage over the mobile Pukhtun in the potential for the development of an infrastructure, but for several centuries this potential was offset by an ideology of pacifism which prevented the holy lineages from acting in an overtly political manner.

The ideology of pacifism was not always followed, however. Several generations ago, a group of men from one of the holy lineages managed to construct a cannon and attack Bodigram, a large village in Upper Swat. They were demanding that the Pukhtun give them better land. This group rebellion failed, and the descendants of the rebels now live in the more remote valleys, having been driven from their best land by the angry Pukhtun. Although the holy lineages as a unit have kept to their subordinate and peaceful role in dispute settlement, some ambitious and charismatic religious ecstatics have contributed greatly to Swat's political history, particularly in periods of crisis, when the Pukhtun need to rally around a leader and forget their own internal rivalries. A holy man, standing outside of lineage oppositions and claiming an immediate relation with the Deity could and often did serve as a focus for Pukhtun military action.

The first such figure known historically was Bazid, the so-called Pir of Darkness. (A pir is a holy man endowed with divine grace, or *baraka*.) He claimed to be the embodiment of Allah and imbued his followers with a sense of immortality. Bazid was opposed by the more orthodox Pir Baba, a sayyid (desendant of the Prophet Muhammad) and his disciple, Akhund Durveza. Both great pirs performed miraculous feats, but the forces of orthodoxy eventually prevailed, though heterodox charismatics have continued to reappear from time to time in Swati history.

This upsurge of religious revivalism coincided with and was stimulated by attempts of the Mughal rulers to take over Swat. Babur the Great entered the valley and demanded submission but, like Alexander, was satisfied with a gift of a woman. Taxes, though requested, were not forthcoming. The great attempt to bring Swat under the yoke was undertaken by Akbar, who in 1586 sent an army of crack troops from his new fort at Attock into Swat. The Yusufzai united against the invaders,

A religious mendicant.

showing a talent for concerted action which was to surprise the British 300 years later. Akbar's expedition was completely destroyed—8,000 of the cream of the Mughal army vanished without a trace. Later, in 1670, the great Mughal Aurangzeb managed to conquer the Yusufzai of the plains, but could not enter Swat.

The Yusufzai resisted not only the Mughuls, but also their successors. In 1725, the Yusufzai captured the son of Muhammed Shah Ghilji, the Afghan ruler of Persia, and held him for ransom. In 1738, the Yusufzai were the only Pukhtun to refuse to acknowledge the Turkoman, Nadir Shah, as their de facto king. Nadir Shah's own Afghan army was defeated by the Yusufzai in the Ambela Pass, foreshadowing a later battle with the British in the same location. However, when Nadir promised the Yusufzai a share in the plunder of India, they gladly joined his army and distinguished themselves in the Mahratta wars and the capture of Lahore.

After the murder of Nadir Shah, the Afghans as a whole elected one of their own to lead them. This was the great Ahmad Shah Abdali. Caroe's account of his election is interesting for the light it shines on Pukhtun politics:

The chiefs of the various tribes . . . gathered in council to select a King. Each in turn was asked his opinion and each insisted his own claims were to be preferred, refusing to submit himself to the rule of any other. Ahmad, the youngest, was asked last. He remained silent, saying not a word. Thereupon a Holy man, Sabir Shah . . . announced that Ahmad alone, having given no cause for dissension, was the proper ruler for the Kingdom. (1965:255)

But the Saddozai dynasty of Ahmad was plagued by the internal fighting which has always been the bane of Pukhtun kingdoms. Racked by feuds between cousins and brothers, it fell easy prey to the army of Ranjit Singh, thus proving Elphinstone's point that "it would require less exertion to conquer all the surrounding kingdoms than [for an Afghan king] to subdue his own countrymen" (1815: 1:233). Even during the reign of Ahmad Shah, many Pukhtuns were in opposition, and the work of maintaining internal order was by far the most onerous duty of the ruler. Plagued by internal treachery and attacked by Ranjit Singh's Sikh army, the Afghan dynasty in India fell. With the taking of Peshawar in 1823, the short-lived regime of Ranjit Singh gained ascendance, only to be replaced in 1848 by the far more permanent rule of the British Raj.

Several characteristics of the Pukhtun have come to light in this account. One is the ability of the Yusufzai to unite to repel invasion, despite fragmentation within, as is illustrated in the defeat of Akbar. But the repeated disintegration of Pukhtun kingdoms, not only in Afghanistan, but in India (the Lodi dynasty), shows that unity is only temporary. The egalitarianism of the Pukhtun will not permit them to acknowledge one of their own number as superior.

With the fall of Muslim rule, there occurred a great resurgence of Islamic fanaticism in the Frontier. For the first time in recorded history, invasion threatened from the south, from the pagan lands of Hindustan, and Islam itself seemed endangered. One of the foremost zealots was Sayyid Ahmad Barelvi, a migrant from Rai Bareilly in Oudh. Seeking a stronghold of Islam from which resistance to the Sikhs and British could be organized, he migrated into the Pukhtun hills and recruited an army of followers from disgruntled Muslims of India. His Pukhtun hosts were also caught up in his cry for a holy war and joined the Hindustani fanatics (as they were labeled by the British) in raids on Sikh outposts, eventually managing to retake Peshawar in 1829. However, Sayyid Ahmad soon overstepped his role. Calling himself the king of the Yusufzai, he began demanding taxes from his "subjects." Even more galling was his order that the Pukhtun should give their daughters to his Hindustani followers without any bride price. In flouting the Yusufzai "sense of shame and modesty" (Caroe 1965:304), Sayyid Ahmad signed his own death warrant. The Yusufzai rose against him en masse, killed most of the Hindustanis, and drove Sayyid Ahmad into Hazara, where he was soon killed by the Sikhs.

One of Sayyid Ahmad's rivals for spiritual leadership of the Pukhtun was a wandering Sufi named Abdul Gaffur. Born to a cowherding family in Upper Swat, Abdul Gaffur had felt a religious call and had migrated to India for instruction with Sufi masters. On his return to his native land, Abdul Gaffur began Sufic practices of renunciation and meditation which won him great fame. Knowledgeable of the customs of the Yusufzai, he did nothing to interfere with local mores, but rather served as a mediator in disputes, the traditional role of religious men in this segmentary society. The Pukhtun who benefitted from his decisions offered him land grants, as did others who simply wished to display their piety. As a result, the ascetic Abdul Gaffur soon became extremely wealthy. His grateful parishioners awarded him the title of Akhund, a messenger of God.

While Abdul Gaffur was building his reputation, the threat of the Sikh had been replaced by the pressures of British imperialism. The Great

Game between empires of Russia and England was played, in large part, in the remote hills of the North-West Frontier of the Raj. Control of *yaghestan*, the land of rebellion, was deemed vital to the thwarting of the supposed Russian thrust to the Indian Ocean. As the threat of colonialism became more imminent, the need for a leader to unite them became evident to the Swat Pukhtun. But, following their historical pattern, the khans could not select a leader from amongst themselves. In 1863, when the British did attack, marching on the Ambela Pass, common consent focused on the Akhund. Traditionally, the Pukhtun have relied on religious leadership when threatened from without. Trusting in the *baraka,* or charismatic power, of the Akhund, the Pukhtun fought the British to a standstill. As a result, Abdul Gaffur's prestige was unrivaled. "There was no doubt that the new place of pilgrimage to the Akhund in Saidu was beginning to gain in popularity at the expense of Pir Baba's tomb" (Caroe 1965:368). Even more land grants were donated to the Akhund, and his word became recognized as the equivalent of Islamic law among the Swati people. In return, the Akhund was careful that his decisions not break local custom, and he avoided seeking secular power, having the bad example of Sayyid Ahmad before him.

After the death of Akhund Abdul Gaffur in 1877, there was a drawn out and complex struggle for the role of spiritual leader in Swat between the family of the Akhund and the descendants of Pir Baba. During this period, the British were quiescent, and the Pukhtun felt little need to support either set of claimants. The region settled back into its previous state of internal strife and "ordered anarchy" as the local khans manipulated against one another in their interminable "hobby" of constant warfare.

The English, meanwhile, had decided that overt action on the Frontier was too costly and inefficient. Instead, they began to pursue a course of bribery and maneuvering in the petty kingdoms beyond their borders. Although there was no central political figure to suborn in Swat, the nearby kingdoms of Dir and Chitral offered fertile ground for colonial intrigue.

"Dir State has always been unique in that there alone among Pathans the tribes acknowledge one of themselves not only as a Khan or Malik, but as their hereditary ruler with power over their persons, indeed as a prince" (Caroe 1965:385). The reasons for this anomolous situation are complex, and I have discussed them in detail elsewhere (Lindholm in press), but revolve primarily around a confrontation in Dir between Pukhtun war leaders and the centralized state of Chitral. This confrontation led to an unusual development of hierarchy in Dir and the rise of a princely family.

Due to the centralization of Dir, the Dir state was regarded as the most powerful region in the Frontier. The Dir Nawab, as the ruler was called, was able to mobilize a large and well-organized standing army at short notice, and this powerful force was destined to play a major role in Swati history.

The valley of Dir runs parallel to Swat and is inhabited by the Melizai, who are considered descendants of Yusuf and therefore cousins of the people of Swat. Though politically more centralized, Dir is much poorer in resources than Swat. The land is dry and the climate is hard. The Dir Nawab has long cast envious glances at the wealth of Swat, and different rulers have welcomed the opportunity to meddle in Swati politics.

Opportunities were often forthcoming, under the conditions described by Schomberg: "There have always been two parties in these lawless lands. When one party weakens, it begins to intrigue with some neighboring ruler, hoping to induce him to come in, occupy the country and enable his supporters to work off their vendettas on their stronger opponents and so redress the balance of power" (1935:242). (The structural roots of this pattern will be discussed in chapter 3.) In Swat, the nearest available ruler was the Nawab of Dir. The Saddozais and a son of Dost Muhammad were also invited to intervene at one time or another (Masson 1842: 1:141). Intervention ended when a balance of forces within Swat was restored and when the intervening party made itself obnoxious by attempting to extort taxes and tribute. The Swatis would then unite to expel the interloper. This pattern of inviting better organized third parties to intervene in local quarrels was not confined to Swat, but is common on the Frontier. For example, the Marwats of Bannu invited the Nawab of Dera into their country, and then discovered that he was impossible to expel.

In Swat, the invitation and later eviction of Dir was repeated several times. But with the entrance of the British and their technical and monetary aid to Dir, the picture changed. The Dir army became more formidable than ever before. The British, however, did not make any overt moves, and appeared content to let the situation simmer.

But, in 1895, the cozy relationship between the colonial power and the petty princes was destroyed. An uprising led by Umrah Khan of Jandul in Dir quickly gained a following and the Dir Nawab was forced to flee his kingdom. Flushed with success, Umrah Khan moved north, entered Chitral, and captured the British garrison. With Pukhtuns rapidly rallying to the banner of the rebel, the British were forced once again to attempt direct intervention. Aided by the Dir Nawab, Lower Swat was invested and a fort set up. Umrah Khan was defeated in Chitral by Kashmiri levies and fled to Kabul. The die had been cast, the purdah of Swat had been irrevocably violated, and a British political agent was appointed to oversee the region.

In response to the overt invasion of the British, the familiar figure of a religious leader arose to rally the Pukhtun against the outsiders. Sadullah, the Mastan Mullah, or Mad Mullah (as he was called by his enemies), was a wandering mystic in the mold of Bazid. He claimed miraculous powers, and his pretensions of a direct relationship to the Diety drove the Swatis to a frenzy. In vain did the Akhund's family try to silence cries for a holy war against the British, fearing that the Mastan Mullah would eclipse them as spiritual leader of the Yusufzai should the battle succeed. The momentum was irresistible.

In 1897, Swat rose under the leadership of Sadullah and besieged the well-fortified British garrisons. "Before Malakand and Chakdara the tribesmen were religious maniacs for eight days and advanced with a bravery which fully entitled those who fell to any reward which such a death may bring" (Neville 1911:249). Almost 4,000 Pukhtun were killed in these futile assaults in the greatest pitched battle ever fought by the British on the Frontier.

The British, despite their victory, were hard-pressed to maintain control. Beset by outbreaks of revolt across the whole North-West Frontier Province, they once again relied on their loyal ally, the Nawab of Dir, to keep Swat pacified. The nawab, following his traditional role, again invaded Swat and was only beaten back after severe Swati losses.

The Swat Pukhtuns, threatened on all sides, once again needed a central leader. Sadullah, who had led the wasteful raids on the British forts, had been discredited. Other candidates were too weak. At last, the khans met and elected Abdul Wadud, the only living descendant of the Akhund, as their leader. This man, Abdul Wadud, was an astute and ruthless politician who had personally killed his two patrilateral first cousins (tarbur). Abdul Wadud organized the Swatis and managed to defeat the Dir Nawab and even to conquer parts of Buner to the east.

However, he realized that the Pukhtun only follow a leader in times of war. In order to solidify his position, he made an attempt to ally himself with the British. After a period of skepticism, the colonial power decided it would be more useful to deal with an already existing leader in Swat than to try to conquer the valley through the aggressions of Dir. With British aid, a telephone system and roadways were constructed throughout Swat. Coupled with a well-equipped private army, these new elements allowed Abdul Wadud, now styled the Badshah, to consolidate his power in Swat. Dir was ordered to cease its attacks, and the new state of Swat came into being under an absolute dictator. The Pukhtuns suddenly found that the man they had elected to defend their freedom had become their despot.

The Badshah now acted to break the power of local leaders by using their own internal rivalries. Filling the role of mediator, he always favored the weak party in any dispute, and the stronger khans soon found their lands under threat of confiscation. The power of the Pukhtuns was broken by their own factiousness and inability to unite. Under the pressure of colonial might, Swat had been transformed from a society without rulers into a tyranny.

In 1926 the British government officially sanctioned the Badshah's rule by giving him the title of Wali and granting him a subsidy. In 1947, Swat was among the first of the princely states to accede to the newly formed nation of Pakistan, but only on the condition of full local autonomy. Functionally, this meant the Pakistan government simply took over the role of the British, providing the Badshah with backing in return for peace among the Yusufzai. The Badshah continued his rule as despot until 1949, when he abdicated in favor of his eldest son, who was titled the Wali, and established a dynasty.

During the military government of Ayub Khan in Pakistan, great favor was granted to the Swati ruling family. In fact, two of Ayub's daughters were married to sons of the Wali. In 1966, President Ayub declared that the Wali was henceforth to be addressed as "Highness" and given a fifteen gun salute on all official occasions. When Ayub fell, the royal family of Swat offered him refuge, and suffered in consequence of their close relationship with the deposed national leader. Popular reaction in Pakistan against Ayub combined with agitation within Swat against the Wali and led to full incorporation of Swat within Pakistan. In 1969, the short-lived dynasty of the Badshah came to an end, and a deputy com-

The oldest khan in Shin Bagh in his *hujera*.

missioner took over the Wali's place. Factionalism once more returned as the order of the day, now that the total power of the Wali had been replaced by a manipulable democratic state (Lindholm 1979).

The era of the Badshah is the period in which the history of the area around Shin Bagh can be traced with some accuracy. Elders of Shin Bagh and the surrounding villages were often participants in the wars with Dir and resistance movements against the Badshah's authority. Although each lineage praises itself and downplays the influence of others, interviews with a number of old men yielded a quite coherent story.

The district of Shamizai/Sebujni in Upper Swat, which includes the village of Shin Bagh, was the area most opposed to the Badshah's takeover. "Although verbally they accepted my authority," the Badshah writes in his autobiography, "yet they did not entertain the slightest idea

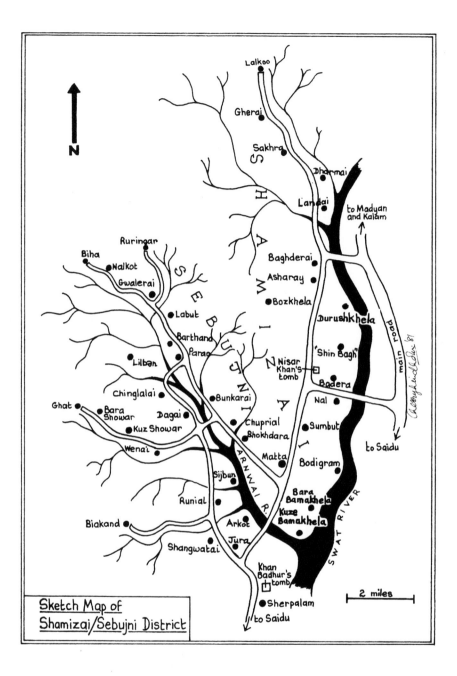

Sketch Map of
Shamizai/Sebujni District

of the principle that all subjects of a State have to live under a certain discipline. . . . They regarded themselves above all temporal laws and moral code. . . . The khans of the area were by no means scrupulous in appropriating to themselves even the lands belonging to me'' (Wadud 1962:54–55).

As in all of Swat, the Pukhtun of Shamizai/Sebujni were divided into two parties, or dala. One party was led by the Malik khel, who now live in Shin Bagh; the other was led by the Mahmat khel, who now live in Durushkhela. Other strong leaders were the Shama khel of Sebujni and the Jora khel of southern Shamizai. Each party had allies in all of the villages of the region and within each other's villages as well. Both parties had ties with Dir, and both had a history of inviting the Dir Nawab into Swat to settle their disputes. Both parties had recruited large bands of fugitives as personal retainers for themselves and their allies, and both parties were alike in their proud disdain of the Badshah's attempts to establish himself as their ruler.

In this intransigent and powerful region, the Badshah could not follow his usual policy of favoring weak elements, for fear of arousing the strong clans to warfare. Instead, he began by favoring the Malik khel, entrusting them with tax collection, and giving a fee to the leading men. However, the Malik khel were not satisfied with the bribe and began appropriating tax money for themselves. The Badshah then aligned himself with the Mahmat khel and drove the Malik khel leaders into exile in Dir, where they requested the intervention of the Dir Nawab. But the alliance between the British and the Badshah kept the nawab immobilized and the power of the Malik khel was effectively broken.

But in defeating one party the Badshah had gained a dangerous ally in the Mahmat khel. Like the Malik khel, the Mahmet khel had no loyalty to the Badshah, regarding him as a mere upstart. They began developing a following of other Pukhtun who opposed the Badshah's rule.

Abdul Wadud, the Badshah, kept up friendly relations with the Mahmat khel and appeared to take no notice of their growing threat. In 1926, the elder of the Mahmat khel was invited to a hunting party with the Badshah. The party ended with the Mahmat khel elder shot dead. The Badshah's private army then moved quickly to disarm the Mahmat khel and drive them into Dir, from which the Malik khel had recently returned.

Now that the two powerful dalas of Shamizai/Sebujni had been overthrown, the Badshah was free to name his own man as leader (Malik).

This man, Khan Badhur, of the Jora *khel,* had previously been in the Malik *khel dəla*. He was a wily and relentless plotter who had covertly supported the Badshah for some time with an eye to gaining power in his own district. Unlike the other khans, he realized that the Badshah was not going to fade into the background. Yet, though he arose by the will of the monarch, Khan Badhur was hardly a puppet. The elements of the defeated parties were still so powerful and so bitter that a strong internal force was needed to control them. In exchange for peace and security, the Badshah was obliged to give Khan Badhur a free hand and unconditional support, thus allowing the construction of what was, in effect, a state within a state. The parallel with the British attitude toward the Badshah is obvious.

According to informants, the Badshah was unhappy with the existence of a powerful separate state within his boundaries, but he trusted that Khan Badhur had no ambitions beyond absolute power within his own sphere. Khan Badhur, on his part, acted as a buffer between the ruler and the abrasive and contentious Pukhtun of Upper Swat. He monopolized all channels of communication and terrorized the Pukhtun with his cruelties, arbitrary judgments, and land appropriations. "The Badshah can never replace me," he is quoted as saying. "I am his protection. I take the blame for all his cruelty."

Beneath the iron rule of Khan Badhur, the old *dəla* system remained dormant. Although obliged by circumstances to support Khan Badhur, the Badshah was careful to keep him from completely destroying his opponents. The ruler reputedly wished to retain at least a potential opposition party within Shamizai/Sebujni for use at the appropriate moment.

This situation continued until 1959. In that year, the son of Khan Badhur's closest ally conspired with the Wali of Swat and the unhappy khans of the district. This man, Major Nisar Khan, had joined the Pakistani air force, and so had a power base outside of Swat. He was able to intrigue against his father's friend (who had forced him into virtual exile out of fear of his abilities) with relative impunity. At the same time, the Wali knew that Nisar Khan's air force duties would prevent him from being the strong leader that Khan Badhur was. The alliance was a success, and Khan Badhur was overthrown at last. Shamizai/Sebujni now returned to its party rivalries, which the Wali carefully manipulated to prevent any party from becoming too powerful. To keep any of the hot-headed Pukhtun from revenging themselves on him for the deaths, exiles, and humiliations they had suffered, the Wali brought a number of them into the civil service and allowed them to share the spoils of statehood. The Wali, however, soon followed Khan Badhur into ruin, as we have seen. (For more detail, see Lindholm 1979.)

After the fall of the Wali, the political arena took on a new form. The parties which had been submerged reappeared and began struggling for the spoils offered by the Pakistani central government. However, the rules had been transformed since the advent of the Badshah. From a purely local drama, relatively uninfluenced by external hierarchies, the participants in Swat now played on the national stage and for national stakes. The intervention of the British in crowning the Badshah and supporting his successor, the Wali, had shown the Pukhtun that it was possible to have a dictator in Swat, provided he had the support of a strong external force. Where the battles in the "hobby" of war had formerly ended in a balance of oppositions, they were now seen to involve a potential for dictatorship.

A further change was the suppression of large-scale warfare. Rather than battling and forcing one another into temporary terms of exile, the parties now warred through the ballot (which is not to claim that violence and threats of violence had ceased to be important, only that violence was no longer practiced on so large a scale).

In Upper Swat, the new party alignments included the old Mahmat khel dala on one side, opposed by the party of the Wali and his supporters among Nisar Khan's party (he was a member of the Nakrudin khel of Badera, cousins and allies of the Malik khel). In 1970, the election returns split between these parties, with the Mahmat khel winning a seat in the Provincial Assembly, while the royal family, in alliance with Nisar Khan, won the National Assembly race. Almost unnoticed was the candidacy of Nisar Khan's younger brother, Dost Muhammad, running on the unpopular Pakistan People's Party (PPP) ticket. Dost Muhammad was a new element in local politics. He refused to follow either party. The Mahmat khel were his traditional enemies, while the Wali's party had relegated his elder brother, Nisar Khan, to a minor role. To the other khans, his stand seemed quixotic and self-destructive, and he received almost no votes.

But Dost Muhammad proved to be at least a temporary prophet when the party of the Mahmat khel, the National Awami Party (NAP) was disbanded by the PPP-dominated central government. The Mahmat khel representative was jailed, and Dost Muhammad suddenly became the conduit for favors from the national government. As a result of his new power, the Mahmat *khel dala* split and Khan Badhur's son, Feteh Muhammad, who had joined the Mahmat *khel* out of hatred for the Wali and fear for his own position, switched sides to join Dost Muhammad. The Wali's party, meanwhile, had run on the Muslim League (ML) ticket, which proved unexpectedly weak nationally. One of the Wali's sons decided to join the ascendant PPP, leading to a serious rift within the family which effectively took them out of politics in Upper Swat. In the 1977 elections, the Wali's sons ran against one another in their own home district of Lower Swat. The field in Shamizai/Sebujni was left to the PPP, composed of the followers of Dost Muhammad and Feteh Muhammad, and the party of the Mahmat *khel*. Essentially, things had returned in form to the pattern prior to the Badshah, with the major difference being that the former Malik *khel dala* was now being led by the Nakrudin *khel*.

But the similarities were, in part, misleading. The alignments took in new elements and new relationships which had been absent in traditional politics. To understand these changes, an awareness of certain transformations in the total society is necessary.

It has been mentioned several times that a money economy had slowly been eroding the economies of barter and the patron–client redistributive network in Swat. This is a fairly recent phenomenon. Even during Barth's fieldwork in 1954 it was possible to state that "the Pakistan rupee, though widely used, is not present in the required volume to serve as a medium for most exchanges in the Swat valley" (1965:43). In 1977 only a very few important exchanges resisted monetization. As a result, there was an increasing pressure to break down the bonds of clientship. Machinery began to replace field labor, and the introduction of new crops often led to reduction of the labor force. Furthermore, in order to purchase newly imported prestige goods, the Pukhtun were inclined to sell their surplus foodstuffs rather than use them for customary payments for services. It was discovered that ceremonies which formerly required a number of dependents could instead be performed privately with a minimum of expense. In this way, servants were severed from their masters and thrust upon the labor market. One result has been the massive exodus of cheap labor out of Swat. Another has been an increased possibility of the poor beginning to see themselves as an oppressed class, whereas previously, as Barth notes, their interests were inextricably attached to the fortunes of their patrons. "Master and servant . . . are unequal and complementary, and the fate and career of the one depends to a very great extent on the actions of the other" (1965:49).

The national policies of the PPP government, which had been elected on a promise of socialistic reform, acted to accelerate the growing separation between the landless and the landed classes. One important measure was a proclamation of land redistribution. While this had little or no effect in Swat, where even the largest landowners are relatively small holders, the program stirred up the fears of the landed and the hopes of the landless. A second, more concrete measure, involved a new emphasis on tenant rights and an end to compulsory labor. This struck at the heart of the old order by challenging the absolute rights of the patrons over their clients. These new ordinances had their most dramatic effect in the highland areas, where herdsmen and farmers began claiming the land as their own. Pitched battles were fought over this issue, and a number of men were killed. In the lowlands, resistance was not so well organized due, no doubt, to the close proximity of the landlords and the close traditional ties they had with their clients. However, many tenants did make use of the new preemption laws to take their landlords to court and to resist eviction from their houses.

The client population, under the twin influences of a changing economy and a socialistically inclined central government, began to be self-conscious. From a society dominated by the vertical splits of the dəla system, in which clients joined their patrons in battles against other patron—client groups, Swat moved toward horizontal cleavages and class conflict. (For similar patterns in Southeast Asia, see Scott 1972; and Scott and Kerkvliet 1975.)

There were several responses among the Pukhtun to this new phenomenon. One was the resurgence of a religious party and a reappearance of the traditional figure of a charismatic religious leader. In the 1970 elections, the religious party of the Jamaat-i-Ulema-i-Islam (JUI) had been a minor factor. But in 1977, with the threat of the PPP becoming more evident, the JUI became the focus of landlord resistance to the demands of the poor. Many Pukhtun suddenly grew beards as a sign of piety and began consulting their religious teachers (imams), who responded by stressing the sanctity of private property in Islamic law and the need for strict punishment of the irreligious. The problem of poverty was left to the charity of the wealthy.

The Mahmat *khel* party, as opponents of the PPP, welcomed the religious JUI into their party. A charismatic imam was even accepted as coleader in the party, to run for office in tandem with the Mahmat *khel* candidate.

But while the rise of a religious appeal had formerly united all the Pukhtun, in the modern case it did not. The cry of the imams against the PPP was seen by the PPP *dala* as merely a plot to gain power. The trickery of the Badshah, who had united the Pukhtun as a religious leader only to rule them as a tyrant, was remembered by all. Instead of joining the JUI against the poor, the PPP sought alliance with the poor. This is not to claim that the Pukhtun of the PPP had any socialistic inclinations. On the contrary, one of the arguments used by PPP leaders to convince wavering Pukhtuns to join them was that the land of PPP landlords would be safe from redistribution. Nonetheless, in public meetings and speeches, the PPP leaders were obliged to use the socialist rhetoric of their national leadership.

Though most of the PPP *dalas* were simply opportunistically making use of their poor constituency, some of the younger men, motivated by the humanitarian precepts of their English-based educations and a desire for personal power, did actually move among the poor, organize them, and make plans for a revolution, with themselves as the future rulers. The poor, though openly skeptical of the motivations of the Pukhtun who had joined them, nevertheless were glad to let the landlords dominate conversations, call meetings, and make decisions about political strategy. Long habits of obedience in combination with a realistic respect for the ubiquitous power and educational training of the young landlords kept the poor in the role of yes men. Yet the fact that some of the landed felt obliged, for whatever reasons, to actively identify themselves with their menials and not the converse was an unprecedented development in Swati politics. The development structurally countered the retrograde motion of the rising JUI.

The two parties, while similar in many ways to those which had existed before the Badshah, had totally new elements within them. The PPP looked to support from below, that is, from the poor who for the first time were seeing themselves as a distinct interest group. The Mahmat *khel* party, now styled by the national leaders as the Pakistan National Alliance (PNA), incorporated the religious segment of the populace who had formerly led in times of external threat, and who had now been conjured up to lead the internal struggle against the nascent demands of the poor.

In the first elections—held in March 1977—for the National Assembly seat in Upper Swat, the PPP candidate, Feteh Muhammad, the son of the former despot Khan Badhur, won a convincing victory over his opponent, the JUI imam. The deciding vote came, not from the Pukhtun, who split equally along traditional *dəla* lines, but from the numerous tenants and laborers who looked to the PPP for help in their battle for rights over land presently held by the Pukhtun.

However, their victory was an ephemeral one. The PNA, defeated throughout Pakistan, declared the elections unfair and began a campaign of strikes and national disruption. For reasons outside the scope of this work, the agitation could not be controlled by the central government. The PPP followers in Swat, who had assumed that the ruling party had as much power as the British Raj, were stunned and dismayed by its impotence. Some began joining the Mahmat *khel*, while others considered founding new parties. Feteh Muhammad's half brother suddenly announced that he had decided to run against the PPP leader, Dost Muhammad, as an independent candidate. Observers believed him to be secretly encouraged by Feteh Muhammad, who was thinking of switching sides once again.

These machinations were cut short when Pakistan's General Zia declared the nation to be under martial law in July. The real power in national Pakistani politics—the military—had taken over. His move was met in Swat with a sense of relief, since it had appeared that large-scale violence was imminent. With the religious men compromised by their membership in the PNA political party, only the central government, traditionally a military-cum-bureaucracy, had the capacity to mediate. The army was seen as a neutral body which would dispense justice during a period of disruption, much in the form of the traditional saintly mediator.

But it was not long before the Pukhtun became tired of the arbitrary military rule. We have seen that traditionally the leader–mediator was replaced after the crisis passed, and Swat returned to internal feuds, fragmentation, *dəla* politics, and business as usual. The Badshah, who was the only man to rule Swat effectively, was kept in place by colonial might. General Zia needed an equally strong force to maintain himself, but one factor in his favor is that the crisis, involving a transformation of the system, not only in Swat, but nationally, threatens to be permanent. (For more detail on Swati politics and its relation to the national politics of Pakistan, see Lindholm 1977 and 1979.)

Despite the novel elements which have been introduced by the influence of the market economy, colonial power, and the nation-state, there is a remarkable continuity in Swati history. The two party system reemerged as soon as pressures from above were reduced. Traditional rivalries, structured by oppositions on the ground between local enemies, gave Swat a fluid yet enduring political structure. The role of the mediator, once held by the so-called saints of holy lineage, has shifted, at least in part, to the government bureaucracy, but the function remains the same. The Pukhtun of Swat, to all appearences, are characterized throughout their history by a remarkable ability to join together to resist invasion and domination, and by an equally remarkable inability to retain that unity after the intruder has been defeated. Struggle and opposition was and remains the way of life for the Pukhtun; a way of life only momentarily altered by an ephemeral state system.

CHRONOLOGY OF EVENTS, PERSONALITIES, AND ALLIANCES

1863   Saidu Baba, a great pir, unites the Swat Pukhtun against British aggression at Ambela. He assumes the spiritual leadership of Swat and becomes a big landowner.

1895   The British invest Lower Swat.

1897   An uprising against the British fails.

1908   The Nawab of Dir, an ally of the British, invades Swat and is expelled with difficulty.

1915   Beset on all sides, the Pukhtun elect Miangul Abdul Wadud, the only living descendant of Saidu Baba, as leader. He allies himself with the British and becomes a despot.

1926   The leader of the Mahmat *khel dala* of Shamizai/Sebujni is shot dead at a hunting party held by Abdul Wadud, who is now the Badshah, or ruler, of Swat. The Mahmat *khel* are exiled to Dir and Khan Badhur is appointed *malik* of the rebellious Shamizai/Sebujni region.

1947   Swat joins Pakistan, but keeps internal autonomy.

1949   The Badshah abdicates in favor of his eldest son, who is styled the Wali of Swat.

1959   Khan Badhur, after three decades of absolute power, is dethroned by an alliance of the Wali and Pakistan air force Major Nisar Khan, the son of Khan Badhur's closest ally. Nisar Khan is unable to control the region and the Wali's strategy is to keep the area in confusion by playing all the parties against one another.

1964   Khan Badhur dies and is replaced as party leader by his son, Feteh Muhammad Khan.

1969   The Wali, closely allied to Ayub Khan, is deposed after the fall of Ayub, and Swat is fully integrated into Pakistan. Feteh Muhammad announces that he is abolishing his party and joining the Mahmat *khel*.

1970   National elections are held in Swat. The main contestants in Shamizai/Sebujni are from the party of the Wali and the party of the Mahmat *khel*. The Wali's son, Aurangzeb, is victor in the National Assembly election, running on the Muslim League ticket, while Muhammad Afzal Khan of the Mahmat *khel* wins the Provincial seat on the National Awami slate. The People's Party Candidate is Dost Muhammad Khan, Nisar Khan's youngest brother, who wins few votes.

1973   Muhammad Afzal Khan, after a meteoric rise to presidency of the NAP in the Frontier, is jailed and the NAP is banned by the nationally dominant PPP. Dost Muhammad, as the sole representative of the PPP in Shamzai/Sebujni, suddenly becomes powerful. Feteh Muhammad splits from the foundering Mahmat *khel* and joins Dost Muhammad, thus reuniting Khan Badhur's old alliance.

1974   Major Nisar Khan dies in Saudi Arabia.

1977   National elections are again held. Dost Muhammad and Feteh Muhammad are the PPP candidates. The Mahmat *khel* run Afzal Khan's elder brother, Muhammad Alam Khan, in tandem with

Maulana Abdul Rahman as Pakistan National Alliance candidates. The Wali's family, split by internal rivalry, does not contest the elections in Upper Swat. Feteh Muhammad wins the National Assembly race against Maulana Abdul Rahman. The Provincial election is boycotted by the PNA, and rioting occurs throughout Pakistan, leading to martial law and the cancellation of further elections.

3. Social Structure

The Pukhtun have not succeeded in being a great nation because there is an autocrat in each home who would rather burn his own house than see his brother rule it.
(G. Khan 1958:46)

Everywhere family is arrayed against family, and tribe against tribe. In fact, one way and another, every man's hand is against his neighbor.
(Bellew 1864:204)

In order to understand society, the main thing to grasp is that it is simple in detail, and complex only in the huge accumulation of detail . . . from a purely cognitive point of view, society is the easiest manifestation to study, and its laws are primitive and accessible to all. If it were not so, social life would be totally impossible, since in society people live by these laws and must necessarily realize what they are.
(Zinoviev 1979:52)

Much of this chapter is a revised version of my paper on Swati social organization (Lindholm 1981a).

VIOLENCE, structured through institutions of feud and warfare, is perhaps the most important formative element in Middle Eastern segmentary lineage societies such as Swat. As organizations of "disequilibrium in equilibrium" (Hart 1970:74), these societies become coherent in relations of lineage opposition. "In other words the tribe is not organised except for offence and defence; except in war and in matters ultimately connected with war, the licence of individual freewill is absolutely uncontrolled" (Robertson-Smith 1903:68).

The ideal form of the patrilineal segmentary lineage system unites groups and individuals through descent from a common male ancestor. Those who share an ancestor are obliged, by the tie of blood, to defend one another against outsiders or more distant relatives. In theory, coalitions in opposition can unite thousands, or even millions, of putative lineal relatives in warfare against intruders, as the British, French and, more recently, Soviet colonialists have discovered. The same mechanism operates at the very lowest level of the genealogy as well, grouping brothers against patrilateral parallel cousins (father's brother's sons). In its ideal form the system has a boundless capacity for fusion and fission, "since even the nuclear family is a miniature of the larger social system" (Murphy and Kasdan 1959:27).

But the ideal pattern in which every segment at every level is structurally equivalent is mitigated in Swat by differentiation in the vital matters of revenge and warfare. Among the Swat Pukhtun the most acrimonious conflict is between individuals and not between groups. Opponents do not often have the comfort of like-minded comrades accompanying them into battle. Instead lone men struggle against their closest patrilateral relatives in personal, perpetual, and sometimes deadly competition over the land of their common grandfather. The Badshah, who killed his own cousins while pursuing his political ambitions, was merely acting within the traditional framework of Swati political life, in which, as the Badshah himself notes, "the only possible course open to us then was to take the initiative and put [our cousin] to death before he did the same to us" (Wadud 1962:8). By killing one's patrilateral relatives, one gains title to their land and possessions.

The action of land rights in forming the social structure and relations of rivalry is recognized in the kinship terminology. Land rights are granted through the patrilineal genealogy, and one who has no land is, in effect, no longer a Pukhtun. Land and personal identity are deeply intertwined in local thought, and efforts to increase one's own holdings form the leitmotif of Pukhtun life. The competition between men who are sons of brothers over land rights is symbolized by the term of reference for the patrilateral parallel cousin, *tarbur*. This term has come to signify an enemy, and the term *tarburwali* means a relationship of enmity. At the same time, implicit in the term is the possibility of alliance in the face of an external threat. The term *tarbur* is strictly a term of reference, and would never be used in address except as an insult. Instead, *tarbur* are called *wror* (brother) or *trə zway* (father's brother's son).

A contrast between the terms of reference and those of address gives some insight into the various areas of conflict and cooperation in village life. The terms of reference are given below (FF = father's father; MMZ = mother's mother's sister; FFBSW = father's father's brother's son's wife; etc.). The kinship charts shown in figures 3.1 and 3.2 give the basic terms of reference.

nikə: FF, FFB, FMB, MF, MFB, MMB, etc.
nya: MM, MMZ, MFZ, FM, FMZ, FBZ, etc.
tror: FZ, MZ, FFBD, etc.
trə: FB, FFBS, etc.
mama: MB, MFBS, etc.
tandar: FBW, FFBSW, etc.
mami: MBW, MFBSW, etc.
plar: F
mor: M
wror: B, MBS, MZS, FZS, etc.
xor: MBD, MZD, FZD, FBD, etc.
tarbur: FBS, FFBSS, etc.
warara: BS, FBSS, etc.
wrera: BD, FBSD, etc.
xorye: ZS, MBSS, etc.
xorza: ZD, MBSD, etc.
zway: S
lur: D

nwase: SS, BSS, BDS, ZSS, ZDS, DS, etc.
nwasəi: SD, BSD, BDD, ZSD, ZDD, DD, etc.
skhər: HF, HFB, WF, WFB, etc.
xwakhe: HM, HFZ, WM, WFZ, etc.
lewar: HB, HFBS, etc.
indror: HZ, HFBD, etc.
yor: HBW, HFBSW, etc.
bən: co-wife
khawənd: H
khəza: W
okhe: WB, WFBS, etc.; also ZH
khina: WZ, WFBD, etc.
sandu: WZH, WFBDH, etc.
wrəndar: WBW, WFBSW, etc.; also BW
zum: DH
ungor: SW

Although most rivalry is focused on the *tarbur*, it is not the only term

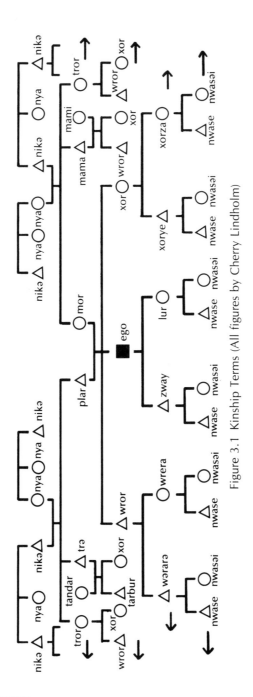

Figure 3.1 Kinship Terms (All figures by Cherry Lindholm)

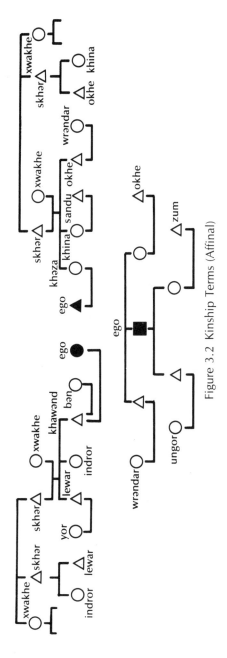

Figure 3.2 Kinship Terms (Affinal)

of reference which is avoided. The same is true for terms which pertain to relatives by marriage. It is, for example, a serious insult to address one's father-in-law as *skhar*. Rather, he should be called ji (sir) or by a respectful nickname, as are all other older men, including one's own father. Women of the wife's lineage should be called *tror*, not *xwakhe*, while her brothers and sisters are *wror* and *xor*, not *okhe* and *khina*. Use of the term *khaza* (wife) is also avoided, replaced either by proper name or by teknonymy (e.g., the mother of my son). The same pattern of avoidances follows for women as well.

The evidence of the terminology is born out by the actual relations between husband and wife and the relations with in-laws. Inside the nuclear family, men and women confront one another in a continuous struggle for power. Women, as incoming wives, seek to retain their lineage honor and to gain a position of dominance in their new home. For men, the task is to subdue the wife or, failing that, to humiliate her. The husband has the trump card in this battle, since he can take a second wife, thereby shaming the first and all her lineage. The woman's response may be violent, as she is not allowed to divorce. Overt fighting, as well as covert use of magical spells against her rival, are the woman's weapons. Should she fail to drive out her co-wife, she may vindicate herself by poisoning her husband, and men with two wives who die of "cholera" are rumored to have been murdered, though public accusations are rarely made.

On the other side of the sexual war, men are permitted and encouraged to beat their wives regularly. Only if bones are broken is a woman allowed to flee to her family, and even then she must return to her husband after a year or so. Outright murder of wives, however, is very uncommon, since the wife's lineage would avenge her death. The few cases of uxoricide have involved women without close male relatives. But there is an exception to the rule of lineage vengeance for the death of a lineage woman: if the woman has been sexually promiscuous or acted in manner which is scandalous, her own male relatives will reject and even shoot her. (For more complete data on Pukhtun marriage see the next chapter and Lindholm and Lindholm 1979.)

The problems of violence between husband and wife make a peaceful relationship between in-laws very difficult. For the wife, the case is made worse by her being coresident with her husband's mother, who makes a new bride's life miserable. Married life in Swat is fraught with tension.

Nonetheless, the woman who arrives in a Pukhtun household as a new bride becomes, in a generation, the mother of the sons in the lineage. The in-laws who are her husband's nemesis become her sons' allies. The term *mama* (mother's brother) is extended to all older men who are not known and with whom one wishes to be on good terms, while the term *mama zway* is extended to all younger men of the same category. Although terms for in-laws are avoided, terms for matrilineal relatives are used as a symbol for a friendly relationship. Indeed, in ordinary life such relatives are considered part of the family, despite the strong patrilineal ideology of the Pukhtun. There is even a term, the *nikanə*, which indicates relatives from the grandparents on down on both the father's side and the mother's side. This is the unit with whom a woman does not keep purdah, the unit from whom one expects aid in trouble (though those on the maternal side are most likely to give financial aid, while those on the paternal side must give aid in cases of revenge), the unit within which one is most likely to marry, and finally, in the persons of the *tarbur*, this unit contains one's most immediate and implacable enemies.

In recognizing, within the *nikanə*, the importance of the maternal relatives, the Pukhtun social structure assumes a cognatic aspect. This aspect is further emphasized in another term *nasab*, which indicates a lineage tied to one's own by marriage. In reckoning genealogies, I was constantly surprised by the ability of men to remember where their great-grandfather's sisters had married, not to mention their awareness of where all the women who had married in had come from in the last four or five generations. Men whose mothers were sisters were expected to be allies, and alliance was often explained in these terms.

In recent times, marriage with other patrilineages has noticeably decreased, while real and classificatory father's brother's daughter marriage has increased. Among the Malik *khel*, for example, the number of father's brother's daughter marriages was 25 percent in the great-grandparents' generation (4 out of 16), 17 percent in the grandparents' generation (5 out of 29), 27 percent in the parents' generation (14 out of 52), and 41 percent in the present generation (19 out of 46). Other *khels* show a similar trend, which is recognized by the elders, who explain it by saying that "since war is finished, we no longer need seek allies outside our own people."

The truth is that, even in the old days, alliances with *nasab* were very tenuous and transitory. The villagers have a special term for a lineage with whom they often intermarry. Such a lineage is called *xpəl wuli*. But, in examining actual marriage links over time, it is evident that such a close alliance was an ideal rather than a reality. The tensions of the affinal relationship are such that close intermarriage between two lineages rarely, if ever, lasts beyond two generations.

The attempt to establish links through the maternal side is an effort to evade the hostilities which prevail on the paternal side. Yet it is the patrilineage which holds land together and which is obliged to stand united against intrusion. Even though one's *tarbur* are, by definition, one's enemies, they also are the people one turns to in cases of external aggression. The relatives in the mother's lineage are comforting and generous up to a point, but they cannot be counted on in emergencies. The relatives in the patrilineage are connected by their common inheritance. This is called being *mirasi* to one another. The word comes from *mirat*, which designates a man who is in the unfortunate position of having no sons. When this occurs, the last surviving brother of the sonless man will receive a double portion of the father's inheritance to pass on to his own sons. If a whole family dies out, its members' land passes on to their nearest patrilineal relatives, their *mirasi*. It is therefore to the advantage of patrilineal cousins to protect the land of their cousins from the encroachments of outsiders while at the same time hoping (and sometimes doing more than merely hope) that the cousin's line will die out. There is a delicate balance here. A man whose close relatives are *mirat* may have a great deal of land, but he has no one to count on to help him protect it. Hostility within the male line of descent is tempered by expedient self-interest. The bond that unites the relatives is not a loving one; they are held together by fear that even more dangerous enemies are waiting to pounce whenever weakness or dissension is displayed.

The patrilineal system of inheritance, with its special twist in giving the last surviving brother of a sonless man a double share instead of dividing the land equally among all the brothers, greatly increases the internal rivalry in the system. The tension between *tarbur* is carried right into the nuclear family itself, as brothers may become rivals for the inheritance of their sonless siblings.

It is well recognized in Swat that the system of inheritance is against Muslim law, but this does not deter the Pukhtun from following their ancient custom. It is said that a man can give land to his daughter while he is still alive, and this land is then inalienable. In practice, such a gift

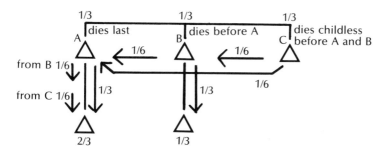

Figure 3.3 Inheritance Rights for a Man Without Sons (*Mirat*)

is extremely rare, and I have heard of only one case, which occurred with a father's brother's daughter marriage. Giving land to a daughter might mean transferring land out of the patrilineage and would be resisted by the other members of the lineage. It could only occur with remote *tseri* (nonclan) land owned solely by the girl's father. While Muslim law, which pronounces that the women of the house should take half shares of the estate, is not followed in Swat, it is reported south of the valley in Mardan and Hashtnagar. According to the Swatis, the result has been that brothers, reluctant to let their land be scattered, do not allow their sisters to marry. Supposedly, the unfortunate women remain celibate and isolated in their brothers' compounds. In Swat, on the other hand, spinsters are rare indeed.

Although the custom is for land to be divided equally among brothers, the absolute rights of the landlord are recognized. As ruler of his tiny principality of farmland, the landlord can decide to give one son more, cut another son out altogether and even, as mentioned above, give land to a daughter. In fact, fathers fear the hatred which such acts would engender among those slighted and therefore do divide the land equally. Men sometimes divide their property before they die, but always keep an equal share for themselves. The old men say this is because they fear that if they gave up all their property, their sons would not feed them. The tendency of old men to hold on to their land as long as possible is a major source of the pervasive tension between fathers and sons. A man is not truly a Pukhtun until he has absolute control of property and, by the same logic, a man who gives up his property, even to his own sons, loses his social identity. Thus, the violence of disputes between fathers and sons, the smoldering resentment of sons toward their fathers, and the complaints of fathers that their sons are greedy, are all based in the identification of a Pukhtun with his rights in land.

A man who can no longer stand the tension and who is especially anxious to show his independence may press his father to grant him a piece of land for his own compound. This was the case with Zaman Khan, who had a particularly abrasive relationship with his father as the son of his father's first, less favored wife. This woman had, in fact, spent much of her married life with her own family in Bodigram village, and Zaman had lived with her there as a child. His pride and resentment played a great part in his strong desire to be his own man and to be free of his father's charity. Furthermore, Qajira Khana, Zaman's wife, had not gotten along at all well with Zaman's stepmother when the young couple lived together in Zaman's father's house in the first years of their marriage.

It was because of these problems that Zaman had gone to work in Saidu Sherif where I met him. Later, in the interests of family peace, his father had agreed to give him a plot for a house and Zaman had constructed his own compound adjoining his father's, but separated from it by a wall, thereby declaring his liberation from his father's influence. Zaman's job with the tobacco company allowed him to earn enough to feed his family without much help from his father (he had been given only land for a house, not land to work as a farm), and he was able to live quite autonomously. Perhaps as a result, his relations with his father were much more amicable, and even Qajira Khana and Zaman's stepmother established a relationship of wary respect.

Zaman, however, was unusual in having an outside source of income that let him buy his own food. Generally, sons who have separated from their fathers either must continue living on their father's charity or else have land given them as well as a house lot. Even when a son is relatively independent, the father may still stop by his son's house and help himself to some onions in his son's garden. The son cannot publicly help himself in the same way from his father's property, but may creep over the father's house wall and snatch a chicken or transplant a seedling removed from the father's fields. If caught, he will merely claim that he is asserting his rights and taking recompense for the fact that his father does not give him his share of food. Theft is often seen simply as a covert balancing of exchange within a family in which the elders are allowed to appropriate what they want openly, but the juniors are obliged to do so clandestinely. The relationship between father and son is seen in purely economic terms, with the father seeking to maintain his position of wealth and power against the demands of his offspring. Rivalry, then, is not only between patrilateral parallel cousins (*tarbur*), but also between brothers and fathers and sons.

Attempts to increase one's own holdings are partly held in check by the rule that land must be kept within the patrilineage. A man may increase his power base within his lineage, but he will find it almost impossible to extend his range beyond his natal village. Although men are occasionally obliged to sell their *dauftar* (clan land), they must sell within the circle of the close patriline. An outsider who came to claim land within the village would find his fields burned and his own life in danger. For example, a man in one ward of Shin Bagh, in need of money, sold a garden plot to a wealthy man in another ward. But when the buyer came to claim his land, he was met by the furious *tarbur* of the seller, who told him, "This land is under my hand. Anyone who wants to work it must be ready to fight me." Fearful of a battle, the buyer demanded his money back and the seller had to resell the land to his *tarbur* at a much lower price. As another example, a man did sell his land to an outsider. However, he kept the sale completely quiet and worked the land himself as a sharecropper of the new owner, delivering payments in secret. This trickery was necessary to avoid the ire of his *tarburs*, who had first rights to the land by custom. At the same time, the new land-owner was forced to accept a relatively small return on his investment since if he complained he might get nothing at all.

A man who sells land in Swat is known as *begherata*, or without honor. It is a stinging insult to suggest to someone that he might wish to sell his land, as it suggests that he is willing to sell his identity as a Pukhtun. More honorable is leasing the land to a relative. This type of lease, called *ganṛa*, is considered almost like a sale, since sometimes the money given cannot be repaid and the land functionally becomes the property of the leaseholder. For this reason, *ganṛa*, like outright sale, is allowed only within the patriline.

Tseri land which is held in shares does not have the same restrictions on sale, since it is not properly clan land. It is possible for a man to own *tseri* and not be a Pukhtun. Men who own *tseri* are allowed to sell it freely to any buyer, but with one peculiar proviso. Shareholders in a piece of *tseri* land must be kinsmen. Therefore, if one shareholder wishes to sell and the others cannot afford to buy, all the shares must be offered for sale. The principle of lineage ownership of land thus carries over even into ownership of land not explicitly linked to the patriline, indicating the strength of the concept. The following story is noteworthy by way of illustration: Two brothers and a cousin held a valuable piece of *tseri* far from Shin Bagh. The Badshah bribed the cousin to sell his share, and therefore the two brothers, though reluctant to give up such a prime piece of land, were obliged by custom to follow suit.

Recently, however, some of the strong men of Shin Bagh have flouted the rules and sold some of their *tseri* and even some *dauftar* to monied landless men, decreasing the total share and making the clan land "like air" (see appendix A, table 7). But the other clan members who have a claim to the land by virtue of their blood tie with the seller do manage to get something out of the transaction. They threaten the buyer with litigation, since such sales can be challenged in the local Swati courts as breaking tradition. To avoid costly litigation, the buyer is obliged to pay bribes to the claimants.

But although the lineage unites to hold land, it struggles within itself over control of land. This struggle is known as *tarburwali*, the opposition between patrilateral parallel cousins. Yet, as we have seen, there is violence as well between husband and wife and implicit hostility between in-laws; furthermore, opposition reaches into the nuclear family itself, though not on the scale of *tarburwali*. Father and son and male siblings have tense relations, despite the formal respect and service the younger must always offer the elder. In a relationship typical of patrilineal society (c.f. Denich 1974), brothers are rivals for the father's land and squabble amongst themselves and with the father for a share.

These conflicts, though the cause of ill-feeling, do not often end in real fighting, because a man's brothers and father are his most certain allies in any outside clash and it would be self-destructive to kill them. Nonetheless, one man did kill his brother within recent memory of my informants. The motive was greed for the brother's wealth and lust for the brother's wife, who was the killer's accomplice. The killer inherited both his desired ends and was safe from revenge since he himself was the closest relative of the murdered man. But without allies he was unable to protect his gains. Soon afterwards, the threats of a local strongman deprived him of both his property and his wife, and he was driven from the village. This was the only case in which the murder was proved, but in Shin Bagh I once heard some men teasing a young khan for poisoning his younger half-brother and thus rendering himself the sole inheritor of his father's land. He vehemently denied this accusation, but the other men exchanged knowing glances and asked him if he would then pray Allah for his stepmother to have another son. "God forbid!" cried the horrified khan.

Killings of fathers and sons are more frequent than fratricide. Two fathers were reportedly killed by their sons in recent memory, and there was an attempt by a son to kill his father during my fieldwork. The attempt failed, and the son remained in jail on his father's complaint (he has since been freed). In another major case during my fieldwork a large landlord in another village coldbloodedly shot and killed his son because the son had refused to give a share of his rice harvest to the murderer's mother, the victim's own grandmother. The wife of the dead man asked that the killer be prosecuted, but her brothers-in-law pressed her to drop the case, which she was obliged to do. These cases were over disputes about property, but sexual jealousy and seduction of wives within the extended family also can cause murder, as Ahmed (1980) notes.

Violence within the family is thus of two types: that directed toward affines and that directed toward agnates. The former is part of a larger pattern of lineage enmity acted out in the hostile relationship of husband and wife and which may lead to a feud if the wife is killed without sufficient cause. The latter derives from internal rivalry over property and women and may also escalate to murder, but does not involve revenge, since the killing has been committed by the closest possible agnate.

But the oppositions within the nuclear family itself are overshadowed by the prevalence of *tarburwali*. Of the seventeen killings of men by men which I recorded in some detail,* seven were killings either of close cousins or the servants of these cousins. In addition, there were numerous fights between cousins which ended just short of death. The potentially deadly opposition between close agnates is so pervasive that Ahmed (1980) sees *tarburwali* as the root of the Pukhtun social structure. Political action, Ahmed says, is always based on "the notion of cousin enmity

---

* The seventeen killings include the killing of a workmate by a young taxi driver, three killings of affines, two killings within the nuclear family, four killings in the ongoing war between tenants and landlords, and seven killings of *tarbur* or *tarbur's* servants. Of these killings six occurred during my fieldwork, while the remainder happened between 1970 and 1977. These are simply killings of which I have good histories, and by no means do they constitute an exhaustive list.

and the desire to maintain honour in relation to him" (1980:183). There is no structuring beyond this basic opposition: "smaller segments do not join with corresponding ones on the same unilineal descent level when threatened or in conflict with other less closely related segments as in many African societies" (Ahmed 1980:128). In other words, the genealogy of the Pukhtun is only structural on the very lowest level, and does not function in any meaningful political way above that level.

Ahmed's characterization of the Mohmand, who are neighbors of the Yusufzai, living just southwest of the Malakand, and who are reckoned as junior cousins of the senior Yusufzai lineage, is similar to Barth's account of social structure in Swat (1959; 1965). Barth, however, does not focus on *tarburwali*, but rather on the primacy of party over descent. Instead of continual fission and fusion along genealogical lines, so typical of segmentary systems in Africa and the Middle East, Swati party allies are supposedly always united. "An ally is an ally in any situation, regardless of whom he opposes. It is inconceivable for a leader, without repudiating an alliance, to be opposed to a person in one situation and allied to him in another" (Barth, 1965:105–6). Barth credits tension between *tarbur* as giving form to the pattern of opposing parties, or blocs, as he calls them, but Swat differs from classic segmentary systems, in Barth's view (as in Ahmed's), because there is no merging of segments at higher genealogical levels:

Unilineal descent, through its relevance to succession and land holding, thus affects the composition of political groups; but it does so by causing rivalry to develop between related persons, not by defining bonds of solidarity and co-operation . . . the structural opposition of the interests of agnatic collaterals prevents their fusion as a solidary political body, and leads to this pattern of alignment in opposed blocs. (Barth 1965:113).

Though in this same passage he contradicts his own point by noting that patrilineal bonds "are indeed defined, and are significant for example in revenge" (113). Revenge obligations, which unite close agnates (Barth 1965:84), take precedence even over alliance. This point, which I will return to later, gives Swat a minimal genealogical structuring that is absolutely central to the system.

The pattern of·opposition between close cousins, combined with a supposed lack of structure above that relation, seemingly sets Swat apart from other Middle Eastern and North African segmentary lineage societies. For instance, among the Bedouin of Cyrenaica close cousins do not appear to have relations of violence. Rather, feuds occur between lineage segments related back to the fourth or fifth ascending generation. Members of this group share blood money payments and are held culpable for any homicide committed by a member (Peters 1960:31). Disputes within this group seem to lead to breaking up the group rather than fighting. A similar distinction is seen among the Bedouin of the Negev, where the *khams* (meaning "five"—a kin group of men related back five or more generations) is responsible for blood revenge (Marx 1967:65). The *shabba* is a coliable five generational group in Iraq (Fernea 1970), as is the *surra* among the Baggara of Sudan (Cunnison 1966). Disputes within these groups do not end in violence, but rather in splitting of the lineage. Blood feuding between close agnatic relatives seems generally to be disallowed in segmentary societies, though the rule is sometimes very laxly observed, as in the Moroccan Rif where "vengeance killings within agnatic lineage groups . . . occurred too often simply to be dismissed as exceptions to the rule" (Hart 1970:70).

Because of *tarburwali*, Salzman has excluded Swat from consideration as a segmentary lineage society: "there is no ideology of genealogical solidarity . . . the genealogy functions only as a pedigree to justify the elite position of the khans in relation to the rest of the population" (1978a:59). Can the theoretical model of segmentary lineage systems then be of any value in discussing the social structure of Swat? I think it can, and I think Salzman's attitude is the result of a misinterpretation of the Swati data.

What exactly is an acephalous segmentary lineage system? As I said in the introduction, it is without head or chief, it is unilineal, it replicates genealogical distance on the ground as physical distance, it establishes rights to land and, most importantly for diagnostic purposes, it establishes relations of "complementary opposition" between lineage segments of equal depth. This is a reflection of the principle of segmentary sociability, which posits that "violence becomes more honorable in proportion to segmentary distance" (Sahlins 1961:332). Implicit in all this is a vision of the lineages as relative social entities, appearing only when aroused by opposition. "The lineage segment cannot stand alone but can only stand 'against'" (Sahlins 1961:333). Structure is genealogical but ephemeral.

In Swat, the first four of these conditions are obviously met. Leaders have risen and fallen, but no permanent centralization or hierarchy evolved until this century with the short-lived reign of the Badshah. The Pukhtun are also strongly patrilineal, tracing themselves back to their apical ancestor, known as Qais or Abdur Rashid, who was allegedly converted to Islam and given his Muslim name by the Prophet himself some fourteen hundred years ago. "The genealogical tree of the Yusufzais is that they descend from Yusuf, son of Mand, son of Khakhey, son of Kand, son of Kharshbun, son of Sorbon, son of Qais Abdur Rashid" (Wadud 1962:xxv).

In general, the people of Shin Bagh do not know their lineages very well, though the more elite families have the best genealogical memories. Among the khan elite several men claim to be genealogists and attempt to trace out their lines back to Yusuf. They claim to be the twelfth or thirteenth generation after Yusuf, while at the same time stating that there are a total of forty generations back to Qais. This is in direct contradiction to the genealogy given by Abdul Wadud and other experts. The fact is that the genealogies given in the village are probably accurate only for six or seven generations, or even less. Beyond that point, they become condensed and mythical. However, errors are not important, since spatial arrangement gives the general genealogical distance of all the clans and since everyone knows, at least vaguely, how the people with whom he is likely to interact are related to himself. While genealogies do not extend with accuracy far into the past, they do extend very widely in the present, and a Pukhtun man or woman is likely to know several hundred people who are patrilineally related to him or herself. A sample genealogy, taken from an elite Malik khel family, is shown in figure 3.4.

By looking at this genealogy, we can give a concrete representation of the constitution of a clan or khel, loosely defined as a group of patrilineally related men. There is no such thing as a Shamizai khel, but within Shamizai District the three main khels are Hassan khel, Mahmat khel, and Mulla khel. Each of these clans occupies several villages within an area. The Hassan khel own six relatively large, contiguous villages: Shin Bagh, Badera, Sumbut, Kuze Bamakhela, Bara Bamakhela, and Bodigram (see the sketch map of Shamizai/Sebujni District). The Hassan khel are then further divided into the Pinda khel and the Nakrudin khel. The Pinda khel are once again subdivided into the sons of Ahmat (Mushur or elder khel), and the sons of Kamal (Kushur or junior khel). The other lines are also named after their founders: Umar khel, Kumbur khel, etc., but they are considered quite junior and their lineage background is

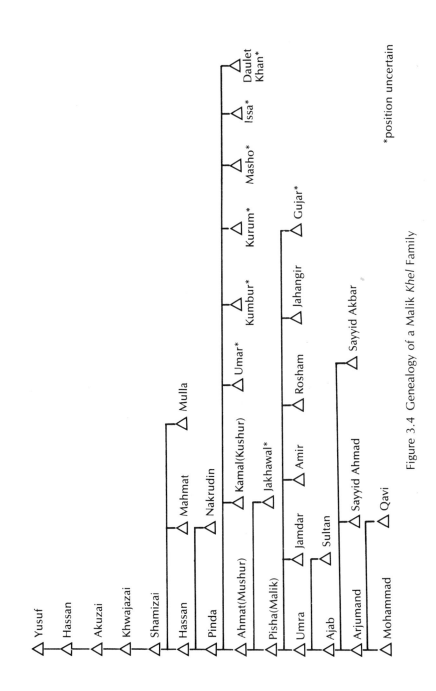

Yusuf
Hassan
Akuzai
Khwajazai
Shamizai
Hassan
Pinda
Ahmat(Mushur)
Pisha(Malik)
Umra
Ajab
Arjumand
Mohammad

Mahmat
Nakrudin
Kamal(Kushur)
Jakhawal*
Amir
Sultan
Sayyid Ahmad
Qavi

Mulla
Umar*
Rosham
Sayyid Akbar

Kumbur*
Jahangir

Kurum*
Gujar*

Masho*

Issa*

Daulet
Khan*

*position uncertain

Figure 3.4 Genealogy of a Malik *Khel* Family

SOCIAL STRUCTURE 71

somewhat uncertain. It is only known that they are, indeed, members of the Pinda *khel*, since they hold land in the villages. The Mushur *khel* are found only in Shin Bagh, while the Kushur *khel* are found only in Kuze Bamakhela. The other, less senior *khels* are scattered throughout the four Pinda *khel* villages. The Kumbur *khel* and Kurum *khel* dominate in Bara Bamakhela, while the Umar *khel* and Masho *khel* hold sway in Bodigram. But, to return to the main line, within the village of Shin Bagh the Mushur *khel* once more divide between the descendants of Pisha, who are called the Malik *khel*, and the Jakhawal, who are rumored to have been born of a slave mother. The Malik *khel* dominate most of the village, but one small *tal*, or village ward, is headed and made up of Jakhawal. Genealogical distance is, to an extent, replicated in physical space. Within the village itself, closely related families live in adjoining houses and are united in wards. The situation can best be visualized with the aid of another chart (see figure 3.5). The genealogical charter is thus replicated spatially, at least in outline. However, in the discrepancies we may see the action of hierarchical principles within the ideologically egalitarian segmentary structure. Although ideally all members of the *khel* are equal, the lesser *khels* such as the Umar *khel*, Kumbar *khel* and, especially, the Issa *khel* and Daulet Khan *khel*, are scattered spatially and recognized as being weaker than the powerful Mushur and Kushur *khels*. The actual background of these clans and their relationship to the Mushur and Kushur *khels* is not known with any exactitude. (The names of these clans are followed by an asterisk in the genealogical chart— figure 3.4). But their membership in the Pinda *khel* is affirmed by the fact that these minor clans are only found in Pinda *khel* villages, and not in Nakrudin *khel* villages, which have their own set of minor clans.

An ambiguous genealogy does not always mean weakness. The Jak-hawal and the descendants of Gujar Khan also have a somewhat doubtful ancestry, the Jakhawal being supposed offspring of a slave girl and the exact relationship of Gujar to his brothers an object of controversy. Yet, Gujar's grandchildren are among the most powerful men of the village due to their large landholdings, while the Jakhawal also hold a good deal of village land and are accorded all the respect due to the Malik *khel*. At the same time, the offspring of Rosham, who is recognized by all as the real brother of Umra, are held in general contempt by the rest of the Malik *khel* due to the present poverty and weakness of the line. The

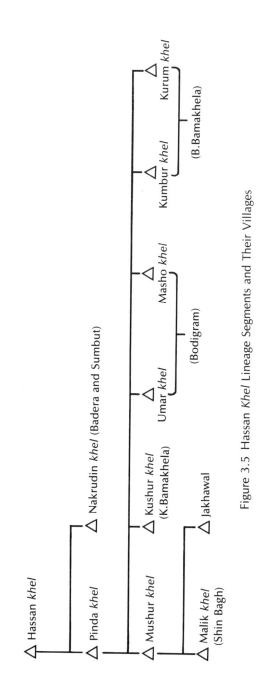

Figure 3.5 Hassan *khel* Lineage Segments and Their Villages

other Malik *khel* will not intermarry with this lineage and their women keep a strict purdah from them.

It is evident, then, that genealogical equality does not mean that all members of a clan are equal in reality. Rather, it seems the genealogies of weaker members may be conveniently obscured, while the suspect genealogies of powerful groups become less suspect over time. The pertinent factor in these transmutations is landholding. The *khels* without large holdings lose their genealogical standing. In Swat, a man without land is no longer reckoned as a Pukhtun, and he loses his place in the family tree. Men who have larger holdings and who are respected are known as khan, while men who have smaller holdings and who act as retainers for their more powerful neighbors are known simply as Pukhtun. Those who have no land are merely *fakir* (laborers).

As mentioned earlier, it is the importance of land for Pukhtun identity, coupled with the genealogical apportioning of fields, which contributes to the virulence of *tarburwali* in Swat. The holdings of cousins are adjacent, and each will try to push the holdings of the other back by trickery or force. As an example, two patrilateral cousins had neighboring plots. The cousin whose field was more distant from the village walked to his field on an ancient pathway which verged on the plot of his *tarbur*. There was a simmering dispute over the right to this narrow path which ended in a gunfight and the death of one of the men's sons.

But disputes arise not simply over land; they concern dominance and power. It is an axiom among the Pukhtun that *tarbur* do not fear one another. They are, after all, of the same blood. A man whose cousin has become wealthy and powerful will feel pressure to pick a fight with him to display his own strength. The most devastating feud ongoing during my fieldwork was one which began with a boy's refusal to let his second cousin play soccer with him. This trivial insult led to a fight which spread to include the boys' fathers. At the close of the fieldwork three men were dead and the fields of both families had either been sold for weapons or else left fallow as the remaining men sought to eliminate their rivals.

Among elite Pukhtun who have a claim to local leadership, a feud must be carried through to its bitter conclusion, which usually entails the ruin of all the participants. Outsiders, who are jealous of a dominant family, will sometimes try to precipitate such a feud. In one village, unauthorized use of a room in the men's house by some young men for a rendezvous with a prostitute led to a beating by the owner of the room, who was the uncle (FFBS) of the young men. This was followed by a series of escalating retaliatory actions, culminating in the jailing of one of the young men. Soon thereafter, the uncle's valuable stand of apple tree saplings was cut down in the middle of the night. The village waited to see what the uncle, a notoriously bad-tempered man, would do; but, after consultation with his brothers, he decided to do nothing. "Thank Allah, I have many enemies," he told me. "They would like to see me ruined in a fight with my *tarbur*. Perhaps these enemies cut down my trees." No blood had been shed, and a feud was avoided. In this history a repeated motif in Swati politics emerges, that is, the role of the manipulatory third party.

Although the elite must carry a feud on to the end, less powerful lineages may allow themselves to be pressured to reach a settlement. In the case of the cousins feuding over the pathway, the village *jirga* (council of elders from elite families) prevailed on the father of the dead boy to accept a blood payment and forswear revenge against his *tarbur*. The opponents in this case were clients of local Pukhtun patrons who feared that they might be drawn in should the feud continue. They therefore pressed their clients to accept a truce. A similar case concerned two landless cousins employed by rival Pukhtun as tenant farmers on adjoining strips of land. A fight between the client families ended in the deaths of two men, but the patrons forced a reconciliation.

It is important for the *jirga* to read a compromise in cases involving poor clients since the honor of the patron is at stake. Even in fights which have nothing to do with his interests, a patron is obliged to enter the fight on his client's behalf in order to keep his credibility as a leader. Fights between servants, like fights between children, can lead to destructive battles between Pukhtun families. Every effort, therefore, is made to arbitrate clients' disputes.

The apparently illogical continuation of fights to the ultimate destruction of all parties involved, especially if they are elite men with pretensions to leadership, is a phenomenon which is not confined to Swat. Black-Michaud has correlated this type of feud with sedentary societies existing under conditions he terms "total scarcity," defined as "the moral, institutional and material premise of a certain type of society in which *everything* felt by the people themselves to be relevant to human life is regarded by these people as existing in absolutely inadequate quantities" (1975;121–22). Swat is certainly a society of this type, as are many segmentary lineage societies, though Black-Michaud, as a student of Peters, ignores the structural roots of the premise of scarcity. Nonetheless, he makes a valuable contribution to the understanding of violence in a social order like Swat by noting important differences between sedentary and nomadic egalitarian communities.

Some of his points are derived from ecological variation in the resource base and the mode of production. Obviously, the Swatis are locked in their land, perpetually facing their rivals, while nomads can simply divide herds and fission off. This reality tends to focus hostility on near neighbors. Sedentary populations also differ from nomads in that a reduction in population leads to increased living standards, since the farmers are generally operating under conditions of severe overcrowding. Land does not multiply as animals do. It is an absolutely limited good. Nomads, on the other hand, rarely suffer from population pressure, and when they do the poor are sloughed off to join the landless peasant population (Barth 1961).

But Black-Michaud does not argue that, because sedentary communities are under more population pressure, violence is just a straightforward way of reducing the population. This would be a debatable point since, as Meeker (1980) says, the nomadic Bedouin were a more warlike people than the sedentary Swat Pukhtun. The violence of sedentary people without overarching authority systems *seems* worse than violence among nomads because it is often within the group, as in *tarburwali*, and because it is very difficult to stop until one side or the other is completely destroyed. In pursuing this end, both sides are often ruined, whereas in nomadic feuds compromise is possible and favored. But the impression of violence is belied by the fact that in most fights, in Swat at least and, according to Black-Michaud, in other sedentary groups as well, the violence is limited to a restricted number of people, unlike the disputes of nomads in which the whole *kham*, or five generations, is implicated. Swat Pukhtun take revenge directly on the killer and then, after he has been killed, perhaps on his sons and father as well. The notion of group responsibility is not developed, and retaliation, even in cases which do not involve *tarbur*, is directed to specific individuals. Pukhtun will wait many years to take revenge on a particular person. As a local proverb states, "a Pukhtun waits for a century to take revenge and says, 'I took it quickly.'" For example, a man was killed in a fight in the early 1950s. His killer offered the victim's family blood money, which was accepted.

But for a Pukhtun, blood money, or even the donation of a woman, is never adequate compensation for death. Blood demands blood. Therefore, after nearly thirty years, the son of the murdered man killed his father's killer while the old man was lying, helpless and immobile, in a hospital bed. This act, which led to the permanent exile of the killer, was much praised by the Pukhtun men.

Rather than making the insupportable claim that violence in sedentary societies like Swat is a direct result of population pressure, Black-Michaud focuses instead on the role of honor as a cause for conflict. Obviously, within systems in which "feud and violence become synonymous with society and institution" (Black-Michaud 1975:172), a code of honor is of primary importance, since it is honor which obliges men to battle one another, even though they know their own death or destruction is the inevitable result. According to Black-Michaud, nomads, who can run away from a fight, are not so concerned over honor and use it as a pretext for starting disputes over practical matters, such as control over water. But in sedentary systems aggression threatens the whole social fabric. The ecological constraints of overcrowding and immobility

are manifestly unfavorable to "the direct expression of antagonistic claims" over land and water which, if allowed, would lead to the appropriation of the best and the most by the strongest, and the complete disintegration of the community as such. . . . Antagonisms . . . are controlled and prevented from spreading throughout the social structure by the existence of the concept of honor which makes it possible to avoid a conflict over real goals by interpreting it in nonrealistic terms. (Black-Michaud 1975:193)

In fights over honor, men display their leadership capacities without drawing in the whole group. The dispute is an end in itself, a "game" in which men reveal themselves and find their identities in the only relations permitted by the system. As Bourdieu says,

Fighting was a game whose stake is life and those rules must be obeyed scrupulously if dishonor is to be avoided; rather than being a struggle to the death, it is a competition of merit played out before the tribunal of public opinion, an institutionalized competition in the course of which are affirmed the values that stand at the very basis of the existence of the group and assure its preservation. (1974:202)

But in Swat, as we have seen, the "game," as played between *tarbur*, had a more demonic aspect. Once blood had been shed, it had to be played out to its bitter conclusion.

According to Black-Michaud, the excessiveness of *tarburwali* is linked to the need of the sedentary community to maintain itself in the face of severe ecological pressures. Violence in the community is really over the scarcity of resources, but is "represented" through oppositions concerned with honor. By these oppositions equality is maintained, while simultaneously the best men display their aptitude for leadership.

Leadership is *both* the dynamic factor which regulates the interaction of co-operating and conflicting individuals *and*, at the same time, the prize or incentive for such co-operation and conflict. The struggle for leadership between individuals and groups is the pivot around which co-operation and conflict revolve. . . . Because in feuding societies no one can opt out of this struggle if he is to survive, feud, that is the struggle itself, is identical with the social structure. (1975:207)

This is enlightening, but Black-Michaud has no interest in the properties of the segmentary lineage system. In fact, most of his examples of sedentary feuding peoples are taken from Albania, which is a country characterized by quite different structural premises deriving from a cognatic kinship system. Because of this, he argues that "in sedentary societies alliance tends to be more sporadic and is dictated by vicinage, whereas among nomadic pastoralists it is a permanent necessity (due to the need for co-operation in herding) and is more frequently based on a combination of kinship and contract" (1975:192).

Swat conforms in certain features to Black-Michaud's schema, but, as I have noted, in a segmentary lineage society like Swat vicinity *corresponds* to genealogical distance. Opposition *is* genealogically structured. Furthermore, Black-Michaud, like Ahmed (1980) and Barth (1959) prefers to look at only the most obvious, because they are the most virulent, levels of opposition. By focusing only on the "demonic" feud, the structure of the system is oversimplified and rendered chaotic above the enmity of *tarburwali*. If violence is the structure of societies like Swat, then the analyst must look at all types of opposition, not just the most prevalent. In fact, *tarburwali* is just one form of violence in Swat. I've already discussed the pattern of violence within the nuclear family itself at a level lower than cousin enmity. I would like now to describe violence at more inclusive genealogical levels in order to demonstrate that Swat is indeed characterized by genealogically structured complementary opposition.

The first level is that of the village, which is divided into three neighborhoods (*palao*); these in turn are subdivided into *tal*, or wards, also usually three in number. These *tal* are dominated by and named after a particular leader who, with his close relatives and clients, heads a faction which must be represented in village *jirgas*. The political organization of the village is perhaps best conceived as small circles of patrilineal kin, residing near one another, and acting together in opposition to other circles of the same scale. The *tals* in a neighborhood, though in opposition, can join together in action against another *palao*. Of course, all is not peaceful within the *tal* either, as *tarbur* compete with one another for leadership and prestige.

So far, the system seems relatively uncomplicated and formal. But the *tals* and *palao* are cross-cut by a dualistic party structure, the *dala*, strongly resembling the *liff* alliances of the Berbers (Montagne 1973). Gellner doubts the existence of the *liff* at the village level, claiming the system functions, if it functions at all, between villages (1969:67). Hart also sees the *liff* working primarily to balance uneven distribution of power within tribal units by external alliances. He notes that " 'temporary' *liff* . . . operating within a clan, a subclan, or a local community, could and did shift and change" (1970:45). The Berbers, like the Pukhtun, speak of the dual parties as if they were concrete entities, and indeed each individual sees the tribal world divided into those who are in his party and those who are against his party. In Swat the parties are named after their local leader's clan, so that the parties have different names throughout the valley. Each village *dala* ramifies in a net of alliances throughout the region, and a powerful leader will be able to name members of what he calls "our party" in fifty villages or more.

But it is important to avoid seeing these parties in too formal a manner. Actually, the party system is simply a statement, couched in universal and abstract terms, of the fluid oppositions and alliances of individuals. A man sees his party as a tool in his own personal struggle against his enemies. These enemies are generally one's *tarbur*, and Barth, as we have seen, has claimed that enmity between blocs, derived from the oppositions of cousins, takes precedence over segmentary merging in Swat. In taking this stance, Barth has reified individual strategy into a structural principle and has given impermanent alliances priority over the unity of patrilineal segments. It is because of this theoretical premise that Salzman, speaking of the Pukhtun, makes the claim that "complementary opposition exists here neither in thought nor action" (1978a:59), and Swat therefore cannot be counted as a segmentary lineage society.

In actual fact, as Barth himself documents (1965:84, 106, 113), party alliances are set aside in cases of blood revenge. Complementary opposition, then, does exist in Swat, since no man would support the murderer of his *tarbur* under any circumstances, even if the killer were a long time party ally. The limited range of revenge rights and the preponderance of *tarburwali* obscures, but does not obliterate, the unity of blood groups in Swat; a unity which is activated in cases of revenge. This does not mean that all of a man's lineage back to the fifth generation will gather to take revenge on the lineage segment of the killer, but it does mean that relatives of the victim will not give direct support or aid to the killer. "There is a difference in the weight of affinal ties between situations in which a man will not support his agnates against his affines and in which a man will actively support his affines against his agnates" (Salzman 1978a:62). Degree of support is the key factor, and Pukhtun do not give overt support to affines or party members in cases of blood. Ahmed, though he argues for the primacy of *tarburwali*, gives data corroborating my viewpoint in his review of actual cases (1980:187–88, 315). As he admits in a footnote, "when there is a clear-cut clan or tribal alternative to chose from, the closer kin may be supported" (1980:371). There appears to be a continuum of allegiance extending from the obligation to blood revenge incumbent on the nuclear family of the victim, aided by his *tarbur*, to withdrawal of the victim's more distant relatives from alliances with the killer and his family. To understand this attitude, it must be emphasized that the *tarbur* relation is ambiguous. He is not only the paradigm for enemy, but also, under proper circumstances, a reliable ally. A man without *tarbur* stands naked to the assaults of genealogically more distant enemies, and while strong *tarbur* evoke jealousy, they also inspire pride.

Besides unjustifiably excluding the Pukhtun from consideration as a segmentary lineage society, Barth's overvaluation of the opposition between blocs has had other effects. Although always aware of structure, Barth's interest in individual action led him to accept without question the ideology of egoism that prevails in Swat. The Swat Pukhtun have been presented by Barth as motivated by what Macpherson (1962) has called "possessive individualism," existing within a Hobbesean world of self-interested manipulation. If only the individual, in his struggle to survive, is portrayed, then the picture is a perfectly adequate description. But this portrayal is not critical; it does not touch upon the cultural

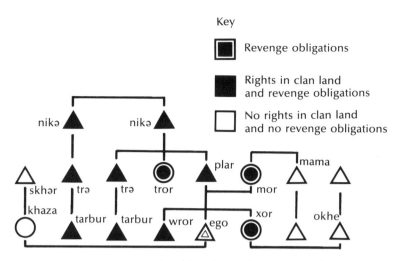

Figure 3.6 Relations of Land Rights and Revenge Obligations

premises which underlie the "rational" worldview. Assuredly, it is rational for the Pukhtun to be an exemplar of a man maximizing his returns as best he can, but the rationality of his behavior is within a cultural context; a context which Barth has presented in static terms (see Cohen 1969). Individualism and maximization are seen as existing a priori, and the Pukhtun is simply a very clear case for the presentation of a model of man the entrepreneur. Of course, there is no doubt that the Pukhtun sees his acts as instrumental, but it is important to note that the very concept of instrumentality is relative and mediated by the implications of the underlying structure. All human activity "takes on meaning as a projection of the cultural scheme which forms its specific context, and its effect by a relation of significance between this contingent reference and the existing order" (Sahlins 1976:21). The end also dictates rationality of means. A suicidal person is rational if he jumps from the tenth floor of a building, irrational if he jumps from the first.

Because of his concern with individual act, Barth has tended to pay little attention to the actual movement of the system. The image he gives of Pukhtun social structure is a frozen one; oppositions balance out in a no-win game as the players' manipulations and defections lead to stalemate (1959). This long-term leveling process is institutionalized in the dyadic dǝla system. But in pursuing this analysis, Barth ignores the triadic patterning of *palao* and *tɔl* and the dialectical principle of uneven development institutionalized within these forms. In the long run, Barth's picture of stalemate is accurate, but in the short run good players can, and do, gain positions of dominance and prestige. Obviously, some families become strong simply by out-reproducing others; some men are particularly brave, intelligent, or Machiavellian; some clans are lucky or skilled at manipulation. Uneven development complicates the picture of balance offered by Barth's concentration on the party system.

To get a more correct view of Swati political process, it is necessary to look at the mechanisms of party formation. Certainly a man opposes his *tarbur*, but he does not have only one *tarbur*. Rather, he has a choice of enemies and allies and joins or wars with his cousins according to his own perception of advantage. The shifting dyad covers a triadic form consisting of ego, his temporary allies, and his temporary enemies. This same pattern is found at every level of Swati society. For example, although each village is divided into two parties, the party lines do not simply bisect the village. Instead, one *palao* will for the most part follow the party of its most able *tɔl* leader; a second *palao* will usually support the rival party; while a third *palao*, weaker in numbers, will oscillate between the two sides, playing off the opponents and hoping they will exhaust themselves in the combat. The same pattern is repeated within the *palaos* themselves as the three *tɔls* vie for dominance. At a regional level, the motif again recurs. Regions are usually made up of three "brother" clans; two strong and one weak, which are cross-cut by *dɔla* alliances. At all these levels the potential power of the weak but manipulative third party is evident, and the role of the troublemaker is seen to be a structural concomitant of the Swati social order.

During political manuevering in the village, violent action is always a potential, but it is rarely actualized. A murder, whatever the cause, leads to revenge. As mentioned above, political alliances then drop away and the affair becomes one of feud between two nuclear families. Much more likely in village politics was exile. Should one family become overwhelmingly powerful, their disgruntled *tarbur* would flee the village to find temporary refuge with a nearby ally. The refugees would encourage their host to plan warfare on their home village in hopes of humbling their proud relatives.

Exile, while sometimes lengthy, was usually not permanent. The exiled party would never be totally accepted by its hosts. In fact, when powerful members of one village party attempted to link themselves to another village in alliance against their *tarbur*, they were occasionally refused, on the grounds that "a man who would betray his own kin would certainly betray us as well." Furthermore, the exiles had no rights in land in their host's territory, while their claim to land within their own village continued in force. Eventually, the exiles would tire of living on charity and return home to claim their patrimony. Sometimes they had to return as supplicants, but more often they were invited back by their *tarbur* in order to maintain the manpower of the village. Sometimes the exiles returned as members of an invading army and used the strength of their new position as conquerors to repay old grievances.

Violence between villages is of several types, according to the genealogical distance between them. Villages which are closely related have a ritualized form of warfare which formerly occurred at the close of the Muslim month of fasting before the feasting of the Eid celebration. Villages were paired according to genealogical and spatial proximity. The young men and boys of the villages would meet in a field to fight with slingshots. There were always a number of injuries and sometimes a death. No revenge was taken for these fatalities, which were seen as accidental. In these fights, the youth of the whole village participated together, regardless of party affiliation.

Fighting between more distantly related villages was considerably more violent, and was known by the people themselves as *jang*, or warfare. Whereas ritual war was within the group of "brother" villages, real warfare was between "brothers." It was to these more distant villages, who could wage real warfare, that exiles fled. Fatalities in these wars could be quite high, as the fighting parties rallied their allies and bodyguards for attacks on opposition strongholds. Deaths in such wars, however, did not involve revenge or even lasting enmity (as Barth notes, 1965:122). Conversely, killings committed by turncoat *tarbur* who had joined the enemy were avenged. For example, in the last great intervillage war around the year 1900 one ambitious man joined his village's enemies. With his help, the enemy group invaded the exile's home village. During this period of occupation, the traitor killed two of his cousin's bodyguards and destroyed a great deal of property. Later, with the aid of allies and defections from the enemy, the defeated party regained strength and recaptured its home base, once again balancing the regional distribution of power. The exile was banished by his allies, who did not want the responsibility of protecting him from vengeance. He was obliged to return home and allow two of his sons to be killed in compensation for his crimes. He accepted this punishment as just, rejoined the village *jirga*, and retained a position of prestige in the village. His grandsons are presently among the most powerful men in their neighborhood. It is significant that the exile's erstwhile allies were not held responsible for deaths which occurred in this war. Also noteworthy is the pattern of betrayal which is a function of the social order. The exile, having failed to win power by manipulation within the village, took the risk of moving the conflict onto the intervillage arena. His treachery was seen locally merely as a political ploy which failed, and not as anything particularly reprehensible. For the Pukhtun, honor lies in vengeance, not in keeping a trust. This matter-of-fact attitude toward betrayal, so difficult for the Westerner to understand, is simply a realistic acceptance of the structurally motivated individualism of Swati politics (Lindholm 1980).

The causes of large-scale wars seem generally to have focused on exiles. Men who had killed a *tarbur,* or women who had shamed their husbands might flee to the protection of a powerful family, who were obliged to offer refuge. If this refuge was violated, then the host would be involved in a feud with people who might be very distantly related to him. Such an event could bring together very large lineage/village groups (see Barth 1965:122 for an example). Also, exiles could instigate a war by throwing themselves on the mercy of their host and demanding that he avenge any wrong which had been done them.

Of course, as Sillitoe (1978) notes, political leaders can manipulate situations to further their own political ambitions. Ambitious and courageous men with aptitudes for strategy favored warfare, since it increased their local authority and prestige. The role of the protector was (and remains) ambiguous and malleable. The host can choose to stress his place as mediator between the refugee and his or her pursuers. As a supposedly disinterested outsider, he could try to work out some sort of settlement to end the situation amicably. Or, conversely, he could use the exile's complaints to justify beginning a war. Then again, the ability of the host to use the situation for his own advantage is limited by external circumstance as well. A host who is reluctant to fight will be forced to it should the refugee be attacked, for instance.

The rewards of war appear, at this level, to have been primarily in the realm of renown. Certainly there were material benefits of success, and

A carved support post in a mosque.

Swati elders recall pillaging the fields of defeated villages. But homes were never ransacked, and men forced into exile left their valuables in the care of local religious men with the full expectation of returning to reclaim them. Successful warriors did not intend to hold on to their conquests, since their very success meant that former allies would defect, join the defeated group, and rebalance the system (see Barth 1959). The end result of the several intervillage wars recorded was a "great name" for the war leaders and their families, but no apparent aggrandizement of their property. In fact, the main purpose of war, according to old warriors, was to carry off the decorative support beams of the opponent's men's house, thus shaming him and demonstrating one's own prowess at war. (For a description of another such symbolic victory see Bourdieu 1974, who describes Kabyle wars which end when the support beam of a guest house is appropriated.) This, of course, fits in well with Black-Michaud's notion of feud as "representation," an end in itself in sedentary society. In this form of war neither land nor property was permanently confiscated, and looting of produce was sporadic and not of great importance in terms of subsistence, as evidenced by the absence of reports of hunger during intervillage wars.

It is in situations of intervillage war that the "saintly" class of religious mediators took on their role as arbitrators. While the village *jirga* mediated disputes between nonelite within the village and feuds between proud *tarbur* were left to run their tragic—but quite restricted—course, war between villages could not cease without the intervention of an external noncombatant "saint" (called *stanadar* by Barth), whose mediation allowed both sides to back off without undue loss of face. The fact that these mediators were rewarded with land grants which lay between the potentially warring villages indicates both the primary role of the "saints" and the relative lack of land pressure during the era of warfare. It is noteworthy that this land was reclaimed by strong Pukhtun clans several generations later when land pressure began to be felt. This reclamation did not infringe on the property rights of anyone except the dispossessed "saints" and so did not lead to increased warfare. Thus, by removing land from the tribal property and deeding it to weak "saintly" lineages the Pukhtun, consciously or unconsciously, provided themselves with a "land bank" from which powerful lineages could draw in the future without violating the rights of any group which could offer serious resistance.

There was another type of warfare which was historically much more destructive. This was war between regions, and it grew from the same causes which led to intervillage war, that is, the exile of a group which then seeks the intervention of an external third party to redress the balance of power. In this case, the third party invited in is not simply another village, but another district. In Swat, as I argued in the last chapter, the external third party was the state of Dir. This state, ruled by hereditary kings, gladly provided sanctuary for Swati exiles. Under favorable circumstances, the army of Dir would join with the exiles, invade Upper Swat, and establish rule there. But Dir was not content simply to "redress the balance." The king wished to annex Swat, and would soon begin exploiting his victory by levying taxes and confiscating wealth. The Pukhtun remember these invasions as times of severe scarcity and hunger. Eventually, Dir's pretensions would lead to an activation of the segmentary principle of unity against invasion; the Swati parties would forget their differences to unite in a war of resistance under the leadership of a religious charismatic, and Dir would be driven out. As mentioned previously, colonial intervention in the last such war led to the ascendance of the Badshah.

A final type of war, also destructive, involved expansion rather than defense. For structural reasons, the segmentary lineage system is one which tends to expand at the expense of its less well-organized neighbors (Sahlins 1961). The Pukhtun of Swat were no exception, conquering the weakly structured, but fiercely fighting, Kohistani peoples to their north. This expansion ceased in the mid-1800s as the harshness of the terrain, the lack of booty and the ferocity of the Kohistani resistance all combined to defeat the Pukhtun armies. Pukhtun wars of aggression were apparently led by strongmen anxious to raise their personal prestige and accumulate a following through leadership in battle and redistribution of spoils. At this late date, it is difficult to discern exactly who followed such men, but it seems that great war leaders were temporarily able to unite fighting men of many different lineages in loose alliances brought together for the sake of conquest. The secular leadership of expansionist war appears to be in marked contrast to leadership in wars of defense, which often arises from "saintly" lineages and relies upon religious exhortation to encourage resistance (see Lindholm in press for more detail on this subject).

Swat, then, does appear to fulfill the criteria demanded by Sahlins as diagnostic of a segmentary lineage system, though it is a system complicated by a land-based agricultural economy. Complementary opposition does exist, but violence at various levels is differentiated along several lines, i.e., the necessity for revenge, the types of mediating bodies and leaders, the virulence of the conflict. Each more inclusive patrilineal segment has its own specific rules of violence for hostilities with segments of equal scale. Violence does indeed become more honorable as genealogical distance increases but with a new concomitant, perhaps unique to Swat, that as genealogical scale increases, the obligation to revenge decreases. Moreover, revenge obligations take precedence over other forms of violence and opposition, so that a death in a village party dispute dissolves the parties and leads to a personal feud between two nuclear families. As Barth notes, "conflicts in defence of honour fall outside the field of alliance. . . . Blood revenge . . . obtains essentially between individuals, and a man's honour can only be defended by his own might" (1965:106). In intervillage wars as well, murders by *tarbur* are avenged, while those by more distant enemies are not. Killing in *tarburwali* is regarded with distaste by the Pukhtun: "No one really is the winner and every enemy death extracts as much sorrow as it does

Table 3.1 Typology of Violence Among the Swat Pukhtun

Location of conflict	Level of genealogical connection	Revenge	Exile	Ritual war	Redressive war	Religious mediator	Secular mediator	Religious war leader	Secular war leader
House	Wife	+							+
House	−1, 0, 1 Son, Brother, Father				+	+			
House cluster	2, 3 Tarbur	+					+ For non-elite		
Village	4, 5			+					+
"Brother" village	6		+						
District	7				+	+			+
Region (defense)	8+ or none							+	
Region (offense)	8+ or none				+				+

jubilation from within the circle of contestants, all close cognatic kin. The prize is negligible, the price is exorbitant. It is a systematic cannibalistic devouring of the innards of the sectional unit" (Ahmed 1980:201). Nonetheless, because *tarburwali* is the most immediate form of confrontation, and because the Pukhtun finds his identity in struggle, it follows that such confrontations may often end in extinction, but extinction only for individuals, not for the whole society. The restricted range of revenge allows the playing out of social values of competition and pride in a small arena, and allows the larger order to continue.

Black-Michaud has seen ecological variables at the heart of the inexorable feuds of sedentary peoples, but it is evident from Swat that the lineage system must also be taken into account. This system means that closely related men are near neighbors, competing with one another for their common patrimony. Other neighbors will not interfere in a fight, for if both sides are eliminated then the neighbors, who are also relatives, will inherit. Violence between cousins is therefore not only violence between the closest and most rancorous of rivals who have the concrete reality of land rights dividing them, but also violence which no outsider will mediate, since the destruction of the battling parties is to the advantage of all related survivors. There is thus another axiom to be derived from the Swati case, i.e., the larger the groups involved in violence, the more likely is external mediation by *jirgas* or "saints."

When comparing Swat with other segmentary lineage societies, especially those with a nomadic economy, it is perhaps best to keep in mind relative scale. Nomadic groups tend to have larger units, the so-called fifth, or *kham*, which functions very much the way individuals function in Swat. This lineage segment is often represented by a hereditary leader, who may also lead more inclusive segments, while in sedentary societies such as Swat leadership tends to be ephemeral and crisis-oriented. This is quite the contrary to the popular view which sees nomads as "free" and farmers as "peasants," but there are good historical and ecological reasons for this variation. Ecologically, herding requires more cooperation than farming and so tends toward larger corporate units (see Black-Michaud 1975:192). Herding societies also rely on scarce natural resources (wells, oases, and so on) which one group can dominate to establish protostates (Spooner 1969; Aswad 1970; Wolf 1951). Historically, herdsmen exist in symbiotic relations with farmers and with states. These relations imply the evolution of representative leaders as intermediaries (Barth 1961; Fernea 1970; Swidler 1977) and the development of corporate groups. Farmers, like the Swat Pukhtun, the Kurds, and the Riffian Berbers, are far more independent and individualistic than their nomad cousins *if* they stand outside a state system.

Nonetheless, the Swatis do have differences of rank within their society, differences so significant that Asad (1972) and Ahmed (1976; 1980) have characterized Swat as a class system, not a segmentary lineage system. Ahmed reserves the lineage model for Pukhtun in more mountainous regions which do not have the luxury of irrigation agriculture or a helot class. Swat, he says, is a taxation (*qalang*) society, resting on the oppression of a landless class and the extortion of surplus by big landlords, while the Mohmand are a people ruled by honor (*nang*), and live by traditional principles of equality and *tarburwali* (1976:73–83; 1980:116–25). To an extent, this opposition is a useful one, especially since it shows the tremendous variation in Pukhtun social systems, but it is too schematic. For the sake of a neat dichotomy, Ahmed has stretched the divergence between societies which are, in reality, variations on a theme. For example, although Swat is said to be a society of taxation, land is still untaxed in Upper Swat. It has not even been officially surveyed. Ahmed claims that *tarburwali* is the essence of *nang*, but he admits that *tarburwali* is *more* prevalent in Swat than among the Mohmand, "due to the tension of *qalang* society wishing to live up to the *nang* ideal but finding it difficult to do so" (1980:118). The real problem for Ahmed seems to be the fact that Swat is a society which purports to believe in equality, but rests on indisputible differences in wealth and power. A similar argument has been made by Black (1972) and also, in a more general vein, by Asad (1978).

In Swat, land, wealth, and power are all one and the same, and there is no question that some men and some lineages have more than others. The list of *khels* given earlier in this chapter shows conclusively that some groups have historically dominated and deprived not only the landless, but their own close kinsmen in the interminable manipulations of *tarburwali*. I was told that "in the old days, strong men took land from their cousins and brothers. The sons of those weak lineages who lost some or all of their land are now retainers and workers."

Strong men not only took land from their relatives, they were also granted land by the whole community. All real khan lineages have special strips of land on the tops of the hills to the west of the village which are outside the clan land, the *dauftar*, and belong to the khan's family alone. This land was supposedly granted by the Pukhtun in gratitude for the leadership of the khan. Along with this land, the khans can also be recognized by their ownership of *tseri* land, which was land originally given by the whole village to holy men in reward for their arbitrations. Khans have acquired this special category of land either through purchase or by force, and it is often rented out to tenants.

A man who is not a member of the lineage cannot hold *dauftar*, and one who loses his share of *dauftar* is no longer a lineage member and therefore no longer a Pukhtun. A man's identity, his pride, and his land are united. At the same time, *dauftar* holders have evolved a sort of truncated hierarchy, as some men have come to be bigger landlords than others and have transformed their smaller neighbors into retainers. This process occurred both by the application of force and by the voluntary donation of land to leaders in return for their leadership abilities.

But even though certain groups did gain positions of eminence, these positions were never certain. Leaders had little real authority and relied on strong personalities, individual ability, and a capacity for intrigue to keep them first among their equals. Even the Malik *khel* of Shin Bagh, who retained local leadership for several generations, were never able to securely grasp a base for power, as is evidenced in their present low position in the region. Instead of being leaders, the Malik *khel* now are followers of other *khels*. Although they are numerous, fairly wealthy, and boast a large and loyal following due to past greatness, the Malik *khel* have been unable to unite and leadership has slipped away from them. As they themselves say, "we are weak because we have produced no great men."

Asad (1972) theorized that power would tend to become more centralized in Swat, giving the society a resemblance to the pyramid structure of class societies in the West. But I have already drawn attention to the role of internal rivalry and the dissipation of inheritance as mitigating against the rise of really large-scale hierarchies. During the monolithic rule of the Badshah, Asad's predictions did seem correct. With the might of the British and, later, of the Pakistani state behind him, the Badshah and his cohorts grabbed land and wealth on a scale never before seen in Swat. But, with the fall of the Badshah's family and the resurgence of party politics as seen in the 1977 elections, it is likely that the holdings of these big landlords will be reduced through the demands of their enemies, who are no longer restrained by the overwhelming power of the central government. Only massive interference by the Pakistani state can halt the trend toward a relative equalization of holdings among the leading khans. This trend could be seen in 1977 in the innumerable suits filed against the offspring of Khan Badhur, the former despot of Upper Swat. In order to keep any degree of political viability, Feteh Muhammad, Khan Badhur's son, was being forced to divest himself of many of the holdings his father had appropriated from other Pukhtun. I therefore conclude that the entrenchment of the structural principles of the segmentary ideology, with its concomitants of internal fragmentation and hostility, renders Asad's straight class analysis oversimplistic. Rather than becoming more centralized, Swat appears to be going backward to the era of petty local parties without central leadership. The nascent class opposition is still dominated by the Pukhtun and is formed by the constraints implicit in the mental model which all the actors have of reality, i.e., a model which posits manipulation, personal interest, and internal dissension and betrayal as the order of the day. This is not to deny that change is taking place; it is only suggesting that change may go in several directions. Although it is possible that class polarization will increase in Swat, it is just as likely (if not more likely) that either class differences will be coopted into a struggle between power hungry junior Pukhtun and the already powerful elite or that the situation will regress entirely and that the old segmentary system will be reaffirmed in the face of external pressures from the state.

Historically, Swat was a society of epic heroes, of hand-to-hand battles, of great courage, and great betrayals. But the party system of constantly shifting loyalties did not allow evolution of a central organization. Only the truncated hierarchy of ephemeral local leaders and their retainers developed. The institution of *wesh* hindered the strong families from founding an expanding power base. Absence of large-scale trade and the lack of easily controllable scarce resources also mitigated against any lineage gaining ascendance in the valley, as did the isolation of Swat, which allowed for easy defense and a general freedom from a steady application of external pressure. Momentary leaders from the category of holy men and religious ecstatics rose to temporary power, but faded from sight with the repulsion of the invaders. The Swati parties, therefore, remained mere conglomorates of equal khans and their Pukhtun retainers, held together by hostility toward their personal enemies. Despite the machinations of master players, the political game remained a draw. Leaders left great names and glorious histories, but were never more than first amidst their peers. No lineage could establish itself as intrinsically superior to the others. As Ghani Khan says, "a true democrat, the Pukhtun thinks he is as good as anyone and his father rolled into one" (1958:47).

But the Pukhtun are not the only people of Swat. There are several other groups which must be taken into account. The first are the landed non-Pukhtun. These are of two types: the first, whom Barth (1965) has termed *stanadar* (literally, those who stand; figuratively, those who are descendants of a charismatic holy man), are the men who traditionally acted as mediators in intervillage disputes. It is this class the Pukhtun rewarded with the noncirculating *tseri* land which lies in strips between villages. The second type are called *mullah*. These are families descended from learned men who could read the Koran. Their claim to honor is through knowledge, not through charisma. Like the *stanadar,* the *mullahs* also hold *tseri* land, but they formerly gave up their land to migrate with the Pukhtun. The closeness of the *mullahs* to the Pukhtun is indicated by the fact that they always live within the village, while the *standar* usually have their own settlements outside the village, called *cham*. Unlike the *stanadar*, the *mullahs* are not prohibited from using violence. They claim to have come with the Yusufzai from Afghanistan. Rather than looking back to a mystically enlightened ancestor as the *stanadar* do, the *mullahs* claim their rights come from religious learning and their previous position as instructors to the Pukhtun on Koranic learning. While the descendants of the *stanadar* as a group do not feel any obligation to concern themselves with religious learning (though some individuals do), the *mullahs* try to educate at least one son in Koranic scholarship. This does not mean that the *mullahs* act as imams in the mosque. This job is the work of a landless man, and a landed *mullah* would consider it a shame to take up such work. Most *mullahs,* like most *stanadar,* are simply small farmers, indistinguishable from the Pukhtun they live among. Because of their history as dependents of the Pukhtun, the *mullahs* are regarded as slightly inferior, and they tend to give more women to the Pukhtun than they receive (seven women taken and thirteen given in Shin Bagh in the last five generations), and the marriage ceremonies when a Pukhtun woman is given to a *mullah* are noticeably tense affairs. The khan elite never intermarry with the *mullahs*.

On the other hand, the *stanadar* regard themselves as superior to the khans. All *stanadar* are descended from religiously inspired men (pirs) in the mystical Sufi tradition. These men partake, to some extent, of the religious mana (*baraka*) of their saintly ancestors, though some, by their actions and discipline, display more of this power than others. Indeed, some *stanadar* are mere landless laborers, without any apparent prestige.

Internally, the *stanadar* divide themselves according to the lineages of their ancestors. Most prestigious are the descendants of the Prophet (the sayyids, such as the famous Pir Baba), then come the *mias* who are descended from disciples of a sayyid, and finally the offspring of local saints, who are called *sahibzadas*. The Badshah of Swat was a *sahibzada*, since this grandfather was the Akhund, a local saint.

Trimingham (1971) has outlined the evolution of Sufi orders from their beginnings in individual revelation to the formation of rules and an order (*tariqa*) to the inauguration of a cult of the saint (*ta'ifa*). In Swat, all three stages can coexist. For example, Abdul Gaffur, who became the Akhund of Swat, was born a shepherd, but was blessed with divine inspiration. Sadullah, the Mastan Mullah, was another such figure, and Swat has abounded with men of this type in its history: wandering dervish mendicants who, in times of trouble can act to unite the Pukhtun. However, Abdul Gaffur was not simply a dervish. He journeyed to Peshawar and studied the *tariqa* of the Naqshabandiyya sect and returned to Swat where he put the ascetic precepts of his sect into practice. His austerities won him followers from the already existing saintly cult of Pir Baba, whose tomb in Buner had become a center of *baraka*, or heavenly grace. After his death, Abdul Gaffur also became a saint, and his tomb vied with that of Pir Baba as a place for pilgrimage and veneration. His grandson, Abdul Wadud, used the *baraka* he had inherited from his grandfather as a rallying point for his followers in his campaign to become ruler of Swat. However, his secularization of the family led to a decrease in the sanctity of his grandfather's tomb, so that it is hardly reckoned as a holy site any more, while the tomb of Pir Baba still holds its place as a sacred location. The descendants of pirs of the different sorts mentioned above may or may not show any religious inclination, but if they do begin to follow austerities and practice the *tariqa* of a discipline, they have a good chance of gaining a following, since they are then thought of as rekindling the spark of *baraka* which resides in their lineage. However, saintly cults of dead pirs are always vulnerable to a challenge by a dervish or *malang*, an ecstatic mendicant who proclaims his personal relationship to God. For this reason, one of the first acts of Abdul Wadud on his ascension to the throne was the exiling of all dervishes from his kingdom. In this way, he destroyed the very class which had given rise to his own lineage and protected himself from internally led religious strife against his increasingly secular government.

Stanadar view themselves as superior to the Pukhtun because of their history as emissaries of the Deity. They rarely give wives to anyone but other *stanadar*. They are willing to take women from the Pukhtun, however. The Pukhtun explain this imbalance in two ways. First, they say they fear the curses of a *stanadar* wife and do not feel comfortable asserting authority over her. Second, Pukhtun men give their daughters to the *stanadar* both as an act of pious charity (for no bride price is demanded), and also in the hopes that the intervention of their new in-laws with Allah will bring them good fortune. Nowadays, the Pukhtun say they would refuse to give a girl to the *stanadar* without a large bride price. The *stanadar* themselves, deprived of their roles as mediators and war leaders by the rule of the state bureaucracy, have become increasingly secularized and rarely are distinguishable from the Pukhtun. Nontheless, the old marriage rule continues to apply. Pukhtun in Shin Bagh in my records took only five *stanadar* women, none from elite sayyid families, while *stanadar* took fourteen women, many of elite families, from the Pukhtun.

The *stanadar* themselves say they prefer to marry inside their own group. Since the source of their power is in their genealogical charter from an illustrious ancestor, and since their stock in trade is the suggestion of mysterious powers, they feel it is wise to keep their lineages as inwardly turned as possible. However, with the reign of the Badshah, whom the Pukhtun saw as betraying his religious role, and with the decline in the importance of the *stanadar* as mediators, the Pukhtun of Swat have lost much of their reverence and awe of the pirs and their lineages. Local shrines, which a few years ago were the site of weekly pilgrimages, now stand empty. Some have even been encroached upon by local farmers for grazing space, cow sheds, and the like.

I have noted above that the power and wealth of the *stanadar* class derived from the Pukhtun's need for neutral mediators of disputes between equals and for leadership in times of invasion. Given the egalitarianism and internal rivalries of the segmentary system, these needs could only be filled by a force the Pukhtun viewed as standing outside their own social structure. After the advent of the state, the role of the balancing element in internal disputes has been transferred to the judicial bureaucratic state apparatus. The basic pattern, however, remains the same, despite the shuffling of the elements involved. The Swati political system, torn by interminable feuds, without a controlling hierarchy, relies on the state as it relied upon the *stanadar*. The role of the state, as the Pukhtun see it, is not to transform the society, but rather "to be a mechanism by which the equilibrium of the political system is maintained" (Evans-Pritchard 1940:43).

Aside from these religiously sanctioned landed groups, there are also the landless—descendants of conquered local people, migrants, or of Pukhtun who have lost their land. In Shin Bagh, 735 of the 1,970 people living in the village have no land at all (see appendix A, table 7). In order to survive, they must work for a landowner. The workers are divided into two broad categories: specialists and farm laborers. Within the specialist field a number of subtypes are to be found. These are referred to either as *khel* or *kam* (occupational group) and define the sort of work the specialist does. But as the economy of Swat has begun to enter the mass market, a number of specialties have been all but eliminated by competition. There is no longer the "high degree of occupational specialization" which Barth noted (1965:119). The tailor (*darzi*), the shoemaker (*chamyar*), the weaver (*jola*), the potter (*kolal*), the oil presser (*taeli*), the ferryman (*jalawan*), and the cotton carder (*landap*) have almost vanished as job categories. The members of these *kam* now are either tenants or casual laborers, and are referred to by other villagers as *fakir*, or landless farm laborers, though they themselves use their traditional *kam* designation. On the other hand, economic change and the introduction of new technology has meant that some new *kam* have appeared, such as the *misri*, who fix mechanical implements. In Shin Bagh itself, the shopkeepers (*dukandar*) form a new *kam*. One villager, from a poor laboring family, has become principal of the local school, and is sometimes said to belong to the teacher (*ustaz*) *kam*.

Although these landless groups are sometimes called *khel* (clans), their genealogical memory is quite short, going back three or four generations or less. Genealogies are unimportant to them since they do not inherit land. The only *kams* which have any extensive genealogies and any notion of clans within clans (that is, of segmentation) are the Gujars and

A *fakir* earning extra money by mending cups in the village street.

Kohistanis, who are actually distinct ethnic enclaves in Swat with their own languages and customs. Gujars often hold land in the hills as clients of the Pukhtun, while Kohistanis are refugees from their own holdings further north, driven south by some feud or family fight. Gujars and Kohistanis are both herdsmen as well, and sometimes have large herds which are passed down patrilineally. Their genealogies derive both from these holdings and from past history as independent peoples holding their own lands.

The *khels* of the landless tend to marry in, and there are traditions that weavers (*jolas*) should marry leatherworkers (*shahkhels*), though in actuality this intermarriage was not found. There are no prohibitions on out-marriage, but there is a vague, generally agreed upon ranking from high to low. People do not like to marry too far beneath themselves, but are happy to marry far above themselves. Commensality is not effected by ranking. Corporate pollution is unimportant in Swat. Pollution occurs through sexual contact, from touching feces, blood, a dog, or some other dirty thing, but not from physical contact with another *kam*.

The recognized laboring *kam* of Shin Bagh are given below in the approximate order of their ranking:

1. *Paracha*: muleteer, often wealthy.
2. *Tarkan* and *Ingor*: carpenter and blacksmith, now amalgamated into one *kam*. They work as general repairmen and wall-builders. They also run the village flour mills.
3. *Zurgar*: goldsmith. Brought into the village two generations ago; often relatively wealthy.
4. *Gujar*: ethnic group; herdsmen or laborers. Speak Gujari language.
5. *Kohistani*: ethnic group; herdsmen or laborers. Speak a Kohistani language.
6. *Darzi*: tailor.
7. *Dukandar*: shopkeeper, often of *paracha* heritage.
8. *Imam*: religious teacher who presides at the mosque. Sometimes a landless *mullah,* but may be originally of any *kam*.
9. *Fakir*: laborer. Not to be confused with religious mendicant (*faqir*).
10. *Chamyar*: shoemaker.
11. *Jola*: weaver.
12. *Kolal*: potter.
13. *Taeli*: oil presser.
14. *Jalawan*: ferryman and fisherman.
15. *Marate*: house slave.
16. *Shahkhel*: leatherworker, butcher, bone setter, and messenger.
17. *Nai*: barber, messenger, bloodletter, and butcher.

The middle range of this chart is very ambiguous, and many would argue that the Gujar and the Kohistani should be accorded much lower places, but it is a fact that Pukhtun men occasionally marry Gujar women; that the Gujars pose the major threat to Pukhtun dominance; and that the Gujars are often quite wealthy. A common abuse is that someone is "like a Gujar," or that something is "fit only for a Gujar." Yet the Gujars are also spoken of with grudging admiration for their toughness and hard work. Kohistani fit in a similar category as an ethnic and not strictly occupational *kam*. The Malik *khel* themselves descend matrilineally from the Kohistani and are closely allied with many Kohistani tribes, so their attitude toward poor Kohistani in their midst as laborers is somewhat conflicted.

One's position in the chart is not immutable, but varies with financial success. The muleteers (*parachas*) were formerly quite a low *kam*. However, their expertise at trade, derived from their traditional work of transporting goods, stood them in good stead with the transformation of the Swati economy. In the larger towns, *paracha* traders have become extremely wealthy, eclipsing even the local khans. In these areas they have managed to buy *dauftar* land and are now claiming the title of Pukhtun. In Shin Bagh, the *parachas* have not reached this height. But they have accumulated wealth and have purchased a small amount of land, and they tend to dominate trade. An indication of their new position comes at harvest time. Formerly, an imam of the mosque would divide the grain into shares at harvest, while the *parachas* would merely haul it. But, in recent years, the *paracha* has taken over this function of the imam, and he now controls the distribution of the crop.

The carpenter and blacksmith (*tarkan, ingor*) were previously regarded as being the closest to the Pukhtun in prestige and honor, and many still regard them so. They are given the unique privilege of free housing by the khans of the village. Like the mullah, it is said that the carpenter and blacksmith accompanied the Yusufzai from Afghanistan. Their centuries of loyalty also wins them respect.

The goldsmiths (*zurgar*) are recent migrants to the village. They were even given land to induce them to stay. The goldsmith is respected because the Pukhtun feel that his is the only work, of all the specialists, that is really skilled.

The imam has never been greatly honored because of his dependence on the charity of his parishioners. But, in 1977, the status of the imams greatly increased, as their mosques became the centers of resistance to the threat of socialism offered by the PPP government. As related in chapter 2, one imam even ran for office under the auspices of the opposition Pakistan National Alliance. It appears that, under stress, the imams have arisen to replace the ecstatic holy men (dervishes and *malangs*) who became pirs and leaders of the Pukhtun in times of war. Some Pukhtun khans, seeing the new power of the previously impotent imams, are sending one or two of their sons to be trained in Koranic studies. In this way, they hope to coopt the political power the imams have begun wielding in the present crisis.

The middle of the list of *kams* is murky in its ranking, but all would agree that the leatherworker (*shahkhel*) and the barber (*nai*) belong at the bottom. Because of some of the attributes of their work and lifestyles, it is flatly stated that no Pukhtun could ever marry into these groups.

Here as well, money, when combined with sufficient distance, can overcome this prohibition, as in the case of a Pukhtun girl who married a wealthy businessman in Peshawar, only to discover his heritage as a barber. Shocked, her family asked if she wished to return to her village but, accustomed to the pleasure of television and a refrigerator, she refused, saying, "Alas, it is my fate." But such an event is extremely rare and may exist only in anecdote.

The low position of these two groups derives from several factors. Both groups are menial servants, and both do demeaning work. The leatherworker is associated with the stench of his trade and, by extension, with death. The barber is despised not so much because of his work, but because of the supposedly lax morality of his wife. The Pukhtun men claim that the barber's wife often serves as the village prostitute, a claim which is, of course, impossible to validate, but one that is nonetheless current. In fact, the barber's wife is called *duma*, a term which is also used for the dancing prostitutes who visit the village at marriage rituals. A great deal of symbolism is attached to these two roles. The leatherworker and barber are among the last *kams* to resist monetarization and resemble the *jajmani* ritual clients found in India (Pocock 1962). Furthermore, each *kam* represents a symbolic alternative to the conflicted family structure of the Pukhtun. The leatherworker is traditionally the foster father of young elite Pukhtun boys. His wife is a wet nurse who provides them with milk, while he is their supportive ally and father figure. I have seen grown men go to their leatherworker foster father when they needed advice, and not to their own father. The leatherworker and his household are a nurturing family of inferiors, as opposed to the Pukhtun boy's real family of rivals. The barber fills a contrary role, representing through his wife the possibility, forbidden in ordinary life, of female sexual promiscuity. In this context, it is noteworthy that one of the barber's duties in the village is to circumcise boys. He also announces, with his drumming, any engagement or wedding. His wife is the traditional go-between in wedding arrangements, and it is she who reports back to the bride's family on the success of the nuptial night. She also has the duty of participating in every wedding by burning a special herb which keeps away the evil eye, and she is able to remove enchantments which have rendered grooms impotent. (For more on the symbolic roles of these *kams* see Lindholm 1981b.)

Table 3.2 will give an idea of the relative wealth of the various *kams*

Table 3.2 Relative Wealth of the *Kams* and *Khels* in Shin Bagh

Khels	Houses	Rooms per house	Total Population	Persons per room	Buffalo and cattle	Dauftar (in paisa)	Tseri plots (in paisa)	Houseowners
Malik	41	2.6	313	3.1	72	522	45	41
Jakhawal	15	1.9	79	2.8	21	129	0	15
Umar	13	1.4	73	4	22	111	1	12
Kurum	39	1.8	277	3.9	99	409	11	39
Daulet	24	1	136	5.7	30	111	4	24
Masho	15	1.1	101	6.1	36	91	1.5	15
Other Pukhtun	7	1.1	35	4.5	5	44	4	7
Kams								
Mia	8	1	50	6.3	13	0	4	3
Mullah	24	1.3	165	5.4	53	0	33	18
Paracha	18	1.3	114	4.9	16[a]	1.5	2	3
Ingor and Tarkan	9	1.1	50	5	6	0	0	0
Zurgar	3	1.3	31	7.8	5	.5	3	2
Kohistani and Gujar	19	1	103	5.4	30	1.5	2	0
Darzi	2	1	12	6	0	0	0	1
Dukandar	3	1.3	24	6	2	0	0	2
Fakir	44	1.2	230	4.4	27[b]	1	0	1
Chamyar	5	1	21	4.2	2	0	0	2
Jola	7	1.3	40	4.4	5	0	0	1
Kolal	2	1	11	5.5	4	0	0	0
Shahkhel	4	1	25	6.3	2	0	0	0
Nai	6	1	41	6.8	5	0	1	2
Other kams	4	1.5	17	2.8	6	0	0	1

[a] plus 60 donkeys
[b] plus 17 sheep

and landowning *khels* of the village. It is evident from this table that the landed *khels,* and especially the Malik *khel* Pukhtun, with their wealth of *tseri* land, dominate the village resources. The *mias* who are noted above are poor *stanadar* who are resident in the village itself. The wealthier *stanadar* who live in their own village just outside Shin Bagh have not been included.

Dauftar is reckoned in Shin Bagh in units of *rupees* and *paisa* (these terms derive from Pakistani monetary units). Forty-eight *paisa* is said to yield approximately 100 maunds (about 8,800 lbs.) of wheat, which equals one *rupee.* Land holdings are thus not reckoned on the amount of land held, but on the yield of the land, though the actual area of a *rupee* is generally assumed to be approximately ten acres, but this only a guess. Shin Bagh itself is supposed to consist of thirty *rupees* of land, though the actual count is quite unclear. A very large holding is fifteen to twenty *paisa.* In actual fact, men are often not sure about the number of *paisa* they hold. They are very sure, however, of where the borders of their various pieces of land lie.

Traditionally, the workers gave their customary services to the other members of the ward, or *təl,* and were paid either by a set percentage of the total yield of the *təl* land or by the rights to cultivate a portion of the land for themselves. Recently, cash payment has tended to replace traditional recompense as some specialists and laborers sell their skills.

Despite increasing monetarization of the economy, some of the specialists and laborers continue, at least partially, to follow the old customs. The carpenter/smith, the barber, the leatherworker, and the muleteer still occupied their traditional *təl* jobs in 1977, though they also accepted paying jobs outside the *təl.* One barber family, who had a son in Saudi Arabia, had become so wealthy that they had been able to purchase some *tseri* land, as well as some buffaloes and a house. Yet they still kept up with their traditional *təl* work.

Those who continue in their customary employment cite loyalty to their patrons as the reason. The patron Pukhtun, however, often complain of the specialists they are obliged to feed and have been seeking ways to cut these dependent *kams* away. It is felt that a monetary relationship is much more advantageous to the employer, since he then need only pay for work done and since his responsibilities for his employees are minimal. The labor market, until recently, has been glutted with cheap labor, and there is no doubt that the patron's view is the correct one, though with the present labor shortage this view may be changing. A traditional client gets a great deal from his patron. He expects food, shelter, bride price, gifts at weddings and ceremonies, protection, and all the other obligatory duties of the patron–client relationship. In 1977, many Pukhtun were feeling that they would prefer money to the dubious loyalty of numerous dependent specialists and workers.

Nonetheless, the patron–client, master–servant relation continued strong. The carpenter still takes 5 percent of all grain he grinds at the mill. In return, he supplies the millstone and transports the grain to and from the mill. He also gets a special piece of land to farm in return for his *tal* work in fixing plows, chairs, and the like. The leatherworker cures leather and makes leather-bottom chairs and beds as well as cleaning grain, butchering, and acting as general household laborer. For this he takes a portion of the grain he cleans, plus the skin, neck, and innards of each buffalo killed. The barber has a similar arrangement, while the muleteer, who carries the grain from the fields and measures it, gets 3.3 percent of the total.

The most important workers in the ward are the agricultural laborers. They are of two types: casual workers and sharecroppers (*dekan*). Elite khans rarely work their own land, unlike Pukhtun with smaller holdings. As an aristocrat, the khan oversees the labor of others and generally prefers not to get his hands dirty, though there are notable exceptions. It is well known that this approach leads to smaller yields, but it suits the khan's image and sense of dignity to be idle.

There are several types of tenancy. One, the most favored, is *ijara,* or straight rental. A certain amount is set as a return for using the land, and this amount must be given regardless of what the land produces. The second type is *braxikor,* and signifies a return of a proportion of the yield. The first type is usually practiced near the owner's own village, where he can keep some control over the man who has rented the land. The second type, which produces much lower returns, is practiced when the field is far distant and the landlord is not able to excercise much influence to assure a just return. In fact, he often considers himself lucky to get any return at all. Land also may be given as *ganṛa,* that is, as a guarantee on a loan. As mentioned earlier in this chapter, this is only done with close patrilineal relatives. No interest is charged, and the land is returned to the owner when he repays his debt. All of these types of land, plus the landowner's own land, may be worked by sharecroppers. A man who has rented a piece of land may work it himself, or he may hire a sharecropper to work it for him. The sharecropper is put in charge of the field. Seed is provided by the man who owns or controls the land. Most sharecroppers either have or can arrange to use a buffalo to plow. Besides working the field, the sharecroppers are also considered to be the employees of their landlord and are expected to do whatever general labor is demanded of them. The wife and mother of the sharecropper may have to help the employer's wife with cooking, sewing, child care, and household gardening, while the sharecropper and his brothers build walls, act as messengers, dig ditches, and the like. In return, 17 to 20 percent of the yield is given to the sharecropper after the traditional allotments to the specialists.

Sharecroppers do not have to be landless laborers (*fakir*), though most of them are. Poor Pukhtun men also take on sharecropping work to augment their incomes (see appendix A, tables 8 and 9). There is no disgrace attached to doing sharecropper work, but a Pukhtun would not be expected to do the household chores demanded of a *fakir* sharecropper. A man can be the sharecropper of one man, yet belong to a ward dominated by a different man.

Some workers do not have the security of being sharecroppers. Instead they must look for whatever work is available. These men find most of their work during planting and harvest times. They are usually paid in cash, though this is a late development. For example, the heavy work of planting rice is paid for at a rate of six rupees (not to be confused with a *rupee* unit of land) a day (60 cents). Unemployed men and boys organize themselves into groups with a leader who negotiates with a landowner for work and wages. The leader, who gets the same wage as his men, does not do any actual physical labor, but rather exhorts his men and chants to drive them on.

A few years ago, at rice planting and at the heavy labor of beating the corn to remove the kernels, cooperative groups of workers called *ashar* went from field to field and were paid by feasting and entertainment. This institution has all but died out except in a few rare cases at corn harvest. *Ashar* on a large scale is now very rare and I have only seen it once. Sharecroppers help one another at peak work periods on a reciprocal basis, and all those with cattle and buffalo have a rotating system in which the owners take turns grazing the animals. But even this mild

Sharecropper women cleaning wheat for their employer.

form of cooperation is now vanishing, since the person herding is responsible for the animals lost; a responsibility most families cannot afford.

To return to the work available for the laborer, one job he may take is that of the *naukar* or servant. This work (also rapidly disappearing) involves attendance on one's employer at all times. A servant is a watchman, bodyguard, sweeper, and carrier in the *hujera,* or men's house. He gives his patron rubdowns, runs confidential errands for him, acts as his house servant and is, in fact, probably closer to his patron than anyone else. Formerly, this sort of work might have been done by a house slave (*marate*), but men of this category are uncommon. Slavery per se was never a popular institution among the Pukhtun, and holding slaves was not necessary for an important man. The house slave, like the servant, was often considered a sort of junior family member. Purdah was not kept from him and the landlord was expected to provide for all his wants. This relation continues with the few house servants and the one slave who remain in the village. The servant who works in the *hujera* and acts as a bodyguard is also diminishing in popularity since he is even more dependent on his employer than the ordinary laborer. The laborer is fed

Sharecroppers and hired laborers sweeping the chaff from corn.

when he works, and his patron has certain responsibilities toward him, but the servant eats with his patron the year round. Only a few wish to continue supporting such a drain on their resources as permanent servants. But, in the days before the state, some great khans had many servants who acted as their private armies. It is claimed that the great Malik *khel* leader, Ajab Khan, fed over one hundred men nightly. Wealthy and politically ambitious khans still maintain such armies, but no one in Shin Bagh had the wherewithal or backing to do so. In passing, it might be noted that working as a bodyguard is considered the most honorable work for an impoverished Pukhtun or an ambitious laborer. The bodyguard is proud to exemplify the Pukhtun virtues of bravery and loyalty, and hopes that these virtues might win the recognition of his patron and, perhaps, a land grant. In fact, this was formerly a major route of upward mobility in Swat.

There is one more category left to discuss; that of the *kandari*. As we have noted on our chart of the different groups in the village, most of the landless do not own their own houses. They are given houses to live in by the leaders of their ward and are thus reckoned as his *kandari*, or householders. Each *kandari* household is obliged to perform corvée labor for the houseowner in order to repay him for the use of his house. This sort of relationship is now very much disliked by the khan houseowners (one mark of a khan is the fact that he owns many houses, while the Pukhtun merely own their own). Instead of labor, they would prefer rent (*ijara*). As a result, there have been many attempts to evict tenants forcibly, and the householders have protested, using the PPP (Pakistan People's Party) government's preemption laws as their support. PPP promulgation of these laws was the prime reason for the poor people's support of that party in Swat in the 1977 elections.

Some families have no able-bodied men and so are without income. These impoverished families should be provided for by the propertied classes as a matter of honor (*gherat*) and, in fact, there was no begging by local people in Shin Bagh. But, with a greater and greater squeeze on resources, coupled with a desire to spend any surplus on luxury goods, the generosity of the landed is becoming strained.

The impression to this point has been of the patrons as benevolent protectors and providers for their clients. But the Pukhtun also extracted a great deal from their workers. Not only was corvée labor given on demand, but the khan of a ward also had the right to fine any of his

A poor old woman mending her clothes on a village street.

dependents for any cause, and often took advantage of this right (backed up by physical force) to impoverish any worker who had managed to acquire a surplus. At marriages, the khan had to be given a payment by the groom's family as a surety against the khan taking the girl for himself. A leg of all animals killed was given to the khan, who could also demand chickens and milk products from his dependents. Because they were able to take milk, meat, and other animal products whenever they wanted, the khan lineage in Shin Bagh still are not very interested in raising buffalo or cattle, leaving that to lesser lineages. Most of the rights of the khans have now been done away with. Fining is done by the courts, and corvée labor has been banned. Nonetheless, the khans are still in an all but omnipotent relation to their underlings, as is indicated by their habit of taking poor girls as their mistresses, snatching things from the hands of poor people, and so on. Men without land are known only by their nicknames, such as "grasshopper," "blue eyes," "dumb one," "traveler," and the like. When angry, a Pukhtun will dismiss such men as "dogs." This is a cruel epithet, since Swati dogs are defiling, live on human excrement and waste, and supposedly think only of food.

The members of the dependent population are, in important ways, the opposite of Pukhtun; that is, they are weak, landless, and potential cuckolds. The Pukhtun defines himself in contrast to his clients, and bends his efforts to keeping them in an inferior state and himself in a state of superiority. But, despite their low state, there is no concept that the clients are a different sort of men than their overlords. Any Pukhtun who loses his land must join the ranks of the laborers and thereby forfeit all respect and honor, while some clients have managed, through intelligence, hard work, bravery, and luck, to purchase or be given *dauftar* and claim equality with the Pukhtun. Mobility was always possible in Swat. The elder Pukhtun men freely grant that any man who holds *dauftar* has Pukhtun status, whatever his previous ancestry, though they say it will take several generations for complete assimilation. It is only fair to note, however, that younger men do not take so sanguine a view, and instead often make vociferous claims that being Pukhtun is a matter of blood, and not land. This difference in opinion between elders and juniors perhaps springs from the greater status insecurity of the younger men, who see *dauftar* land being sold more and more often and some of their previous clients becoming relatively wealthy due to their work as migrant laborers, a sort of work which, in the past, was regarded as beneath the dignity of an elite khan. The younger men feel that such upstarts should be barred from the respect offered a blood Pukhtun.

Nonetheless, the muleteers of the larger towns who have become wealthy and purchased land claim and receive the title of khan. The basic principle is that all men are fundamentally the same. A man with land has been blessed by Allah and is worthy of respect; a man without land is an unfortunate, cursed for some unknown reason. Loss can strike any man at God's will. With this ideology, the poor are never dehumanized, while at the same time they still provide the Pukhtun with an example of all that is degrading and to be avoided. The poor, in turn, look to the Pukhtun as exemplars of the proper life which, as poor men, they are unable to live. Their complaints against the elite are that the elite do not "act Pukhtun," i.e., they do not live up to the ideal.

Here is the nexus of the problem of class among the Pukhtun. Certainly, as Asad predicted (1972), there has been a trend toward proletarianization of the poor. The money economy has cut many of the emotional ties between patron and client, as we have seen. There have even been armed confrontations between the landless and the landed. Yet the client does not question the value system of his society, any more than the patron questions the system. The social premises which motivate the elite are the same premises by which the poor would like to live. The hope of the poor is simply to become exactly like the Pukhtun landlords who dominate them. Since these landlords are organized on the fragmenting principles of the segmentary society, class unity both among them and among the poor who emulate them is presently an impossibility, since the segmentary ideology divides men at every point. Just as the Pukhtun cannot unite except through the efforts of a religious *stanadar*, so the poor look to their patrons or, more recently, to the state bureaucracy for leadership. The only leader who has arisen from the poor is a wealthy Gujar, who has extorted land from his fellow Gujars, who lives like a Pukhtun, and who demands to be addressed as khan. The main difference between the Pukhtun and their clients is that the Pukhtun are able to try to live out the ideal life, while the poor are prevented from doing so by their weakness. Were the situations reversed, the system would remain the same. Only through a transformation of consciousness and an awareness of class solidarity could real change come about, but this does not seem likely at the moment. As one laborer said, "there will always be landlords on the necks of the poor. God grant that I may become a landlord."

In order to understand the constraints under which the system operates, it is useful to look at the factors which differentiate the landed from the landless. We can see a continuum of sorts running from the elite—who are concerned with their lineages, their land rights, and who find their identity in these two concepts—to the laboring classes, who care little for lineage, have no land, and are identified primarily by their work. This continuum is paralleled in treatment of women. Among the landlords, women are exchanged with great reluctance. They are viewed as repositories of family pride and kept in rigid seclusion. The lower the ranking of a *kam*, the less seclusion women observe, reaching the nadir of the *duma*, who is a dancing girl and a prostitute. Seduction of a Pukhtun woman leads to death for both parties, while seduction of a lower class woman by a Pukhtun carries no penalty at all and seduction by another lower class man leads, at most, to a fine. Purdah among the elite is joined to a desire to have as many wives as possible, a strict prohibition on divorce, and the custom of levirate. Women as wives are an object of strong competition among the Pukhtun, especially among the elite khans, who view taking women as an aspect of their "hobby" of warfare and one-upmanship. Having a wife reveals one's capacity to dominate and subordinate another elite clan. In contrast, the poor cannot afford two wives, are allowed divorce, and feel no shame in marrying a widow with sons by another man. Land ownership, the ideology of patrilineality, and the protection of one's women are all tied together in the same complex of associations which governs Pukhtun life. The poor observe this complex and wish to emulate it, but are disallowed by their condition.

I have noted in this chapter some of the attributes of the social organization of the village. The basic structure is that of the segmentary lineage system, with its premises of equality and unification in opposition to external pressures. Conquest and a rivalry over land have led to some hierarchization within the system, the development of *tarburwali,* and the two fluid but ubiquitous parties. The conquered client population has provided an image of weakness as the symbolic opposite of the Pukhtun's concept of themselves as powerful, independent, petty lords. This image is shared by the clients themselves, who seek to imitate the Pukhtun principles.

The Pukhtun live within a system which obliges men to present themselves as completely self-reliant. The articulation of land rights brings close relatives into constant conflict; no one is to be trusted and each man is on his own against a hostile and threatening world. This view of the world is, without doubt, a perfectly "rational" one from the standpoint of the people who live within the system. Suspicion, defensiveness, bravery, vengefulness, pride, envy, a Machiavellian aptitude for intrigue, and a Hobbesian vision of the world are all eminently practical and reasonable stances for the Pukhtun, given the circumstances of his life. The essential fact of the worldview which knits Pukhtun society together is the individualistic ideal of a strong, lonely man, struggling against all others for survival and personal honor. Having revealed the structural premises from which this belief arises, we can see that it is assuredly the only realistic attitude for a Pukhtun man to adopt.

4. Exchange

A tribal marriage, in some sense hard for an outsider to comprehend, is seen as exposing a family's sense of shame and modesty.
(Caroe 1965:304)

A Pukhtun would rather give up his life than surrender his land or his wife. They both are sacred.
(G. Khan 1958:45)

Women have no noses. They will eat shit.

One's own mother and sister are disgusting.

Women belong in the house or in the grave.
(Pukhtun proverbs)

EXCHANGES of various sorts are the stuff of social life. Human relations are inescapably relations of exchange: exchange of goods, of words, of women given in marriage, of affection or hostility. The patterns of exchange do not simply reflect the social structure; they are, in a very real sense, the essence of the structure, since social elements can never exist in isolation.

And yet this is not the view of the Pukhtun, who believe that individuals stand alone, independent of the world. As Elphinstone was the first to note, the Pukhtun's "highest praise in speaking of a well governed country is, that 'every man eats the produce of his own field,' and that 'nobody has any concern with his neighbor'" (1815: 1:327). But this pose is itself the artifact of the social order outlined in the last chapter: an order in which every man stands in opposition to his nearest neighbor.

This chapter will show how the structure is expressed in some typical relations of exchange, but I do not want to imply a priority of structure. In actuality, the entire complex of structure and exchange is a unity; it is the relational world in which the people of Swat live and attempt to make some understandable order for their lives.

One form of exchange relation is a recent innovation due to the intrusion of the money economy into Swat. This is the relation of employer to employee. Previously, Pukhtun confused this relation with that of master–servant or patron–client, and therefore refused to demean themselves by seeking jobs. But recently various opportunities in Swat have opened up, not only in the bureaucracy (called "service" by the Pukhtun), but in private industry as well. My friend Zaman Khan, for instance, worked as a representative of the tobacco company. His job was to try to get people to contract to grow tobacco. Others work in textile factories in Mingora, in Lower Swat. Education, a desire for cash, and the impersonal tie with the employer have combined to lead many younger Pukhtun into the expanding job market. In fact, the plea of the Pukhtun to me was to help them organize a factory in Upper Swat, perhaps for manufacture of matches, so that the men could find jobs without being forced to leave their homes.

There continued to exist, however, many remnant beliefs deriving from the underlying segmentary system that have prevented the Pukhtun from becoming either good bosses or good workers in the new capitalist economy. The position of wage earner is still considered to be of much lower value than the traditional work of overseeing a farm. As an illustration

A textile mill near Saidu Sherif.

of this value difference, it is believed that grain purchased with wages will last only half as long as grain raised in one's own fields.

Furthermore, Pukhtun carry their rivalries into their business life and are unwilling to work for other Pukhtun. Punjabis and Kashmiris, who are considered inferior from birth, are suitable employers, since the Pukhtun, though demeaning himself by working for them, still believes himself to be intrinsically superior. But, if a Pukhtun works for another Pukhtun, he admits the other as his better.

Pukhtun also find it very difficult to begin businesses, since their pride does not permit them to practice wheedling or obsequiousness for the sake of gaining customers. If a customer is troublesome, the Pukhtun will as like as not offer him his merchandise for free as a way of shaming the customer. But this is not a profitable way to run a store.

Another type of business relation is the partnership, which is eagerly entered into in the hopes of profit. Men will join together in order to pool their resources and spread the risk of a new enterprise. However, partnerships are rarely successful due to mistrust among the partners. For example, several men in Shin Bagh purchased a tractor and planned to farm cooperatively. When one of the partners took the crop to market, the return was smaller than had been anticipated. The other partners then accused the seller of pocketing some of the profits for himself. Later, when the tractor needed repairs, the partners accused one another of causing the damage. The tractor was eventually sold at a loss and the partnership dissolved with ill-feeling.

A favorite mode of exchange among men is barter, or *adal-badal* (give and take). Men are always on the alert for the possibility of bartering one of their possessions for something better. Often the exchange is like for like: a radio for a radio, sunglasses for sunglasses, a watch for a watch. However, unlike objects can also be exchanged, such as, in one instance, a bicycle for two donkeys. *Adal-badal* is always practiced with nonrelatives and affords men a great deal of pleasure as they attempt to get the advantage over their exchange partner. A good exchange, in which a man feels he has gotten the better of the deal, is cause for bragging and pride. If the exchange is bad, the recipient tries to renege on the deal or, failing that, to palm off the faulty object on someone unsuspecting. The best partner in *adal-badal* is someone who is distant spatially and will therefore have little opportunity to complain. *Adal-badal* is a one time occurrence between two otherwise unconnected men. Mistrust prohibits the development of permanent bartering partners, nor are there any chains of barter between villages and regions. All barter is strictly dyadic and nonrecurrent. In this, it resembles marriage, though in other ways it is quite different, as will be discussed.

Aside from barter, there is also gift-giving to outsiders. This type of gift is called *swori*, or charity. Under this heading come such actions as lending cattle to a man for plowing without expecting any return. While *adal-badal* is morally neutral, since each man is trying to outwit the other, *swori* has moral connotations. A man who gives without return is said to be "loved by Allah," while the man who receives without giving is "disliked by Allah." *Swori* resembles the giving of *gherat* (feasts and food for the poor) and *zakat* (pious charity). In all these cases, the giver is regarded as morally superior to the taker. This is true in every

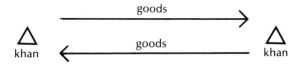

Figure 4.1 Barter (*Adal-Badal*)

situation, with two important exceptions: the guest and the holy man. These will be discussed in my concluding chapter.

Loans of money are often arranged with outsiders, though sometimes a well-to-do relative linked through a female will give a money loan. It is not easy to get a loan among the Pukhtun, even though one of the oft-quoted definitions of a good man is "a man who gives loans easily." Loans have a certain moral connotation, and the lender is "loved by Allah." The debtor is also "loved by Allah," but not to the extent of the lender and only when he repays the loan. If the loan is not returned, the debtor has admitted his inferiority to the lender and is equated with a mendicant. Because the lender gives out of honor, he should not dun the debtor. Rather, he should wait patiently for a return, satisfied with the heavenly credit he has accrued by his generosity. An impatient lender makes use of an intermediary to ask the return of the loan. Requesting a loan is also done through an intermediary. Both requests are embarrassing for the Pukhtun, since the implication is that the person asking has a need and is therefore not self-sufficient. To avoid this embarrassment, Pukhtun often get loans or run up credit with shopkeepers and, more recently, with banks and government agencies.

There is no shame attached to owing money to such people who are, by nature, inferior. But, by the same token, the storekeepers and bankers are not bound by the Pukhtun code of honor and have no compunctions about demanding return of their loans. By avoiding the humiliation of asking for a loan from a fellow Pukhtun, the debtor is later subjected to the discomfiture of public dunning. Banks and government agencies have even threatened to foreclose on land in repayment for debts accrued by the Pukhtun, though this threat had not yet been made good in 1977. The Pukhtun, meanwhile, use every subterfuge possible to avoid repay-

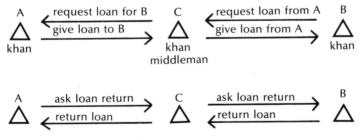

Figure 4.2 Loans

ment to their non-Pukhtun creditors, in keeping with the saying that "a Pukhtun would rather steal than beg" (G. Khan 1958:47). Debts to other, equal Pukhtun, however, are scrupulously repaid on the threat of being regarded as dishonorable. Thus, there are then two patterns for loans: one is with those who are not one's equals and who therefore have no honor and need not be repaid, the other is with fellow Pukhtun who must be repaid or else admitted as one's superiors.

One evident pattern is that exchange between Pukhtun which might involve an overt or covert admission of inferiority by one party must utilize a mediator. The arrangement of loans is a paradigm case, and a middleman is used between the borrower and the lender. Mediating in a loan is not a dishonorable position, since one is in the center of an exchange which will, in time, become equal. In fact the role of middleman is sometimes assumed by the actual borrower in order to avoid the shame of appearing in need. The borrower pretends he is asking the loan for a third party. The convention of silence that keeps the lender from asking the debtor for return of the money lent can allow the actual borrower quite some time to enjoy his cozened funds. When the lender finally does discover that he has been manipulated, he should laugh the incident off, since it would be shameful to show great concern over money lent under any conditions. By such chicanery, begging a loan is transformed into the more respectable form of a confidence game. Nevertheless, although the loan was gained under false pretences, it must be repaid if the borrower wishes to retain his honor. Trickery in itself is not dishonorable and, in fact, is rather an admirable trait. But failure to repay would be shameful unless, of course, the lender were an inferior person.

Mediation in a loan is regarded as honorable, and middlemen in such transactions are considered the equals of the loaner and the debtor. But mediation in other affairs is not honorable, and Pukhtun are willing to act only as middlemen in loans, not in other exchanges in which the inequality of the two parties is implied. For instance, the role of middleman in marriage negotiations is always taken by the most despised of *kams*, that of the barber (*nai*) and his wife. Giving a woman is a shameful business, and the *nai*, as a shameless man, is the logical candidate as marriage arranger.

The dancing girl (*duma*), performs another mediatory role. Dancing unveiled in front of the village men at a marriage party, she represents sexuality without commitment. During these dancing parties, men pub-

A *duma* performing.

licly express their solidarity with their lineage mates, placing money on the foreheads of their lineage brothers to be snatched away by the whirling dancer. Only at this event do men give freely to their brothers, and the gift is diverted into the hands of the dancing girl, the woman who will sleep with a man in return for money. Here, it seems, is a symbolic recognition of the fact that marriage and the sexually exclusive tie between wife and husband is seen as dividing brother from brother. The dance represents an antimarriage, in which the brothers unite and show their solidarity by giving money to a woman who can sleep with all of them. It is very important for a clan to give high payments to the dancers, since it is a matter of rivalry with other clans as to which has given the most. At one small party in Shin Bagh 1,600 rupees were given. The dancing girls are so demanding that a man must pay even to have tea with them, and the amount paid is something to brag about. The most attractive girls are discriminating, and will not accept a man as a lover if they find him distasteful. A khan can be humiliated by such as refusal, but nonetheless many have wasted their fortunes in pursuit of the ideal the dancing girls offers.

The *duma*, then, is the converse of the ordinary wife who must sleep only with her husband upon demand, who must remain in purdah, and who, ideally at least, is the slave of men. The *duma* is sexually free and shameless. Following the opposition further, it is the wife who is always blamed for the breakup of the patrilineal joint family; a break which is in fact largely caused by the enmity and personal ambitions of the brothers. But the *duma*, out of purdah and sexually promiscuous, unites the brothers in a reversal of marriage. They buy her attentions for one another and thereby overcome, if only temporarily, their own opposition. The contrast becomes even clearer when it is realized that only a few years ago the role of the *duma* was taken by dancing boys who were passive homosexual men dressed as women. The realm of sexuality is removed not only from marriage, but from the female sex itself (see Lindholm 1981b for more on this).

Barbers' wives and dancers are both called *duma*, and it is assumed that all barbers' wives are promiscuous. The duties of the barbers' wives involve aiding marriage negotiations, and they are therefore the agents who supposedly destroy brotherly unity, especially in father's brother's daughter marriage. The *nai* himself, as the circumciser, also has his role in that ceremony of transformation in which a boy assumes the attributes of a man. He and his wife are ambiguous figures, charged with sexuality and shamelessness. As mentioned in the last chapter, the barber's wife is often the boy's sexual initiator. Her husband shapes the boy's manhood and she tests out his ability to function.

Associated with the *nai* are the *shahkhel,* or leatherworkers. To quote one local saying: "There was a disturbance in the village, but the barber and the leatherworker benefited." The *nai* is associated with sexuality and marriage. The leatherworker is associated with death, with nurturance and, in a circuitous way, with sexuality as well. In other parts of Pakistan, the Leatherworker reportedly is a professional washer of bodies, and even in Upper Swat, where he does not have this job, the leatherworker has dark connotations. It is believed that if the body of a dead leatherworker is disinterred and washed, the water used is an infallible love philter. Thus, death and sexuality are symbolically equated as the leatherworker, who mediates in death, provides in his death a potion for love (see Lindholm 1981b).

The leatherworker and the butcher also officiate at all sacrifices. At every major event a buffalo or at least a cow or bull should be slaughtered. The *nai* and the *shahkhel*, acting together, are the butchers. These two thus act as mediators in the sacrifice which connects man with the Deity. Allah is, in fact, the only superior being acknowledged by the Pukhtun. The leatherworker and the barber, already contaminated by their mediating roles in death and marriage, also take on the symbolic stigma attached to the admission of inferiority that is implicit in sacrifice.

The *stanadar,* who are actual religious practitioners in the Sufi tradition, are the more conventional mediators with Allah. Like the *nai* and the *shahkhel*, they also are viewed by the Pukhtun as suspect and ambiguous. *Stanadar,* who preside over tombs and holy places, and pirs, who claim charismatic power to intervene with Allah, are believed able to influence the future if given proper payment. Interestingly, these men also have reputations for sexual promiscuity. A favorite outing of the women is a visit to a famous tomb or pir, and the men are suspicious that these visits are merely pretexts for a sexual liaison with a member of the *stanadar* class. One of the major blessings sought from holy men is the blessing of a son, and the holy man often takes personal responsibility for fertilization.

Women who are childless will visit various faqirs [not to be confused with *fakir* laborers], whose prayers have a reputation for being efficacious for the removal of sterility. They write charms, and dictate elaborate instructions for the behavior of the woman till her wish be fulfilled, and they take the gifts which the suppliant has bought with her . . . and when a child is born in due time, the husband of the woman cannot always claim paternity. (Pennell 1909:238)

Several men in the village, recognizable by red birthmarks on their faces, were pointed out as the results of such a union. Stories of the sexuality and salaciousness of holy men abound in Swat, not only concerning Sufi types, but also the more orthodox imams as well.

Wandering mendicants, *malangs* and dervishes, who can blossom into pirs given the discipline of an order, also have the power to give sons. Women, in the absence of their husbands, ask the *malang* to rub them with his mirrored charm and give him food in return. The mendicants also bless boys of the neighborhood, rubbing their heads and saying, "God willing, you will have sons," and then striking the boys on the back. The *malangs,* who wear patchwork clothing in the style of the early Sufis, allow their hair to grow long, and wander from place to place. They spend much of their time inebriated from hashish (*charas*). These men, who were much more numerous in Swat prior to the Badshah, who exiled most of them, are greatly feared by the villagers as cannibals. Children are frightened into good behavior with the cooking pot of the *malang* as a threat. Yet, the blessings of a mendicant are regarded as the mythical source of the power of each great clan. The *malang* and the *stanadar* are thus viewed as composites of sexual seductiveness, holiness, fertility, and cannibalism.

In this extraordinary mixture, which corresponds in its outlines with the attitudes toward the barber and leatherworker, the social distaste for the mediator (aside from the Pukhtun who mediates in loans) is evident. The *malang,* the pir, the barber, and the leatherworker are alike in that they act as arbitrators in unequal exchanges involving either the Pukhtun and his equals (marriage or a dispute), or the Pukhtun and his only superior—Allah—in the rites of death, sacrifice and blessing. As we have seen, the ideology of the society is such that each Pukhtun visualizes himself as either the superior or, at least, the coequal in any relationship. The relations utilizing these arbitrators belie this ideology. The Pukhtun wish to have no such relationships, but reality dictates that marriages must be entered into, that man must acknowledge the power of God, that death reduces the lineage, and so on. The admission of inequality, even with the Deity, can only be made palatable through the offices of mediators, who themselves take on the taint of ambiguity, as can be seen in their contradictory attributes.

Hatred of ambiguity, of mediators between unequal elements, of things which are not "one thing or the other," is strongly marked among the Pukhtun. Ambiguity is hated and feared as a threat to the structurally given posture of personal isolation, independence, and self-sufficiency. Douglas (1966; 1970; 1975) has noted that highly structured societies dominated by public systems of classification and characterized by powerful social pressure will mistrust ambiguity. Swat is a society of this type, and the distaste for the equivocal is manifest throughout the culture. The ephemeral arc of the rainbow is considered ugly and dangerous because of its blending of many elements and its transitory character. It is said to cause the reversal of the gender of anyone standing beneath it. Children stringing beads automatically separate all the beads into color and shape categories, and do not mix them. Bangles of two different colors are carefully divided, and an equal number of contrasting colors are worn on each arm. A third color cannot be worn, since it would disrupt the symmetrical opposition. The English word "normal" has been coopted into the Pukhto language to designate a passive homosexual. This is because their English textbooks define "normal" as "in between," therefore ambiguous. The Pukhtun seek to deny, in every avenue of life, the necessity of dependence, loss, transformation, complexity, and ambiguity. Life should be neat, isolated, and confined to well-defined categories.

The same problems of repulsion for relations of exchange that are not clearly between coequals is evident in the Swati marketplace. Previously, as elsewhere in Asia, markets rotated on a weekly round, but there were no permanent shops. Durushkhela was the site of one such marketplace, which even in 1977 continued to meet weekly in its new location at the district capital of Matta. But in former times, the market was essentially a place for barter. Money was very little in evidence, and there was no opprobrium attached to engaging in such exchange. Even the great khans felt no disgrace in carrying on long-distance trade and enriching themselves by importing cloth and other luxury goods which they exchanged for local produce.

Recently, however, cash has intruded into the economy, and the relations of the marketplace have been greatly transformed as the local economy has evolved from one of reciprocity and periodic relations of barter to the far more encompassing economy of the monetarized free market. The equality of all buyers and sellers, regardless of social status, now poses a grave threat to the Pukhtun notion of reciprocity between equals, while inferiors must suffer appropriation and be rewarded through redistributive largesse. Yet a Pukhtun who enters the marketplace is selling himself, and must offer himself and his goods or services to all comers. It is interesting to note that relations of buyer and seller generally exist between Pukhtun and non-Pukhtun. Among themselves, Pukhtun do not buy and sell, but rather give their wares without payment. Few Pukhtun are merchants, but some are lawyers and doctors. It is expected that a professional Pukhtun will give his advice gratis to his fellows, while exacting a fee from a laborer or a storekeeper. There are several reasons for this. The professional Pukhtun dislikes taking money from his equals for his services since this implies that he, the professional, is a sort of servant. Also, the man who gives a service places the recipient under obligation to him, and this is considered more gratifying and more honorable. On the other hand, payment given by an inferior is not tainted, but instead ratifies the professional's superiority. Of course, some lawyers and doctors may donate their services to the poor as *gherat* (charity) as well; a gift which again testifies to superiority. But giving services to fellow Pukhtun is hardly *gherat*. Instead, the parallel is with a loan which must be repaid for the debtor to retain his honor. This attitude appeared to be changing in 1977, as some lawyers decided they preferred money to honor and refused to take cases for Pukhtun equals unless paid in advance. Such a stance, while understood as practical, was still regarded as "the act of a dog" by the Pukhtun in general.

A discussion of exchange relations outside the family brings several issues to light. The predominant one is the preoccupation of the Pukhtun with avoiding relations of dependence on their equals, while at the same time striving to render their equals dependent. This attitude makes part-

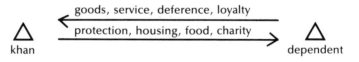

Figure 4.3 Appropriation and Redistribution

nership impossible and prevents barter from being anything more than transitory and not repeatable. Another issue is the mortification men feel at asking loans from their fellows and the consequent use of intermediarites and recourse to loans from non-Pukhtun. We have seen that taking from non-Pukhtun, even in the context of a loan, is viewed as honorable, since taking from inferiors vindicates the Pukhtun's own superiority. In the same context, giving without return is an absolute moral good while the reverse is morally reprehensible. Even asking a Pukhtun to perform a professional service is viewed in the same light, and the one who asks is considered morally similar to a Pukhtun who has requested a loan. Relations of exchange outside the family appear to have a double dimension: relations with those who are inferior and who therefore either receive charity or are forced to give payment (which is viewed by the Pukhtun as a form of tribute and as evidence of his superiority), or exchange between equals, where each seeks to place the other under obligation while at the same time maintaining a pretense of one's own absolute self-sufficiency. The result of the latter is a balanced reciprocity, as exemplified by the popular exchange of adal-badal, in which each tries to gain advantage over the other, in which ties are easily broken and only made for purposes of self-aggrandizement, in which both sides are equal, and in which there is no possibility for the development of hierarchies. The introduction of a money economy has transformed this system to some extent, but the underlying values remain powerful, as is demonstrated in the reluctance of the Pukhtun to accept another Pukhtun as employer. The system leads to a strong distaste for mediating figures, save in the case of a loan, when the exchange partners are equals.

The way these behaviors fit into the picture of the village social structure is evident. The individualistic image that is the central image of Pukhtun society portrays the ideal man as one who takes from his inferiors and then redistributes to them through charity (see figure 4.3). At the same time, he competes with his equals and seeks to dominate them. Mediation which implies inequality is despised.

Exchange with outsiders is, however, perhaps the least important sort of exchange in Swat. Most exchange is either within the lineage or with affines, and is much more complex and emotionally charged than relations of barter or business.

Relations within the patriline vary along sex lines. Cross-sex relations (brother–sister, father–daughter, mother–son) are affectionate and giving, while same-sex relations are generally cool and distant, though much more so among men than women (see Fortes 1949 for a discussion of this pattern). Despite marrying out and being severed from their father's estate, women continue to revere their lineage and to consider themselves as partaking in its glory. Women who marry into a village from outside lineages are often referred to by their village of birth, i.e., Dharmi Bibi, Sijbun Bibi, etc. The close association of a woman with her patriline is seen in several rules. In the rare cases in which a woman is given land by a doting father, the land reverts to her patrilineage if she dies without sons. Furthermore, if a woman is killed, it is her own lineage, not that of her husband, which is responsible for revenge. A woman's honor derives from the position of her lineage, which she stalwartly defends against the insults offered by her husband and his people. Arguments in a household are very often concerned with past deeds and misdeeds of the respective lineages of husband and wife. This is true even in a father's brother's daughter marriage. In such a case, the virtues and vices of the brothers who are the fathers of the couple are invidiously compared. A woman looks to her patrilineage for help and support, and, in return, she offers loyalty to her lineage brothers, giving the needy ones money when she can find it, steal it, or wheedle it from her husband. She also offers moral support at all times to her own family. The disgrace of her lineage is seen as her disgrace, and the rise of her line swells her own pride.

The women of the lineage, who have no claim to land, are intensely loyal. The men of the lineage, who are rivals over inheritance, are often treacherous and cold with one another. Given a situation in which women are essentially strangers in an enemy camp, looking to their own patriline for a sense of personal identity and pride, and in which the men of the lineage are unified only in bonds of enmity to external threats, it is understandable that close emotional ties should be across sex lines. The relationship of brother and sister is considered the most powerful bond in Swati society. At death, it is expected the sisters will grieve the most for their brother, and vice versa. When a boy's mother dies, his grief is not reckoned to be as profound as that of the dead woman's brother. The relation between sisters, like the relation between brothers, is one of rivalry, but this rivalry is not based in the struggle over land

Brother and sister.

and is therefore not very deep-seated. Sisters also may be scattered in several villages after marriage, and have little opportunity to interact and excite one another's jealousy.

A man's sister is loyal to the patriline but, as a noninheritor of land, she does not partake of the patrilineal rivalries and is a reliable ally as a result. There is a proverb that says: "a Pukhtun will not beg, but if he does, he will beg from his sister." In fact, a Pukhtun man in trouble goes to his elder sister first, both for advice and for financial aid. The sister will even sell her wedding jewelry to aid her brother. The helping relationship of the sister is an extension of her relationship to her brothers in childhood. She is taught from infancy that the strength of the lineage resides in her brothers, and that her duty is to defer to them and serve them. For the sake of the lineage, the young girl carries her baby brother, gives in to his every whim, caters to his needs, allows him to beat her without striking back (every male–female relationship has elements of violence in Swat) and, generally, is totally submissive and self-denying in relation to her male siblings. In return, the brothers will give presents to their married sisters, take them in if they are expelled from their

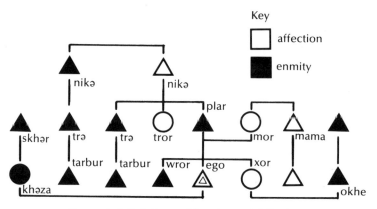

Figure 4.4 Relations of Enmity and Affection

husbands' houses, and stand as sponsors and protectors of their children, a relation which will be discussed later in this chapter.

A further indication of women's position is seen in the levirate. A widow without sons is obliged to marry her husband's brother or one of his *tarbur*. She is not allowed to marry outside her husband's lineage. But the tensions within the line are also well illustrated by the widow's actions should she have a son. She is then prohibited from ever remarrying. Instead, she will flee her husband's village and go to live with either her own family or that of her *mama* (mother's brother). There are two reasons she does not marry if she has a son: one is that the husband's lineage does not want her to marry any man outside of the lineage for fear of setting up a new contender for her son's land; the other is that she does not want to marry within her husband's lineage for fear that her son will be killed in order to invoke the rule of inheritance. Therefore, she runs to the haven of her own family or that of her *mama*, who have nothing to gain from the death of the boy. Later, when he is a young man, the son will try to gain allies in his home village and reclaim his patrimony. He may succeed, but if he does not he will remain in his adopted village as a weak dependent.

Another rule, indicative of women's place in Swat, pertains to adoption, which is absolutely prohibited for boys, though allowed for girls. Only a blood tie can permit sharing in lineage land.

In comparing the relations of the men in a lineage to the relations of brothers and sisters, an interesting dichotomy appears. Women of the lineage are loyal and giving to their brothers, while brothers (and sisters, to a lesser extent) are envious and grasping among themselves. Yet a man can count on his male relatives if there is a fight or a need for vengeance, while female relatives can offer only sympathy and, perhaps, money. Women, imprisoned in the house and regarded as mere pawns in games of alliance, are impotent except in their power to humiliate their husbands. Affection between brother and sister, while sincere, is corrupted by the culturally decreed weakness and repulsiveness of all women. Affection is further tainted by the very fact that the sister, in marrying and leaving her natal home, is the symbol in her person of the shameful necessity for giving up one's own women. The ideal of the total self-sufficiency of the Pukhtun is met with an absolute contradiction in this necessity.

The mother, too, fills an ambiguous place in the lineage. She continues her identity with her own people, yet gives birth to sons who will carry on the lineage of her husband. This contradiction, so fundamental to all patrilineal societies, is recognized in the Pukhtun ideology of blood, for half of a man's blood is said to come from his father and half from his mother. Children have divided loyalties from infancy, as the mother occupies herself in making scurrilous comments on her husband's lineage, while he inveighs with equal vehemence against her family. If the mother comes from a clan distant from that of the father's, the children will be plagued continually by people they meet with the question, "Which clan are you?" This will usually be met with shy and confused silence.

Loyalties may be further divided if a woman leaves her husband, which occurs quite frequently among the khans when the husband brings a co-wife (ban) into the house. In such cases, the first wife may flee to her parents' house, taking the children with her. She will care for the children until they reach puberty and perhaps longer, with the father only having an obligation to make sure the children are married. By custom, the father can bring the children back to his house when they are seven or so, but this is rarely done. The boys only return to their father's home when they are old enough to protect themselves. The fact that children tend to accompany their mother shows that the importance of her lineage is admitted.

There is a sex difference in the strength of childrens' divided loyalties. While children of both sexes look to their mother's lineage for protection, the tie is much stronger with boys. Mothers and sons have a common enemy in the husband/father. The mother is an outsider in her husband's house, while the sons are the father's rivals for his land. Boys therefore look to their mothers for affection and guidance. Pennell's experience in Bannu holds true in Swat as well. When he asked the boys of his mission school which parent had the most influence in molding their lives, the unanimous response was, "Of course, our mothers have all the influence" (1909:201). While boys must be respectful and obedient with their father, they are allowed to cavort and joke in front of their mother. She, in turn, protects them from the father's wrath, praises them, and soothes them. This does not mean mothers are exempt from violent attack by their sons; each year several cases are lodged for just this offense. Mothers, like all women, remain basically contemptible and irritating to men.

Girls, in contrast, are much beloved by their fathers, who cuddle them, tease them, and roguishly rub them and bite them; which again is not to claim that daughters are not beaten by their fathers. But the relation is a loving one, and the little girls are coquettish with their fathers. Father and daughter remain close in later life. It is said that a woman respects and obeys only her father and, to a lesser extent, her brothers. The mother gives her daughters little affection. Instead, she is generally harsh and demanding. There is certainly an element of jealousy in the hostile relationship between mother and daughter, for the daughter is treated more sensually and lovingly by her father than the wife is ever treated by her husband. The jealousy is not always unfounded, since cases of father–daughter incest are often the subject of local gossip. Of course, since incest is a domestic offense, the village takes no action against the offender, but his daughter will find difficulty in marrying. In one case in Shin Bagh, the girl ended by being engaged to a very old man living near Peshawar.

The movement from the home into married life is the major event of a woman's life. The play of little girls is most often an enactment of the marriage ritual: faceless dolls are dressed in finery and placed in a decorated replica of the wedding palanquin (dolie). Girls' songs (boys do not sing) are concerned with marriage and wedding gifts. Girls' talk is often about marriage, as they speculate what presents they will get, and whether their husbands will be handsome, young, and rich.

Weddings are arranged by the parents, and the bride and groom have little to say in the matter, though girls have been known to refuse to marry a man who is ugly, extremely cruel, or malformed. Boys also can resist their arranged marriage. But resistance is rare, since both boys and girls must rely on their parents to organize the drawn-out exchanges which characterize Swati nuptials.

Sometimes, among the elite, marriages are arranged before a child is even born by men who wish to solidify an alliance or maintain an already existing relationship. Brothers, especially, arrange that one son and daughter (i.e., first cousins) will marry. These agreements are considered binding, and breaking the contract causes great anger, though no legal action can be taken. One village man had been betrothed to his father's brother's daughter from birth, but left the village to work in Peshawar, where he met and married a Persian woman. Whenever he returns to Shin Bagh, he is still reviled by his uncle as a *taliki*, a divorced man, for failing to fulfill his obligation.

Men marry much later than women, who are generally prepubescent when they leave their family compound to join the husband's household. The event itself is very traumatic, and the girl, more often than not, must be carried weeping into the palanquin by her kinsmen.

The wedding is said to be a sad event for the household giving up the girl, and the *dolie* is spontaneously likened to the houselike coffin used to carry the dead to the graveyard. Significantly, the Pukhtun say of a family with whom they have a close relationship: "We go to their weddings (*khadi*) and funerals (*gham*)."

The wedding is not only sad; it also has warlike aspects. The drum which the barber beats to announce engagements and weddings is beaten with the same roll that is used to announce an enemy attack in the days of warfare. The gesture that symbolizes fighting within a family is a manual imitation of this drum rolling. The hostility implicit in marriage was formerly overtly enacted by the bystanders along the path the *dolie* followed from the bride's house to the house of the husband. It was customary for these uninvolved onlookers to pelt the bridal procession with stones to try to knock the palanquin down. Of course, the more distant the bride's house, the more stones were thrown. It was considered dangerous business to carry the *dolie*, and at least one man was killed within memory during a procession in Shin Bagh.

Another custom now in abeyance also sometimes led to fighting, though the fighting would not be between the procession and spectators, but rather between the new affines. This was the customary demand that the bride (newai) be given the place of honor by the hearthside of the groom's house. This demand was often refused by the groom's family if they felt too much bride price had been demanded. A fight would then ensue.

Although these customs are no longer practiced, the entrance of the bride is still a dangerous moment. For example, some years ago a mullah family arranged a marriage with a Pukhtun girl despite a high bride price. As noted previously, marriages between mullah and Pukhtun families are noticeably tense. In this case, when the mullah men came to get the girl, the Pukhtun family proudly denied them entrance to their house, bringing the girl out in the dolie themselves. In retaliation, the mullah men decided not to allow their new in-laws into their compound. A fight then broke out in which a number of men were severely injured. The bride was dragged ignominiously into the groom's house and the two families did not speak for a number of years, though they are now on good terms. A more serious incident erupted in 1969 among the Malik khel. A bus bringing a bride from outside the village caused some accidental damage to the hujera of the groom's tarbur. A fight occurred in which a servant of the groom's family was killed and a feud began between the two Malik khel segments which continued into 1977.

Although the wedding is sad for the bride's family and dangerous for both families, it is a happy occasion in the groom's house. When the procession approaches, boys of the house throw candy and nuts from the rooftops into the street, guns are shot off in celebration, and the women of the house dance, drum, and sing with happiness. It is the only time women are allowed such pleasures. Ideally, the drumming, singing, and dancing should have been going on for some months prior to the wedding itself in preparation for the big day. Even the men sometimes dance a few steps at a wedding. But not all the women of the groom's household dance. The women who have married in do not dance, except for the mother of the groom. Dancing is done by the groom's mother, the women he calls sister, and the female servants.

Before the wedding procession leaves the bride's house, the family provides entertainment with dancing girls and drumming for the procession members from the groom's house. Tea and snacks are also given. But the big celebration is at the groom's house, where a huge feast of rice, ghee, meat, chicken, and curd is provided for all, along with a

Girl drumming in the groom's house.

night of dancing girls and music. All those who are related or associated with both families must attend these celebrations, but especially the celebration at the groom's house. For three days those with whom the groom's house celebrates *ghəm-khadi* (the reciprocal obligation to attend funerals and weddings) will arrive to say congratulations (*umbarikshaw*) and to be given food. Failure to show up is seen as a calculated insult.

The procession itself is made up of men from the clans of both families. The girl, completely veiled and clutching a Koran, is carried from her bed and put in the *dolie* by her brothers and patrilineal cousins. The *dolie* is met in the courtyard of the bride's house by men from the groom's party, who help to carry it. Other men collect the possessions the girl is bringing with her into the marriage. These include such things as her personal clothing, utensils, quilts, pillows, some furniture, and the like. The wealth of the girl's family is displayed in part by the public parade of the gifts they have given her as they are carried through the streets behind the palanquin. Arriving at the groom's house, two of the men who carry the *dolie* must be brothers or cousins of the girl. The palanquin is taken right into the house and the girl is lifted out by her patrilineal relatives who put her on the cot. The bride's kinsmen (the father does not accompany her), along with the barber's wife from her village, sit alone with the girl for ten or fifteen minutes in silence. They then leave her and the barber's wife to join in the feast being provided.

Neither the bride nor the groom gets any pleasure from the festivities. The girl is expected to sit motionless and completely covered for the first day. She has avoided drinking or eating for some time previously, so that she will not have to relieve herself. The women of her new household jostle about her, trying to see her face. A child considered lucky is brought to the bride's room, and this is the first person she should see. Meanwhile, her new in-laws coax her with sweets and cajole her to show herself. Nonetheless, she should remain covered, only allowing her face to be seen on the third day. A generation ago, the wife refrained from showing her face to her husband for much longer, and two generations ago some women reputedly hid themselves for a year.

While the bride is crouching motionless on the bed, the groom is expected to be secluded in the *hujera* of some relative. He is not permitted to take part in the celebration or to show himself, for to do so would be shameful. This custom, however, is dying out and at least one "shameless" young man has brazenly attended his own wedding. Previously, young men would run away to another village, usually that of their mother's brother, and would remain there for a month or more. Their kinsmen would have to come and tease the reluctant youth into accepting the responsibilities of marriage. Even after the marriage was consumated, the groom would continue sleeping in the *hujera*, visiting his wife secretly by night.

Custom is no longer so strict, but the groom is expected to remain in the men's house for three days. He visits his bride on the third night, a visit eagerly awaited by his sisters, who may drill a hole in the wall in order to view the defloration. The bride, if she is a khan woman, probably will be completely inexperienced sexually. Her mother has given her

Unveiling the new bride at a carpenter's wedding. The barber's wife is to the left, behind the "lucky" child.

instructions on the proper treatment of a husband, but this counsel is primarily magical in nature and concerns ways in which the man can be kept in the woman's power. For example, the wife should always greet her husband first and always place her hand behind his head when the two sleep together. In this way, the husband will never be able to forget his wife. But practical advice about sex, according to elite women, is nonexistent. The bride awaits her husband, whom she may have never seen before, in an agony of fear that he may not like her, that he may humiliate her by taking another wife. The husband, often a decade or so older and with some sexual experience, may arrive inebriated. He gives the girl a gift of some sweets and a watch or some jewelry. He then should have sex with his new and very young wife. It sometimes happens that a man will find his wife repulsive, malodorous, or ugly and be unable to have intercourse with her. This problem is remedied by magical rites involving the scattering of water from a hookah used for tobacco. Sometimes the husband has been enchanted by a male lover and turned into a *bedagh* (passive homosexual) who is incapable of having sex with a woman. This unfortunate situation is not grounds for divorce, and the girl must continue to live with her impotent husband. Several such cases were known in Shin Bagh. There is no importance given to the fact that the girl might dislike her husband. Her main fear is that he might not like her and shame her and her lineage by marrying again.

Marriages are arranged by the parents of the groom, usually through the mediating efforts of the barber and his wife. Before the engagement is settled, the father, elder brothers, and friendly cousins visit the house of the prospective bride. Sitting in the mens' house or *batuk*, they negotiate the bride price and the *mahar* (money and land given to the bride herself from the husband's family). Once this is decided, the bride's kinsmen are invited to the groom's village for a big celebratory feast which marks the formal engagement. The bride and groom are now considered unbreakably bound to one another. If the two families are close relatives and do not normally keep purdah from one another, a restriction on allowing the engaged couple to meet will be enforced from the time of the engagement. In initiating purdah the new relationship which marriage brings between patrilineal kinsmen is symbolized, for marriage separates agnates.

After the engagement is announced a cycle of exchange begins between the two families. The boy's family sends gifts of cloth and jewelry to the girl at the major holiday of Eid, the Muslim feast at the end of the month of fasting—analogous, because of its gift-giving tradition, to Christmas. The boy should visit the girl's family during Eid celebrations where he will be entertained and given a watch, a ring, or some clothes. These exchanges should be approximately equal. Visiting at Eid symbolizes among the Pukhtun an expression of loyalty and inferiority. Big khans simply remain home during this celebration, while their dependents come to drink tea and pay homage. Interestingly, although men are supposed to continue visiting their in-laws at Eid after marriage, very few of them do so.

The engagement may last for several years. The groom's family often needs this time to raise the funds necessary for the marriage and to prepare a place for the young couple to live. When marriage does take place all the people of the groom's *tal* (ward) must provide food and service for the celebration. These contributions are carefully recorded and must be returned exactly or with interest if the groom wishes to maintain his prestige. For instance, at a recent wedding of an important Malik *khel* man in Shin Bagh ninety-five families in his *tal* and in the

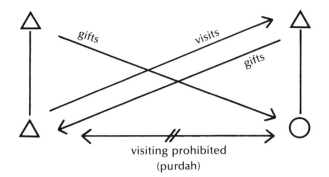

gifts

visits

gifts

visiting prohibited
(purdah)

Figure 4.5 Engagement

village sent food. Prestations kept coming for ten days, all of which were noted for future return.

While food is given by one's fellow villagers, cloth is brought for the bride by the Pukhtun women who have been invited for the ceremony. These clothes are kept track of and must be repaid exactly or with something of greater value for fear of losing prestige. Money is also given to the bride by the groom's female relatives, including his elder sisters. The bride bows down before these elder women, touches their feet in an expression of obeisance, and greets them. In return, money is given to her through the intermediary of the barber's wife, who counts it carefully and stores it away. This money, which may amount to 4,000 rupees for the very wealthy, is the inalienable property of the wife. However, after the wedding night the girl is supposed to show her appreciation of her husband and her submission to him by offering to give him this money which, if he is wealthy, he will refuse. But if the girl is sexually dissatisfied or angry, she may elect to keep the money for herself. This is considered a very unfortunate beginning for a marriage.

Sometimes friends and relatives of the groom give him money at the time of the wedding. This gift, like the procession which carries the bride, is called *junj*. It is a display of solidarity with the groom and his family and an indication of the pride and honor of the donor. Sometimes the *junj* gift is more of a gesture than an actual exchange. For example, a rather poor Pukhtun borrowed 500 rupees to give as a wedding gift to the brother of a man who had lent him 1,000 rupees which he still owed. When the gift was given, the recipient thanked the donor, accepted the extravagant gift, and then returned it later the same day. This nontransaction was an honorable one for both parties. The debtor lived up to his Pukhtun status by giving a large gift while the groom's family, knowing the relative poverty of the donor, did themselves honor by returning it. There is a subtle distinction here. The groom did not insult the donor by refusing the gift. Rather, the gift was accepted, then returned. The image of reciprocity was enacted. Accepting the gift would also have been honorable, but repayment of the original loan would then have been much delayed. *Junj* gifts, like other prestations, must be reciprocated.

Occasionally a very wealthy family of the bride will also give cash to the groom. This gift, called *jora,* does not need to be returned, and so is unlike the other gifts mentioned. *Jora* may amount to several thousand rupees, but the usual sum is two or three hundred. This donation is seen as the reverse of bride price, and aims at giving an impression of balance in the marriage exchange. But in actuality it is never anywhere close in amount to the bride price. Were the *jora* larger than the bride price, this would be a great shame for the groom's family.

The bride price is the largest prestation at marriage. Formerly called "money for the girl's head," it used to be paid outright by the groom's family to the bride's father. Recent religious propaganda has made the Pukhtun aware that the practice of purchasing girls is contrary to Islam. Previously, the situation was much like that reported by Pennell in Bannu: "A man practically buys his wife, bargaining with her father, or, if he is dead, with her brother; and so she becomes his property, and the father has little power of interfering for her protection afterwards, seeing he has received his price" (1909:193). In Dir, bride price is still given openly. The father of the bride stands in the public square and demands a price for his daughter. In an auctionlike setting, the friends of the groom then promise money to meet the father's demand. Nor is the ruler of Dir exempt. In a recent marriage with a merchant family of Peshawar, the nawab received 300,000 rupees in a public ceremony from the groom. His honor and the value of his daughter having been validated by this presentation, the nawab later privately returned the money to the groom.

In Swat itself a few lower-class families openly sell their daughters, and it is commonly believed in the rest of Pakistan that any Swati girl can be purchased for the right price. Indeed, there is a flourishing racket among some unscrupulous families who sell their daughters to outsiders (Swati girls are much desired in Pakistan for their fair skins and supposedly passionate natures), encourage the girl to run away, and then sell her

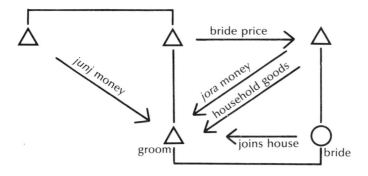

Figure 4.6 Bride Price, *Jora* and *Junj*

again. Girls from Swat and the North-West Frontier Province also provide a large number of the prostitutes in Pakistan, but these are not girls who have been sold. Rather they are runaways who have left their husbands and fear returning to face the anger of their natal families.

In Shin Bagh, the Pukhtun now recognize that bride price is forbidden in Islam. In any case, they would never allow any of their women to be married by an outsider, whatever the inducement. However, among themselves bride price is still given covertly, and men joke with one another about the profits to be made in selling their daughters. Bride price used to be openly given in the form of livestock, wheat, and money. Beautiful and intelligent girls could get a high price and were much prized. The situation is not so different today, though bride price is now given under the pretext of money donated by the groom's family for the purchase of household effects for the bride. This money, up to 10,000 rupees, is given the bride's father to spend as he wishes. Very little is spent on house furnishings for the bride, since most of these things are made by the servants of the bride's father as a part of their *tal* obligations.*

Aside from the bride price given to the bride's father, there is also the

---

* In the Peshawar Valley this pattern has been transformed among the wealthy professional elite. A young man with a good future, such as a doctor, is greatly prized, and the bride's family does not expect any bride price. Instead, they must provide huge dowries, including televisions, washing machines, and refrigerators. The Pukhtun professionals still marry mainly within kin circles. However, if the marriages of non-Pukhtun merchants are any indication, the pattern of in-marriage will also break down. Marriages of these city merchants show a marked shift in the last two generations from marrying relatives to marrying wealthy outsiders. "We are modern. We marry for money, not for blood," they said.

presentation of *mahar* to the bride herself. *Mahar,* which consists in Swat of jewelry and land, is not considered to violate the Islamic code since it is given to the bride and is her inalienable property. Discussion of *mahar* is extremely important in marriage negotiations, for an adequate *mahar* is a guarantee to the bride's father that his daughter will not go unprovided for once she has left his house.

Mahar should ideally be given in jewelry, but in Swat it is usually given half in jewelry and half in land. For example, in a typical exchange, a new bride was given 4,000 rupees worth of gold and the rights to a garden worth 6,000 rupees. Theoretically, the girl is allowed to do any-thing she wishes with her *mahar.* It is possible for a woman to sell the jewelry, buy land, and keep the profits she realizes from selling the produce. If she dies without issue, the *mahar* land and jewelry belong to her patrilineage, and the husband and the husband's family must give cash recompense. If a woman has children, she hands the *mahar* jewelry down to her daughters, while the land goes to her sons. Her husband is not allowed to give the land to his sons by another wife or to sell it. The rights of women's own patrilineages to *mahar* are not mere talk. Many court cases over *mahar* by women who have returned to their natal villages tesify to the importance of the institution. These cases are un-dertaken by the woman's patrilineage on her behalf and are heard by the district council. If the case is judged in favor of the woman, the money value of the *mahar* land (never the land itself) and the jewelry or its value in money goes to the woman's father or her brothers.

Like the money given to the bride by the groom's female relatives, the *mahar* should be returned to the husband by the new bride. After the wedding night, the girl is supposed to say to her husband, "I give you my *mahar.*" But, unlike the money from the groom's sisters and aunts, the donation of the *mahar* back to the husband is not unconditional. If the marriage deteriorates, the woman can demand that her *mahar* rights be honored, regardless of what she said to her husband.

In general, the *mahar* land is given by the groom's father and he simply keeps working it, especially if the new couple live within his compound and eat from his produce. But if the couple move to their own compound, then the groom's father should give them the produce from the *mahar* field. This donation may make all the difference in the diet of the new household. In effect, the husband is being fed by his wife, through her *mahar* rights.

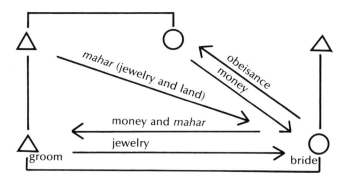

Figure 4.7 *Mahar* and Money for Obeisance (Ideal Pattern)

Mahar and the rights over *mahar* provide the grist for endless arguments in the family, especially if a man takes a second wife. When this happens, he will have to offer the second woman a large *mahar*, since she is entering a troubled household. This will further increase the fury of the first wife, who sees the large *mahar* given the second wife as yet another insult from her husband. She will then demand that her own *mahar* claims be met. In an ideal situation, *mahar* is a parody of reciprocity; a gift which is given only to be immediately returned. But, in reality, the tensions between husband and wife sometimes lead the wife to assert her own individual rights and thus short-circuit the reciprocal image.

I have now come to a central problem in Swati exchange. The ideal form of exchange between equals, one which satisfies both sides, is the exact and preferably immediate return of what has been given or its equivalent. In this way, a balance is maintained. But among the Pukhtun of Shin Bagh the exchange of women is prohibited. Instead, bride price and *mahar* as well as the obeisance of the groom at the celebration of Eid are given. But these things are not the equivalent of a woman. A woman is an active agent, a member of her own lineage with her own loyalties, pride, and sense of self. We have seen that historically the giving of a woman was an emblem of defeat or subordination, and that marriage is viewed as exposing a family's sense of shame. The wife, then, enters marriage as a representative of her own line and a reluctant hostage to her husband. Despite the rituals of reciprocity, she can disrupt the entire facade by demanding her *mahar*, running from her husband, and causing him to be shamed. Before considering this problem, I'd like to continue the discussion of the pattern of affinal exchanges.

I have mentioned above that exchange of women is prohibited among the Swat Pukhtun, and especially among the khans of Shin Bagh. This exchange is known by the same name as barter, that is, *adal-badal*. It is seen in other parts of the Frontier, as Pennell notes: "Suppose in each of two families there is an unmarried son and an unmarried daughter; they then frequently arrange a mutual double marriage without any payments. In such cases the condition of the wives is a little, but only a little, better than in the marriage by purchase" (1909:193). In Dir, *adal-badal* is common, and in the neighboring valley of Sebujni I recorded several cases among the elite. But these Sebujni marriages were always arranged between classificatory patrilateral cousins who lived in neighboring villages. Animosity between *tarburs* who live at a distance is greatly lessened, and *adal-badal* was viewed by these families as a way of cementing friendship. But in Shin Bagh, where *tarburs* are living next to one another, *adal-badal* is forbidden. It is considered to be disgraceful on two accounts: since no payment is made, it indicates that the exchanging families are poor and unable to arrange a proper marriage; further, if a man gives his sister to his wife's brother, then he will be afraid to beat his wife since his sister will be beaten in retaliation. Another reason, though unstated, is that *adal-badal* implies a continuing and friendly relation between the two families, a relationship that the Pukhtun of Shin Bagh find impossible to maintain in reality.

In refusing marriage of this type, while simultaneously avidly practicing *adal-badal* with goods, the Pukhtun of Shin Bagh have admitted covertly that women are not merely commodities, but entities in themselves. Whereas with goods the ideal is escalating exchange and continual trade, women, once given, do not circulate further. Indeed, the perfect stituation would be one in which women were not given at all, only taken. Of course, the continuation of society makes exchange a necessity, and sisters must be given up to other families.

A generation ago, as mentioned in the last chapter, marriage ties in Swat were over a wider circle than at present. Women were used for making alliances within warring parties, and men descended from sisters were expected to be friends. With the cessation of warfare, this centrifugal tendency has been countered by the desire of the Pukhtun to marry as close within the patriline as possible. In this, the attempt is to unify the lineage and deny the entrance of external loyalties as represented by outside women. But, at the same time, marrying one's father's brother's daughter poses new problems and introduces new divisions into the patriline. This type of marriage does not lead to reduced bride price or *mahar*. Indeed, according to some reports, the *mahar* given in a parallel cousin marriage should be higher than that given to a woman from outside the lineage. The reason stated is that an offer of marriage within the lineage can cause a great deal of hostility and embarrassment if it is rejected. The large *mahar* and bride price is the sugar on the offer, designed to prevent a humiliating refusal. Payments to the bride and her family indicate the distance between the two families, not their unity, despite the intention of the parties.

Furthermore, as we have seen, the relations between patrilineal parallel cousins (*tarbur*) in Swat are the paradigm for relations of hostility. Marriage with the father's brother's daughter simply ratifies a separation that already exists. It is thought that marriages with the real father's brother's daughter tend to be unsuccessful, with the girl dying young, or with the groom never taking any sexual interest in her and the marriage remaining childless, or with the groom taking a second wife. "We like to marry our father's brother's daughters," one man told me, "but we do not like to have a friendship with them." The closeness and hostility of the *tarbur* is added to the hostility of affines to make for marriages which, more than most, are violent and strained.* Yet these marriages are sought, not only for the illusive unity of the patriline, but also because the father of the girl wishes to keep her near him and give her some protection. That this attempt reportedly leads to even more misery than is usual does not deter men in the attempt. More successful is marriage with a classificatory "sister," such as an FFFBDDD. Rivalry between the families is then more attenuated, and the two families may even belong to the same *dala*. This type of marriage is now in the majority in the village.

In looking at marriages, one fact stands out above all: the lack of any consistent model. Some men say that mother's brother's daughter marriage is the best, since the mother's brother is an ally. Others favor the

* The hostility of FBD marriage is not only proverbial in Swat, it also seems to have some statistical validity. If we accept the local notion that taking a second wife indicates an unhappy marriage, then there is a very suggestive difference between men who have married real FBD and those who have not in the last five generations of Malik *Khel* marriages. Of the 115 marriages recorded for men, 4 of the 8 marrying real FBD later took second wives, whereas only 19 of the remaining 107 men married a second time. In the present generation, 2 of the 3 men who have married their FBD have married again, while only 2 of the remaining 39 men have done so, one by levirate.

father's sister's daughter, since this lineage "owes" a woman to ego's lineage. The truth is that there is no repeated alliance, aside from the favored father's brother's daughter marriage. Looking at Malik *khel* marriages over six generations, counting 94 Malik *khel* women who have married 97 times (48 marriages outside the village) and 115 Malik *khel* men with 150 marriages (21 men with 2 wives, 7 with 3 wives, 90 marriages outside the village), we find the results outlined in Table 4.1.

Other marriages with relatives include one with classificatory MZD, two real MZS marriages, and one classificatory MZ marriage. Looking at both men and women, we find that of the 247 marriages recorded for the Malik *khel*, 129 could be traced to relatives of different sorts. Of these marriages 84 were within the village, 82 within the patriline, while the remaining FZD–MBS marriage can also be seen as a classificatory FBD–FBS marriage. There were a total of 17 marriages following the pattern of generalized exchange (MBD–FZS), the majority (13) made by village men. It is evident from the low number of FZS marriages (4) that generalized exchange is not a continuing cycle in the Malik *khel*. Delayed exchange (FZD–MBS) has a more equal balance, with 10 men taking FZD and 14 women marrying MBS, but the pattern as a whole is too chaotic to allow the assignment of any elementary structure. Rather, it is perhaps accurate to see Swati marriage as an attempt at a different structuring of exchange, an attempt that inevitably fails. The people say that it is rare to marry with the same group for more than two generations. Hostilities between affines and animosity between husbands and wives lead lineages continually to seek new partners. The only pattern found in the genealogies is that of a lineage segment forming a marriage re-

Table 4.1   Malik *khel* Marriages (Six generations)

In village—male		In village—female	
FBD marriage (classificatory)	33	FBS marriage (classificatory)	33
FBD marriage (real)	8	FBS marriage (real)	8
FZD marriage (real)	1	MBS marriage (real)	1
Out village—male		Out village—female	
MBD marriage (classificatory)	7	FZS marriage (classificatory)	4
MBD marriage (real)	6	FZS marriage (real)	0
FZD marriage (classificatory)	8	MBS marriage (classificatory)	7
FZD marriage (real)	2	MBS marriage (real)	7
Total	65		60

lationship with another line, marrying intensively with them for a generation or two, and then breaking off the relationship.

The difficulty of maintaining an exchange of women with another clan is a function of the social myth of independence. Historically, weaker parties in disputes gave women to the stronger in order to gain a truce. Taking a woman from another is a central symbol of superiority in the worldview of the Pukhtun. It is for this reason, among others, that purdah is so strict among them (see chapter 6 for more detail). By keeping strict purdah the Pukhtun demonstrates his control over the women of his house. Conversely, when a man gains political power, as General Zia did in his military coup in Pakistan in 1977, the Pukhtun say that "he has taken the women of his enemies." Given this symbolism, the difficulty of the Pukhtun in having a continuing marriage relationship with another family is understandable.

Not only is it difficult to continue exchange with another lineage, it is also difficult merely to keep control over one's wife. The woman, though she is effectively severed from her father's estate by marriage and the payment of bride price, does not submissively join her husband and admit his superiority. Although the Pukhtun have a saying that "husband is another name for God," and claim the Koran relegates women to the status of servants, the women hardly fill the ideal role. Earlier, I noted that women have their own set of loyalties and are emotionally closely tied to their patrilineages. Like their male siblings, they are raised to believe in the honor of their family above that of every other. Pukhtun women are anything but servile, and are quick to take umbrage at any infringement of what they consider their rights. They are willing and able to fight for their rights and resist humiliation. For example, a man sold a cow which his wife had been given by her father. She demanded the money from her husband, saying he had no right to make the sale without her permission. He refused, claiming the money was needed for food. Enraged, she began insulting him and his lineage, tore off his shirt, and fought him until he managed to knock her down. These sorts of fights are considered perfectly normal, and a man who does not beat his wife regularly will be abused by both men and women (including his wife) as "a man with no penis." These beatings and fights provide the drama in Swati life.

Both parties can escalate this domestic war. The man, if he has sufficient funds and land for *mahar*, can utterly shame his wife by taking another woman into the house as co-wife. There is a saying in Swat that may be translated as "I may be a fool, but not such a fool as a man who has two wives." Yet men continually talk of talking a second wife and those with the wherewithal try to do so. The idea is not so much an increase in sexual pleasure, but rather the mortification of the first wife. Like a fight with one's *tarbur*, this course is recognized as self-destructive, both financially and for the tranquility of the husband's home life, since the two women will quarrel day and night. But the satisfaction derived from shaming the first wife and her lineage, coupled with the image of greatness to be gained by having the resources to afford two wives, is enough incentive for men to dream of taking another woman into the house. Once this fantasy has been realized, the man will then be obliged to look for a third wife. This is because the two wives will make his life so miserable that he hopes to drive them both from his home by bringing in yet a third woman, and starting all over again with just one wife. In this, he will be encouraged by his first wife, who wishes nothing more than that her rival should be shamed as she has been shamed.

The tensions of marriage and the likelihood of a marriage break-up are paralleled by a stringent prohibition on divorce. To call a man *taliki*, or divorced, is a deadly insult, and the man who merits it must leave the valley. The convention of alliance is protected by custom, but this custom only prevents an embarrassing public rupture and confrontation. It does not prevent fights, nor does it keep men from bringing in new wives or women from leaving their husbands.

The mechanics of separation are complex. A man cannot send his wife home to her own family, though if she leaves of her own accord he is not obliged to ask her to return. Sometimes, men resort to trickery to get a disliked wife to leave the house. In one instance, a man convinced his wife that her mother was dying. The woman hurried to her natal village, only to find that the report was false. Her husband then refused to invite her back to his house and married another woman. When a wife does go to her own family and is not asked to return, she is quietly reabsorbed. However, she is not considered divorced and is referred to as the guest of her father (there were three such women in Shin Bagh—see the key to appendix A). Her husband should contribute to her maintenance, though a contribution will not be demanded, since it would then appear that her own family was too poor to support the woman. Discreet messages will be sent to her husband, asking him to reconsider. But, if he does not, the family may swallow their pride and keep the woman at home while waiting for a chance to avenge themselves. Less proud lineages may demand *mahar* payment, but for the khans a suitable revenge would be inducing a woman from the husband's own lineage to abandon her husband, or else poisoning the husband surreptitiously.

Although a woman who goes to her natal home with her husband's permission must be provided for by her own family, a woman who runs in anger from her husband's home is a different matter. If the woman has had a bone broken or other serious injury done to her, her running is considered within Pukhtunwali, the code of honor (see chapter 6). But if the injury is to her pride, then her running defies the code of male domination and shames not only her husband, but her own family as well. A woman who is sent home brings shame, but not by her own will, and her husband is held blameworthy by her family. When a woman runs, she is expressing her individuality and personal rebellion. She is denying her role as a pawn, and asserting herself. In this, she reveals the great contradiction in Swati marriage, i.e., that women are thought of as inanimate objects despite their training as self-willed individuals. The granting of *mahar* to women is an acknowledgment of their individuality. The customary return of the *mahar* to the husband is an attempt to have the woman herself negate that individuality, and the prohibition on divorce and the sanctions against a woman running from her husband are recognitions that this negation is not sufficient to insure male dominance. The woman's right to reclaim her *mahar* also shows her power.

Marriage is permeated with stress, as we have seen. Nuclear families are forced by the rules of exogamy to open themselves up to accept women with external loyalties while giving up their own women to outsiders. The men seek to obscure this problem by making marriage a matter of purchase. The men of the groom's family and the men of the bride's family are, in a sense, coconspirators in an attempt to negate the individuality of the bride for the sake of male pride. But an adult woman, far more than a man, has the potential to be a free agent. She is cut away from her family estate and yet not absorbed into the family of her husband. By the act of walking out on her husband, she can expose the male pretense at total control and self-sufficiency as a lie. It is no wonder then that the penalty for such an act is rejection by her own family, which allows the outraged husband to murder his runaway wife without taking revenge on him. They even threaten to kill her themselves should she appear asking refuge. Nor is it any wonder that some Swati women who find their home lives intolerable and flee their husbands end as prostitutes in the brothels of Karachi and Lahore.

Marriage, then, is a major problem for the Pukhtun, who seek exact reciprocity in all matters concerning their equals. Giving a gift, and then getting it back again is the ideal form of exchange. But a woman, once given, cannot be given back, and bride price is not the equivalent of a woman, no matter how high it may be. Some wealthy khans seek to ignore the woman altogether, and give a dowry (*jora*) to balance the bride price, though the match is never exact. *Mahar* also may be seen as an attempt to enact the ideal pattern with the wife herself, since *mahar* should ideally be returned to her husband. However, as we have seen, the woman's own pride may lead her to expose this reciprocity as a sham, demand the *mahar* and to assert herself through protest.

Relations between husbands and wives tend to be warlike. Even in sex, tenderness is said to be absent. As women say, "I asked for a kiss, and he gave me a bite." All romantic encounters, even those between lovers, have similar sadistic undertones, as the man forces the woman to submit and demonstrates his own superiority. Although men claim that women love sexual intercourse, the women vehemently deny this. Simultaneously, many men complain of early impotence. Each sex is dissatisfied with the other. Women say that "Swati men are no good," while the men claim that their women are lazy, ignorant, and cruel. People, then, believe that the unfortunate hostility between the sexes is not inherent in human nature. Rather, it is seen as resulting from the particular conditions of Swati life. "Gujar women are better than ours," the men assert, while the women say the men of their own families are kind and good. The problem of sexual antagonism is characteristic of Muslim society in general. As Mernissi says, "the whole Muslim social structure can be seen as an attack on, and a defense against, the disruptive power of female sexuality" (1975:14).

The problem of sexual relationships is understandable given the ideology that all women are, in themselves, repulsive and inferior, and have the potential to shame men. The repulsiveness of women is linked to the conundrum they pose in the social structure as the foci of the contradiction between the necessity of exchanging women and the social ideal of the self-sufficient nuclear family. Also linked is the prevalence of homosexuality among the men, who find a relationship with a boy less demanding and more pleasurable than with a woman. Yet, though women are despicable, men know they cannot survive without them. A woman can chase her husband from the house by simply refusing to cook for him. Women are powerful, despite the ideology of their inferiority. This ambiguity further stirs the disgust of the Pukhtun, who hate things that are equivocal and not clearly "one thing or the other." Each Pukhtun likes to imagine himself and present himself as monolithic and consistent. A woman not only exposes the contraditions of the patrilineal pose of splendid male isolation and domination, but she is also in herself a contradiction, embodying both weakness and strength. (For more on the Pukhtun marriage relation, see Lindholm and Lindholm 1979.)

The contradictions of the role of women in Pukhtun society are clearly brought out in the attitudes taken toward relatives linked by marriage. But, where a wife contains within herself attributes which are both needed and hated, these attributes are distributed among affines, so that some are liked, others disliked.

One's own in-laws are often either actual or potential enemies. They will support their own child in any disagreement, regardless of questions of right and wrong. As noted in chapter 3, the tension of the relationship is demonstrated by the fact that the term of reference for in-laws (skhər) is considered an insult if used in address.

The ideal relationship of a man with his wife's family would be one of mutual help. Occasionally, especially if the brothers-in-law are from the same dəla and distant enough not to be rivals, this relationship actually exists. However, more often than not, the two men avoid one another for fear of becoming embroiled in arguments over the husband's treatment of his wife. At the same time, if the wife really is causing trouble and it is feared that she might run away and shame both families, then her brother or father is called in to settle her down. For example, young married women are sometimes possessed by invisible demons. While possessed, the woman may attempt suicide or run out in the street in a frenzy. She will heap abuse on her husband's family and generally vent her spleen without restraint. The usual cure is to invite a religious practitioner who painfully squeezes her hand until she comes to her senses. The new wife of a khan suddenly became subject to these fits soon after her marriage in 1970. When the fits kept recurring, her father

Making bread.

was invited to speak to her. He told her that if she continued he would bring her back home and give the khan her younger sister as wife. The fits never occurred again. But this was a special case, and generally the woman is supported in all she does by her family, unless, of course, she shames them by running from her husband.

Women have a much more difficult time with their in-laws than men do, since they are obliged, at least in the beginning of marriage, to live in the husband's natal household. A woman must show respect for her husband's family, covering her head in front of his father and following the orders of his mother and elder sisters. Ideally, she should be silent, obedient, and hard-working. The husband's mother "trains" the girl to do household chores, and does not spare invective and abuse. It is in rejection of such treatment that young women, especially those who have not yet had a child, are afflicted with demons. This is, of course, in line with Turner's "power of the weak" hypothesis (1969). See also Freed and Freed (1964) for discussion of similar cases in north India.

The girl is usually cowed by her mother-in-law until she begins having sons. Then she starts to assert her own identity and loud fights may start. An especially proud girl from a good family may even come to blows with her mother-in-law. The intensity of the fights in the house sometimes becomes so great that the young couple are given their own compound, so that interaction can be cut to a minimum. This is essentially what happened to my friend Zaman. His proud wife, Qajira, could not get along with Zaman's equally proud step-mother. After the couple moved out, relations between the two women improved.

If relations between a person and his or her in-laws is one of barely concealed hostility, the relationship with one's maternal relatives is one of affection and trust. I have already noted that boys in particular look to their mothers for affection and, furthermore, that the closest emotional ties in the society are between brother and sister. The boy and, to a lesser extent, the girl, look to the maternal line for help and refuge in difficulty. If there is a dispute between brothers over land rights, it will be mediated by their mother's brother. It is assumed that, since he has no interest in the land and only has the well-being of his sister's children at heart, he will mediate fairly. Children who are orphaned are brought up by the mother's brother, who protects them against the greed of their *tarburs*. Women who are expelled from their husband's house also live with their brothers or with the mother's brother, and the children are then raised in that household until they they are old enough to claim their rights.

The close relationship of a brother with his sister's son is illustrated in the role of the former at the latter's circumcision ceremony. This ceremony, necessary in Islam, is usually performed before a boy reaches the age of seven, and is the occasion of much rejoicing. Previously, circumcision was observed by the Pukhtun with large feasts and a dancing performance, second in scale only to the feast of a marriage. Recently, the ceremony has declined in prominence, as the Pukhtun tend to take the child to be hygenically circumcised by a doctor rather than having the traditional public event with the *tal* barber performing the operation. Although now often the only audience is the doctor and his assistants, the mother's brother continues to fulfill his ritual part. Accompanied by a representative of the boy's lineage (not the father), the mother's brother is the one who is delegated to arrange for the circumcision, take the boy to the doctor, and see that everything is done properly. Payments for services and gifts to the doctor and his assistants (which take the place of giving a feast in the *tal*) are paid out by the boy's lineage, but it is the mother's brother who presides over the ceremony and whose presence is indispensable. Sometimes, if his sister and her husband are estranged, the mother's brother will even pay for the ceremony himself.*

The role of the *mamagan* (people of the mother's lineage) is important politically as well. They are expected to be political allies of their sisters' children. This expectation extends to mother's sister's sons as well. The tie with the *mamagan* becomes more important with distance, since there is then less reason for dispute. For example, the ancestor of the Malik *khel*, Umrah Khan, married a woman of the Narel Kohistani of Bahrain village. These Kohistani, who are matrilineally related to the Malik *khel* by a marriage four generations ago, and who are a good sixty miles from Shin Bagh and completely out of the Malik *khel* sphere of influence, still visit the Malik *khel* regularly and are visited in return. Both sides vow

---

* Formerly the custom was to have a feast at the father's house after the circumcision, which would be performed just outside the house compound wall. Relatives and dependents of the family would donate money, as well as making a collection to pay the barber. Special food would be provided, especially a bright red ghee. After the cutting, which is done with a dull knife and watched avidly by the children (the men avoid watching), the foreskin would be hung on the rafters of the house. This custom is still followed by the more traditional Pukhtun. Poorer people keep exact track of the donations given at a circumcision, but khans do not. The circumcision differed from the wedding in that only neighbors, *tal* members, and the *mamagan* (mother's lineage) of the boy attended, whereas at a wedding the attendance was much larger.

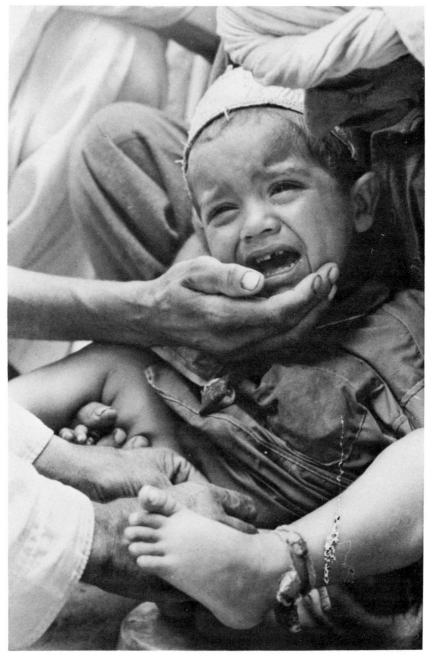

Circumcision.

political support for one another, though these vows have been, to this point, quite meaningless.

The closeness of mother's brother and sister's son may also be seen in an incident which occurred in the village. A sister's son of some Shin Bagh men had been having difficulty with his *tarburs* in his home village. His *mamagan,* who could not intervene physically, offered to give the young man a share in their *dauftar* land and a house to live in. In other words, they were offering to incorporate him into the Malik *khel.* The boy refused the offer, however, preferring to maintain his honor by fighting it out with his enemies in his home village. The incorporation of outsiders into one's own lineage by marriage is not unknown in Swat, though the outsider would usually be a religious *stanadar* or pir. "A man who marries into a tribe not his own always among Pukhtun casts in his lot with his wife's people. It is unusual for the Yusufzais to admit strangers to marriage, and is only done (and that rarely) with Sayyids and holy men" (Caroe 1965:363). The possibility that a boy may leave his own lineage to join his *mamagan* accounts, in part, for the strong propensity of the Pukhtun for in-marriage, which would thereby negate this possibility. An event that occurred three generations ago illustrates this danger. Shahbaz Khan had been contesting with his *tarbur* Habibullah Khan for paramountcy in the Malik *khel.* To win the struggle, Shahbaz relied on aid from his wife's people, the powerful Mahmat *khel.* In return, after his victory, he allowed the Mahmat *khel* to make good their claim on some large *tseri* (non-clan) plots within Malik *khel* territory. While his acts built his own name, Shahbaz Khan's alliance depleted the land of his village, to the ultimate detriment of his descendants. In 1977, the Mahmat *khel* were the strongest lineage in Shamizai because of their lack of external entanglements and their internal unity. The Malik *khel,* on the other hand, were seriously weakened by internal dissension and Mahmat *khel* encroachments, encouraged by Shahbaz Khan's policy. In fact, the Mahmat *khel* held the largest single piece of land in Malik *khel* territory, which they rented out to tenant farmers. Shahbaz Khan later repudiated his affines and waged war with them, but the land he had allowed them to take could not be taken back. Thus, the help of one's affines, while useful for gaining personal power, at the same time weakens one's patrilineage, which is the root of power in Swat.

Aid given by in-laws and even by one's *mamagan* is, however, generally unimportant in Swati political activity. The relatives tied through a female are helpful insofar as they are disinterested, since they do not inherit or have a share in one's land (excepting, of course, in-laws who are agnates as well). They are not obliged to take revenge and therefore their help, like the help offered by one's sisters, is feeble. If it comes to a fight, a man can rely only on his lineage mates, not on his *mamagan*, who will offer sympathy and refuge, but will not risk life for their sister's sons. Noteworthy here is the fact that loans given to the sister's son are actually given to the sister, not to the boy himself. A man cannot apply to his mother's brother personally for a loan; he would not be trusted. Rather, he must ask his mother to intervene with her brother, for a man cannot refuse giving aid to his sister. The same tactic of applying for help through the woman when making a request of female-linked relatives holds true in asking aid of a sister's husband or wife's brother, though these cases are much rarer. Linked by women, one's affines must be approached through women, and are correspondingly associated with women and somewhat despicable.

Women are, in fact, the mediators within the family as well. A boy who wants something from his father or who wants to avoid punishment pleads with his mother to intervene. She will then represent her son to her husband. Like the religious practitioners, or the barber and leather-worker, women are middlemen (or middle women) in relations between unequals. Their own ambiguous position makes them appropriate for this contemptible role. As "women in between" (Strathern 1972) Pukhtun wives and mothers have considerable manipulatory power, and their ability to shame their husbands by acting shamelessly themselves makes them covertly feared by men. Because of her ambiguity, because of the contradictions she embodies, because of her mediating role, because of her subtle power, the Pukhtun wife is always viewed with suspicion and unease by her husband, and all women, even loved mothers and sisters, are distanced from men by insurmountable ingrained antagonisms.

The distance between husband and wife in Swat is mirrored in the rituals which accompany death. It is forbidden for a wife to wash the body of her dead husband, and vice versa. An elder lineal relative of the same sex as the deceased should perform this task. Only lineal relatives may kiss the corpse or display sadness, though a woman's children are considered of her line in this instance. Of the mourners, a man's sister is the most disconsolate. Children seem remarkably unaffected by the death of their father, and treat the event as something of a holiday. Men are forbidden by custom to show any grief, even at the death of their sister or mother. They sit quietly in the *hujera* and form a silent procession carrying the body to the grave. The women, meanwhile, remain in the house, keening verses in honor of the dead, and describing their own grief. They may not accompany the burial procession, but must say their goodbyes to the dead man as he lies in state in the vestibule of the house. The shrieks and moans from the house offer a startling contrast with the silence of the motionless men in the *hujera*.

As mentioned at the beginning of this chapter, death is spontaneously likened to marriage in its rituals by the people themselves, who compare the wedding palanquin to the sarcophagus in which the corpse is interred. Like marriage, death is a rite of separation and, like marriage, it is the occasion for a gathering of all allies. After the death of an important man, all the families related to him and all the families who have had political dealings with him must send representatives. Close associates must arrive on the day of the funeral (*gham*), which must be within twenty-four hours of the death according to Muslim law. It is astonishing how quickly the news of a death travels, and hundreds of men and women are soon thronging the dead man's house and *hujera*. The women enter the house, embrace the women there, and begin keening and ritual weeping. The men go to the men's house and sit quietly, awaiting the arrival of the body which they will carry to the graveyard. The body is carried on a bed and buried in a houselike coffin. The corpse, perfumed and dressed in special white clothes, is lowered into the coffin, which has been placed in a wooden frame underground. The top of the frame is then covered over with slate and mud and a mound is built over the grave. All is silent until the slate is put in place. Then an imam begins recitations from the Koran.

Those unable to come on the day of the funeral must send representatives within three days, just as at a wedding. Attendance at a funeral is even more important than attendance at a wedding. A great deal of the time of elder khans is spent at funerals. Some of the women who come to a funeral will stay two or three days with the bereaved family. The funeral, especially of an old man, is like a vacation for them, and they visit with female relatives in the dead man's village, exchange gossip, and help out with the chores in the dead man's house. Men who are

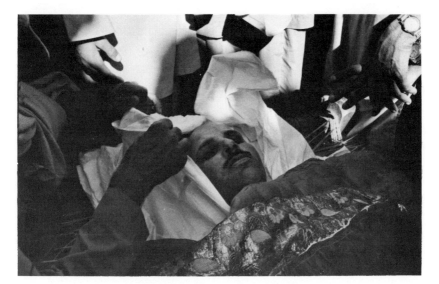
A young khan prepared for burial.

close to the family should return for several days to offer their prayers for the dead. This is a formal event. The visitor goes to the *hujera* where the dead man's relatives are sitting. He offers the prayer, which is called *las niwa*, soon after he arrives, saying, "May God bless him, he was a good man." The visitor may then leave or stay and have tea and quietly talk politics and reminisce about the deceased. It is said that if three hundred men follow this ritual, the dead man will go to heaven.

There is a sequence of gifts and sacrifices which should attend the death of an important man. A special bread is made by the women of the dead man's house and given to the poor of the village for three days. An animal may also be killed and sent to the mosque, where the poor gather to collect their bounty. On the Friday after the death a buffalo or cow is killed and given to the village and to visitors who have come to pay their respects. The immediate family of the dead man generally fasts for three days, and in some parts of Swat the entire village is obliged to fast as well. This does not occur in Shamizai/Sebujni, but there is a feeling that it is rather shameful for a man to eat in the house of a bereaved family. The food is consumed primarily by the poor.

For forty days after the death of an important man, a male buffalo (the local symbol of virility) should be killed every Friday. Close associates

Women gathered for a funeral.

and dependents of the dead man should show their respect for him by donating buffalo for these expensive sacrifices. Women whose brother or father has died try to nag their husbands into sacrificing buffalo as well. On the fortieth day, a big feast is held, and another feast, with a buffalo sacrifice, should be held one year after the death. This latter feast, called *tlin*, may be held every year for a decade, but ordinarily is held only once. In these feasts, the redistributive largesse of the dead man is celebrated and the food is eaten by the poor dependents of the dead man. Members of his family also eat. Equals of the dead man do not attend these feasts unless they were his close associates.

The death rites for women do not involve such elaborate rituals. They are enacted by the immediate family with few, if any, guests, and only bread is distributed.

Death is a subject which preys on the minds of the Pukhtun. They consider it an insult to address a man as "grandfather," since this suggests that he is near death. Between husbands and wives, the most common bantering abuse is that the other has grown old and ugly. When a man is kind to his wife, other men say that "his wife is making him old." People often curse one another with a wish for an early death, saying "God drown you," "God destroy you," and so on. Men publicly wish that their wives would conveniently die and release them from their nagging. The women do the same, and when the husband comes home late, the wife jokingly tells the children to mourn, "for your father has died." She will never admit to fearing widowhood, though she does fear the death of her brothers. It is a common complaint by both sexes that the spouse and the spouse's family "will laugh over my tomb."

These complaints, curses, and insults are indicative of the fear always present between husband and wife that one may kill the other or drive the other to death. Angry women have reputations for poisoning their husbands. Arsenic poisoning resembles cholera, and a death by cholera is always suspect. Men, meanwhile, severely beat their wives, though they fear to kill them because of the revenge the wife's family would take. Nonetheless, the statistics of the 1972 census show that in the Swat subdivision, which includes Shin Bagh, there are 149 men per 100 women aged over sixty, while for those under sixty, the proportion is more equal: 108 men per 100 women. This large discrepancy among the aged suggests that violence, malnutrition, and continual childbearing weaken women to an extent that their average age at death is much lower than that of men. These statistics give the hostility between men and women in general and husband and wife in particular a very concrete dimension.

Within the Swati social order, then, all relationships contain elements of hostility or contempt, or both. All women are contemptible because they embody within themselves the odious contradictions of all patrilineal societies, i.e., the centrality of the womb in a system that denies the existence of women as independent entities. One's own women are, however, friendly figures, while one's wife is often actively hostile. One's mamagan (mother's people) are also friendly, but weak, like women, while the sister's husband and wife's brother are men to be avoided for fear of disputes over treatment of women. All of one's agnates are rivals, and the closer the relation, the greater the rivalry. Those who are distant are relatively neutral, and can be tricked and cheated in barter. All those who are inferior are contemptible for their weakness, while the only Being admitted to be stronger than oneself is Allah, and He is dealt with through ambiguous and otherworldly mediators.

The stress is on individuality, fragmentation, and struggle. The pattern of structure and exchange offers *no* paradigm in the lives of the Pukhtun for a relationship of mutual trust, respect, and generosity. Charity offered to the poor is the other side of appropriation, and validates the superiority of the giver. Kindness from one's sisters, or mother, or mother's brother, is tainted by the weakness of the givers. Sexual relations are laden with hostility. Individuals, of course, do care about one another, and the tears shed by women at funerals are not always pure convention. But the stoical silence of men at death rituals is a reminder that life in Swat does not permit much concern over the tragedies of others. Each man is too well aware that he has his own tragedy to enact.

5. From Child to Adult

Let us take a knife, and cut through the flesh of our arms to the bone; and when we have mangled and mutilated ourselves, no one can reproach us with mangling and mutilating others. (Masson 1842: 3:370, quoting the plotters against the Afghan king, Dost Muhammad)

Where there is the sound of a blow, there is respect.

When the flood waters reach your chin, put your son beneath your feet. (Pukhtun proverbs)

Neither friendship nor kinship exist,
All is deceit . . .

I've come to know how children act:
They are all scorpions and snakes.
(Khattak 1965:16, 113)

I WOULD like now to flesh out my portrait of the Pukhtun through a discussion of birth, infancy, childhood, and adolescence, and a review of the attitudes and behaviors of adult men. The experiences of growing up are a preparation for adult life. Children who do not learn the proper attitudes of toughness, egoism, and self-reliance will not grow into adults who can survive in the world of Shin Bagh. The way children are raised, as Mead and the other Culture and Personality theorists tirelessly pointed out, deeply indoctrinates them in the social order, and thus is the mechanism through which the culture reproduces itself.

But, although I agree with Culture and Personality theory as to the importance of socialization processes, I want to avoid their emphasis on "national character," "basic personality types," or even on the more statistical "modal personality." As DuBois, whose work on Alor is a model for Culture and Personality studies, says, the effort to show "a demonstrable relationship between the personalities within a group and the socio-cultural milieu in which they lived . . . failed to reveal any very high degree of consistency between the aspects investigated. It is doubtful that any culture is fully integrated in this sense" (1961:xviii). The attempt to show that personality is a reflection of culture, or that it is influenced by certain basic institutions of child care which are more or less synchronous with the child's own physical development (Kardiner 1939), has not been particularly successful. The difficulties are in definition of the problem. The notion of personality itself has proven to be vague and refractory (Hall and Lindzey 1957), and discrimination of basic "primary" institutions from reflective "secondary" institutions also proved impossibly difficult (Barnouw 1973). Furthermore, analysis tended to be simplistic and did not lend itself to generalizations. The problem is evident in DuBois' exemplary work on Alor where maternal neglect was seen as the dynamic for the Alorese personality, although other societies having instances of maternal neglect did not generate similar personality types. Finally, as Wallace has written, the variation of personalities within a culture is as great as the variation of personalities between cultures. In his view, cultures are far from being homogenous, but instead make "possible the maximal organization of motivational and cognitive diversity" (1970:38).

In order not to get lost in definitional problems, and to avoid the unsupportable (and patently untrue) claim that the people of Shin Bagh have the same general personality, I would like to follow DuBois' advice and focus on "beliefs and attitudes" (1961:xxii). People may not have the same personalities, but they do share an attitude toward life that makes human relations in Shin Bagh predictable and regular. Beliefs, attitudes, and values are learned through childhood training. They are not thereby ingrained for life but, given no great social change, the training of children functions to shape their perceptions of possibilities for the future, and to give them the rules of the social reality in which they must, if not thrive, at least survive. Perhaps, following Freud and Kardiner, interruption of infant suckling, lenient toilet training, or other events which are unsynchronized with a postulated "natural" series of stages in child development, will have definite and predictable consequences for adult character, but I must leave interpretation of this type for those who are qualified in that area. My own interest here is less analytic than descriptive, and begins with childbirth.

The Pukhtun say: "Our women make bread and produce children. They need do no more. They are like cows in their stalls." But the production of children is a hard and dangerous job. Fourteen village women were remembered to have died in childbirth in the last decade, usually while having their first baby. Many infants succumb to disease, neglect, or malnutrition. One woman who lived near us had seven children who died, and 338 infants and small children were recollected as having died in the last ten years. The actual number of deaths may have been considerably higher, since people often forget the death of an infant. Illegitimate children, who are abandoned in the graveyard to die of exposure, be eaten by wild dogs or, rarely, to be found and adopted by poor people, are also not counted among the infant mortalities.

Nonetheless, children, and particularly male children, are the *sine qua non* of a woman's life. Without sons, a woman is not respected. Her husband will beat her and insult her more than ever, and will begin to look for another wife. Even her own family will revile her for her failure to produce an heir. But if a woman has many sons, she is entitled to special marks of respect. She will sit near the matriarch of the house at family feasts, men will stand when she enters a room, her advice will be asked. A productive woman is a woman with honor.

Because having a baby is both dangerous and necessary, women have conflicting feelings about the process. Pregnant girls who are having their first child often have hysterical fits, thought to be caused by evil spirits, in which they insult their husband and his family, rush into the streets, and try to throw themselves into the well or the fire. Exorcism is done by specialists, but such fits usually cease after the birth of the child. Women who have had several children sometimes have secret recourse to an abortionist. The abortionist is an old woman, often a former prostitute, who also functions as the midwife. Abortion is reportedly induced by the introduction of foreign substances into the uterus, with a mixture of chicken manure and opium being the favored abortifacient. It is impossible to say how much business the abortionist actually does. Men suspect it is a common practice, while women say it is rare. It is a fact that modern methods of birth control, assiduously promoted by the Pakistani government with enormous aid from the United States and the United Nations, were spectacular failures in Swat. The free contraceptives given by the family planning officers are often sold as balloons to children, and some women said that birth control pills are only taken during the fast month of Ramzan in order to prevent menstruation during that holy time. Given these facts, it is likely that abortion is rarer than the men assume, though there is no doubt that it does occur occasionally. The lowest rate of abortion is certainly in households in which there is more than one wife. In these circumstances, the rival wives enter into a competition to see who can produce the most sons. By being more productive, one wife can dominate the household and drive the other wife to her natal home in shame. For this reason, polygamous households tend to be more prolific than monagamous houses.

The women of the village, whether in a monagamous or polygamous house, are generally quite fertile. The number of deaths in the village in the decade of 1967–77 was 457, while the number of children born and surviving was 899, so the birth rate is nearly double the death rate. Of the women in the village, 46 had between 6 and 10 surviving children.

Although birth is dangerous, a woman is not given any special treatment to prepare for it. She continues to work as usual, and her belly is so well hidden beneath the folds of her huge shirt that those outside the immediate family may not even realize that she is pregnant. There is no couvade for men, and they appear to ignore the birth process. Husbands reportedly may continue to have sexual relations with their wives up to the time when the baby is actually born.

The blasé attitude toward birth changes when the moment of parturition arrives. Men are barred from the scene of the birth, and only elder women are allowed. The mother sits or stands during the birth of the child. If the

A midwife/abortionist.

baby does not come out easily, it is pulled out. This practice is a common cause of death for the mother and the child. A clean string is tied to the umbilical cord and it is cut with an ordinary knife. The mother is fed ashes to force her to vomit and push out the afterbirth, which is subsequently buried.

After delivering a baby, the mother is subject to extensive food and bathing taboos. These prohibitions are extensions of prohibitions enforced after menstruation when the woman is not permitted to wash herself for five to ten days. After birth, this ban on washing is lengthened to forty days. Only washing of the hands is tolerated, and the husband will complain of the woman's bad smell, despite the perfume with which she douses herself. After menstruation and childbirth, women often put a small cotton cloth, soaked in red wine, into their vaginas. This is supposed to keep the passage tight and pleasurable for intercourse (though women deny that they enjoy sexual intercourse, and say this practice is simply to keep their husband's interest). Sexual contact is forbidden during the time when a woman is not bathing, but some men still have sex with their wives during menstruation. This act is not favored, since it is thought to be dangerous for the man and to cause bad terms between the couple. The strictures against bathing are in strong contrast to the injunction that both men and women must wash their genitals immediately after sexual contact, a rule that is strictly followed.

The ban on bathing and sexual contact after parturition is concurrent with a set of dietary restrictions. The husband's sister prepares sweets with clarified butter the first week. These sweets, with tea and boiled water, are the new mother's only food. In the second week, she is allowed to drink chicken broth, which is the standard remedy for colds. After two weeks, she can eat chicken, and she gradually resumes a normal diet. The foods given a woman who has just had a child are considered "hot," and no "cold" foods, such as rice, would ever be eaten.* This diet is not

* Swatis share with other Pakistanis and South Asians a firm belief that food, drink, and even people are either "hot" or "cold." The logic by which these divisions are made is by no means clear, and sometimes people disagree as to whether a particular unusual food is "hot" or "cold," but there is widespread agreement about the major parameters of the system. It is central to Yusufzai beliefs about health, and it is presumed that most illness and almost every natural death are caused by ill-considered mixing of "hot" and "cold" foods. Drinking water, eating fruit or rice, or any other supposedly "cold" thing after tea is thought especially dangerous, causing immediate sickness and possibly death. Cold foods must always be eaten before hot foods, never after.

followed by all families, since few can afford chicken, but all families will try to give the new mother "hot" foods, since the woman is considered "hot" after childbirth, and the "cold" foods would do her harm. The woman should also stay in bed for two weeks. This treatment can be compared with the treatment given cattle and buffalo after calving. These animals, like women, are given no special treatment before birth, but are kept warm and secluded afterwards and fed on special "hot" feed (residue from ground flour) and given well water, which is considered warmer than stream water, for a period of thirty days.

The husband avoids his wife and the baby during the lying-in period. His supposed possession of the evil eye makes his glance dangerous. Even his clothes are unsafe, and it is believed that if a small child is covered by material which belongs to the father, it will develop a nasal blockage. This condition can only be cured by a supernatural remedy: the father silently opening the sluices to three rice fields three mornings in a row.

The beliefs about childbirth make an interesting combination. Women are considered to be "hot" by nature and much more passionate than men. In the female process of childbirth and menstruation, this heat becomes so strong that men should avoid their wives completely, and the woman is not permitted to bathe for fear of injuring herself with the cool water, while men bathe, at least partially, every day before prayer. At the same time, the prohibition on bathing makes the woman rank-smelling, validating the male view of woman as loathsome. Unlike some other patrilineal societies where the couvade allows men to pretend that they are essential factors in bearing a child, the Swati system affirms that having a child is an ugly and painful thing, which renders the mother seriously ill and physically offensive. There is no attempt to imitate female fertility; in fact the negative power of the male to harm the newborn infant is stressed. Childbirth, for men, is an event which is largely ignored since it demonstrates the importance of women.

The temperature of various common items is as follows: greens and most vegetables are hot, peanuts are very hot, chana dahl is hot, potatoes and onions and eggplant are hot. Garlic is extremely hot. Wheat is hot, but corn and rice are cold. Fish is hotter than meat. Eggs are very hot if boiled, less hot if fried in ghee. Ghee is hot, as are sugar and salt. Milk products are cold, but become warm if heated. Snow is very hot. Oranges and apples are cold. Carrots and pumpkins are cold. Tea is hot, charas is hot, opium is very hot. Naswar is slightly hot. The hottest of all is green tea, usually drunk just before bedtime.

As in most Muslim societies, the difference in status between male and female in Swati society is marked immediately after birth. The birth of a boy is the occasion of rejoicing in the family and congratulations and gifts from outsiders. The birth of a girl is not even announced, and can only be inferred from the dour faces of the new baby's family.

Despite the difference in the effects of their births, male and female infants are treated and dressed in approximately the same manner. Children are swaddled in layers of clothing and tightly tied up until they are a year or even a year and a half old. It is said that if the baby is not swaddled it will not sleep, and that an unswaddled baby may put out its eyes with its flailing hands. Among more westernized Pukhtun, the time a baby is left swaddled is decreasing, but the custom continued to be universal in 1977.

Although babies are restricted in their activities, they are encouraged in their demands for attention. A baby is picked up and fed by its mother and given the breast whenever it cries. There is no attempt to train a child to be hungry at a certain time, and more or less continuous crying is considered perfectly normal. Women keep breast feeding the child long after it has been released from binding and, in fact, ordinarily go on giving the breast to a child until another is born. It is not uncommon to see a five-year-old still taking mother's milk, although it is believed that taking mother's milk for too long makes a child susceptible to disease. Weaning is sudden, and often results in a rapid weight loss, especially among older children. Some children even die after weaning.

Because a child is always picked up and given milk when it cries, it soon learns to expect an immediate response to crying. If the mother is otherwise occupied, an elder daughter or a servant girl is asked to carry the baby and quiet it. Little girls who are able to carry a baby without dropping it (about age six or seven) seem to have a baby on their hip for the whole day. This baby is considered to be the total responsibility of its young caretaker. If the baby begins wailing and refuses to stop, (a rather common occurence) the girl carrying it is likely to get a beating. As a result, the girls are very concerned to keep their charges entertained and silent. At the least noise the baby is picked up, bounced, soothed, and pacified in order to prevent a tantrum.

This technique of child care discourages the infant from displaying any curiosity or from actively exploring its environment. If the crawling or toddling child is investigating something and cries out of frustration at

Newborn infant, tightly swaddled.

not being able to reach whatever has attracted its interest, the mother or elder sister will immediately pick the child up and return it to the breast or hip. The result is that the infant is trained to meet any new or unexpected event or object with immediate bawling, which always elicits the comforting stereotyped response. This method trains the child to cry and whine a great deal at even the slightest irritation or stimulation, and crying soon becomes habitual and even forced. The amount of crying which goes on among infants on the breast or recently weaned is astonishing to an outsider. It does not even cease at night; the mother is constantly awakened by her demanding baby. These crying fits evolve in later life into tantrums of kicking and shrieking among young children, and even among older children and preteens. Such fits occur whenever the child is denied or frustrated in its wishes, and they are the precursors of the adult tantrums which may end in broken dishes and broken jaws.

Children not only cry spontaneously, they also learn the art of faking tears. Older children sometimes pretend to cry to see if they can coerce their parents or siblings into given them what they want, or simply for the fun of pretending. Tantrums, whining, and nagging are used by children to force their demands on their parents, for parents find it difficult, if not impossible, to refuse their childrens' tearful pleas. A public tantrum is especially effective, since a man feels ashamed to reject public entreaties by his children. To escape such irresistible demands, parents often make promises to their children merely to placate them. These promises are rarely fulfilled, and the child soon learns to be wary of the word of others.

Although attention is invariably gained by crying and fits of temper, the form the attention takes is not always pleasurable. The mother, who sleeps with the baby, soon tires of being awakened throughout the night by cries for the breast; the sister wearies of the heavy burden on her hip. Meanwhile, the infant itself becomes increasingly hard to please and is dissatisfied with the narrow range of responses it can elicit. It may begin bawling for no reason at all, simply to give vent to its feelings of restlessness and general frustration, and will not be comforted. The mother may take to slapping and pinching the child in irritation at the same time as she gives it suck. The sister surreptitiously punches and teases her exasperating little encumbrance.

When the baby is not howling, on the breast, or on the sister's hip, it is often called upon to perform. It is taught to make faces, which convulse the family in laughter. Later, when able to toddle, a little girl may be encouraged to dance and she will be asked to dance whenever music is heard. (Note the contrast with adult women, who are allowed to dance only at the weddings of their kinsmen.) Children soon learn to withhold these tiny favors and to show stubborness and willfulness.

While some amusing antics are taught, there is no effort made to teach the child motor coordination skills. The child will learn to walk or crawl on its own, without parental encouragement. Nor is there any toilet training beyond expressions of disgust. Children, especially boys, soon learn that their aggressions can be expressed by strategically defecating in their mother's bed, in the pathway, or in some other awkward place. Girls are much more likely to be punished for such behavior if it is recurrent. A child is also not taught to speak, though it is taught facial mimicry. Indicatively, the first words spoken are those most heard and most necessary, "ma la," which means "give me."

Children are seen, at best, as amusing little animals who need very minimal care, though their tantrums must be catered to. After they are able to get about on their own, they are left to forage for food during the day. There is usually a store of stale bread for them to fill themselves with in a special spot in the house. Up to the age of seven or so the children are known as *warukəi* (boys) and *wara* (girls). Children in this

Playing with a baby. The mother is showing it a dead bird.

category are not considered able to feel or reason. Their personalities are said to be fluid, and they are particularly susceptible to the evil eye and to *jabǝi*, a disease thought to be caused by deprivation that leads to wasting away. Not much is expected of young children. The idea that children of this age group can learn is amusing, as is the idea that young children might be upset or disturbed by being lied to or insulted. "Children have no feelings," the people say.

However, it is understood that children do have some feelings: these are feelings of fear. Training is by frightening the child with punishment or with stories of fearsome monsters. Praise is uncommon, for the Pukhtun, like the Rajputs of India who have a similar social structure, believe that praise will spoil children (Minturn and Hitchcock 1963:325). Praise also may be a prelude to affliction by the evil eye and so should be avoided. Punishment, though, is easily meted out, and is often quite harsh by Western standards. Children are slapped hard across the face for stumbling or bumping into something. They may be tied up and hung from the rafters of the house for spilling tea, coming home late, misplacing something, or any other reason. Adults see nothing reprehensible in publicly beating a child, or in showing pleasure at giving a child a beating. One of the privileges of a khan is catching and beating children of poor people who may stumble into his path or follow him too closely. Men brag, "the children of the village fear me," and use violence to increase that fear. Children are encouraged to beat each other as well. For example, a six-year-old spilled a bowl of curd; her father punished her by making her do deep knee bends while she held her ears (a punishment he had learned in elementary school by being subjected to it) until she collapsed. He then asked her elder siblings to kick her, which they did with gusto. This story was told with great glee, much as stories of wife-beating are told. Each spouse complains that the other is too harsh with the children but, in fact, both mother and father treat the children cruelly or kindly according to their mood of the moment. Children are not permitted to justify their acts or to argue back to their parents. Punishment itself is quite arbitrary, a situation reported in an Egyptian village as well, where "in administering punishment, there is no consistency or regularity" (Ammar 1970:243). Behavior that leads to a beating one minute is passed off with a laugh the next. For example, when one child stumbled in the yard, the father leapt up and gave it a slap. A few minutes later, another child also stumbled, but the father did nothing. When this inconsistency was pointed out, he laughed and said, "Too many children make a man crazy." The randomness of punishment, combined with its severity, keeps children wary and frightened. But showing fear invariably increases the ire of the punisher, so the children maintain a trembling bravado and rarely cry when struck, in contrast to the ease with which they cry when denied something.

Punishment in Swat is not given for offenses that might be punishable in the West. Stealing from outsiders, lying, fighting, and so on rarely lead to disciplinary action. Rather, carelessness, clumsiness, stumbling, and any kind of awkwardness is often very cruelly dealt with. Boys in particular are apt to be beaten for public behavior that shows a lack of self-control. Putting one's hands near one's face while talking to an adult, or even having a vacant expression, are punishable for boys, who are pressed to display a manly reserve in public and in front of their fathers. Girls do not have to show such decorum, and may giggle and play where a boy would have to be scrupulous and stern. But if boys have to show more reserve, girls have much more responsibility, and are beaten for shirking, for letting a younger sibling cry, or for any number of delinquencies.

It is evident from the above that treatment of boys and girls begins to vary as soon as they are released from swaddling. Boys are treated by all with much more deference than girls. They are allowed and even encouraged to beat their sisters. If a girl hits back, she is liable to be severely punished. When a meal is served the boy gets the best portion as a matter of course. In this he emulates his father, who also eats the choice food. But while the boy eats with his mother, the father eats separately. The boy has the best clothes and is the better groomed child, although he does not know how to keep his clothes clean or how to wash himself. The girls, on the other hand, are left to wash their clothes themselves and to bathe whenever they want. These are tasks the girls often ignore, and filthy little girls are a common sight. When her brother soils his pants a girl is delegated to wash them for him. The little boy is raised like a prince among his subjects.

Not only is the boy pampered and trained in his own superior position, but he also hears the anger and disgust with which his father often refers to his mother and picks up the sexual insults that make up a large part of ordinary childish conversation. He learns that his mother and elder sisters are prisoners of the house, and that he can evade their anger by simply stepping out into the public street. He sees his sisters working carrying the baby, cleaning the rice, sifting the corn flour, and helping the mother with the myriad tasks which are a woman's lot, while he is expected to do nothing more than help his father to entertain a guest by bringing tea, cushions, and so forth. Both boys and girls may be asked to deliver messages and goods, but a boy who fails in such a mission will only be reprimanded, while his sister is likely to be beaten.

Little boys are not so well developed mentally as little girls. Their toilet training is quite retarded in comparison with girls of the same age, as is their self-reliance and general aura of mental capacity. Presumably, the backwardness of young boys, who appear much more juvenile than girls of the same age, is due to their almost complete inactivity, enforced by custom, which encourages a dull affect. A boy, even among the poorest families, is not expected to *do* anything while he is waited on by his doting mother—who sees her son as the agent of increased prestige—and by his subservient sisters, who are trained to cater to his every whim. This training is inaction stands the Pukhtun boys in good stead in later life, since much of the Pukhtun's life is spent in motionless silence lounging in the *hujera* or *bətuk* (guest house). The names of the boys reflect their exalted status. Names like Shah (king), Nawab (ruler), and so on are normal. The family's attitude toward its sons leads the boys to feel themselves to be specially privileged beings who can gain their desires simply by stating them or, at most, by whining.

But if the boy is pampered and indulged by his family, he also has to begin to live up to certain standards of behavior, as mentioned above. Men are proud to have sons, but they like their sons less as the boys grow up, because of their resentment over the fact that the son will replace them. The relationship between father and son is too strained with rivalry to be affectionate (see Fortes 1949). The boy looks to his female relatives for comfort and warmth. When the boy is five or six the father begins to demand that he present himself as a Pukhtun, that he learn the name of his clan and clan genealogy. He instructs him in the rituals of greeting and politeness, and punishes him for lapses. The boy is expected to behave honorably in public and not shame his family by unmanly bearing. Fathers often abuse their slow-learning sons as homo-sexuals (bedagh), and laugh at their pretensions to manhood. Public humiliation is considered a good way to teach a boy his proper role. The stress is on learning a part which can be enacted to other Pukhtun in order to demonstrate the boy's grasp of Pukhtunwali, the Pukhtun code of conduct. However, whining and demanding attention in private is still acceptable and even expected as a function of a boy's assertion of his privileged position. In learning these two modes of behavior, one for public consumption and one for private life, the boy is becoming set in a pattern which will continue in the future. Furthermore, the boy has been trained to believe and behave as if his desires, as he expresses them in the home, will be met if he reiterates them long enough and with sufficient emotion. Grown men have the same attitude, but are unable to find in their wives someone who will cater to them as their mothers and sisters did. The high expectations of the boy are bound to be thwarted in his adulthood.

The boy is therefore trained to demand a great deal of his home environment without being obliged to contribute, though among the less well-to-do families, an older boy will be expected to help with the field-work. But among the khans, even this labor is not demanded. Simultaneously, the boy is taught to fear exposing himself to public shaming, to keep an impassive face outside the house, and to follow the Pukhtun code of conduct. He is taught to be restrained, to walk rather than run, to control his emotions in public.

The girl does not expect so much from her life. She learns to accept serving and to acquiesce in her own inferiority (though never in the inferiority of her lineage). She understands that her life will be one of work and drudgery, with little relief. However, like her brother, she is instructed in family pride, and her most severe punishments follow when she plays with unsuitable companions. If a girl sees herself as less than her brother, she also learns that her family is the best of all families, and that all other men are not up to the standards of the men of her own lineage. Like her brother, she sees herself as "the center of many encircling emotional walls, each of which stands against the world in general, and each of which stands against the world directly outside" (Newman 1965:11).

The discrimination between boys and girls continues when they enter the next phase of childhood. This phase, which begins at approximately the age of seven, is recognized linguistically as the girls are now called *jinai* and the boys are called *halak*. It is at this time that the girls begin spontaneously to wear the *sadar* (shawl) over their heads at all times, rather than just wearing it sporadically. Accompanying this change is an enforcement on the prohibition against leaving the compound without specific permission. The girl's life now becomes even more like that of her mother, as she spends her time in the compound working and gossiping.

The boy, who has by now learned the rudiments of proper public behavior, goes in and out of the compound quite freely. The change in his life is marked primarily by his joining a gang of local boys and beginning to take part in the pranks and fights which make up a boy's life. Like the general society, these gangs are quite democratic, and a boy's father's position makes little difference to his place in the gang. The strongest and most daring boys rule. At the same time, hierarchy has its place, as the boys hesitate to beat the son of an important khan severely for fear of his father's wrath. But this sword cuts two ways. The father will be angry at his son for being weak, while the son wishes to show self-reliance and tries to settle his disputes on his own. If he runs to his father he is exposing himself to ridicule as a milksop.

Boys' gangs are roughly divided between prepubescent boys and unmarried teenagers. The younger boys, and often the older, are never to be found without their slingshots, which are used both for killing birds and for pelting enemies. The gangs are made up of boys from the same ward. They run without supervision over the roofs, causing trouble by stealing fruit and by various other small depredations. When they get older, their misdeeds may become more serious. In the village, one gang kidnapped a poor girl and raped her, while another group of boys secretly kept a prostitute in an abandoned hut.

The period of adolescent play is full of wrestling, tests of courage, and invective. Pranks can be cruel; a favorite one is cutting the tail from the cow owned by a man who has insulted the boys or caused them trouble. Men remember these days of their youth with nostalgia, but also with distaste, since there was an ever-present fear of a fight and of humiliation. Adolescence is seen as a very dangerous time for the boy's family as well, since the boys are trying to prove their strength and bravery among their peers. A rejected friendship, a careless insult, or a sudden fight can lead a boy to take up his father's gun in order to redeem his honor, thus initiating a ruinous feud. For example, a twelve-year-old boy was humiliated by a companion, who pulled off his trousers in public. The boy went home, took his father's rifle, and killed the other boy, thereby forcing his own family to precipitously flee Swat. Such deadly fights are most often between khan boys, since their sense of honor is most easily sullied.

In the gangs, boys learn the skills they will need in later life. Weaker boys learn to attach themselves to those who are stronger. Leaders learn the necessity for establishing a loyal following. Boys learn stealth and bravado in gang activities, as well as having their fears of humiliation reinforced.

Formerly, the boys spent all their time in gang activities, though the poorer boys had to help in fieldwork as well. In modern days, some of the boys, especially the khans, have been sidetracked from their gangs by other activities, particularly by schoolwork. Most of the khan boys and a few Pukhtun and worker boys went to the local school in 1977. The schools, founded by the Wali, teach Urdu, Islamic studies, and basic skills in math, the sciences, and social studies. The learning is completely by rote, following the example of study of the Koran, in which repetition without understanding is the traditional mode of instruction. In the schools, there are no essays, nor is there any questioning of the teacher— only parrotlike imitation. As a result of this technique, it is perfectly possible, as I have witnessed, for a student to know that 22 plus 22 equals 44, since this sequence has been taught, but not to know that 22

A gang of boys playing in the graveyard.

plus 23 equals 45. As an aside, this form of education continues in the universities of Pakistan, where creativity is discouraged and passive echoing is the norm.

Education is viewed in a characteristic way by the Pukhtun. It is seen as a sort of status activity which can lead to a role as an elite doctor. It is not understood that learning is something which cannot be purchased; Pukhtun brag about the bribes they paid in order to gain a high score for their sons' examinations. Cheating is considered quite honorable, since by cheating a student can avoid the public shame of failure.

Girls in some of the more elite families have also been to school in recent years. This is a novel development. Qajira Khana, who was twenty-six in 1977, was unusual for a woman of her age because her doting father had hired a private tutor to teach her to read the Koran when she was a girl. It was not thought necessary to teach her to write, nor to use numbers, but she was able to piece together articles from Pukhto books and newspapers. Nowadays, it is prestigious to send girls to school, though the schooling almost always stops at puberty. Qajira Khana and Zaman Khan have made a special effort to have their girls educated, and have arranged to have their eldest daughter, Shagufta, study at the elite private school across the River in Sangota.

Schoolboys.

Wealthy Pukhtun men want educated wives, and a prerequisite in elite marriages is that the girl be able to read and write. Some of the very wealthy families in Lower Swat have sent their daughters on to college. But not even college educated girls are permitted to use their learning in any meaningful way. Education is regarded as a status symbol that will increase the girl's value on the marriage market, and there are many stories of young women who had been brilliant in school who then became locked into traditional marriages with completely illiterate, but rich, men. Some girls from poor, and therefore "shameless" families, have broken out of this mold and managed to get jobs as teachers. Unfortunately, this takes them off the marriage market, and they are condemned to lives as spinsters.

The fate of educated girls is doubly unhappy from my perspective because they are by a large margin the best students. Teachers say girls are more hardworking and better at schoolwork than the boys, undoubtedly because school is the one place where a girl can surpass a boy on merit. The institution of purdah, so dear to the hearts of the Pukhtun, cuts off from active participation in social life the most creative young people in the schools. Here is the place where the vitiating influence of the system is most evident.

Whether the students are boys or girls, however, the schools still emphasize rote learning and de-emphasize creative activity. This parallels a striking aspect of children's attitudes. Whereas a Western child passes through a stage of interminable questioning, the Swati child does not. It is unheard of for a child to ask a question of an adult which is not purely instrumental, such as "Where is the teapot?" Reality is an absolute given for the Pukhtun, and there is no need or incentive to question anything. It is worth noticing here that the word for "thought" in Pukhto is the same as the word for "worry" (soch). When I asked schoolboys in a questionnaire what they thought about, the reply was often "I don't think." Among adults as well as children abstract questioning is never heard. Lack of curiosity about the natural world is marked among the Pukhtun, who are generally uninterested in those things which are not of direct advantage to them. People have no notion that the caterpillars which appear in the spring later become butterflies; nor do they realize that tadpoles and frogs are different forms of the same creature. Whatever exists, always exists.

This is not to imply that there is no questioning at all. One of the most frequently heard words in the village is "wuli?" or "why?" But this interrogative is always addressed toward a particular action of another person and is never abstract. For example, on meeting an acquaintance a typical exchange might run as follows:

"Greetings brother."
"God bless you."
"Where are you going?"
"To the hujera."
"Why?"

Most often the reply returned to the question of "why?" will be either "sakh" or "asai." The first means "I don't know" or "because I feel like it." The second means "I know, but don't want to say. It is my business." The reply of "sakh" is most appropriate in response to factual questions and indicates that the speaker does not want to bother answering. "Asai" is most heard in response to questions which concern motivation. For instance, a mother may ask her son why he threw his newly washed clothes in the mud, and his reply will certainly be "asai." Or a child may tell someone that "I have broken my friendship with you," and when asked why he will answer with "asai." Questions are therefore

A schoolgirl.

met with a reply which is not a reply at all, but rather a closure of communication. These conversation-stopping answers are felt to be perfectly legitimate in the talk both of children and adults. In fact, "sakh" and "asai" are seen as perhaps the best possible answers to most questions of "wuli?"

Girls have a different attitude toward questions than do boys, since they are used by their mothers as reporters on the latest events in the village and are trained to give voluminous reports on recent scandal. Questions about domestic crises in the village elicit long and detailed responses. In learning to report local incidents, especially incidents of fighting in or between houses, the girls develop talent for gossiping and rumor-mongering which will serve as sources of entertainment and solace in later life. The hard lot of women is greatly lightened by the amusement and sense of sharing they get from hearing about the troubles of others. Boys, on the contrary, should not spread gossip. It is seen as beneath male dignity to show an interest in household quarrels. Boys, like the men they emulate, pretend that what goes on in the house has no relevance for their masculine concerns, which involve, in large measure, daydreaming about wealth and glory.

As they reach the age of reason, children are quite different in the way they are expected to perform in daily interactions. The girls do not have a public face. When they are small, they behave in public the way they behave in private; giggling and flirtatious with people they know, shy with those who are unfamiliar. When they are older, the girls cease to appear in public at all, but continue to be emotional and volatile at home and among friends.

There are two sets of expectations regarding the bearing of boys who are over seven and have become *halak*. The first is that they should be silent and shy among their elders, looking down meekly and not offering an opinion. This is called *sharmigi*, or being ashamed, and is considered the proper and praiseworthy bearing of a young man in public. Yet, at home and among his gang a boy who is inarticulate and reserved is criticized as being *aghəl* or *mazub*. These terms indicate someone who is retarded or dull, and a boy who is *mazub* will certainly be the butt of many taunts and pranks.

The opposite of being dull is being a joker, or *khandaroya*. Parents actively train their children to be funny and, as I have noted, the only training given small children is the art of making faces. Later, when the

Self-confident young girl.

182 FROM CHILD TO ADULT

child is able to speak, the parents will teach it verbal abuse, and the child, especially if it is a boy, will make the parents laugh heartily when he insults them. Furthermore, a child may escape a beating by joking and being charming. A funny boy is highly valued in his gang. With humor comes the role of prankster; it is the joker who thinks up the gang's escapades. A boy who is a *khandaroya* is favored as a potential husband because it is thought that such a boy is "hot" and therefore a good worker and fertile, while a silent child will be a slow worker and possibly sterile. Although the joker is encouraged in his defiant and mischievous character, he is also verbally abused as being a *shaitan*, or devil. He is the boy who will disobey his parents and turn the joking insults of his youth into serious abuse and fights when a teenager. The public presentation of the shy boy, who is held up as an ideal, is in complete contradiction to this other ideal of the joker. The boy who has learned to be insolent as a child is also expected to be taciturn and servile in his relations with his elders when he becomes a young man. A similar pattern is found in Egypt. "The behavior pattern and motivation of the learning situation where adults are involved are different from those of the age-group learning situation. In the former, subservience, respect and fear are expected, while in the latter rivalry and reciprocity on equal terms are the norms" (Ammar 1970:230). This contradiction plays a large part in developing the worldview of Pukhtun man.

Children are trained from infancy to be self-reliant and possessive. Playthings are few, and the mother will not make any effort to see that they are shared. Rather, the stronger children will be encouraged to take from the weaker. The mother plays the same game, and will take anything she fancies that a child brings into the house. Thievery from neighboring houses, or from other nuclear families in the same compound, is also encouraged, either overtly or covertly. For instance, a man took his son to visit his brother. On leaving, the boy picked up a toy belonging to his father's brother's son. The father, far from telling the boy to return the toy, helped his son to conceal it, justifying the theft on the grounds that his brother should have been generous enough to give the toy away. Stealing from one's own house, however, is not considered amusing, as one six-year-old discovered to his dismay after he took some of his mother's pots and generously gave them away on the street. "He thinks he is a big khan already" his angry father said.

Within the house, the main conversation of children consists of dispu-

Boy embarrassed at being seen with no pants.

tation over possessions, and cries of "That's mine!" and "No, it's mine!" are often heard. Children have hiding places for their meager belongings to protect them from the demands of their siblings. A toy given to one child soon circulates to others who are stronger or more demanding, for children, like adults, cannot stand repeated demands. The child who is more persistent in his or her demands usually gets the coveted object. Of course, if a girl has something a boy wants, she should give it to him immediately or face a beating from her parents.

Rivalry and jealousy is the normal state of affairs within the house as the children struggle among themselves for privileges and to avoid beatings. Siblings betray one another and are rewarded by being allowed to participate in beating the miscreant. They also learn to lie and pass blame onto others without a qualm. Survival is for the fittest.

Enmity within the family is exacerbated by the blatant favoritism of the parents, who make no effort to pretend they like all their children equally. One child may be especially signaled out as a *taliman* (good luck charm) because of the good fortune which followed its birth. Or a child may be favored because it is eldest or youngest, or resembles the father, or for any other arbitrary reason. The favored child may not be the most well behaved and, in fact, is likely to be the worst because of pampering. Boys are naturally more favored than girls, and a girl in the middle of a large family is often virtually ignored by her parents. But boys who are in a household with many sons may suffer the same fate, especially the sons of a co-wife who is in disfavor, for it is well recognized that the children of a disliked wife will also be disliked. Even in households with only two sons, there is always a definite favorite who continues in that role even when the sons are grown men. "My father hates me," is a common complaint, and it is understood that nothing can be done to alter this hatred. Women are not far behind in expressing distaste for some of their children, calling them *nakara* (ugly) or *sxa* (disgusting). More than men, women are prone to curse their children, saying "may God drown you," or "may God make you childless."

Although some children are liked more than others and are given preferential treatment, the life of all children is far from comfortable. The stress is on training the children for the severity of Pukhtun reality, an emphasis which is acknowledged by Ghani Khan when he writes that the Pukhtun is trained to accept many things as more valuable than life and is "forbidden colorful clothes or exotic music, for they weaken the arm and soften the eye" (1958:30). Children are left to themselves, and get no advice from their elders beyond that necessary to teach proper manners and work habits. When it rains, they huddle, shivering, in the house, since no one tells them to change into dry clothes. In the summer accumulated dirt and the heat combine to cause boils and running sores which they stoically endure, since such afflictions are viewed as normal for childhood. The noise level in the house, with the baby crying, the other children fighting, the women gossiping and haranguing, and the animals making their various cries, is extraordinary. The environment is unhealthy: overcrowded and dirty. Mosquitoes and flies abound, beds are full of children, who are often afflicted with worms and parasites which make them weak and sluggish. But, in this atmosphere of pressure and physical discomfort, the child is learning to take for granted and to withstand without complaint the conditions that will make up the future.

Added to the environmental hardships are other difficulties. The child must continually fear arbitrary punishment and random violence from his or her parents. This punishment can only be avoided by deflection onto another sibling. There is also the sense that one's few possessions will be appropriated as soon as they are seen by someone stronger or more demanding; the belief that one's own family stands in a relation of enmity with every other family; the disputes and occasional savage fights of the mother and father; the lack of creative activity and the high level of complete immobility and tedium; the rigid standards for public behavior; the jealousy and mistrust both within and without the household and the fights and vituperation of one's peers. As one Pukhtun said when asked what some children were doing: "They are abusing and complaining. That is all they ever do." Children are trained by their society to abuse and complain, and in this way they are conditioned to survive in a hostile and dangerous world.

In the above pages a pattern of training has been outlined which fits children to the actualities of Pukhtun life. To reiterate, children are taught to be assertive and aggressive, jealous and possessive. They have been taught, by repeated examples, to mistrust the words of others, while at the same time their unrestricted and prolonged suckling in infancy and the willingness of their parents to give in to repeated demands has given them a "whim of iron." Boys are raised to present themselves as paragons

Children on the street.

of Pukhtun virtue in public, but encouraged also to be jokers and hell-raisers among their peers. They have been taught in their families that they deserve to be served the best of everything on demand, while sisters are trained to serve and submit to the men of the family. Both sexes are also taught that their own household is the only refuge in a dangerous world, and that even this refuge is problematic. All other houses are more or less despicable and fair game for thievery. Children soon realize that lying and clever talk are useful methods for avoiding punishment for themselves and transferring punishment onto an enemy sibling. As Ammar notes in a similar situation, "the effects of these techniques of fear as forcing children to resort to lies and deception are reflected later in the prevailing atmosphere of adult life which is charged with suspicion, secrecy and apprehension" (1970:244). The children learn to hide fear, because fear will elicit attack, but simultaneously they learn that throwing tantrums and nagging is a useful tactic for getting what they want. All teaching in school focuses on particulars rather than abstractions. Children are taught not to question, but to accept.

The value structure developed by these training methods is a volatile one. In Western society there is the notion of a privatized conscience, but the Swati is apparently not burdened with problems of guilt and self-reproach. As in many cultures, shame and a fear of public humiliation replaces the Western concept of guilt and conscience. Any methods are permissible to escape public shaming, which occurs when one is shown not to live up to the ideals of strength, pride, and self-reliance. The attitude of the Pukhtun man, and especially the khan, is formed by a childhood made up of a mixture of pampering and arbitrary violence, of expectations that he present a manly public face combined with a constant fear of humiliation. In his gang, he has learned to stand up for himself, to organize others, to be a leader, a plotter, a joker. He has developed great expectations and opinions of his own value, but these are tainted with an undercurrent of anxiety inculcated by the random punishment and rigid rules of public performance, the necessity for maintaining his own honor at all costs, which made up his childhood training. The pattern correlates, it appears, with the pattern of weak infant discipline and severe later discipline postulated by Goldfrank (1945) and later used in the Middle Eastern context by Ammar (1970). As a result, any questioning of society's standards reveals an inability to act upon these standards and is shameful in itself. Public enactment of the rituals of Pukhtunwali (the code of honor) is everything to the Pukhtun, who exists in a divided world in which his public part, consisting of reserve and manly solemnity, is in strong contrast with his plots, demands for a dominant role, and his inevitable disappointments. The Pukhtun man is accustomed to a lack of affection, hardened by a harsh physical environment, and prepared for a life of struggle, betrayal, and cruelty. To survive, he must strive to subdue and rule his fellows, who all have the same desire. As we have seen, this struggle must end in failure, and the Pukhtun is fortunate who can simply maintain himself with honor, much less reach the paramount position that is his dream. Nevertheless, the struggle must continue if a man is to continue to have the right to call himself Pukhtun. A proverb clearly expresses the philosophy behind raising a male child: "The eye of the dove is lovely, my son, but the sky is made for the hawk. So cover your dovelike eyes and grow claws" (G. Khan 1958:12). What the Pukhtun man must present to the world is the hawk, the bird of prey. What he must conceal is the dove, the sensitive victim. The egocentricity of the Pukhtun is a fragile facade, hiding the insecurity that is its opposite and its dynamic.

The attitude of the woman is, in many respects, equivalent to that of the man. She too is trained to be self-willed, jealous, avaricious, and aggressive. But she does not suffer under the same weight of expectations as her male counterpart. She anticipates very little in life beyond her traditional role of breadmaking and childbearing, and her dream of having many sons is likely to be realized. If she has boys and is clever, she will win respect and achieve her goal of dominating the home. Her husband, older than she and surrounded by enemies, gives up the fight for rule in the house and the woman ends as victor in her personal battle.

Women also do not have the relations of enmity with their equals which keep men apart from one another. As inferior beings, imprisoned under the will of their husbands, they are united in their complaints against all men, who are characterized as bad, ugly, and cruel. The community of shared grievances provides solace among women during the gossip sessions which are their only entertainment. Men, though they say their women are bad and lazy, cannot properly even deign to notice the petty doings of the household, but rather must affect complete lack of interest in women and women's affairs. Only with a close ally may a man reveal the wrongdoings of his wife and the anxiety she has caused him. Even then, he simply talks as if a good beating followed by sexual

A powerful matriarch.

intercourse is all the wife needs if she has been misbehaving. In polite greetings, a man never asks another about his wife. Rather, he says "How is your house?" Men try to act as if their female relatives and wives did not exist, and will not greet them if they see them returning from a funeral or wedding feast. Women are quite the opposite, and greatly enjoy roundly criticizing their spouses to anyone who happens to be in the house, including her children, the servants, female guests, and even saleswomen and Gujar milksellers.

Women are further united by the fact that they do not hold land and therefore participate only at a distance in the rivalry which divides men. Even *mahar*, a bone of contention between co-wives, functionally belongs to the husband, and goes to the wife's male relatives in case of separation. Other women, with the exception of the co-wife, do not threaten the honor and livelihood of a wife. This is not to say that women are not rivals. There is strong competition among neighboring women, especially if they are lineage mates, over who has the most possessions. Women, like men, love to excite the envy of others. But hostility between women is never so deep as to incite a feud. Women only murder their husbands, stepchildren, or their hated co-wife.

Paradoxically, despite their isolation and inferior status, women are much less conflicted than their husbands. They have the advantage of a community among their sex, even if it is only a community of complaint. Their expectations are not unrealistic and it is relatively easy for a women to achieve her ideal. They do not have to struggle against the machinations of powerful enemies and are in no position to do much political manipulating themselves. In their isolation, their lives, though devoid of much of what a Westerner would feel are the necessities of affection and interest, are also quite sinless in the Islamic sense. Most women are confident of their religious merit. Men, operating in the stern reality of the world and seeking to defend and protect themselves while simultaneously struggling to conquer their ubiquitous enemies, are obliged to cheat, steal, betray, and lie. Sometimes, they must even kill. They can only pray continually in their dotage and hope for the mercy of Allah.

Women are also always in private, where they can freely give vent to their anger and frustrations. Men are public creatures, and should present a stoical face in their public encounters, even though internally they may be boiling over. Even at the most emotional of occasions, such as the

Women eating together.

funeral of a son or a sister, the man must never let a tear fall or show any feelings. The conflicts of the men, which are greater than those of the women, are made even more of a trial by being bottled up. No wonder then that Pukhtun men are famed for their fits of temper and sudden outbursts of violence (see Newman 1965).

The Pukhtun man is thus more caught in the contradictions of his social order than the woman. The Westerner, raised in a much softer and more lenient environment, must admire the toughness of the Pukhtun men, their resolute efforts to live up to an impossible image of freedom, independence, and bravery. But, beneath the romantic picture of the lone man standing his vigil against the might of the rest of the world, is an underlying despair. Men, unlike women, can never make their dreams come true. The woman can rule the house, but the man cannot rule the world, nor can he even manage to rule his cousin. The dreams of conquest, respect, wealth, and honor, which give the Pukhtun strength to continue fighting, eventually fester and sour life. Men complain bitterly in private that their lives are "narrow" and that they are "imprisoned." The claustrophobia of the valley is not just from the surrounding mountains. The women, who literally are imprisoned, are much more reconciled to their fates, and do not make such complaints. Elder men, who have gone beyond the realm of political strife, may reach a plane of philosophical distance, but the younger men, immersed in their struggles, cannot afford such a stance. It is this sense of malaise that leads, in part, to the Pukhtun's willingness to migrate, and to the quickness with which he is able to drop his tribal ways and assume a new lifestyle once he has managed to flee his native land. For an outsider, the Pukhtun men seem larger than life, with their pride and clear-cut codes of honor. But the truth is that many of them hope and dream that they may leave that romantic-seeming life behind them and find a new life that will offer a measure of respite from eternal hostility and poverty.

The results of the socialization process can be seen in a review of the characteristic behaviors of adult men. Their childhood has prepared them to engage in a struggle for survival in which many weapons must be used. Trust, generosity, tenderness, humility, creativity, kindness; all are disallowed by the necessities of living. Mistrust and betrayal, for example, are pervasive themes. The struggle of local leaders for dominance has always been marked by treachery, even among the closest relatives. Such behavior is expected and is not greatly censured. "This attitude is not illogical in the orbit of frontier politics where war, assasination and treachery are never treated very seriously. Every man is ready to embrace one or all of them given a favorable opportunity" (Schomberg 1935:235). Betrayal is especially common among close relatives. Warburton's description of the Afridi can be extended to the Swat Pukhtun as well: "The Afridi lad is taught from his earliest childhood by the circumstances of his existence and life to distrust all mankind, and very often his near relations, heirs to his small plot of land by right of inheritance, are his deadliest enemies. Distrust of all mankind and readiness to strike the first blow for the safety of his own life have therefore become the maxims of the Afridi" (1900:49).

> To me all my relatives are reptiles;
> Those I've helped repay with trouble.
> (Khattak 1965:49)

Perfidy within the patrilineage is in keeping with the principle of *tar-burwali* (enmity between brothers' sons), but breach of faith is not limited to relatives within the lineage. Affines also may play one false, and the deceit of one's wife's family is the subject of many proverbs such as: "Enemies reconciled by marriage are the most fearful of treachery."

A successful elder.

Burnes gives the example of Feteh Khan, the famous prime minister (vizier) of Kabul prior to the reign of Dost Muhammad:

An individual . . . had insulted Futteh Khan, and even knocked out one of his front teeth. The injury had to all appearance been forgiven, for he had since married a sister of the Vizier; but the alliance had only been formed that Futteh Khan might easier accomplish his base intentions. . . . He seized upon his brother-in-law and put him to death. . . . The Vizier's sister threw herself at her brother's feet, and asked why he had murdered her husband? "What!" said he, "have you more regard for your husband than for your brother's honor? Look at my broken teeth; and know the insult is now avenged. If you are in grief over the loss of a husband, I'll marry you to a mule driver."
(Burnes 1834: 1:129)

Feteh Khan's sentiments would be echoed by the people of Shin Bagh, who would deplore only the stupidity of Feteh Khan's brother-in-law in allowing himself to come under the control of his wife's brother.

Within this Hobbesian world even one's own nuclear family is not to be trusted. Men are in constant fear that their wives will betray them sexually and render them *begherata* (without honor). Men fear not only betrayal and trickery by their wives, but also treachery from their own brothers and sons. It is not uncommon, according to the villagers, for a man to be cuckolded by his own brother. A case of this kind occurred in a neighboring village during my stay, and ended with the murder of the girl and the exile of the brother (see Ahmed 1980 for other cases.) Sexual seduction is not the only form of perfidy practiced by brothers on one another. In another recent incident, a hill dwelling family secretly dug up a Buddhist ruin which happened to be lying on their property in the hopes of selling any antiquities they might discover. The brother of the man digging up the stupa was jealous of the profits that might be realized and informed the authorities, who confiscated the few articles which had been excavated. A similar anecdote concerns three brothers who discovered an emerald mine. One brother stole the loose emeralds and decamped, but not before he had betrayed his brothers to the police, who put them in jail.

With betrayal a constant threat, suspicion is the watchword and secrecy the norm. "In this country the traveller invariably conceals his route and time of departure. Thus, if going direct from Mardan to Peshawar by night he gives out that he leaves for Nowshaira in the morning" (Bellew 1864:214). While people are no longer quite this secretive, they are very reticent. A Pukhtun man is trained from youth to maintain a calm and unperturbed demeanor and not to reveal his inner feelings. I once asked some men to imitate someone experiencing fear, joy, suspicion, and so on. The men entered into the game with enthusiasm, but to my eye, all the expressions were the same; tight-lipped and stoical. Nor could the other men tell what emotion was being counterfeited. The ubiquitousness of the belief in the necessity for concealment is indicated by the results of an attitude test I administered to seventh and tenth graders in the area schools (see appendix B). To the question, "Should a man keep his thoughts and activities secret?" 127 out of 140 replied "Yes."

Even within the nuclear family a man is not free of the need for dissimulation. One of the most frequent complaints men make about their wives and families is that they reveal family secrets in the course of gossip.

By morning the whole village knew
The secret words I'd used
The night before, intimately,
When talking to my son.

If it's your hope never to be
Shamed before anyone
It's best to keep within your heart
Even your least affair.

Let your heart bleed within itself,
Khushal, if bleed it must,
But keep your secrets well concealed
From both stranger and friend.
(Khattak 1965:36)

The underlying cause of treachery is generally viewed as envy. "If they are to be believed, their ruling vice is envy, which besets even the nearest and dearest of relations" (Burnes 1834: 1:144). Burnes' observation was validated in Shin Bagh by the statements of the villagers themselves. As a quantitative check, I included the question, "Are most people jealous?" in the attitude test mentioned above. Out of 140, 116 replied in the affirmative.

Elphinstone gives a characteristically good account of the origin and workings of Pukhtun envy: "Their independence and pretensions to equality make them view the elevation of their neighbors with jealousy, and communicate a deep touch of envy to their disposition. The idea that they are neglected or passed over, while their equals are attended to, will lead them to renounce a friendship of long standing, or a party to which they have been zealously attached" (1815: 1:329).

The importance of jealousy is shown by its unconscious working through the medium of the evil eye (nazar). Here envy accomplishes the downfall of others without even the intercession of volition by the one who envies. Every person is considered to have some ability to give the nazar to something by admiring or praising it. It is for this reason that new houses in Swat are disfigured by skulls of cows hanging from the eaves; fields are dotted with flapping black clothes; children have open holes in their ears to make them imperfect. These defacements aim to take the edge off the evil eye by rendering unsightly whatever might excite envy.

Children are particularly vulnerable to the evil eye, since it is said that their personalities are not yet rigid and hard, like an adults', but rather are fluid and open. Women greatly fear the working of the nazar and keep their young children wrapped with magic cords and holy amulets to ward off the baneful influence of envy.

Although everyone has some power of the evil eye, it is khan men who have the most nazar, and, among khans, those who most nearly fit the ideal image of what a khan should be have the strongest nazar. Tall, fair, blue-eyed men who are strong, rich, generous, pious, and brave may win terrible reputations for the evil eye. This involuntary power of envy is parallel to the real power of the big khan to practice betrayal in the realm of politics.

Interestingly, the evil eye is especially dangerous to one's own sons, and men avoid praising or fondling the future inheritors of their land for fear of sickening them. Only a few years ago, a local khan famous for his nazar forgot himself and praised the strength of his son in carrying a load of wood. The boy reportedly immediately fell unconscious and died. When the son of one of my acquaintances became sick, the man lamented that he had caused the illness by admiring the little boy's healthy cheeks. The tense relationship between father and son, with the son envied as the rival and eventual supplanter of the father, is here perfectly symbolized.

The ability to give the evil eye is publicly considered a burden, but in private men will gloat over the strength of their nazar. When an envied man falls from a high position, other men feel pride in the part their *nazar* took in his downfall. The whole village also has a collective ability to *nazar*, and this power is often cited as the cause for the ruin of an overbearing villager. Jealousy, symbolized in the evil eye, thus acts as the incentive in willful acts of betrayal and functions in fantasy to destroy those who are admired and envied (for theoretical statements on the evil eye, see the articles by Spooner, Maloney, Garrison and Arensberg in Maloney 1976; also Foster 1972).

But despite the leveling power of jealousy, men are still motivated to raise themselves above their peers through acquisition and hoarding. "The love of gain seems to be the Afgaun's ruling passion. . . . The influence of money on the whole nation is spoken of by those who know them best as boundless, and it is not denied by themselves" (Elphinstone 1815: 1:327).

Desire for wealth and the struggle to fulfill that desire is a major theme in Pukhtun life. Venture capitalism and entrepreneurship are nothing new in the village. Traders from Swat traveled as far as Yarkand in what is now China only thirty years ago, while big khans increased their wealth by taking caravans of rice and grain down to the plains to trade for cloth which could be exchanged in Swat for enormous profit. Fruit, timber, and honey were also traditionally exported in return for salt, indigo, spices, sugar, cotton, silk, shawls, and weapons.

After British irrigation schemes enriched Mardan and cut the market for exported food, the Swatis were obliged to experiment with other trade items. The recent craze for apple orchards, tomatoes, and opium shows that the entrepreneurial spirit is very much alive in the Swat Valley. Any successful venture immediately attracts a horde of imitators, and there is a thriving trade in the futures of commodities as diverse as mushrooms, lentils, emeralds, tobacco, and valerian root in the trading houses of the business capital of Mingora in Lower Swat.

The villagers of Shin Bagh try their best to earn extra money, though they are now far from the trade centers. Great poverty and a desire for gain has prompted many of them to leave their homes and join the massive labor migration to Karachi and the Middle East. In hopes of earning money, men are willing and eager to abandon their wives and children to work incredibly long hours under unbelievably arduous conditions. Labor recruiters in Karachi have informed me that their Arab contractors specify their preference for Pukhtun labor because of the stamina of the men and their willingness to work even in the most difficult circumstances. Within Pakistan, the most strenuous labor, such as cleaning of canals, is carried out by Pukhtun men. Other Pakistanis say that "only Pukhtuns can do such work," and indeed it does seem that only Pukhtuns are willing to undertake such difficult and ill-paid labor. The willingness of Pukhtun to work is certainly partly a result of poverty, but other Pakistanis are nearly as improverished. The Pukhtun themselves believe their ability to work is a result of their childhood training, and link it to a deep desire for acquiring and hoarding wealth, a desire doubtless fostered by the difficulty of keeping possessions as children.

Khushal Khan Khattak has commented ironically on his countrymen's love of gold in this quatrain:

What is it that works miracles? Why gold!
Gold makes the dead alive, the timid bold,
Changes maid to mistress, slave to lord,
And softens the hardest steel while yet cold.
(1965:200)

Love of gain once led many khans and other wealthy men to violate the precepts of Islam and charge high interest rates for loans. For a debt of 1,000 rupees, 20 maunds (approximately 20 bushels) of corn annually were demanded as interest, with a maund valued at 20 rupees. If only part of the interest was paid, the remainder would be added onto the debt. Thus, if only 10 maunds were given, the price of the remaining 10 owed would be added onto the original debt, giving a debt of 1,200 rupes upon which 24 maunds of corn would have to be paid the next year. Small landowners who needed cash for a court case, a wedding, or for warfare would often be forced to accept these onerous terms and, eventually, might be obliged to sell their land to clear the debt. The recent influx of money from migrant labor has increased the availability of liquid capital in the area, and interest rates have decreased as a consequence. The introduction of the bank and of government loan programs has also cut the importance of lending for interest, though it still occurs occasionally.

Acquisitiveness manifest itself in hoarding. "Most of the chiefs prefer hoarding up their great but useless treasures to the power, reputation and esteem which the circumstances of the times would enable them to command by moderate liberality." (Elphinstone 1815: 1:327). An amusing example of this tendency was found in the local bank president who carried his private accumulative character into his work, and hesitated to permit his customers take their money out of his bank. Hoarding wars with the entrepreneurial spirit and makes long-term investment a rarity. Return must be immediate or else absolutely certain for the Pukhtun to invest. He much prefers to buy land, if possible, or to leave his capital in the bank. As we have seen, friendly loans are very difficult to arrange, even (or, perhaps, especially) among close relatives, and men often prefer to borrow money at interest from the bank to borrowing at no interest from a cousin or uncle.

Money is not the only item which is hoarded. Status goods such as shoes, pretty clothes, and books are purchased in overabundance both by those who can afford them and those who cannot. They are then stored away and rarely used. Well-to-do women are great buyers of clothes, which they keep locked away in their private trunks. Most of these clothes are never worn at all, but are revealed to women visitors to excite their admiration and envy. The constant demands of the woman to have more clothes to put in her trunk are a major cause of fights between husband and wife. These demands are often completely unrealistic, since the women rely on the opinions of other women to ascertain value. They do not seem to take much account of their husbands' real income. If the worth of the husband's gift is judged low by other women, then the wife will cause a scene, throwing the gift in the dust and crying that she has been insulted by such a mean offering. The demand for gifts, coupled with the angry rejection of whatever is deemed inadequate, is an assertion of the wife's honor and pride and a humiliation for the husband. Men exhibit the same set of traits, but to a lesser degree. While only very poor men ever overtly demand a gift, all men make a practice of denigrating any present they receive.

Another expression of acquisitiveness, noted previously, is found in the widespread prevalence of theft. Theft is considered wrong only when one's own possessions are missing. One's relatives may be roundly cursed as thieves when, after a visit from them, a number of small items (and perhaps some which are not so small) are found to be missing. However, it is not considered wrong to steal some things back. Preferably, one should be able to steal more than was lost in the first place.

Children are actively encouraged to steal, both from other houses and from each other. Successful theft is considered a mark of commendable self-reliance on the part of the child, and the mother will defend it against all accusations, even swearing on the Koran as to the innocence of her light-fingered offspring.

Grown women are also sometimes thieves. When visiting relatives, their voluminous *sadars* are extremely useful for hiding stolen goods, and the man of the house will detail his wife to keep an eagle eye on the visitor. Within the walls of an extended family's compound nothing is safe. Personal possessions must be locked within a cabinet or else risk being snatched by a sister, brother, or in-law. If a man steals from his brother or father, he excuses himself with a laugh, saying the stolen item is a part of his share of the family property anyway. If captured, the thief who is a close relative (as is usually the case, since only close relatives have access to the house) will simply return the things he or she has stolen. Or the thief may try to brazen it out, claiming that the chicken, or shawl, or teacup is really his or her own, and is simply being reclaimed.

While men steal only outside their own nuclear family, women also appropriate from their own husbands. The woman's chore is the cleaning of grain, and she will often secrete as much as she dares in a hidden place to sell privately for her own pocket money. The husband considers this theft, but the wife considers it her just dues for her work.

Servants also steal, as do workers, and the khan must carefully oversee all work to prevent pilferage. When a servant or worker is caught stealing he may be insulted and dismissed, but he is not beaten. The offense is not serious enough to warrant violence.

Professional thievery is considered a somewhat low but not greatly dishonorable occupation and young men who cannot extract money from their fathers sometimes steal cattle or break into the stores (*dukans*) of neighboring villages. Daring theft is admired as showing courage and resourcefulness. Thirty years ago, prior to the imposition of the state, robbery was a way of life for many khans. With their armed retainers they plundered caravans and took whatever food and cattle they liked from their weaker neighbors. A man's reputation derived, in large measure, from his ability to organize and implement such raids, which are now a thing of the past.

Although the days of raiding parties and ambushes are over, khans still demonstrate their power by simply taking whatever appeals to them in the village if it is held by someone weaker. If a khan sees a boy with an apple, he may take it without a word. If the wife of a poor man is delivering some bread, the khan may stop her and break off a piece. If he notices a handsome knife belonging to a member of his faction, he may demand it. These are relatively small things, but the khan may also take the wife or daughter of a weaker man as his concubine, or force a man off his land and claim it as his own. Taking land, women, and goods is a display of power which demonstrates the strength of the khan and the weakness of his inferiors who are compelled to accept these depredations. Acquisition, in the form of pure appropriation, indicates the might of the khan. In collecting things, he shows he has the requisite force to extract from others and validates his own position, for the power to take without return is the mark of his rank. It is for this reason that gifts are not acknowledged with gratitude, but rather with complaints. A gift is not taken by force, but is instead given from plenitude, indicating that the recipient is needy and, therefore, inferior. Complaints offset this implication and equalize the relationship.

If Pukhtun society fosters deceit and acquisitiveness, it also fosters violence. The Pukhtun themselves characterize one another as cruel, but those who are not violent are castigated as weaklings. Casual violence is regarded as a normal part of everyday life, and the use of force is considered a legitimate sensual pleasure. For example, in an incident in which several young men were beaten for illicitly taking a prostitute into the men's house, those who did not participate in meting out the punishment were upset. "We missed our chance to enjoy striking those boys," they lamented.

Casual violence is common, especially among the childrens' gangs. Fighting and displays of strength are the order of the day for the boys, who beat one another and the girls they run across. Adult feuds are often sparked by childrens' disputes, and a child's bloody nose can easily escalate into something really serious. Boys who have had an offer of friendship rejected or who are publicly humiliated (a favorite humiliation is pulling off the trousers) can also start serious trouble, and may even kill their tormentor.

Men are very rarely involved in public fights. In over a year and a half in the Swat Valley, I only saw men fighting once. The disputants were *tarburs* and old enemies. One claimed the other had insulted him. They were quickly separated by their Khan. Men are usually polite, even to enemies, because fights quickly jump to a dangerous level, since men carry knives and guns, which they do not hesitate to use to avenge any insult. Most violence between men is planned as revenge and is enacted from hiding. In the village streets, however, there is often the uncomfortable feeling that a dangerous fight might erupt at any moment. But ordinarily mens' casual violence is directed toward their inferiors, and especially toward children, who may be slapped hard if they get in the way while a man is walking down the street. Of course, the strength of the child's family may have something to do with whether he or she is slapped, but poor people's children are struck with impunity.

While men never fight unless in earnest, women sometimes wrestle playfully with one another. Men would not indulge in such play for fear it might develop into a real fight.

As we have seen, most of the violence of the society is meted out within the family. Children are punished by hard slaps across the face, punches, and kicks for minor infractions, such as stumbling or spilling something. Rigorous punishment is handed out by the husband to his wife, who reciprocates in kind. Fights between spouses usually begin with a long torrent of invective and complaint from the wife, whose skills at nagging have been honed by a lifetime of practice. The husband, less adept at verbal attacks, will eventually strike his wife, or she may work herself up to such a pitch that she makes the first move. In these fights, the man and wife slug it out like two amateur boxers. She struggles to tear his clothes and humiliate him, while he tries to hit her hard enough to silence her insults. A man may also throw stones at his wife, aiming at her face; or he may take a club, set aside especially for that purpose, and beat her. He must be careful not to kill his wife or injure her too severely, since that would involve her family in revenge, but scars, bruises, and perhaps a few minor broken bones are not considered particularly serious matters. These are seen as a normal part of married life, and women will point with some pride to the relics of their domestic battles.

Until recently, retainers and laborers were punished like children, i.e., by being tied up or beaten. Sometimes men were bound up for two days. With greater independence of servants and workers, these punishments have fallen into disuse. Still, beatings, houseburnings, and even murders are by no means rare when a *fakir* (landless laborer) tries to make a legal case against a khan. Violence and the control of violence remains the court of last resort in Swat.

Cruelty is also offered to animals, and a favorite children's sport is torturing the pye-dogs that infest the village by showing some food to the starving animal and then striking it when it comes close to eat. At the age of a year and a half, children are already amusing themselves by throwing stones at dogs.

Tenderness, is rarely, if ever, seen. Even in a romantic mood, the man communicates with his wife by bites and skin-twisting pinches. In language, invective and nagging is as common as praise is unusual. Toughness, the ability to bear suffering, and a willingness to inflict pain are all valued traits to the villagers, while kindness is a dangerous demonstration of weakness.

The ubiquitousness of violence and the acceptance of the pleasures to be found in the use of force, coupled with the stoicism children learn when they are beaten, gives the Pukhtun an attitude of bravery and heedlessness in deeds of valor. Yet, when it comes to defying custom, bravery vanishes. "A man may resist an army," states one proverb, "but he cannot resist the force of custom." The Pukhtun, and especially the khan, must observe the outward forms at all times, and the prime cause for punishing a boy is the boy's failure to maintain the proper Pukhtun posture and demeanor. As noted earlier, a boy who looked away when speaking to someone or who sucked his fingers in company would be severely punished and insulted. For an adult, any deviation from social norms results in ridicule and contempt from his fellows. A man who was overtly affectionate with his wife, a man who allowed his daughter to take a job, a man who sold a part of his land in order to go into business: all these men would be objects of ridicule, as they would for performing far less serious acts, such as shaving off one's beard or wearing a new style of hat. Custom and the pressure of the village can force men to act directly contrary to their own feelings. As examples: a man in a neighboring village was obliged to kill his wife, whom he loved, because village gossip accused her of being unfaithful; another man shot his own mother for the same reason; an educated khan who wanted schooling for his family of daughters gave up the idea for fear of shaming himself; a husband and wife who hated each other were compelled to live together because custom does not allow divorce. People sometimes curse the force of custom, but they do not seriously consider any alternatives.

Conformity accompanies a lack of innovation and creativity. Teaching is by rote, questioning is actively discouraged, and knowledge which is not directly instrumental in the struggle for survival is not pursued. Discussion among men revolves around crops, cattle, and political tactics, while the women gossip and talk about the failings of their men. Abstraction and thought which is not of the moment is unheard of. There is never any question that one's way of life is inevitable.

Among Pukhtun, shame is the most feared thing, for their self-esteem rests on their public enactment of given roles. The reason given for every failure to innovate is that "people will laugh at me behind my back." Exciting jealousy and envy, while dangerous, also validates a man's superiority. He is proud that others envy him. But if a man becomes ridiculous, he cannot bear it. As a trivial example of this pervasive stance, a man preferred walking four miles to work or else catching the bus rather than riding his bicycle. This was because his brother had a motorcycle and he did not want to risk being compared to his brother. Fear of being shamed or thought a fool gives men a morbid fear of failure and a timorousness in regard to custom, which is in strong contrast to their martial air and attitude of independence and individualism. The freedom from restraint that the Pukhtun are so proud of is actually the freedom from paying tribute or acknowledging another as a superior. It is a purely negative concept, an absence of ties. But, among themselves, freedom is rigidly circumscribed by the rules of the social order which are more unbreakable than any government edict. Entrepreneurship and innovative farming techniques are allowed, if they succeed, since they propel men toward the shared goal of domination and power; but change in personal relationships is an impossibility.

If men fear being laughed at, they greatly desire to laugh at others. Men state that their aim in life is to avoid the derision of their brothers and the only way to do this is to rise above the brothers, and so be in a position to do the sneering. From the position of dominance one need no longer fear shame, but rather can shame those who are inferior. This internal rivalry and one-upmanship is a pervasive theme, as Bellew notes: "Even amongst themselves, each man considers himself equal to, if not better than, his neighbor." (1864:209). Much of a man's life is spent trying to prove his own superiority.

The Pukhtun, therefore, has none of the self-effacing character made famous by studies of "peasant mentality" (Foster 1967). Instead, at every opportunity, he seeks to show himself as a great man, a man to be reckoned with, and will exaggerate his successes and lord them over his inferiors, even at the cost of greater demands on his resources from his dependents. This is called being *mas,* and is an accusation leveled at all well-to-do or lucky men. The proud Pukhtun struts and makes a show of ignoring his less fortunate former peers.

Part of this proud posture is the stance of total independence and self-reliance which the Pukhtun affects:

If it means an obligation
Eat no man's sweetmeats, Khushal;
A crust of dry bread is much better
Than any sweets in such a case.
(Khattak 1965:48)

Men continually strive to give the impression that they are completely autonomous and self-contained. Yet, as they attempt to avoid dependence, they seek to make others dependent upon them, thereby demonstrating their own individual power and dominance. The man who has a record of achievement therefore may be avoided assiduously by his peers who do not wish to enact the humiliating role of sycophant. The arrogance of the successful man limits further success, since it offends the sensitive pride of potential followers. It is assumed that followings are purchased and not won over by admiration and respect. For example, when some men were informed that the daughter of Mr. Bhutto, then leader of Pakistan, had been elected head of the Oxford Student Union, the immediate response was that "she must have given many presents."

Arrogance is also expressed in egotism and lack of concern for others. The individual is interested in himself and his own personal elevation, and resents the good fortune of anyone else. The traits of deceitfulness, envy, and greed which I have already mentioned may be seen, in some sense, as emanations of the egoistic self-interest of the Pukhtun, and especially of the elite khans. Perhaps the most graphic example of the extremes of egocentricity in the Swat valley was told to me by a doctor in the main hospital in Saidu Sherif. The doctor informed me that conditions in patients who required a blood transfusion were quite often fatal in Swat due to the lack of blood donations. Blood had to be imported from other parts of Pakistan, diluted, and built up with chemicals to reach even half the recommended hemoglobin count. The reason for the dearth of blood was, quite simply, the unwillingness of the patient's family and neighbors to be donors. Although assured that the blood will replenish itself, people are unwilling to make even a temporary sacrifice to save the life of a close kinsman. According to the doctor, people say, "Let them die. I will not weaken myself." (For an interesting discussion of donation of blood as a metaphor for social responsibility, see Titmuss 1971). For the Pukhtun to give to another is to weaken the self and conversely, to take is to build one's strength.

The life of the Pukhtun is thus characterized by deceit, envy, acquisitiveness expressed in entrepreneurship, hoarding, and thievery; violence, conformity, and the morbid fear of being shamed; and, finally, arrogance, which reveals itself in proud domination over the weak, and in a stance of total independence and egotism. These are behaviors inculcated by childhood training, and they are necessary for survival within the social structure and physical constraints of Swat. I am not claiming here that the villagers are "naturally" cruel and greedy. In fact, they are capable of great kindness and self-sacrifice. Nor am I even asserting that they have characters which are molded by circumstances to be violent, rigid, and egotistic. My point is simply that people are trained to behave in a certain fashion, and to have attitudes which are consistent with their behavior. Individual personalities are varied, but actions are stereotyped, patterned by the framework in which they take place. In all societies, sane people act in a manner compatible with the pathways offered by the cultural matrix, and in Swat the cultural demands are severe indeed.

6. The Code of Honor

Only the man who follows Pukhtunwali [the code of honor] can be called a Pukhtun. (Pukhtun proverb)

. . . one of the most remarkable characteristics of the Afghauns is their hospitality. The practice of this virtue is so much a national point of honour, that their reproach to an inhospitable man, is that he has no Pooshtoonwullee. . . . All persons indiscriminately are entitled to profit by this practice; and a man, who travelled over the whole country without money, would never be in want of a meal, unless perhaps in towns. (Elphinstone 1815: 1:295)

It is the greatest of affronts to an Afghaun to carry off his guest; but his indignation is never directed at the guest who quits him, but at the person who invites him away." (Elphinstone 1815: 1:297)

I HAVE now arrived at the crucial juncture of my argument. To this point, I have drawn an unrelenting portrait of the Pukhtun forced by circumstances to endless relations of opposition, contempt, and hostility. It is a picture that Hobbes would recognize. The Yusufzai, given their social order, are seemingly driven by a "perpetual and restless desire of power after power that ceases only in death" (Hobbes 1958:86). It is a society where apparently

> there is no way for any man to secure himself so reasonable as anticipation—that is, by force or wiles to master the persons of all men he can . . . [where] men have no pleasure, but on the contrary a great deal of grief, in keeping company where there is no power able to overawe them all. For every man looks that his companion should value him at the same rate he sets upon himself; and upon all signs of contempt or undervaluing naturally endeavors, as far as he dares (which among them that have no common power to keep them in quiet is far enough to make them destroy each other), to extort a greater value from his contemners by damage and from others by the example . . . [where there is] continual fear and danger of violent death; and the life of man solitary, poor, nasty, brutish, and short. (Hobbes, 1958:106–7)

But this "war of every man against every man" (1958:108), while an accurate picture, is not a complete one. As Hobbes himself recognized, man, even in his hypothetical "state of nature," lives according to codes of honor, though the form honor takes will be consistent with men's lives, "that is, to abstain from cruelty, leaving to men their lives and instruments of husbandry" (Hobbes 1958:140). Black-Michaud (1975) has also called attention to the importance of honor in societies characterized by feud, and Bourdieu (1974) has given eloquent testimony on the concept of *nif* (point of honor; also, the nose) among the Kabyle. Swat has its own code of honor, called Pukhtunwali, which is perhaps the most formal known among Middle Eastern tribal groups.

This code is far more complex than that hypothesized by Hobbes, and covers behavior on all public occasions. The demands of this code are well known to all, and provide a charter for public action which both ratifies the necessities of the social structure and conceals its contradictions. It is by reference to Pukhtunwali that the villager will define himself and his culture to outsiders, and it is by adherence to Pukhtunwali that a man makes his claim to a place of dignity among his peers.

Looking from the perspective of the previous chapters, some aspects of Pukhtunwali seem quite anomalous indeed. As Bellew wrote, "The existence of such sentiments of honor among them is very strange, for they glory in being robbers, admit they are avaricious, and cannot deny the character they have acquired for faithlessness" (1864:211). Particularly odd are two of the so-called three pillars of Pukhtunwali. These are the three aspects of the code that the Pukhtun themselves see as essential to their way of life. A man who does not act upon these focal rules has, in local thought, no right to call himself a Pukhtun. These pillars are said to be *badal, melmastia, nanawatia,* or revenge, hospitality, and refuge. Revenge makes immediate sense since, as discussed in chapter 3, it is an integrating and necessary value in a segmentary lineage system, providing the basis for shaping what seems at first glance to be a world of pure anarchy. But what of hospitality and refuge? Although they are seen by the Pukhtun as of prime importance in ratifying his definition of an ideal self, they appear to stand quite outside the main thrust of the social order.

The three pillars, though they are the heart of the code, do not exhaust its range, and texts have even been written elaborating the many fine points of Pukhtunwali, much as the medieval principles of chivalry, which so resemble Pukhtunwali, were elaborated by scholars and troubadours. The points most often mentioned, aside from the three pillars, are equality, respect, loyalty, pride, bravery, purdah, pursuit of romantic encounters, the worship of Allah and, most importantly, the unselfish love for the friend.

The question this chapter has to ask is whether these aspects of Pukhtunwali can fit within the world of oppositions and jealous hostilities which I have depicted as characteristic of Swati life. My answer, as the reader knows, is that the principles of the code can be shown to be rooted in the social order, that is, except for the principles of hospitality, refuge, and the various forms of romance, worship and, especially, friendship. In my view, most of Pukhtunwali is an expression of, or a mask for, the realities of the highly politicized, isolated, and competitive life of the Pukhtun man.

In order to demonstrate my point, I will discuss each aspect of the code of honor in turn (omitting revenge, which has been dealt with elsewhere), showing the working out of the injunctions and connecting each particular rule to the underlying order (and underlying contradictions) implicit in the segmentary system.

Equality is a central value in the segmentary order. The belief that all men who are of the Pukhtun lineage are, at least potentially, coequals is deeply ingrained in local consciousness. As Black (1972) and Ahmed (1980) have shown, this ideal persists even when actual hierarchization has occurred. Why this should be so has, I think, been interestingly discussed by Salzman (1978b) who argues that in the long run, historically, segmentary societies build up hierarchies as the central state strengthens, but the hierarchies crumble as the center periodically disintegrates. The concept of equality, therefore, is a realistic notion which maintains an alternative social order during relatively short term periods of state domination. This fits with my own data on Swat and is, of course, a restatement of Ibn Khaldun's cyclical theory of history.

Rituals expressing Pukhtun equality are quite pervasive. The most obvious are the elaborate greetings men offer one another whenever they chance to meet. The man who is walking toward the village must be greeted with "Baxair raghli" (You are welcomed), to which the response is "Khodai de obaxa" (God bless you), or "Loy shi" (Become great) if the person is a child. Failure to give or return a greeting is a serious matter and never occurred in my experience.

If the two men meeting have not seen one another for some time, the greeting is extended by an embrace. The men will hug one another three times, fervently inquiring of one another's health and families. These inquiries are not answered, but rather are repeated in a sort of antiphony between the two men.

The politeness and ceremoniousness of Pukhtun greetings was noted with surprise over one hundred years ago by the rather sour H. W. Bellew: "The Yusufzai observe many outward forms of courtesy towards each other and strangers that one would not expect in a people living the disturbed and violent life they do" (1864:213).

This unexpected courtesy is not reserved only for one's actual equals. Instead, it is a gesture extended to all, from the richest to the poorest. The landowning powerful aristocrats of the society, the khans, feel no compunction at embracing the lowliest shoemaker or barber. There is no concept of corporate pollution in Pukhtun society. A striking incidence of the enactment of the ritual of equality occured in Karachi when I was working with Pukhtun college students, all from elite families. One of the boys introduced me to a young man from Bajaur. Only much later did I learn that the man from Bajaur was not a student or an elite khan. Instead, he came from a landless family and made his living shining shoes. But there was no evident indication of his inferior position in the attitude or behavior of the other young men or in his demeanor toward them.

Equality is expressed in public discourse as well. In discussions men of any class feel free to offer their opinions, even if they differ from the opinions of their patrons, and talk is remarkably free and unrestrained by servility among the Pukhtun.

Equality is also displayed in feasting at weddings, circumcisions, and other celebrations. As mentioned above, corporate pollution has no part in Pukhtun life. All people eat together at feasts, and there is no aversion to sharing food with Christians or even to accepting the hospitality of local Hindus—though people say they would not eat with a sweeper, but this statement has never been tested, since there are no sweepers in the village.

Another demonstration of equality is found in attendance at the mosque. All men mingle in worship, following the Islamic precept that all Muslims are brothers and coequals. Any man who wishes can volunteer to stir the village with the call to prayer. Men of any background can study the Koran and become religious teachers. Prior to the advent of the Badshah, and now, perhaps, once again, men of any background could become mystically inspired and gain followings as pirs. The Badshah's own grandfather, the famed Akhund of Swat, was himself born a poor cowherd.

Not only religious men can develop hierarchies out of the egalitarian structure, though their hierarchies are doubtless among the most durable (Hammoudi 1980). As we have seen, the secular khans and, in fact, all the Yusufzai, also aspire to positions of leadership. The possibility of hierarchy is implicit in the structure, since elders have precedence over their juniors, and the principle of respect, which is the converse of the principle of equality, expresses this internal differentiation. It is a public statement of the potential for hierarchy. The respect offered to a khan is modeled after the respect offered to an elder and, in fact, the term for an elder and for a powerful leader are the same, *mushur,* while a follower or a younger person are both called *kushur.*

The principle of rank is seen alongside the principle of equality. Although all men eat together at public functions, the seating is arranged so that the *mushurs* get the best seats and the choicest pieces of meat. When a powerful man enters the *hujera,* the other men stand for him and do not sit until the *mushur* has seated himself. In former times, the *mushur* of the *hujera* had a thronelike chair which physically raised him above his cohorts. Or, if the chair were absent, the *kushurs* would turn over their cots and sit near the ground. The *mushur* also had a special turban which symbolized his position.

Within the mosque there is also precedence. The *mushur* of the congregation stands in a place of respect behind the imam during services. He also controls the utilization of the funds collected by the mosque from its parishioners.

However, in general, powerful men are not easily distinguished from their dependents. All men wear essentially the same clothes; the *mushur* does not have any spectacular trappings to set him off from other men.

But if the political *mushur* is not obviously marked, respectful relations between elder and younger are very much in evidence. The principle of respect for an elder often overrides other differences, so that a young khan will address an old landless laborer as "ji," or "sir." Among the elite landowning clans, such as the Malik *khel* of Shin Bagh, even slight age seniority is acknowledged in conversation by the avoidance of the *mushur's* real name. Instead, standardized titles are used which often refer to some physical attribute of the *mushur*. Common titles are Spin Dada (White Father), Lala Gul (Lala Flower), Tor Khan (Black Khan), Khiesta Dada (Beautiful Father), and the like. The *mushur*, on the other hand, always uses the junior's real name.

The prohibition against using the real name of one's *mushur* is strongest in the case of one's own father. Traditionally-minded men will refuse to give their father's name even when the old man is absent. They will sometimes profess not to know the father's real name.

Women, after marriage, are addressed by younger members of the husband's family by an honorific name, always ending in "bibi." These names often commemorate the village the incoming girl hails from. Men avoid referring to their wives, and the polite circumlocution simply denotes the wife and children as "kor," or house. If pressed, a man may mention his wife as "the mother of my son so and so." Women also refer to themselves and to other women by this form of teknonymy, but not so frequently as do the men. But in the home, husband and wife call each other familiarly by name. Women, who are rarely if ever in public, are not as careful as men are about formal names. Elder women are sometimes addressed by name. Children, on the other hand, are strictly trained always to show respect for all elders. Older relatives are addressed by their relationship term followed by a "ji" to indicate respect. Thus, the mother is always called "maji," the elder sister is "xorji," and so on.

Besides address, respect is also shown in the circumspection and grave demeanor which must be displayed in relations between elders and juniors. The attitude of restraint, which begins when children reach the age of nine or ten, is reciprocal, unlike the usage of address terms. Younger people must not play or joke in front of their elders, nor should the *mushurs* allow a break in their own respectable mien before their juniors. The juniors should stand when an elder arrives, offer the best seat available and, if they are quite junior, maintain respectful silence. When boys become men, they are allowed to speak and even argue heatedly with their elders, but never to be overly familiar or insulting. If the discussion goes too far, the elder can silence his juniors simply by calling attention to the speaker's inferior age ranking.

Not only should men display deference to their elders, but they must also refrain from enjoying themselves within their sight. The spectacle of a forty-year-old khan with several wives and a dozen children hurriedly snuffing out a cigarette or hiding his chewing tobacco at the entrance of his father is typical. The elder also should not indulge himself in front of his juniors. For this reason music parties are always attended only by men of approximately the same age.

Deference is not only shown by constraint and displays of abstinence, but also by the offering of services. Children act as silent servants and younger brothers are commandeered to prepare the *hujera* for guests, help set up feasts, and perform other menial duties. Requests from the elder should be complied with immediately. It is in this context that the younger boys and men of a household are introduced to a guest as "your slaves."

While both equality and respect express contradictory, but very real, implications of the social structure, the principle of loyalty is an attempt at reconciliation of these opposing and contradictory tendencies. Given the premise of equality, men are able to develop hierarchies only on the basis of ties of personal loyalty. Even men with great ability, wealth, and power cannot compel others to follow. Poor men can and do shift allegiances if they feel it is to their own advantage. Of course, powerful men can use many methods to place the weak under obligation, but there is no sense that followers are somehow naturally inferior, and there is a continual competition among the khans for followings, as Barth has ably documented (1965). Since leadership is, in reality, so ephemeral and followings so fluid, there is a great emphasis by a man with pretensions to leadership on displays of loyalty by his adherents. Only by such performances can the leader feel his position is secure.

Previously, loyalty was demonstrated by attendance at the *hujera* of one's khan. The khan provided a place to sleep, food, entertainment, and protection. In return, the men who stayed in the *hujera* were declaring their support for the khan in any battle or dispute that may arise.

In the period of my fieldwork, the men's houses had decreased in importance, but demonstrations of loyalty continued within them and within the *betəks* or with individuals. Men come and sit or lie on cots while poorer men squat on the ground. Politics and local affairs are freely discussed and the host's opinion is asked. Perhaps a quarrel will be aired and the host will make a conciliatory decision. One of the poorer men may give the host a rubdown while looking lovingly at him.

It is expected that certain men, kinsmen and dependents of the host, will turn up every night to talk or simply listen, smoke hashish (*charas*), take chewing tobacco (*nəswar*), and perhaps hear the news and Pukhto songs on the radio. Often long hours are spent in silence, just sitting. Yet, if one of the men rises to leave, there is a flurry of protests. If a man does not turn up one night, an excuse is required. The men were amazed when I told them that in America we do not visit the same people every night. This seemed impossibly rude and dangerous, in that divided loyalties would be set up. When a man visits another within the village, he is expressing loyalty and membership in the faction of his host. If he visits someone else, he is announcing that he is considering switching sides.

Loyalty is further demonstrated by work. The loyal faction member will help his leader with ploughing, wall-building, and other labor, as well as providing physical force in a dispute. In return, the patron can be asked for loans or to intercede with authority on behalf of his faction members.

The pride and bravery of the Pukhtun is also connected to the pivotal conflict of equality and hierarchy. In the real world, a man who does not present a proud and even insolent figure is doomed to be taken advantage of by his more aggressive neighbors. Equality means that each

A poor herdsman.

man in theory has an equal chance to subdue his fellows. Each man struggles to conquer and rise in the shallow hierarchies the system allows. Although he may not succeed, the Pukhtun can, at the least, hope to ruin his enemies as well. Only pride, courage, and an implacable belief in one's own honor enables a man to continue the eternal and usually fruitless battles of ordinary life. A man without bravery and pride is soon destroyed, as there is no room for the weak-willed in Swat.

Pride is demonstrated in the ordinary bearing of the men, who carry themselves erect, walk with a swagger, and look one another straight in the eye. There is no evident servility or caste consciousness. "Every Euzofzye is filled with the idea of his own dignity and importance. . . . Their pride appears in the seclusion of their women, in the gravity of their manners, and in the high terms they speak of themselves and their tribe, not allowing even the Dooraunees to be their equals" (Elphinstone 1815: 2:32).

Even impoverished men carry themselves like royalty. If a man is accused of dishonorable dealing, he will defend himself, not by evidence, but by a recitation of his lineage and the cry of "Am I not a Pukhtun!" Legends of the doings of the ancients are told and retold, illustrating the generosity and courage of the lineage. It is assumed that the Pukhtun are more intelligent, braver, more hospitable, more religious, and more of everything than any other people. Among Pukhtun, as Elphinstone noted, the Yusufzais claim first place. Among the Yusufzais, the khans of Upper Swat claim the most illustrious heritage, and among these the Malik *khel* of Shin Bagh assert their ascendancy. Each famous clan pursues the same line of reasoning and argues the aristocracy and superiority of its own ancestors. Even poorer clans have great genitors to look back to and regard their lowered state as the work of an unfortunate fate.

Seclusion of women, as Elphinstone noted above, is an indication of pride and family honor. Only the poorest, who cannot afford to do otherwise, allow their women to leave the compound and work. In the building of a house, the first part constructed is the compound wall, to insure the privacy of the women. When the British first invaded Swat, it was said that they were violating the purdah of the valley. In 1977 the reformist political party was accused of wanting to eliminate purdah. This is an emotional subject, and one which lies close to the heart of every Pukhtun. It is believed that rigid seclusion of women is enjoined in the Koran and that the licentious nature of women (who are seen as being ten times as passionate sexually as men) would compel them to cuckold their husbands were the women not kept under close guard. Furthermore, in secluding his women, the Pukhtun demonstrates his power over them by totally removing them from circulation.

Purdah is kept very strictly in Upper Swat and Kohistan. Local doctors report many cases of osteomalacia among the local women. This severe bone disorder is a direct result of their lack of exposure to sunlight. The village of Shin Bagh, as an aristocratic village, is famed for the harshness of its purdah. As a result, women are rarely seen in the village streets unless they are very poor. The Pukhtun women go out only to special events such as the celebration of a wedding, a circumcision, or a funeral. Even then, they must beg permission from their husbands, who can refuse on a whim. When they do leave the house, they are enveloped in a voluminous *sadar* which covers them from head to foot like a shroud. As they walk down the village streets, accompanied by a child or an old servant lady, (a man would never accompany his wife), the women efface themselves, looking demurely away and covering their faces if a man chances to pass by. If a woman reveals herself to a man outside her or her husband's family, or if she speaks to a man beyond her wall, she is liable to be harshly punished.

The most popular Pukhto song during my fieldwork in 1977 was the story of a woman who, moved by the pleas of a beggar, revealed her arm as she handed him alms outside her compound door. The beggar, enraptured, went into the fields where he told a group of men what had happened. One of the men was the woman's husband. He hurried back to his house, asked his wife if the story were true and, finding that she had indeed broken purdah, regretfully shot her. The song, with its catchy beat and rather cheerful tone, captures the Pukhtun's own notion of ideal behavior. Naturally, reality does not always live up to the ideal, but, as Pennell (1909) reports, women who had their noses sliced off as punishment for breaches of purdah were often patients at his clinic. I don't know if this form of mutilation was ever practiced in Swat, but my informants do recall women being stoned to death only thirty years ago, and men do keep clubs to keep their wives in line. For a woman who will not mend her ways, the gun still remains as the ultimate sanction, and women are killed by cuckolded husbands (though less often than the Pukhtun themselves like to claim, since in reality a man may prefer to send the woman home to her parents or to her *mamagan* rather than take the risk of shooting her).

Women are regarded as chattel. This view of women is reinforced by the institution of bride price, which severs the incoming woman from her natal family, and the prohibition on divorce, which prevents her from ever cutting her ties with her husband. The prohibition exemplifies the ideological position of the wife as totally submissive and dependent.

The wife acts out the ritual of subordination to her husband by never asking him any questions and by allowing him his freedom. Wives should not be jealous and, in actuality, do not seem perturbed at their husbands' extramarital affairs. Men with guest houses or guest rooms may occasionally have parties with prostitutes or promiscuous girls of the village. Such entertainments are regarded by the wives as the prerogatives of their husbands. Nor should a wife even inquire as to her husband's whereabouts. A sophisticated Pukhtun, who had lived in England for some time, told me about his affair with an English girl. He admired her intelligence and beauty, but could not accept her questioning him about his activities. Eventually he broke off his relationship with her and married his cousin.

The women and girls express their deference to the men in other ways as well. The men and boys are routinely given all the meat, the choicest curd, the fruit, and anything else which is considered delicious. Except for special occasions, the girls and women wear tattered clothes, while the boys and the men will usually have on relatively new, clean outfits. The best bed in the house (aside from the bed for guests) is reserved for the husband. The wife is expected to give up her jewelry, her only personal wealth, to her husband if he should demand it.

Men demonstrate their view of women not only by keeping the women in strict isolation from other men, but also by avoiding all reference to women in conversation. The visitor, lounging in the *hujera* and talking of politics and genealogies, might easily forget that women even exist were he not reminded of them by the pot of tea which miraculously appears at intervals. Although ordinary conversation is peppered with sexual references, actual talk about sex is rare and confined to joking about the size of a promiscuous woman's genitals. Men much prefer to ignore women altogether whenever possible.

The purdah of Swat goes far beyond anything enjoined in the Koran. It is stretched to signify a prohibition on divorce, a taboo on female

Women in purdah preparing a meal.

inheritance of land, and the complete dominance of husband over wife, all of which are contrary to Koranic law. The severity of purdah and the violence with which women are treated are also extraordinary, even in comparison with other Pukhtun areas.

Looking at purdah within the context of the social structure and exchange pattern, the peculiarities of the custom become more intelligible. Women in Swat function as counters in a game of marriage exchange and, as such, threaten the image of the self-sufficient patriline. As Murphy and Kasdan have noted (1959), this threat can be offset in two ways, both of which occur in Swat. The first is by endogamy (FBD marriage) and the second is by debasing female status. The integrity of the woman's lineage is maintained by completely cutting the woman off from her lineal estate through the prohibition on divorce, the levirate, and the ban on female inheritance of land. Strict seclusion of women is an emblem of the control of the household men, and emphasizes the men's denial of women's status in order to maintain patrilineal unity.

The ideology of the monolithic patriline, which is threatened by the hateful necessity of marriage, is demonstrated and ratified by the isolation and low status of Swati women. The strict Swati purdah is a reflection of the conflicts of a society torn between the ideology of patrilineal unity demanded by the segmentary order and the undermining influence of marriage. Because the threat that women offer is a serious threat, the tensions that attend the essential exchange of women are also great. These stresses are counterbalanced by relegation of women to low status, rigid purdah, and the severance of the woman from her patrilineal estate. The disruptive effect of female exchange, felt most at marriage but continuing within each nuclear household, is publicly negated by Swati custom, which seeks to lower women to the status of chattel by the institution of bride price. At the same time, the strictness of seclusion admits, by its very harshness, the potential power of women to challenge the social order. A woman, like all dangerous creatures, must be kept well caged otherwise she may break out and render her husband *begherata*—without honor. Purdah in the Swati context is therefore formed by the social framework I have outlined, and is a reflection of the tension implicit in the exchange of women within a strictly patrilineal society; a tension made even more severe by the rivalries inherent in the land-based economic structure and the scarcity of land.

The romance of the Pukhtun is the mirror image of purdah. It pervades local poetry and legend:

> Your curls are a swing,
> Your forelock a snare,
> Your face a lamp
> That draws the moth . . .

> If the world asks about my sickness
> And the one who has stricken me asks not,
> Then what use are all the others?
> (Sher Azim Khan, Malik *khel)*

The romantic stories of the region often concern star-crossed lovers who die of love but who never actually have sexual intercourse. In real life, men are perfectly capable of falling deliriously in love with a barely glimpsed eye or an accidentally revealed ankle. Romance can never be with one's own spouse or fiancée, but must be with a mysterious stranger. In stories, the beloved woman is always one of the elite khans, but in reality the khans usually guard their women too well to allow for many actual love affairs, though secret passions may run high. Romance which ends in a sexual encounter is most often with girls from poor households whose fathers do not have the strength or the courage to protect them. Or, occasionally, a father may hope for some remuneration from his daughter's lover. Men who cannot protect the chastity of their women are considered to be without honor. Sometimes, a poor and weak man will acquiesce to his daughter's defloration, either from fear or cupidity. But more often an affair, even with a poor girl, is a risky business that can end in murder. Nonetheless, romantic adventures are a favorite sport of the Pukhtun young men. But it is not a one-sided pursuit. Women, both married and single, may be passionate as well, and sometimes take the active role in arranging assignations with a desirable man. In the histories of romance that I collected, I was surprised at how often the man was essentially entrapped by a single-minded, scheming woman. She, of course, is much braver than her lover, since she is far more likely to suffer if the romance is discovered. But my impression is that very few of the khan women are so careless of their honor, while women of poorer families are far more apt to have affairs.

Love affairs may be numerous, but they are rarely long-lived. The spice is in the chase and the unveiling, not in the subsequent mundane sexual encounters. The girls often have greater hopes from their romances, and try their best to entrap their lovers into marriage. One method for accomplishing this end is for the girl to present herself, with her newborn baby, at her lover's house. He is then obliged to take her in and acknowledge her as his wife. However, this technique is too shameful for most women. They either practice abortion or abandon their illegitimate children.

No doubt the distasteful complications of reality explain why the romantic tales of the Pukhtun inevitably end in the deaths of the lovers. In death the romance lives, whereas in marriage romance is dead. This concept of romance is not far from that of the medieval French troubadors, who borrowed it from the Muslims of medieval Spain and North Africa. It also resembles the notions of romance found among other Muslim peoples, such as the Marri Baluch (Pehrson 1966).

However, the Pukhtun code of romantic love differs from that of the troubadors and the Baluch in one essential: perhaps because of pervasive relations of hostility between men and women, the loved one for Pukhtun men is quite often a boy or handsome young man. Homoerotic relationships were much more common a generation ago than they are now, since Western influence has brought a sense of shame about homosexuality, at least among the more educated.

Formerly, guests in the *hujera* were entertained and sexually serviced by dancing boys, and a powerful man might keep several passive homosexuals (*bedagh*) in his retinue. No aspersions were cast on men who had sexual intercourse with a *bedagh* and, in fact, anal sex with a passive homosexual is still considered by some men to be the most satisfying form of congress. In contrast, anal intercourse with women is strictly forbidden, unlike the practice of the ancient Greeks (see Dover 1978). But even those men who prefer sex with a *bedagh* are still expected to father children, and it is shameful for a man to be impotent (though it is not grounds for divorce). Men who are *bedaghs* are laughingstocks, but they also marry and are not socially ostracized. In Shin Bagh, the lover of a local *bedagh* became the lover of the man's wife and sired his children. This was thought disgraceful but no overt action was taken. It is noteworthy that in this and other similar cases, local mythology had it that the husband had become *bedagh* as a result of his wife's promiscuity. "He loved her too much and let her have other men in the house, and so he became *bedagh.*" If a man is too fond of his wife, she will emasculate him. Whether this sequence is actually true or not, I have no idea, but it is firmly believed by the Pukhtun themselves. There are some men, however, who have been supposedly enchanted by a male lover and rendered permanently *bedagh,* while others are thought to have simply been born *bedaghs.*

In 1977, homosexuality was very much less in evidence in Swat than it had been. Dancing girls had replaced dancing boys, and transvestites had become rare. Nonetheless, the first sexual experience of many, if not most boys, is with one of their passively inclined peers, or with an older man who is a confirmed *bedagh.* Older men still may cultivate a handsome young protégé who will accompany them everywhere, though the practice is hardly universal. Male beauty is much admired and the same word, *xkuili,* or beautiful, is applied to both men and women. Pukhtun poetry is often frankly homoerotic, following the Persian model.

Yet the sexual element is hardly the foremost aspect of male–male relationships. The word *minae* (love) and *yar* or *dost* (friend) can be applied not only to sexual relationships, but also to worship and, most properly, to friendship, which has no sexual content.

In the religious poetry and prose of the Pukhtun, God is viewed not as the Father, but as the Friend and Lover.* In former times, worship was often directed toward men who styled themselves as God's representatives on earth. These men, who are called pirs, built followings by performance of miracles and inducing ecstacy through chants and dancing. In Upper Swat, a famous pir named Kohnawal inspired his followers to the extent that some of them are said to have killed themselves in his honor, expecting rebirth. When he died, his disciples went to the extreme of praying toward his tomb rather than to Mecca. This heresy was only stopped at the intercession of a more orthodox pir, the great Pir Baba.

In the saintly cults of the Pukhtun, the aspect of a personal and immediate relationship with God the Friend and Lover was stressed, to the exclusion of the mundane round of orthodox ritual and recitation. Allah was often described in explictly homoerotic terms, and the quest of the initiate was a complete loss of self in God's love, just as the lover seeks oblivion in the embrace of his beloved or the friend in total devotion to his comrade.

* Conrad Arensberg notes that the Zoroastrian term for God is "Friend." He has also suggested that the men's house, where violence is absolutely prohibited and where hospitality and male community are celebrated in group rituals is, in a Durkheimian sense, a more authentic church than the often contentious mosques (personal communication).

Intoxicated by love
My consciousness has vanished . . .
(Rahman Baba 1977:103)

Even those who did not go so far as to join an ecstatic sect still paid service to the personal concept of God in their respect for holy men and their tombs. These tombs formed important places of pilgrimage in Swat, and were visited by supplicants every Thursday. Offerings were left and gifts given to the tomb guardians in the hope that the dead pir would grant a boon.

At the time of the fieldwork, saintly cults had greatly decreased, and some tombs in Shin Bagh have been encroached upon for building space, but it is still believed that the desecrated saints will punish the sacreligious builders. The local tombs have only a few supplicants, always women, visiting them, though the major shrine of Pir Baba continues to be popular. Orthodox religion has triumphed for the moment, and the emphasis is on prayer and repetition of the Koran rather than on ecstasy and mystical union. The idea of God the Friend remains current, however, and the repentant sinner hopes that Allah will be merciful, understanding, and forgiving, just as a friend would be.

Like the relationship with a lover or a friend, the relation with the Deity is also ambiguous, for the petitioner knows he has sinned, and he has to hope for absolution. But he also fears that dispensation will not be granted.

A man is a fool who seeks forgiveness
When his own heart is a stone.
(Sher Azim Khan, Malik *khel*)

Both the notion of romance and the concept of worship are derived from the image of the friend, who, as we shall see, is a more perfect image of the Pukhtun's desire to have a relationship without the taint of rivalry or domination. Romance and worship are secondary because both contain elements of disjuncture, hierarchy, and separation. Romance, in Pukhtun verse and myth, is never consummated, for consummation means the end of the quest and the loss of the ideal. In sexual union the Pukhtun see domination and subordination. This duality destroys the essence of the hoped-for relation, that is, complete mutuality. For this reason, unlike the Greek case, friendship is never mingled with homosexual love affairs, since sex affirms separateness. Lovers cannot truly be friends.

In a similar manner, the union with the Deity, which is at the heart of the Sufi mode of worship, is usually feared by the Pukhtun, since God is clearly superior to the worshipper, just as the dominant lover is superior to the submissive beloved. Only in periods of external threat does Sufism become popular (Lindholm in press). If the concept of romance is spoiled by the hierarchy which actual sexual contact entails, so is worship contaminated by the absolute power of God. The Pukhtun cannot reconcile himself to seeking the Deity as a meek servant implores his master. Rather, tries to enter heaven by way of magical rituals and incantations. When Allah must be supplicated, it is done through pirs and dervishes, who take on themselves the dishonor of begging for favors, as well as the charisma of association with the Supreme Being.

Remembering this, the role of the dervish and pir as beggar begins to make some sense. The holy man acts out his submissiveness on the temporal plane by begging from the Pukhtun who, like God, dispenses bounty. The Pukhtun thus becomes analogous to God and is rewarded with a blessing. The blessing of a beggar pir who has been treated with generosity by a Pukhtun is cited as the cause for the elevation of the great clans of Swat, including the Malik *khel*. It is also relevant to note here a Malik *khel* myth, in which a mother was reluctant to send her favorite son, Kamal, to be blessed by the pir because she feared he would be abducted. Ahmat, the less beloved son, was sent instead. The boy, though poor, begged his mother to kill the household's only cow to offer hospitality, and as a result his lineage, the Malik *khel*, was blessed with greatness. This story shows the dangers and rewards of dealing with holy men. It also shows how the Pukhtun reconciles his weakness in relation to Allah through the analogical reasoning of myth.

In the myths of the region, giving often occupies an important position. There are many legends of men who gave up everything, including their wives and children, to demanding guests. As a result, Allah miraculously interceded to double all their possessions. Truly generous people now no longer exist, the villagers say, but in the last generation there were men who were so generous that their cooking pots refilled themselves by supernatural means.

Generous hospitality is thus used as a validation for greatness in the present, and powerful lineages must continue to offer hospitality if they wish respect. Naturally, generosity has its instrumental side. It was and is certainly hoped that the guest will look favorably on his host, and that the relationship will deepen into a friendship. The friend will, of course, help out and give aid whenever it is needed (Jacobson, 1975). Pukhtun workers and students try to bring their employers and teachers to the *hujera* as guests with the ambition of turning these superiors into friends, or at least into well-wishers, through the offering of hospitality.

But these instrumental values are hardly the causes of hospitality and refuge, any more than are the other hypothetical causes cited in my introduction, i.e., protection of trade, winning a dependent following, Islamic rule, and cultural symbol. The instrumental value is purely secondary, and the hospitality offered to a wayfarer who will certainly never reciprocate is equal to that offered the president of the bank or the principal of the school.

Within recent memory, all guests were put up and fed at the neighborhood *hujera* at the expense of the local khan. The whole neighborhood would contribute to the care and feeding of the guest in a display of communal help. It was a point of pride that the guest should receive a sumptuous welcome and return to his home with tales of the generosity of his hosts.

Traditionally, whenever an important guest arrived, such as the *malik* (headman) of another village, he would be greeted by the ceremonious rolling of war drums. The local leaders would meet him at the village entrance and vie with one another for the honor of providing *melmastia* (hospitality). Such a guest, with all his retinue (which might amount to fifty men) was obliged to remain at least three days with his host on pain of giving insult. All guests would be fed lavishly; people would store food for just such an occasion. It is said that a guest would sometimes try to hide to avoid having to eat yet another feast, but they would be found out and fed. The competitive potlatch aspect of feasting is obvious, but the Pukhtun themselves focus on the cooperation of the neighborhood in feeding the guest, which shows that there is "great love" among the neighbors.

Generous treatment was not meted out only to the elite, though in the days of war usually only men who could afford a bodyguard ventured out of their villages. Mendicants were also put up at the *hujera* or, if religious, at the mosque.

At the time of my fieldwork, cooperation in the neighborhood had greatly diminished, following the decrease in the importance of the *hujera* and the power of the khan over his clients. Donation of hospitality has become individualized. Some people still gave milk and rice or a chicken if requested but, more often than not, they will try to beg off. Foodstuffs are no longer saved for guests; rather the surplus is sold to get money for the purchase of status items.

The site of hospitality has also shifted as moderately well-to-do villagers have built their own guest rooms (*betəks*) adjoining their houses. The responsibility of entertaining guests has thus shifted from the khan who controlled the men's house to individuals with their own guest rooms. In Shin Bagh I counted thirty-four *betəks*, three of them doubling as shops. Most were owned by middle-level khans, but a number were held by successful laborers and herdsmen. Guests are not provided for on the scale of previous years, nor are there the large-scale entertainments and feasts of twenty or thirty years ago.

Other customs have also gone into decline. It was formerly a point of honor to provide for unknown persons in the *hujera*. One famed khan was known to give hospitality for three months before ever asking the name of his guest. But, in 1977, guests were almost invariably distant relatives or acquaintances men had made at work, either in other parts of Pakistan or in Swat itself. It is significant that one of the reasons Pukhtun whom I interviewed in Karachi said they liked the city was that they could make friends there. In fact, it was often said that in the slums of Karachi where the Pukhtun laborers lived there was "much love," and this was contrasted to the rivalry of village life. The reason for this reversal of the Western image of the city as a place of alienation and anomie is, of course, the attenuation of kinship oppositions and the availability of people who are outsiders as candidates for friendship relations.

In Shin Bagh itself, few outsiders ever appear. I certainly would never have gone there had I not chanced to meet Zaman Khan in Saidu Sherif, gained his friendship, and consequently been invited to his village. Several other foreign "guests" have been entertained in Shin Bagh since I first went there in 1969. They were all young travelers, some of them mystically inclined and seeking a guru, others more interested in the cheap opium and hashish Swat has to offer. None of them, apparently, had gone beyond the role of guest, and some of them had abused their privileges by injecting themselves with morphine, wandering through

Taking tea in a guest room.

230 THE CODE OF HONOR

town half-dressed, insulting their hosts, and generally behaving very badly, so that the Pukhtun had become leery of offering them hospitality, and the institution continued to decrease in importance.

Despite the gradual diminution of hospitality as a vital ritual in Pukhtun life, the rite continues in its central place in the consciousness of the people. When it is enacted, it is to the fullest extent allowed by the circumstances of the host. The visitor will be treated with a cordiality which belies the poverty of the village. He will be placed on the most comfortable cot in the *betǝk* or *hujera* where he has been received. The children and younger brothers and sisters of the household are introduced as slaves of the guest, and see to it that he is made comfortable. Large pillows, ornately embroidered, are slipped behind his head, and sweet tea is served in the family's formal crockery. The host will sit attentively with his guest, apologizing to him for the failings of his hospitality, or *melmastia,* and urge him to rest himself and take more tea. If the guest wishes to walk, the host will walk; if the guest wishes to sit, the host will sit, despite any other business which might be at hand.

The *melma* (visitor) will be requested to stay for a meal and to sleep overnight. In all likelihood, a chicken (the most expensive and desired food) has already been killed and is being prepared in honor of the guest. If the host has no cow, he has sent someone to his dependents and allies in the neighborhood to ask for some of the best quality curd with the explanation that "a guest has come." Any other luxury not immediately at hand will be borrowed and prepared into a feast meal. The host, meanwhile, will not leave his guest, but rather will sit with him, discussing whatever they can discover to be of mutual interest. Or perhaps they will simply sit in silence. Other men will also drop by to pay their respects to the guest and to express their loyalty to the host. When the meal comes, it will certainly be the best the family can prepare. Preferably, it will consist of chicken, rice, clarified butter, curd, and some vegetables. The guest will be expected to eat all the best portions while the children or servants bring more. The host will refuse meat and curd and himself pour large amounts of clarified butter on the plate of the guest. The *melma* will be encouraged to eat as much as possible in order to show his appreciation for his host's hospitality, although the more the guest eats, the less remains for the host and his family. Afterwards, some sweet green tea will be drunk, the radio turned on, some *charas* may be smoked, and the guest will be entertained until he signals that he wishes to retire. If the guest is not tired, the host will happily sit with him all night.

When the *melma* finally does go to bed, he sleeps on the best bed in the house, with the newest and cleanest quilt and the best pillow. The room in which he sleeps (either in the *betэk* or a room in the *hujera*) will assuredly be clean and well kept. Although the rest of the host's house may be built of mud and stone, the guest room will be of concrete if at all possible.

Though hospitality is offered in a formal way, the feeling behind it is sincere and friendly. The host places himself wholly at the whim of his guest and assures the guest of his wish to become his friend and intimate. Affection and friendship are given without reserve by even the poorest host. "Look at the warmth of my eyes and not at the hardness of the corn bread before you" (G. Khan 1958:59). And although the resources available for entertaining are more difficult to come by, there is still competition over the right to entertain a newly arrived guest. If the guest is lured from his initial host to stay with another, this insult can cause a feud between the two hosts just as it did in the days of large-scale hospitality.

The rules of hospitality are indicative of the relationship. In theory, the host should give his guest whatever he requests, and the polite guest ought to avoid showing too much appreciation of any of his host's possessions for fear of precipitating a gift. Sophisticated Punjabi tradesmen are well aware of this Pukhtun trait, and many valuable items have been extorted from generous hosts by the simple strategy of excessive admiration.

It is considered extremely bad form to attempt recompense for hospitality, or for any form of freely granted help. The host wants absolutely no return for his kindness, not even the name of the guest. The wise guest brings a gift with him, which is presented before hospitality is accepted, for it would be insulting to offer anything after taking hospitality. The Pukhtun are very adverse to appearing to be offering themselves for hire. "They will do anything that is wanted of them with much more zeal if a present is made to them in advance, than if it is withheld in the hope of quickening them by expectancy" (Elphinstone 1815: 1:330).

The attitude of self-sacrifice is not restricted only to the men of the house. The wife also feels that her honor and respect are at stake in offering hospitality (*melmastia*), though she will never even see the guest

A khan in his *hujera.*

unless she spies on him through a hole in the wall. She is proud of the entertainment given to her husband's guest, since it reflects well on her abilities. She works hard to keep the guest well supplied with tea and food and does not begrudge giving him curd and meat, although she herself does not taste such luxuries.

But too much hospitality wears on women. The husband is often willing to wreck the finances of the household with his open-handedness, and I have seen men ruin themselves through their generosity. When this occurs, the wives protest, but to no avail. Once the guest has arrived, the woman must cook and provide for the sake of her own pride.

As a complement to hospitality, the principle of refuge is the third pillar of Pukhtunwali, completing the basic trio of concepts by which the Pukhtun usually defines himself. The idea of refuge (*nanawatia*) is also linked to the guest–host relationship, but in this case the host is defined as the guardian of the guest, whereas in the case of *melmastia* the host has the role of provider. The guest must not only be entertained, fed, and housed, but also kept as safely as the host's strength will allow. This principle extends to any guest, even one unknown to the host. It operates regardless of the rank of the guest, his nationality, religion, or personal characteristics. If the guest is insulted, injured, or killed it is a stain on the honor of the host, who must take revenge on the perpetrator. There is a Pukhtun joke about this principle which has to do with a Hindu who was the guest of a Pukhtun. The rest of the village became irate over the presence of an infidel and resolved to kill the Hindu. Terrified, he asked his host how the host intended to cope with this threat. "Do not fear," the host replied. "Your death shall be revenged."

The principle of refuge is extended to its fullest logical limit, to the point that a man should give refuge to the killer of his own son if the murderer appears at his door. Cases are cited in local history of just such situations occurring, and of the bereaved father offering shelter and hospitality as required by custom. *Nanawatia* thus supersedes even the notion of revenge, at least while the guest is within the property of the host. However, as soon as the guest leaves the host's estate, he becomes fair game. Protection only extends to the limits of the host's own holdings and "there are undoubted testimonies of predatory tribes entertaining a traveller and dismissing him with presents, and yet robbing him when they met him again, after he was out of their protection" (Elphinstone 1815: 1:297).

Women may also apply for *nanawatia,* and a truly desperate family will send a woman to beg for refuge and aid. A request from a woman would be extremely dishonorable to ignore. Rather than sending the woman herself, a *sadar* may substitute. Women who run from their husbands may occasionally apply to a powerful man for refuge on their own account. If the woman is of a respectable family, such an application becomes a source of great pride to the recipient and great humiliation to both the girl's own family and the family of her husband. Women are sometimes forced to resort to this appeal when life with the husband becomes intolerable and when her own family refuses to offer shelter. There were two such cases I knew of personally during fieldwork, and others were reported. It is, however, very much a desperate measure, since the woman is thereafter assumed to have become the concubine and servant of her host. She will never be allowed within her own home or her husband's house again.

Nanawatia implies more than simple protection. It also can be applied as a lever to force a favor. A man who arrives as a guest may refuse to sit or take tea until the host grants him what he requests. The host must grant the petitioner's wish or be reproached for not being a true Pukhtun. "So far is the practice carried, that a man over-matched by his enemies, will sometimes go Nannawautee to the house of another man, and entreat him to take up his quarrel; which the other is obliged to do . . ." (Elphinstone 1815: 1:296). An example of this aspect of *nanawatia* occurred recently in Swat, when a father and his sons sought refuge with a powerful khan after they had killed the father's first cousin in a quarrel. The khan was obliged to take the side of his guests in the dispute and to attempt to reach a mediated settlement with the family of the dead man. The host had to act as the representative of his petitioners despite the fact that they were generally regarded as being in the wrong in the case.

The principle of refuge was formerly applied in Swat to recruit armies from the ranks of fugitives seeking asylum. Many of the laborers of the village are the descendants of men who fled their own homes pursued by their enemies and threw themselves on the mercy of the Shin Bagh khans. By accepting the role of permanent wards of the Malik *khel,* these men became part of the warrior retinue of their protectors. Again, refuge, like hospitality, has its instrumental side—but refuge must be offered even if it is politically ruinous and, as in the case above, the host can be forced into fights he does not want by the demands of *nanawatia.*

While I have demonstrated that the refuge/hospitality complex is not, in essence, a political action, it does have in common with political life the effort to display mastery. The relation between the host and the guest is the relation between controller and controlled. As such, it reflects the social order, which is a continual struggle for control. In the host–guest interaction, the dominance of the host is complete. The relation of hospitality is not the reciprocal flow of Western visiting. Rather, it is a one-way flow of prestations which is passively received by the guest, who may never reciprocate while he is in his guest role on pain of insulting his host. The host's unreciprocated giving is central to the ritual, as is his abstemiousness. One man even told me that the essence of honor was "never to eat any of the food one has given to a guest." Although the host is obliged to remain with his guest and follow the guest's whims, the dependent position of the guest is never in doubt. He is accompanied in all his movements, and his every need is seen to according to custom. Visiting another person besides the host is impossible for the guest, as is simply going out for a solitary walk. Protests that the food is too rich, the bed too luxurious, are futile. In a very real sense, the guest is the prisoner of the host. Once hospitality has been accepted, the guest must reconcile himself to passivity. Even in the ritual of refuge, in which the guest seems to take an active role in forcing his host to take up arms against the guest's enemies, the reality is that the guest is admitting, in the most graphic way possible, his weakness and reliance on his host. In the one-way flow of prestations from host to guest, and in the jealousy with which the host guards the guest and keeps him isolated in the *betak* or *hujera*, the ascendance and control of the host is paramount. The guest is not a personality. He is a mirror which reflects the host's generosity. As the mirror or shadow of the host, the stranger-guest is ideal, since he is, by definition, an unknown factor without a given reality beyond his role as guest.

But, again, this is not to assert that the hospitality offered is cold and unfeeling, a mere ritual gesture. On the contrary, the hospitality of the Pukhtun is notably warm and sincere, and the host typically radiates his joy at filling his role and his friendliness to this stranger in his midst. This warmth is similar to the empathy generated between two solitary strangers meeting on a voyage. The trust and intimacy which are a feature of this relationship derive from its very impermanency. Unlike a friendship in the usual Western sense of the term, friendship with the stranger-guest takes no risks, since nothing is really at stake. The stranger will soon disappear into the limbo from which he came. Absent, he cannot betray the intimacy of his host.

The rituals of hospitality and refuge are obviously formed by the social order of Swat. The host, in his dominance over his guest, displays his mastery and control, two attributes highly desired in the competitive world of Swat. Furthermore, the concept of the stranger-guest emphasizes once again the pervasive mistrust of the Pukhtun, who can only warm to one who is soon to vanish. But hospitality and refuge cannot be explained by these formative pressures. These pressures only explain the particular form of the host–guest relationship in Swat. The question still remains concerning the cause for the reversal of ordinary life in the offering of hospitality.

I have noted that the host is undeniably the overlord of his guest. In ordinary life the powerful and dominant first exploit the weak and submissive and later redistribute their gains in charity. Being exploited and being the recipient of charity are both equally shameful positions, for they indicate one's inferiority. But the guest, who accepts a submissive role, is honored for accepting the largesse of his host. The guest is far from being shamed at being the powerless recipient; he can actually shame his host should he refuse his prestations (c.f. Mauss 1967 on the significance of refusing a gift). Unlike mundane exchange relationships, the guest deliberately enacts a powerless role, and is rewarded not only with gifts, but also with respect and regard, as well as affection. My explanation of this anomaly is that the hospitality ritual offers something very important to the host. In giving hospitality to the passive guest, he can enact the pivotal requirement for friendship, that of selfless giving without restraint or greed. Hospitality is the outpouring of gifts and food to the completely self-effacing other. If the guest were to offer a return, the disinterestedness of the host would be impugned. What the guest provides is not any material benefit. Rather, he gives the host an op-portunity to show his capacity for the self-sacrifice that Pukhtun see as the root of friendship. Otherwise, the ritual of hospitality could have no meaning within the Swati context, for despite the molding effects of the social structure, the central aspects of the generosity of the host and the regard offered the passive guest remain inexplicable.

The importance of hospitality and refuge, and their relationship to the notion of friendship, can be seen in Pukhtun definitions of honor. Honor, of course, is the enactment of all the injunctions of Pukhtunwali with resolute courage. But honor also has a more narrow sense discernible in the two distinct terms used for it. *Nang* means being willing to die or otherwise sacrifice oneself for Pukhtunwali, but it has the specific mean-ing of sacrifice for a friend. This is the quintessence of *nang*. *Gherat*, on the other hand, has the more positive meaning of living up to the prin-ciples of the code, and the man who is *begherata* (without honor) is the man who pimps for his wife, sells his land, and is too incompetent and lazy to defend his rights. But *gherat* has a special significance as well. The term in its core has to do with generosity, feasting, and the free giving of the host, which is an enactment of the free giving expected of a friend.

To summarize, the code of Pukhtun honor seems largely to be under-stood as a reflection, and sometimes as an effort to mask or to reconcile, the realities of the social structure. Revenge unites men and gives the minimal form necessary for social life. Equality and respect rituals enact the two opposing potentials in the segmentary system, while the demand for expressions of loyalty is an effort to reconcile those potentials. Pride and bravery are needed attributes of men isolated and engaged in continuous competition, while purdah is an effort to mask the anomalous and dangerous place of women within the Pukhtun patrilineages.

But there are elements not so easily understood, and they all revolve around the ideal of friendship. Romance and worship have been discussed as secondary forms of friendship, tainted by qualities of hierarchy and domination. Hospitality and refuge, two of the three pillars of the code of Pukhtunwali, though formed by the demands of the social structure, seem inexplicable from a purely structural viewpoint. They also point toward friendship, and appear to be ritualized enactments of the friendship ideal. What is this ideal, and how can it exist within the Swati world?

7. The Friendship Ideal

How can a person ever claim
To be in love, when first of all
He worries about life and name?
That man is not in love at all.

I always contemplate Sultan Mahmud
Whose love made him a servant of his slave.

I want to give the world to my beloved
Lest I myself become desirous of it.
(Rahman Baba 1977:151, 93, 89)

Oh God, grant me a true friend who, without urging,
will show me his love!
(Pukhtun proverb)

THE concept of friendship is essential to the Pukhtun: both God and the lover are metaphors for the friend; hospitality is a ritual enactment of friendship; the notion of honor itself hinges on the generosity and sacrifice demanded of friends. All men desire a true friend who can be trusted, loved, even venerated, despite the laments of classical and modern poetry that the ideal is unattainable. "How can you rejoice in the fidelity of one who's faithful first, but soon betrays you?" (Khattak 1965:1). It is far removed from the casual Western concept of friendship, and entails a complete devotion and loyalty to the exclusion of every other relationship. Friends should be together constantly; they should completely trust one another and reveal all their secrets to one another; they should always help one another in any circumstances and must be willing to sacrifice for the sake of the other. The code of friendship supersedes even the Koran, since it is considered honorable for a man to lie for his friend, even with his hand on the Holy Book.

> True friendship's first condition it must be
> That come what may, they will burn together . . .
> (Rahman Baba 1977:95)

> Separation from the friend
> For one moment is like Judgement Day.

> Should their love take them to Hell
> For the friends Hell is paradise.
> (Rahman Baba 1977:55)

For the Pukhtun, the metaphor for the friend is the identical twin. As exact replicas of one another, twins will, in Swati thought, be the best of friends. A similar belief is found in Africa, as Brain (1971, 1976) attests. But in his cases, identity is not demanded. Rather, the ideal twins are dialectical opposites: "In Africa and ancient myth twins are not god-like beings because they are identical, so as to be interchangeable, but because they were born as two, from the same womb, at the same time, and are complementary" (1976:126). The Swati ideal is more Platonic, as elaborated in the *Symposium*, in which the friends become a single body, as it were, and are lost in love for the other; a love that is, in Plato's theory, love for one's own higher spiritual self. In this sense, as Brain admits, "the image of twins is also a narcissistic one, the pair of friends only trying to mirror their own identity in each other, at the same time seeking in undividedness an attempt to repeat the unity of the mythical androgyne" (1976:143–44). The metaphor of the identical twin means that the friend is seen as a reflection of one's self. His every desire should coincide with one's own desires. Like the guest, the friend does not properly have a personality of his own. He is an emanation of one's own wishes.

To elaborate on this theme, the attributes of the ideal friend offer instructive evidence. The friend should be willing to sacrifice himself in total devotion to the will of the other. His affection must be spontaneous, without reservation, and all-consuming. The true friend is called "naked chest" because the hearts of both parties are bared to one another, thus sweeping away the pervasive secrecy and mistrust of Swati society. But this complete trust is accomplished only because the interests of the other are identical with one's own, and there is consequently no need for concealment. The proverb which begins this chapter states, "Oh God, grant me a true friend who, without urging, will show me his love!" The friend must display his love without invitation. His identification with his comrade is such that he can intuit the other's needs without the necessity of a request. The relationship is so unmediated that even the humiliation of asking is eliminated, for a request establishes need and thereby develops into a hierarchy of dependency. In effect, the friends merge into a single person in their perfect mutuality and identification; concern for the other is the same as concern for one's self, since both are united in their desires and anticipate the needs of the other as their own. It is a relationship of total generosity which at the same time involves no loss whatsoever, since the friend's generosity is equal to one's own. The life of the other is more dear than one's own, and therefore one may confidently trust the friend with one's life. Each holds the other more precious than the self and finds gratification in the pleasure of the other. Naturally, in such a relationship there is room only for a dyad.

How can a man pay the price of friendship
With a thousand friends spending his love?

The true friend loves only one
And ignores the rest.
(Rahman Baba, my translation)

The friends hoard one another and exclude the rest of the world.

The pertinent factors in the picture offered here are the possessive jealousy and the totality of the friendship ideal. There is no middle ground for friendship, just as there is no middle ground in the society itself. Furthermore, what is found in the friend is the friend's utter self-abnegation, so that in giving everything to the friend, one is in fact taking no risk at all, since the friend has no desires for himself. The ideal then is giving up the self to one whose only concern is the very self which has been relinquished. The friend combines equality with a complete selflessness. In a very real sense, the friend *is* ego, and this is the meaning of the metaphor of the identical twin.

This concept of the friend as purely passive image of ego is obviously a result of the social order which rules Swati life. Like the guest, the friend is a cipher, an empty category to be filled by one's own will. In completely absorbing the friend into the self, the self assumes absolute mastery of the other. This is the final fantasy of domination. Other interesting ties with ordinary systems of exchange may also be relevant. The immediate return that the friend offers is paralleled by the reality of exchange between equals (*adal-badal*) in which an equivalent return is always sought. Ideally, *adal-badal* is a matching exchange, though, as we have seen, each party actually attempts to cheat the other. The friendship ideal is also analogous to the gifts of *mahar* and money donated to a new bride, which she is supposed to return to her husband after he has successfully consummated the marriage. Again, reality does not necessarily follow the ideal pattern, as the woman uses the gifts to assert her own rights and individuality and oppose her absorption into her husband's lineage. Both *adal-badal* and the *mahar* payments seek, with no great success, to assert self-sufficiency while simultaneously engaging in exchange. What is given should be returned, so it is as if nothing had ever been given. In the ideal relationship with the friend, this same effort is again enacted in its fullest sense. In giving to the friend, the donor is, in effect, giving to himself, and self-sufficiency is reconciled with exchange. The dream of friendship, in its particular all-encompassing form, may be seen as an attempt on the mythical plane to unite the major contradiction of Pukhtun life, that is, the contradiction between individual pride and the necessity for exchange. In the sexless ideal of the friend who merges with ego into one psyche, albeit with two bodies, these opposites are painlessly harmonized.

Another important attribute of the friend is his position as an outsider. Failing twins, Swati parents hope for an even number of sons, since it is believed that those closest in age will be friends. In fact, brothers, and especially half-brothers, who are about the same age do have a special relationship of trust and mutual help. This relation, however, is not very strong or enduring, and is often tested by self-interest. I have never seen adult twins, but I imagine that their relations would also not meet the ideal. The rivalries of adult men within the local patrilineage keep them from the mutuality and trust that is the basis for Pukhtun friendship. The men linked to one through the mother or, to a lesser degree, through the father's sisters, are one's allies, but not friends. They can only be approached through the medium of the women who link them with one's own lineage and are therefore touched by the inferiority and contempt implicit in such a tie. Furthermore, their concern for one, though disinterested and generally positive, is neither profound nor totally committed. Of course, no woman can qualify as a friend, since all women are contaminated by their contradictory role in exchange and their consequent repulsiveness. Other Pukhtun men who are distant relatives cannot properly be friends because all equals are continually trying to assert dominance, while the essence of friendship is concord. At the same time, inferiors cannot be friends in any real sense, though it is with inferiors and especially with personal servants that the Pukhtun man comes closest to the ideal relationship. "The tie between master and servant is usually an extremely close and intimate one—much more so than between brothers, friends, or even father and son—apparently far the closest emotional tie between males that Pathans ever experience" (Barth 1965:49). Barth has mistaken allies for friends in this statement, but it is otherwise quite correct. The servant is a friend in his acquiescence, his willingness to make the desires of his master his own, but his base position renders his commitment suspect. He is a friend out of weakness, and his friendship therefore bears the poisonous trace of compulsion.

Friendships are struck up among boys, who are relatively free of the intense rivalries of men over land and who roam their ward in egalitarian gangs. Predictably, friends are age-mates (umzoli), so that the respect that must be offered an elder does not enter in. Boys who are friends hold hands and caress one another quite unself-consciously. This type of relationship seems to be prevalent among young teenagers, as I discovered through questionnaires I distributed in several local schools.

One questionnaire asked the boys who they personally liked and who they disliked. It also asked who they thought were the most popular and the least popular members of the class. The adolescents of the seventh and eight grades responded well to this test, but the older boys did not, merely saying that they "liked everybody" or not answering at all. Of the ninety-seven seventh and eighth graders, there were ten pairs, that is, twenty boys who had dyadic friendships, each liking only the other. These pairs were the object of jealousy and rivalry by the other boys, who often singled out one of the pair as personally disliked or as the least popular boy in class, while simultaneously characterizing the other as most popular or as a personal friend. There were even several romantic triangles, with A liking B who likes C who likes A who, unfortunately, hates him as his rival for B. These youthful attachments, while extremely passionate (though not sexual, at least to my knowledge), are subject to the sudden breaks, betrayals, and tragedies that one might anticipate, given the prevailing atmosphere; and the older boys have learned not to reveal themselves to "one who's faithful first, but soon betrays you." Friendship with those who are close by becomes recognized as impossible.

If all neighbors, both equals and inferiors, are summarily disqualified from consideration for friendship, who then is the friend? The friend cannot be more powerful than ego, for this would imply servitude. Nor can he be less powerful, for then he is a servant. Nor can he be an equal, for then he would be a rival. Obviously, he must be of a different order altogether, outside the realm of the struggle of Pukhtun society. There is a potent irony here. Pukhtun society has historically been one of "predatory expansion" (Sahlins 1961), increasing its territory at the expense of its weaker neighbors. Yet, though the society at large acts with rapacity to those who are exterior to it, the individuals in the society look to outsiders as the only people who can possibly fill the role of friend.

As I have documented elsewhere (1980), British administrators in the tribal areas during periods of indirect rule were sought out as friends by the Pukhtun. These friendships, of course, had an instrumental side, but their primary value, for the Pukhtun at least, was emotional. These administrators were suitable as friends since they stood outside the rivalries of ordinary life and did not become involved in politics except as mediators. The relationship is perhaps best described by Warburton, who worked with the Afridi Pukhtuns for many years. "If you can overcome his distrust and be kind in words to him [the Pukhtun] will repay you by great devotion, and he will put up with any punishment you care to give him except abuse" (1900:342). His words were proven true when the British, contrary to his advice, invaded Afridi territory. He rode alone among the tribesmen while the British army destroyed their homes and despoiled their land.

> When I told the old men of the Afridis in reply to their cry, that it was out of my power to help them, the *jirga* [council of elders] replied: "Never mind, Sahib, whatever happens we are earnestly praying that you should not be injured in this campaign." These old men were witnessing the destruction of everything that was dear and sweet to them in life. . . . And yet in that supreme hour of their distress they had a thought for the safety of the Kafir who had done nothing for them, except to try to be their friend. (Warburton 1900:344)

Caroe (1965), who also was an administrator during indirect rule, gives a similar portrait of Pukhtun friendship, as do Elphinstone (1815) and Masson (1842), who filled the passive role of guests. But the British, who entered into political competition with the Pukhtun, who sought to suborn or rule them, told a different story, if they survived to tell any story at all. Comparing Burnes (1843), Bellew (1864), and Nevill (1911) with Warburton, Caroe, Masson, and Elphinstone, it seems the writers are portraying quite different people, though all worked with the Pukhtun. Those who were guests or mediators write of the courtesy, trustworthiness, and generosity of their hosts and friends, while those who attempted to manipulate, conquer, or control see treachery, greed, and malice. The reason for the apparent discontinuity is simple: outsiders playing the game of domination with the Pukhtun have forfeited any claim to friendship and will be treated as the Pukhtun treat any rival; while those who remain outsiders, who do not claim superiority or offer competition, fill the criterion for becoming the sort of comrade dreamed of as the ideal.

In Shin Bagh, the Pukhtun men who claimed to have friends all took them from different social orders. One had a friend who was a landless Hindu shopkeeper, another had a friend who was a Kohistani laborer, another friend was the Punjabi manager of a local firm, while a fourth man claimed as his friend a goldsmith who worked as a teacher. Pukhtun workers in Karachi and elsewhere find friends among their coworkers from distant places. The foreigner is much sought after as a friend, since he fits, more than any Pakistani, the necessary qualifications of strangeness, equality without rivalry, and an absence of conflicting interests.

Thus, the concept of the friend is formed by the pressures of the Swati social system. It expresses the desire for mastery, the total domination of another. Furthermore, the image of the ideal friend resolves, on the plane of myth, the interior contradictions of the society. Finally, the friend, like the guest, is a stranger, an enigma, outside the hostilities of ordinary life and lacking his own personality. But, despite the fact that the pattern of the ideal can be understood by reference to the social structure, the essence remains a mystery.

Although the notion of friendship is fashioned by social reality, the premise of generosity, of giving up the self within a relationship, cannot be discovered by analysis of social causes. Granted that the giving up of the self is, in reality, not a giving at all, but rather an expanding of the self to engulf another, nonetheless there is no model for such an act in any other area of the society. From whence comes the notion that another human being could be perfectly understanding, perfectly accepting, perfectly forgiving, perfectly trustworthy? We have seen that in the society at large these qualities do not exist. Historical, ecological, and social pressures oblige the men of Swat to view all their relations with their fellows as dangerous and threatening. The daily reality is one of struggle and betrayal. In the framework I have outlined in the previous chapters, this daily reality is easily grasped, for it fits with the overwhelming predisposition of the entire social structure. A relationship of giving and trust is an obvious impossibility within this framework, yet the fantasy of just such a relationship is found in the ideal of the friend.

The way Pukhtun look at friendship became evident during my own long friendship with Zaman Khan. When the relationship began, I was a lone, rather alienated young man wandering across Asia. Zaman's offer of friendship, his sincerity and warmth, coupled with the intriguing exoticism and masculine quality of Pukhtun life, drew me into a very intense emotional experience. At the time, I was quite willing to accept Zaman's word on everything and to trust him completely; nor was I ever disappointed in my trust. In a sense, he and I were perfectly complementary, since I had made myself into an empty canvas where his generosity and honor could be portrayed.

After coming back to America, I had time to think about our friendship. I continued to feel a tremendous pull back to Swat, a pull which, as I mentioned in my introduction, was instrumental in my beginning graduate school in anthropology. But during the intervening decade, I grew and changed; I learned what I wanted to do in my life; I no longer suffered from the crisis of identity that had led me to the Orient originally. And when I returned to Pakistan, I discovered how much Zaman's memory of me was built of dreams and impossible images. "You are no longer the same," he said. "You no longer follow me." It was some time before our friendship could mature beyond fantasy into a more realistic sharing.

The passion and jealousy of the friendship given by the Pukhtun is difficult to imagine. Perhaps those who have been in the Middle East and who have had a Middle Eastern friend angrily reproach them for seeing another friend will have an idea of how very different the concept of friendship is. For Westerners, friends are many. They may last a long time, or they may change; some friends are closer than others. But for the Pukhtun and, I believe, for other Muslim people, friendship is a far more focused and vital matter. For instance, Zaman was once speculating what he would do if, by some luck, he was able to come visit me in New York. "There would be so much to do that I would only come to your house once or twice during the day!" The lure of New York would be so powerful that it could do the ultimate; separate two friends for a few hours.

In reality, of course, the perfect friend does not and cannot exist. An ideal friend must be willing to cut himself away from all other ties, to submit utterly and uncritically to the love of the one who has offered his devotion. The absence of the ideal in the real world is recognized by Khushal, who laments its lack:

Friendship and kinship are both found
Only in outward form,
While everybody has in view
His personal desires.
(Khattak 1965:7)

The ideal of the man who will give up his "personal desires" for the sake of another is rarely actualized in any culture. In our own society such a man would be either a saint or a lunatic. In Swati society which is, if anything, more competitive than that of the most cutthroat Western businessman, such an ideal image is more than unrealistic; it seems absurd. It is as if a wild card were thrown into the tidy picture of the Hobbesian world of Swat, with its rivalries, hostilities, and fears. The dream of the friend, that is, the dream of an unmediated relationship of complete empathy, seems to have no roots in the structure I have described. Yet it exists. Why?

Friendship, generosity, affection, attachment; these are hard things for an anthropologist to write about. It is far easier and more contemporary to subsume sentiment into structure; to say, with Lévi-Strauss, that "contents which can be assigned to such and such an attitude are less important than the relations of oppositions discernible between coupled pairs or attitudes" (1976:86). "Impulses and emotions explain nothing. They are always *results* either of the power of the body or the impotence of the mind. In both cases they are consequences, never causes" (1963:71). Therefore, instead of emotions we have "the attitude of the creditor [and] of the debtor" (1967:47). If structuralists see emotions as byproducts of exchange relations, then functionalists have an equally narrow view, envisioning, for example, ties of affection between sister's son and mother's brother solely as mechanisms for linking unrelated lineages while keeping the integrity of the patriline (Radcliffe-Brown 1924). "Sentiments," writes Radcliffe-Brown, "are related to the cohesion of the society" (1958:40), and that is an end to the matter. One does not analyze the content of the sentiments, only how the sentiments add to social cohesion. For neither the structuralist nor the functionalist do the emotions have any autonomy or authority.

The effort to excise human emotional life from the field of anthropology arises perhaps from a fear of being unscientific, of having the material become too personal and uncontrolled (Spindler 1980:27). As Durkheim and Mauss wrote:

A concept is the notion of a clearly determined group of things; its limits may be marked precisely. Emotion, on the contrary, is something essentially fluid and inconsistent. . . . [Emotional states] lose themselves in each other, and mingle their properties in such a way that they cannot be rigorously categorized. (1967:87)

According to Lévi-Strauss, "affectivity is the most obscure side of man [and] . . . what is refractory to explanation is ipso facto unsuitable for use as explanation" (1963:69). Furthermore, as White (1949) argues, emotions are everywhere a constant, and constants cannot explain cultural variation. "Since all men are equipped with the same psychobiological tendencies, all sociocultural systems should be the same" (Harris 1968:531). Even psychological research, which one might expect to try to redeem the study of emotion and, especially, of affection, focuses instead on the rationality of greed and manipulation, while relations of friendship are portrayed as masks for egoistic self aggrandizement. A review of personality theory noted that "if affect or emotion is found at all in the indexes of recent personality textbooks, the reference is to fear, anxiety, or aggression, and often in the context of conditioning. Researchers who treat the subject more broadly take pride in the fact that their theories of emotion are 'cognitive'"(Helson and Mitchell 1978:566).

Nor does psychological anthropology have much to say about affect. The emphasis instead is on developing a method for understanding psychological differences between populations. For instance, in one standard text, the fundamental problem is considered to be the "lack of reliable indicators of personality disposition," while the elements which make up the personality are left undefined and unexamined, though it is considered that "personality is a system with its own internal properties, interacting with the sociocultural system in a relation of limited interdependence" (Levine 1976:288, 97). But what is this "system" and what are its "properties"? Wallace frankly writes that "it does not seem possible at present to make very satisfying generalizations about human nature" (1970:132), while Spindler laments that "we have rarely examined the roots of our theory" (1980:30). Hsu (1972) is rather unique in his effort to correlate the emotional content of kinship with cultural patterns of thought and behavior. He has focused on the nature of strong dyadic relationships in various societies, looking at "the feelings of individuals toward each other in kinship, and the extent to which each member of the group allows others to enter into and share his private life" (1972:513). He presumes that each basic dyadic relationship, such as that between mother and son, "possesses inherent and distinctive attributes" (1972:514) and that in every culture one dyadic relation is dominant, and thereby modifies the behavior of people in the society in certain definite ways. But Hsu's work is essentially about social needs and attitudes toward self and other. He assumes certain basic traits, but DuBois's statement that the major problem in psychological anthropology is the discovery of "which aspects of human personality are universal, which are very frequent, and which are unique to given socio-cultural groups" remains accurate (1961:xxv).

Lacking a comprehensive theory of emotional structure, social science cannot get at the heart of human experience. It is simply not enough to claim that man is a social animal who lives in communities and leave it at that, moving on to the tidier realms of efficient food production, symbolic structures, or integration of institutions. To understand the development and continuance of human culture, social science must grapple with the messy and vague realm of sentiment because without a theory of emotional need we cannot begin to grasp the driven quality that has pushed us into the creation of history. Men and women are motivated beings, as Burckhardt says, "suffering, striving, doing"; we are compelled by desires and fears, loves and hates; interior demands that we may think about, but that are not thoughts, that are structured, but are not structure.

The effort to grasp the deep springs of social life has been the historical mission of the social sciences, from Kant's affirmation of the moral law, Weber's concept of elective affinities and charisma, Durkheim's work on social solidarity and the collective consciousness, Freud's community of shared guilt, the notion of human sympathy found in Rousseau and Adam Smith, and on to Marx's ideal of a class of itself and for itself and Parson's harmony of roles. These theories are often contradictory, but have in common at least a minimal consideration of the emotional ties that bind human beings together. All these writers felt some necessity of discussing the why, and not just the how, of human community. But the question is perhaps too hard, or not suitable for quantification, or gives the lie to the individualistic and manipulative ethos of modern social science, and so is presently set aside. Yet by denying the importance of this question, social science commits itself either to the technicalities of what the Frankfurt School has called instrumental reason, or else to contemplation of society as "an apparatus which knows no activity other than repetition, and which lacks a goal. It is a knowledge of the void" (Paz 1970:126).

This is not to say that anthropology has totally ignored the study of emotion in general, and of friendship and love in particular. There is a large literature on *compadrazgo*, a formal bond between coparents in Latin America and Southern Europe, while trade friends and "blood brothers" have been well documented worldwide. A new interest in existential anthropological writing has led to a focus on the relationship between informant and researcher that often explores the permutations of friendship in a cultural matrix (see Rabinow 1977 for an example). But so far as I am aware, most of the work done on relations of affection has been concerned with the functions of the relation. For instance, Rosenblatt, in a survey of incidence of romantic love, says it occurs where there is non-neolocal residence and

serves to promote the integrity of a marriage by protecting it from divisive pressures of nearby relatives, to unite groups by providing a relatively strong bond between them, and to provide cohesion in a marital relationship in the face of the lower level of economic dependence of spouses that may be common where residence is non-neolocal. (Rosenblatt 1967:479)

Cohen has done a similar survey of friendship, demonstrating that inalienable bond friendships are most likely to occur in what he terms a "maximally solidary community" where community membership is ascribed, while close friends are found in solidary communities where membership is not fixed, casual friendships in nonnucleated communities, and expedient friendships in individuated societies such as modern America. Swat would undoubtedly be a maximally solidary community, but there are no bond friendships. In fact, friendship, as we have seen, is an ideal, and not a reality. Still, the image of the friend conforms in certain respects to Cohen's schema, in that there should only be one friend, not several. According to Cohen, this is because "in establishing the emotional propensities which are actualized in inalienable friendship, the maximally solidary community also creates a threat directed against itself; but it protects itself against this threat by arbitrarily limiting the range and extent of inalienable friendships" (Y. Cohen 1961:375). But Cohen's findings also show that emotional support is *less* important than economic support in maximally solidary communities, and this is certainly not the ideal in Swat. (See Wolf 1966 for a similar view.)

Simply because Swat does not fit Cohen's categories does not invalidate his work in any way. It may only mean that the character of friendship within the solidary community will shift as internal pressures within that community grow. Cohen's emphasis, though, is not on the roots of attachment, but on the way in which attachment is formed by social structure. Nonetheless, he goes further than most anthropologists in saying the need for friends is a predisposition that "derives from experiences with kinsmen and nonkinsmen during the formative and later years" (1961:352), and he even steps beyond this, noting that friendship in its most powerful form cannot be fully understood in terms of function: "What is especially curious about friendship is that—at least in its institutionalized or inalienable form—it is not a sociological or cultural imperative" (1961:372).

One of the few anthropologists to bring emotions overtly into theory is the idiosyncratic Turner, who has blended Freud and Lévi-Strauss to produce his own unique, but sometimes confusing, brew. In an interesting paper, Turner draws attention to similarities between human and animal ritual behavior. In both cases, ritual is seen as a method for channeling emotions, particularly those of sex and aggression (1969). Here he comes close to Freudian instinct theory. According to Turner, the symbol is the "molecule" which, linked to other symbols, makes up human ritual life. Symbols, in Turner's view, are multivalent, and serve to bring together and reconcile the opposing sides of human nature. These opposing aspects he terms variously the emotional and the cognitive, the id and the superego (with ritual as the mediating collective ego), the natural and the cultural, and, in his own phraseology, the "orectic" (or physiological) and the ideological. "It is hard to locate directly genetic ritualization in man. Nevertheless, as Freud has shown, certain 'innate' drives, such as sex and aggression, when they reach public expression or threaten to do so, provoke (like grit in an oyster) the growth of elaborate cultural (symbolic) formations. In the polarization of ritualized symbols there is great tensile strength and bonding power; they command both men's minds and their emotions and relate thought to feeling and action" (1969:19). "The norms, values and ideas at the 'ideological pole' become saturated with emotion, while the gross and basic emotions associated with the physiological referents at the 'orectic' pole become ennobled or 'sublimed' through contact with social 'bonding' notions and values" (1969:21). "The exchange of qualities makes desirable what is socially necessary by establishing a right relationship between involuntary sentiments and the requirements of social structure" (1974:56). Thus, "one aspect of ritual is shown . . . to be a means of putting at the service of the social order the very forces of disorder that inhere in man's mammalian constitution" (1977:93).

So the emotions, which are physiological, are socialized through ritual, but Turner seems a bit unsure of his ground, as the quote marks in the phrase "certain 'innate' drives," demonstrate. Are the drives "sex and aggression," and are they natural or cultural? Turner ignores the former question. As for the latter, the link with ethology would suggest an instinct theory, but he later makes quite a different claim: "Once culture provides the crucial symbols of human interaction, phylogeny ('nature') itself becomes a concept rather than a determinant, and the *idea* of bodily processes becomes a cultural polarity" (1969:23). And again, "culture fabricates structural distinction; it is culture too that eradicates these distinctions in liminality, but in so doing culture is forced to use the idiom of nature" (1974:253). Nature as a symbol has assumed priority over the body as a sensual reality, and the "gross and basic emotions associated with physiological referents" are now "ideas" or "idioms" culture uses to maintain itself; they are never determinants with their own force. Culture disembowels nature. But, despite his inconsistencies, Turner has confronted the problem.

Other anthropological accounts of emotional relations have been primarily ethnographic and descriptive. For instance, among the Hausa of the Sudan "formal bond friendship between persons of the same sex is a symmetrical relationship of equals in status and age, with a variety of reciprocal obligations" (Smith 1954:33). The Hausa form of friendship, quite common in Africa and elsewhere, is lifelong, and involves gift exchanges and a slowly growing trust between the parties. This is a far cry from the Swati case, where the friend is preferably a stranger, and where reciprocity is forbidden.

There are many other variations. Among the Saraktsani herdsmen of Greece close cognatic family units are uniformly suspicious of outsiders, and friendship is only permitted with a first cousin (Campbell 1963). A more familiar pattern occurs among Guatemalan Indians, where unmarried men become passionate (but not sexual) intimates, exchanging confidences and continually seeking out one another's company. The relationship "is maintained not for economic, political or practical purposes, but only for an emotional fulfillment" (Reina 1959:48), a fulfillment that is generally absent in the harsh, suspicious, and internally divided world of the village. The tie is strong and is intended to be lifelong, but jealousies and violence cut it short: "There seems to be a recurrent pattern in which a close *camarada* relationship is followed by hostility" (Reina 1959:49). The parallels with Swat, particularly in regard to the enmity of ordinary village life, are strong, though the Guatamalan Indians have at least the luxury of attempting a friendship within the village itself, a friendship characterized, once again, by reciprocity. But Reina (1966) simply accepts the quest for "emotional fulfillment" as a given; he does not explore the source of the quest. A similar pattern is noted by Brain (following Piker 1968) in Thailand, where "emotional friendships make possible a degree of vicarious gratification of a desire for love which is strongly felt but often frustrated in the selfish, backbiting world of everyday life . . . these passionate relations between best friends survive most strongly when the geographic distance between them is great" (Brain 1976:43).

Brain's work (1976) is the only anthropological writing I know to attempt to deal explicitly with the problem of attachment and friendship, and he has collected a great deal of fascinating material from his own fieldwork with the Bangwa of the Cameroons and elsewhere. His work demonstrates that close emotional attachments need not be sexual and, in fact, even claims that "sex, especially when it is associated with a romantic passion, is destructive of real love" (1976:210). The book is essentially an insightful polemic against romantic love and in favor of a wider range of affectionate relationships, perhaps established through formal ties. As a polemic, the book is effective, but it leaves something to be desired as theory. Though he rails against Freud, who supposedly "regarded hate as a more spontaneous urge, a more ineradicable appetite than love" (208) and who "was the bearer of a capitalist ethos" (209), Brain has little to say himself about the dynamics of affection, and what he does say is often contradictory. At one point, he claims the existence of "bonding mechanisms in individuals [that] derive from a basic trust deriving from bonds established in early childhood, usually with the mother, and from this trust we derive our fundamental attitudes of sociability and our capacity for commitment to people" (209). So friendship comes from bonding, which comes from trust, which comes from bonding. Later, friendship is seen as learned: "We can learn aggression as we learn cooperation and friendship, but we are not born with either" (211). Then again, friendship is a Hobbesian contract: "Men, therefore, cooperate because they would destroy themselves if they didn't" (215); or else a function of exchange relations: "Friendship need not derive from an unconscious sexual drive but a cultural imperative to exchange ideas, sentiments, and goods" (233). And finally, in conclusion, he propounds an innate needs theory: "Close loving contacts between two individuals are basic needs, as basic as any need to belong to a group" (262). "We come into the world preprogrammed to need love. . . . I have no qualms, therefore, in elevating friendship into an imperative" (264–65).

But confronting Brain with the hodgepodge of theories he has fallen back upon is not really fair to him. His theoretical confusion mirrors the confusion of theories about affection and attachment to be found in psychoanalytic literature, which is the only place where the problem is dealt with seriously. As an anthropologist with no clinical training, I hesitate to enter into this thicket of opposing opinions, especially since each position is often obscured by an exuberant foliage of jargon.

Nonetheless, at this juncture I must alter my argument and delve into the psychoanalytic literature. I can go no further with a social structural approach. My work to this point has shown that the friendship ethic, with its enactment in the hospitality/refuge complex and the notions of worship and romance, simply does not fit in with the dominant ethos of the Swati system. In actuality, the ideal of friendship as a perfect communion of souls appears to totally contradict social reality, and I have been unable to find any satisfying sociological explanation for this contradiction. As a last resort, I have turned to psychology. It is a last resort because psychological explanations in sociological works have been anathema since Durkheim declared society an object "sui generis". But I do not wish to commit the reductionist error of deriving social structure from a hypothetical set of innate needs. This is a fruitless and even foolish task, since diversity can never be accounted for in such a schema. My argument is that human emotions must be taken into account, and that they have their own reality and their own structure, just as society has its own autonomy and organization. The one informs and motivates the other, and without a theory of human emotions the study of society is one-sided and sterile.

In my research I can perhaps liken the Swati situation to an experimental setting. Because of the extreme conditions that prevail there, it is a perfect place for uncovering the influence of emotional structure on social structure. But first I need to outline what psychoanalytic scholars have discovered about the pattern of human emotional life.

The concept of emotion has had a controversial history in the literature of research psychology. The most accepted early theory was that proposed by Lange and James (1922), who asserted that emotional states are byproducts of physiological changes. This seems to be the view of Turner as well when he sees emotion as a derivitive of the physical appetites (the "orectic" pole). But this reductionist view has been permanently laid to rest by Cannon's critique (1927), which shows that induced physical changes do not necessarily arouse emotion, and that the same visceral changes occur in different emotional and nonemotional states.

Darwin (1873) was perhaps the first to link emotions with instinct, claiming that emotional expressions may be a remnant of formerly adaptive behaviors. This theory was elaborated by Dewey (1894), who prefigured a supposition that was to dominate the thirties and forties when he suggested that emotions are a sign of conflict and interfere with adaptive activity. Behaviorists, meanwhile, attempted to eliminate the term altogether from the vocabulary of psychology, stating it was too vague and subjective. Duffy (1941) said that emotion is simply a change in energy level, and that emotions cannot be analytically distinguished from any other form of response.

The vogue of "hard" behaviorism was fairly short-lived, and Leeper's proposal of a motivational theory of emotion (1948) carried the day against the theory of emotion as disorganized response. Emotion thus became a causal factor, and Leeper (1968) went so far as to consider the emotions as a type of perceptual process, distinguished from physiological motivation by complexity, responsiveness to change through learning and, among higher animals, priority over physical need. Other writers pursuing the same tack, such as Lazarus (1966), and Schachter and Singer (1962) go on to stress the cognitive aspect of emotion, that is, that emotional states follow cognitive appraisal. There is little discussion of emotion as having any form of its own, or of the roots of emotional states. As mentioned earlier, the cognitive orientation continues to prevail in American research psychology.

Arnold and Gasson, however, have the beginnings of a theory of a pattern of oppositions in their definition of emotion as "the felt tendency toward an object judged suitable or away from an object judged unsuitable, reinforced by specific bodily changes according to the type of emotion" (1968:203). The emphasis is on judgment, but, unlike the cognitive theorists, Arnold and Gasson stress that only intuitive judgments give rise to emotion, leading in turn to action, either positive or negative. Feelings and moods, on the other hand, do not incite to action, but merely indicate an inner state. Like Freud in their dualism, Arnold and Gasson postulate a polarized theory of emotional structure, though they oppose Freud by denying that emotions can be reversed; that positive can become negative and vice versa.

Having clarified some of the history of the concept of emotion, let me return to psychoanalytic theory and the Freudian dialectic. As Freud said, "our views from the very first have been dualistic" (1961:47), and even in his earliest work he postulated opposed forces working against one another in the human psyche. At first he opposed sexuality to self-preservation, but the discovery that the ego could take itself as a sexual object (1911), led him to modify this theory considerably through the "metapsychological papers" of 1911, 1914, and 1915, culminating in the publication of *Beyond the Pleasure Principle* (1920) and *The Ego and the Id* (1923). In these controversial late works, he made the "far-fetched speculation" (1961:18) that the basic drives underlying not only human action but all life were anabolism versus catabolism, Eros versus Thanatos or, in other words, love (sex) versus hate and aggression (death).

Freud put forward this theory very tentatively, since, as he said, it touches on the "most obscure and inaccessible region of the mind . . . [therefore] the least rigid hypothesis . . . will be the best" (1961:1). The theory was based partly upon his own clinical experience with repetition compulsions and masochistic behavior that seemed not to be explicable in terms of neurosis or repression, and partly upon his own notion of the evolution of life that he derived from the prevailing concept of energy in the physical science of his era. In this "hydraulic theory" all energy strives for release, all tension aims at reduction. Life, as a state of excitation, must be a result of external causation, and must continually press toward death. Self-preservation is only a way of dying properly, since "the organism wishes to die only in its own fashion" (1961:33).

But life, however it came about, exists, and struggles through Eros to maintain its existence. "The emergence of life would thus be the cause of the continuance of life and also at the same time the striving toward death; and life itself would be a conflict and a compromise between these two ends" (1960:30–31). Important for my picture of Swat is Freud's image of Eros: it is a uniting force, "it seeks to force together and hold together portions of living substance" (1961:54). In other words, Freud posits a pressure toward community. Individuals remaining alone die, whereas when individuals unite tensions develop that permit the creative continuation of life.

According to Freud, the life instincts, because they press for connection with others, are more easily seen. But the death instincts also "are diverted toward the external world in the form of aggression" (1960:44).

Both instincts are often mixed together in actual behavior as, for example, in aggressive sexuality. Checking external aggression leads to internal aggression, and the work of sublimation done by the ego, which diffuses the erotic drive, aids the death instinct, as does the repression enforced by the superego (which Freud says is the only really human part of the mind). Anxiety, and this is central to my theory, is seen as resulting from the ego's "fear of being overwhelmed or annihilated" (1960;47). Later anxiety states derive from "the first great anxiety state of birth and the infantile anxiety of longing—the anxiety due to separation from the pro- tecting mother" (1960:48). Anxiety is provoked when one is no longer sheltered, protected, and loved.

In his earlier work, Freud had paid little attention to the tie between mother and child, but in his later writing this tie assumed greater and greater importance, so that he could describe this bond as "unique, without parallel, established unalterably for a whole lifetime as the first and strongest love-object and as the prototype of all later love relations— for both sexes" (1949:188). But, because Freud's concept of instinct was physiological, he saw the tie as secondary, arising from the mother's role as the giver of food and reliever of tension. "Love has its origins in attachment to the satisfied need for nourishment" (1949:188). Whatever the source of attachment, in Freud's late work, the withdrawal of the loved object became central to his theoretical stance. Anxiety over that loss, rather than repression of instincts, is prior. Repression occurs when the loved object is absent and cannot protect the infant ego against its own instinctual appetites (1949:164–72).

Many of these late ideas of Freud's were rejected by his followers. The death instinct especially was repudiated, except by Klein and her school, who made it central to their theory. Other analysts generally agreed with Guntrip, who wrote that Freud had mixed up his categories: "sex is primarily biological and then becomes personal, aggression is primarily personal and then becomes biological" (1973:37), and with Winnicott:

"Death only becomes meaningful in the infant's living processes when hate has arrived, that is, at a late date, far removed from the phenomena which we can use to build a theory for the roots of aggression. . . . It is difficult to get at the roots of aggression, but we are not helped by the use of opposites such as life and death that do not mean anything at the stage of immaturity that is under consideration" (1965:187).

Oddly, though, these arguments seem prefigured by Freud himself:

Death is an abstract concept with a negative content for which no unconscious correlative can be found. It would seem that the mechanisms of the fear of death can only be that the ego relinquishes its narcissistic libidinal cathexis in a very large measure—that is, that it gives itself up, just as it gives up some *external* object in other cases in which it feels anxiety. I believe the fear of death is something that occurs between the ego and the superego. (Freud 1960:48)

The fear of death, then, is a late form of anxiety derived from the anxiety of separation from the loved object, and can only occur after the ego has developed narcissistic self-love as a defense against abandonment. But the fear of death and the death instinct are quite different matters, and I think Freud would argue that the death instincts continue their "mute work" from the beginning. Aggression, either externally or internally directed (through the medium of the superego), is a secondary development derived from the interplay with Eros; but basically, in Freud's view, death seeks solitude, immobility, and silence.

If most analysts denied or minimized the death instinct, Klein and her group gave it major importance. Klein's effort was to demonstrate the workings of the instincts from the earliest possible age, and the portraits she has given us of human infancy stress the internal world of the child rocked by the competing pulls of Eros and Thanatos. Unlike Freud, she did not see anxiety as arising from an early fear of separation from the loved object, but instead interpreted the death instinct quite literally as a fear of personal annihilation: "I differ from Freud in that I put forward the hypothesis that the primary cause of anxiety is the fear of annihilation, of death, arising from the workings of the death instinct within" (Klein 1975:57). Hate is thus internal to the infant, as is love, but both are projected outward to the mother, especially to her breast, which "inasmuch as it is gratifying, is loved and felt to be 'good'; in so far as it is a source of frustration, it is hated and felt to be 'bad'" (Klein 1975:62). Like Freud, she emphasizes the mother's role as feeder, and the sadistic component of the child's orality.

Klein's work is seen by her critics as too focused on an unproven preexistent internal war in the very young child, and as underestimating the importance of the mother–child tie. But many who did not follow her instinct theory or her reliance on projective mechanisms did find insight in her portrait of the child's relations with the external world.

"What [Klein] really did was to display the internal psychic life of small children not as a seething cauldron of instincts or id-drives, but as a highly personal inner world of ego–object relationships, finding expression in the child's fantasy life in ways that were felt even before they could be pictured or thought" (Guntrip 1973:59).

Other figures who have kept the Freudian postulate of the death instinct have not been psychoanalysts, For some reason, perhaps because the concepts are so general and so dialectical, Freud's later work has been especially popular with social theorists, particularly Brown, an historian, and Marcuse, a philosopher.

Brown (1959) attempts to rescue Freud's work from too literal an interpretation by interposing human institutions between the universal instincts of life and death, which touch all living things, and the development of those instincts in mankind.

We shall have to say that whatever the basic polarity in human life may be— whether it is the polarity of hunger and love, or love and hate—this polarity exists in animals, but does not exist in a condition of ambivalence. Man is distinguished from animals by having separated, ultimately into a state of mutual conflict, aspects of life (instincts) which in animals exist in some condition of undifferentiated unity or harmony. (Brown 1959:83)

This development of ambivalence is an ontological situation derived from the very conditions which give man his humanity, i.e., the institution of the family, the intense emotional ties fostered by long infant dependency, the ability to symbolize.

In man the dialectical unity between union and separateness, between interdependence and independence, between species and individual—in short, between life and death—is broken: The break occurs in infancy and is the consequence of the institution of the human family. . . . Objective dependence on parental care creates in the child a passive, dependent need to be loved, which is just the opposite of his dream of narcissistic omnipotence. . . . It is the dialectic formed by this contradiction which produces what Freud calls the conflict of ambivalence. . . . Anxiety is a response to experiences of separateness, individuality and death. The human child, which at the mother's breast experiences a new and intenser mode of union, of loving, of living, must also experience a new and intenser mode of separation, individuality and death. (Brown 1959:113–15)

For Brown, the human project is the overcoming of dualism, a project that he sees as possible since, unlike Freud, he does not view the instincts as radically discrete. Rather, in his view, love seeks to reestablish unity with death and an overcoming of repression.

This utopian vision is shared by Marcuse, who sees the fear of death as "the ultimate cause of all anxiety" (1965:74), and as the primary tool for manipulation of the masses by oppressive states. Like Brown, Marcuse also believed that a liberation from repression could confound separation and anxiety (1962). Love and union, for both Brown and Marcuse, are real possibilities if aware men and women can conquer the ambivalences ingrained in them through their indoctrination in the family. Thus, though both begin with essentially Freudian premises, these thinkers reject Freud's pessimism in favor of what Becker (1973) has called a "flaccid" vision of reconciliation. He attributes this failure of nerve, I think rightly, to the impossibility of being a "tragic revolutionary." Brown and Marcuse want to change the world and must present a utopia. Freud, the pessimist, is not under this obligation, and his image of the possibilities of the human condition is bleak indeed.

Though most psychoanalysts are not utopians, they too shy away from Freud's austere vision of innate drives constantly at war. The iconoclast Reich, who is perhaps as close to a utopian thinker as psychoanalysis has produced, was willing to retain a dialectic of innate drives, but repudiated the death instinct as a purely social construct. Rather, the basic opposition for Reich is between the ego and the outer world: "The first antithesis, sexual excitation—anxiety, is merely the intrapsychic reflection of the primal antithesis, ego—outer would, which then becomes the psychic reality of the inner contradiction: 'I desire—I am afraid'" (Reich 1972:275). The movement of life is expansion and withdrawal, libido and anxiety, love and hate. Aggression and masochism are a result of frustration by the outer world of ego's efforts to make contact. "The driving force behind all these measures taken by the ego is, in the final analysis, fear of punishment" (Reich 1972:157).

But Reich was almost alone in retaining the concept of energy, tension, and relaxation at the heart of his theory. The whole notion of instinct and the homeostatic pleasure principle came under attack as unproven extensions of a rather dated physical science model into psychology. As Guntrip says, the hydraulic tension reduction theory of pleasure and motivation "reduced any psychological consciousness of experience to the level of a mere accompaniment of bodily processes. . . . This is not psychology at all, but brain physiology" (1973:33). There was a general movement away from the instinct theory and the Freudian topology of the mind toward a psychology of the ego, led by Hartmann, on the one side, who stressed structure and system, while Sullivan and others focused more on the development of personhood.

The major new theory relevant to this discussion was the work of the object-relations school, perhaps the most influential contemporary movement in psychoanalysis. The movement took form from the work of Klein (though rejecting her focus on innate instincts), Anna Freud, the Balints, and others who had worked primarily with children. Their work has concentrated on the development of children and has led, under the influence of Fairbairn in England, to a concern with the mother–child tie as sketched in Freud's later work.

Because of the interest in the child's growth through relation with others (object-relation), this school has downplayed the role of innate drives or instincts at war. Rather, "the human infant [is seen as] a unitary dynamic whole with ego-potential as its essential quality from the start" (Guntrip 1973:93). An instinct, then, is not an entity, but simply "a characteristic dynamic pattern of behaviour" (Fairbairn 1954:218). This is not to say that there is no dialectic; but it does mean that the dialectic is provided more by experience than by internal drives. The fundamental premise is that the infant is whole by nature, but that experience in the world leads to a later split between good and bad stimuli and the development of ambivalence. An anthropologist who has been influenced by the object-relations school sums up the position of the infant: "though the mother gives, she also denies; she rewards, but she punishes; she is at the command of the infant, but sometimes she does not respond" (Murphy 1979:32).

Where Fairbairn and his disciple Guntrip took rather strong positions against the theory of innate instincts, Winnicott made an effort to link the two positions. Though he notes that "there is no id before ego" (1965:56) and stresses the central importance of reliable "good enough" mothering for individual development, he also notes that "being and annihilation are the two alternatives" (1965:47). For him, the infant is "an immature being who is all the time *on the brink of unthinkable anxiety*," metaphorically described as a fear of falling forever or of losing the body (1965:57). But this fear, which is a function of physical motility and a beginning sense of self, occurs after the mother has held the baby and given it a feeling of its own integrity. Only then can the child fear disintegration. Yet Winnicott still retains an underlying dualism, aside from the developed dualism of being and annihilation: this is the dualism of "the erotic and motility impulses" that derive from the body itself (1965:127).

Mahler, though more of an orthodox Freudian than Winnicott or Fairbairn, focuses on the same relation between mother and child, noting that "the gratification and frustration sequences promote structuring" as the infant becomes aware of its separateness and autonomy (1969:18). "The normal sympathy on the part of the mother is the human substitute for those instincts on which the animal is able to rely for survival" (1969:34). The infant discriminates between bad (pleasurable) stimuli and good (painful) input. The latter leads to aggression and ejection, the former to bliss and reaching out; the two being visualized as centrifugal versus centripetal. Mahler, like the object-relations theorists, hedges between supporting either the nature or the nurture position, recognizing an innate timetable of maturation and an opposition between good and bad stimuli, but noting that the maturation process can be confused and even destroyed by bad mothering. For her, as for other theorists, the ideal is the development of what Erikson (1950) has termed "basic trust," that is, a belief in the reliability and consistency of the world, as modeled after the reliable and consistent "good mother." The child, through learning trust and internalizing an image of the mother, is then able to be alone and to develop a sense of individuality.

Modern psychoanalytic theory, then, looks primarily at the evolution of the child's identity in his or her relation to the mother. It is essentially the ambivalence of this relation that provides the dynamic for emotional growth, while the notion of innate instinctual drives to love and hate are played down. Nonetheless, there is no assertion that the child is a tabula rasa. Instead, the child is seen as having certain underlying predispositions, a certain ability to discriminate between stimuli, a predetermined rate of maturation, and so on. The assumption that children *need* attachment and, later, also *need* to be separate is implicit in all object-relations psychology.

The theorist who has made the most specific contribution to clarifying these assumptions about attachment and separation is Bowlby. Operating essentially within the framework of the object-relations school, Bowlby has made it his life's work to uncover the roots of human emotions, using material from many close studies of infant behavior (particularly the cross-cultural work of Ainsworth 1967; 1972; Stayton, Ainsworth, and Main 1973), as well as the theories and observations of ethologists.

For Bowlby, the main problem is "Why should a young child be so distressed simply by the loss of his mother?" (1969:34). In order to understand this distress, he has looked at the various theories of the origin of the mother–child tie, including the infant's association of the mother with food and warmth, a craving for the womb, a need to cling, a need to suck (1969:178). But for him these theories do not take account of the fact that infants attach themselves even if not adequately mothered. For example, the emotional attachments of children in a nursery "remain undeveloped and unsatisfied but . . . are latent and ready to leap into action the moment the slightest opportunity for attachment is offered" (Burlingham and Freud 1944:43). Infants seem to have an "inborn endowment to extract every drop of human stimulus, of environmental nutrient, every bit of human contact available" (Mahler 1969:50). Even severely traumatized institutionalized children will form attachments, perhaps with an older child or with a peer group.

In order to account for the presence of attachment even without the physiological tie to the mother, Bowlby has postulated a new theory of instincts taken from ethology. Instincts are seen as more complex forms of behavior, set out in systematic "plans." "Instinctive behaviour is not inherited: what is inherited is the potential to develop certain sorts of systems" (Bowlby 1969:45). Feelings associated with these behaviors serve to bind them and to provide a disposition for action, but are not causes in themselves. For Bowlby, attachment and the feelings of love that accompany it are a result of the proximity of the loved object. Proximity is the goal of the instinct. The origins of this attachment behavior remain obscure, though Bowlby thinks it may be a remnant of the archaic necessity for the infant to be protected from predators.

Bowlby's work has, quite naturally, been taken up by sociobiologists, who focus on emotional reactions as innate and genetically derived. In an interesting way, sociobiology is the logical counter to modern academic psychology. Psychologists look for cognitive reasoning beneath emotional stances; the sociobiologists see emotion as prerational and genetic, while cognition is secondary and often merely justificatory. "The less rational but more important the decision making process . . . the more emotion should be expended in conducting it" (Wilson 1978:68).

Wilson sees phobias, romance, aggression, and so on as genetic attributes of human beings, and follows Bowlby in finding their source in man's long prehistory as a hunter and gatherer.

This is not the place for a detailed critique of sociobiology, but I might note in passing that Bowlby's documentation is far better than that of Wilson, who relies on a few case studies which happen to support his hypothesis (the !Kung and Yanomamo) while ignoring less favorable studies (the Eskimo, the Montagnais, the Tapirapé to name just a few), and who bases his theory on totally unjustified cross-species comparisons and the untenable concept that man exists outside of culture as a pure genetic construct (see his discussion of replicating human beings in a test tube and his claim that feral children would somehow formulate their own language and culture, 1978:18, 24).

While Wilson takes a tack opposite to that of cognitive psychologists, his basic position, like theirs, is mired in the cultural matrix of the West. The psychologists search for rational economic motivations behind every action, mirroring the technical rationality of our society. Wilson looks at human nature as a mechanical structure, a "marvelous robot" (1978:54) technically programmed to achieve the highest level of reproductive success. Aside from this economic view of man, Wilson also makes dubious assertions based on his own conception of the human condition, without knowledge of cross-cultural variation. For instance, when he claims that "love and sex do indeed go together" (1978:141), he is certainly not speaking for the Pukhtun.

The real flaw of sociobiology is that it claims far too much from too little, as Leacock (1980) has pointed out. The effort to search for biological roots of human activity is, nonetheless, a laudable one. Far more important, however, is to discover what the range of human behavior actually is. Without that knowledge, the sociobiological writers are merely building castles in the air.

Bowlby's work, however, is much more substantial than Wilson's, and includes a number of interesting correlatives. One, which may be applicable to Swat, is that children who are insecure seek to "confine all social behaviour to a single figure" (1969:308). In treating separation, Bowlby sees it essentially as the absence of attachment. It is the source of anxiety and the cause of infant protest, despair, and detachment. "In so far as attachments to loved figures are an integral part of our lives, a potential to feel distress on separation from them and anxiety at the prospect of separation is so also" (Bowlby 1973:56). The fear response and the anxiety resulting from separation are viewed as instinctive and genetic, like attachment behavior. Again, there are interesting correlatives as, for example, the child who is abandoned becoming particularly jealous and aggressive.

Bowlby has greatly broadened the theory of instinct and has brought it back to some measure of repute in the psychoanalytic community, though his work remains quite controversial. His data, however, is most impressive, and he has conclusively demonstrated that attachment is very deeply rooted and not derived from simple physiological gratification, and he has shown that the anxiety aroused by separation from the loved object is also a deep and primary experience. But, like all genetic theorists, Bowlby lacks a dynamic. There seems to be no concept of the child's efforts to separate himself and develop his own autonomy. The evolution of the self, with its painful contradiction of wanting to be at one with the loved object and yet desiring to be an independent individual, is left aside by Bowlby. His concentration on physical behavior alone leaves him without a theory of internal conflict and maturation, and the ambiguities of relationships are simply ignored. "There is no other point where the clash between metapsychological and descriptive thinking becomes as obvious as it is here. It leads to the apparently paradoxical result that what in terms of the libido theory is the apex of infantile narcissism, appears in Dr. Bowlby's descriptive terms as the height of 'attachment behavior'" (A. Freud 1960:56).

The aspects Bowlby lacks can be found both in Anna Freud (1936) and Reich (1972) in their discussions of defense mechanisms in the building of character. Both clearly note that defense is not only against anxiety deriving from the internal suppression of the instincts, but also from objective circumstances and from the demands of the superego. Particularly relevant is Anna Freud's discussion of altruism. While most theorists have focused exclusively on repression of sexual urges or the projection of aggression, she writes that the projection of "altruistic surrender," with consequent selflessness and intimacy, also occurs. The type case is Cyrano de Bergerac, who overcomes his own "narcissistic mortification" through self-sacrifice.

She also writes that play is a public fantasy of children, a way of reversing the unwanted realities of daily life, something that Klein and her school have studied in depth. Following Beidelman (1966) and others, perhaps it is permitted for anthropologists to extend this insight and see ritual as, in part, a sort of adult play, an enactment of liberating fantasies of escape from or reversal of cultural constraints.

A few basic points seem to stand out in the psychoanalytic literature, as I understand it. There is a very general consensus, even among the object-relations school, that human beings have a dual nature. Character is evolved through gratification and frustration; bliss, reaching out, love, expansion, union, attachment, the erotic are associated around the pole of interdependence and community, while independence is linked variously to anxiety, separation, hate, withdrawal, fear, motility, aggression, and individuality. The polarity is stated in many different ways. For Anna Freud, "love, longing, jealousy, mortification, pain and mourning accompany sexual wishes; hatred, anger and rage accompany the impulses of aggression" (1936:32), and the relation between the opposites is ambiguous, since "the distinction between the two classes of instincts does not seem sufficiently assured" (S. Freud 1960:32). Hatred may enter into relations that appear to be loving, and vice versa, and the matter of the dialectic between these poles is extremely complex.

Despite the complexities and ambiguities, despite disputes over the source of human duality, there is nonetheless a very striking correspondence of terms, and I take it as given that human beings do indeed have an emotional structure, visualized as dialectical, and consisting of sentiments associated with separation and independence on the one hand and attachment and interdependence on the other. This emotional structure, which may derive from the experience of extended nurturance and an intense mother–child tie, or from innate instincts, or a combination of both, is seen as existing independently of any particular social structure, though it can be modified in its expression by social circumstances. All humans everywhere will need to feel autonomy, and all will need to experience attachment. This is implicit in the definition of humanity offered by the psychoanalytic literature.

Given this structure, the next postulate is that its elements must find some form of expression within the cultural framework. The mechanisms of ego defense can distort and transform the ways in which the structure will find expression, and the mechanisms of the society itself can and do exert tremendous transforming influence. Yet the very convolutions of defense so ably documented by Anna Freud (1936) and Reich (1972) demonstrate the power of the emotional substrata, and the necessity for release. I am not making the claim here, as Roheim has done, that social organization is a secondary phenomenon, the "colossal efforts made by a baby who is afraid of being left alone in the dark" (1943:100), and that culture must therefore be interpreted psychoanalytically. Culture has its own being and motion, and can be viewed profitably from many nonpsychoanalytic perspectives, as I myself have done and hope to continue to do. But Roheim is right when he says that human beings eternally repeat "the fundamental pattern of separation (anxiety, aggression) followed by union" (1970:43). Culture does not function simply to give form to that pattern, as Roheim asserts, but I claim that culture *must permit* expression of these universal emotional needs.

Returning to Swat, I have described in some detail a particular social order based upon a segmentary lineage system as it has evolved in a situation of land scarcity. The resulting social structure and pattern of exchange is such that the reality in which people exist is one of individual egoism, fear of others, jealousy, hostility, and contempt. In the course of this work, I have demonstrated repeatedly that most of the activity and ideology of the society can be traced to the necessities of this stern social order. However, I have discovered that hospitality and the pervasive male ideal of friendship, though molded by the social reality, cannot be traced back to this reality.

If we accept an underlying emotional structure as pan-human, then, of course, this structure must exist in Swat. In my picture of Pukhtun society, separation and the concurrent aspects of independence, individuality, and aggression are all expressed unrestrainedly in daily reality. The emotional coloring surrounding the pole of separation is complementary with the general tendencies of the social order itself. In contrast, the emotions associated with attachment clash with the trend of the society at large. Trust, love, and intimacy are not found in Swat once the child has been weaned. Rather, he must face a world in which women are contemptible in general and often hostile in particular, and where all equal men are rivals, while all superiors are feared and envied, and all inferiors are despised.

It is important at this juncture to recall again the strong relations between a young child, especially a boy, and his mother. Hsu (1972) has characterized the strong mother–son tie as primary in South Asian society in general and other psychoanalytic writers, particularly Kakar (1978) and Roland (1980), have focused on the development of the self in this cultural context. Although the subjects of these studies have been caste Hindus living in strongly hierarchical worlds, dependent on authority and accepting of subservience, there are many striking parallels with Pukhtun life. Especially important is the very powerful relationship with the continually forgiving, doting, always available mother figure, who provides her infant son with a security he is never to know again in later life. This tie is much stronger than that found in Western societies, and is reinforced by the social order, which emphasizes the importance of sons for the mother's own sense of selfhood and value. But, as the son grows up, is weaned, and begins to be socialized into the hard world of adulthood, the encompassing loving relation with his mother is made impossible by social conditions. Men are not dependent in Swat (the relation is, of course, much different in caste India, where the cult of the mother attests to her continuing power), and women are repudiated as objects of affection. No other object is available, and love is then displaced onto the realm of the ideal. In India, where the pattern is, as I have noted, somewhat different, the ideal figure also exists. He is the guru at whose feet the disciple wishes to sit. In Swat, where no man can accept sitting at the feet of any other, the ideal is the friend, and his image, the guest.

It is within this framework that the ritual of hospitality and refuge and the ideal of total friendship must be seen. The ritual is a playing out of fantasy, an enactment of relations that the conditions of real life make impossible. The altruistic surrender (to use Anna Freud's terminology) found in hospitality and friendship are expressions of emotional needs prohibited by a social structure which is competitive and exceptionally insecure. As Bowlby notes, insecure relations of attachment give rise to focusing on a single figure, and to jealousy and aggression. In Freudian terms, the love offered in Swat is narcissistic, since it seeks to find in the other a mirror for the self, but this is no wonder, since "basic trust" of others, lauded by Erikson, would be folly in Swat. Yet the love offered, though molded by social circumstance, is real enough. The outpouring of affection found in hospitality and friendship relations shows the power of the underlying need, a need kept dammed up save for the few highly restricted breaches socially permitted in the wall of repression.

But if attachment is generally disallowed except in ideal and ritual, might we not expect tremendous anxiety? The consensus of the psychoanalytic literature is that isolation, separation, and independence must lead to apprehension. Since Swati men idealize independence and autonomy, and since the release of affection is greatly limited, one would expect some evidence of internal tension and fear.

At first glance, the assumption of anxiety and tension seems incorrect. The Swati men appear either stoical in their ordinary lives or else extremely friendly and affable when entertaining a guest. Also, the Durkheimian indicator of anomie, a high suicide rate, is absent in Swat, as suicide, despite romantic songs, is decidedly rare. But it must be remembered that anomie, a sense of the loss of self, does not occur in Swat. The rigid social structure has the beneficent effect of assuring everyone of exactly who they are and what they should do in all situations. There is no confusion over who one is in Swat society, no muddling of self-image, and therefore no anomie.

But what does exist is quite a different thing. This is an overpowering fear of suffocation by a terrifying invisible demon. Beneath the men's exterior presentation of self, there is a sense of tension which breaks out in what appear to be classical attacks of acute anxiety. These attacks, which are common, especially among younger men, are rarely discussed because men fear that discussion will trigger further attacks. The cause of the attack is said to be the predatory and (sometimes) amatory attentions of a succubus which preys on men just as they are dozing off to sleep. Called a *xapasa*, or noseless one, this horror lies atop the hapless victim, fitting her noseless face to the face of her victim, stopping his breath, making his heart race madly, while at the same time rendering him completely impotent and immobile. An attack, which may last for twenty minutes, leaves its victim shaken and trembling with fear. In these frightful events the underlying anxiety of Swati life reveals itself.* The *xapasa* is said to live primarily in the Swat Valley. This is significant because Swat, with its great population pressure, has perhaps the most competitive and internally hostile social order in the region. It follows, then, that anxiety would be highest there. It also follows, from my argument, that hospitality would be most highly developed in Swat. This indeed is a claim that Swatis make for themselves, but it is impossible to validate.

* Alan Roland has suggested that the form of the *xapasa* might be related to the close mother–son relationship, and expresses the son's fear of her suffocating attentions (personal communication).

Apropos of this point, however, there is an interesting and generally accepted characterization of the people of Dir; a characterization believed in Dir as well as in Swat. The people of Southern Dir, who have the reputation of being peaceful and honest, also have a reputation for miserliness in hospitality. In contrast, the Pukhtun of Northern Dir are warlike, treacherous, and hostile, but are warm and lavish in treatment of a guest. To explain this contrast, it is said that "where there is much fighting, there is also much hospitality." The local understanding thus parallels my own.

Where there is less hostility within, there should also be less emphasis on hospitalitity and the friendship ideal. This correlative is validated by the Dir case, and can clarify the female concept of friendship and hospitality as well. Women and girls would be expected to differ from men, since they have a much less conflicted life. They have the advantage of a female community within which complaints may be shared. They do not suffer the travails of inter- and intrafamilial rivalry over land. Their ambitions (having male children and eventually becoming dominant within the household) are quite easily actualized. Their enmity with one another is shallow and short-lived, and is greatly overshadowed by the universal female war with men, which unites all women in a deeply felt bond of shared misery.

As private creatures, and as creatures of a lower order, women are free to vent their anger and release their hostilities in gossip with other women. They are also allowed, and even expected, to display emotion in hysterical crying at funerals and in other outbursts, while the men must maintain a stoical face. Because women are not so emotionally repressed, and because they are not so conflicted or under such emotional pressure as their men, the ideal of friendship and the enactment of hospitality is not so important to them, and they are also less subject to attacks by the xapasa. Women are hospitable, but their hospitality is for the sake of their own honor; to fail to provide for a guest would reflect badly on a woman. But women do not particularly desire guests, as their husbands do, and they are known to argue with their men against grandiose displays of hospitality. Furthermore, women do not appear to have the ideal of friendship which has such an important role in the fantasy lives of the men. This comparative indifference to the central rite of men's lives indicates the women's relative satisfaction with their existing relationships, and their lack of any emotional need to enact an idealized relation of attachment. This attitude of women was tested among twenty girls at a local elite coeducational school. The same test of liking and disliking mentioned earlier in this chapter was given to the girls as well. Their answers differed strikingly from the boys'. There was only one pair of friends, and most named a number of other girls as equal friends. There was no rivalry over friendships, and dislike was reserved for certain boys in the class. Like the men of Southern Dir, women fight less and also have less of a need to enact rituals of attachment.

My hypothesis is a tentative one, but it seems to make sense of contradictions that a purely social analysis could not comprehend. Empirically, it would be valuable to look at similar societies to see how friendship or romance is elaborated. There has been a beginning in this direction in studies of the American family, where the elaboration of romance is seen as a response to increasing competitiveness and lack of community in the society at large (see Lasch 1977). The Ik, recently forced to settle in the barren mountains of northern Uganda, are perhaps the most famous anthropological example of a society which stresses separation and egoism. According to their ethnographer, the Ik are a people for whom "cruelty took the place of Love." "The Ik have successfully abandoned . . . those 'basic' qualities such as family, cooperative sociality, belief, love, hope, and so forth, for the very good reason that in their context these militated against survival" (Turnbull 1972:159, 289). This seems to refute my argument, but Turnbull notes in passing that the Ik have strong dyadic friendships with men of other tribes in which "each individual vows to aid the other, without any right of refusal, for the rest of his life" (1972:162). In the totally selfish Ik society, friends must be generous with one another, and Turnbull admits that friendship is "the one bond that stood up in the midst of an almost total collapse of society. . . . It was . . . a sort of bedrock below which even the Ik could not sink" (1972:181). It is precisely this "bedrock" that I am seeking to understand.

The theory of emotional structure might also be extended to extreme societies at the other end of the spectrum, i.e., those that demand community and cooperation while denying aggression and separation. There I would expect a hypostatized and ritualized treatment of the prohibited emotions, an expectation validated in the horrific demonology of the Lepcha (Gorer 1967) and the Semai belief in harmful spirits and their panic at thunderstorms (Dentan 1968). The Semai case, in fact, has led two anthropologists to attempt formulations of emotion (Robarchek 1977; Paul 1978), the first a cognitive cultural account, the second a theory of instinctive aggression. My own understanding is that these excessive societies stressing the interdependence pole of sentiments have found a means for releasing other emotions prohibited within the general cultural framework.

Once again, I repeat that I am not proposing a reduction of anthropology into psychology, nor am I claiming that the actions of men and women within their social system can only be grasped through psychoanalytic insight. In fact, social structure has an overwhelming influence on individual action, as this book has demonstrated. Even our emotions have been structured, according to ego psychology, the object-relations school, and utopians like Brown, through a long history of social interaction, and are themselves thus a social product of that most human of institutions, the family. But whatever the origin, I claim that there is a universal pattern of emotions, a dialectic between love and hate, union and separation, community and individual, that must find expression in every society. Friendship and hospitality in Swat can then best be understood as the expression, in a world of hostility and fear, of the necessary counterweight to the Pukhtun man's inevitable sense of isolation: love.

Appendix A
Survey Data

KEY TO TABLES

Pukhtun
MK: Malik *khel*
J: Jakhawal
UK: Umar *khel*
KK: Kurum *khel*
DK: Daulet Khan *khel*
MS: Masho *khel*
OK: Other *khels*, including four households of Kushur *khel*, one house-
       hold Issa *khel*, one Nakrudin *khel*, and one Pukhtun family from
       Dherai. All are immigrants to Shin Bagh.

Stanadar
Mi: *Mias*
Mu   *Mullahs*
Sb: *Sahibzadas* (only on table A.5.)

Laborers and Specialists
P: *Parachas* (muleteers)
T: *Tarkans* and *Ingors* (carpenters and blacksmiths)
Z: *Zurgars* (goldsmiths)
G: *Gujar* (ethnic group: laborers and herdsmen of cattle)
Ko: *Kohistani* (ethnic group: laborers and shepherds)
Da: *Darzis* (tailors)
Du: *Dukandars* (shopkeepers)
F: *Fakirs* (laborers)
C: *Chamyars* (shoemakers)
Jo: *Jolas* (weavers)
Kl: *Kolals* (potters)
S: *Shahkhels* (leatherworkers and butchers)

N: *Nais* (Barbers and messengers)

OL: Other laboring groups, including one household of *taeli* (oil presser), one of *jalawan* (boatman), one *marate* (slave), and one *ustaz* (teacher).

House Guests at Time of Survey

MK: 3—a widow with her son and daughter for 11 years.

KK: 3—a daughter returned by her husband for 3 years, and a sister and her husband for 7 years.

P: 1—a daughter returned by her husband for 2 years.

F: 2—a dead brother's daughter returned by her husband for 3 years and a father's brother's wife on a visit for 10 days.

Table A.1 Population of Shin Bagh by Household

	Pukhtun							Stanadar		Laborer and Specialist														
	MK	J	UK	KK	DK	MS	OK	Mi	Mu	P	T	Z	G	Ko	Da	Du	F	C	Jo	Kl	S	N	OL	Totals
Total resident	331	81	75	227	136	101	35	50	166	114	50	31	85	18	12	24	231	21	40	11	25	41	17	1,970
Family	313	79	73	277	136	101	35	50	165	114	50	31	85	18	12	24	230	21	40	11	25	41	17	1,946
Servants	18	2	2	0	0	0	0	0	1	0	0	0	0	0	0	0	1	0	0	0	0	0	0	24
Family																								
males	152	38	32	135	62	50	16	23	89	58	26	14	42	10	6	11	111	11	23	6	11	20	8	953
females	161	41	41	142	74	51	19	27	80	56	24	17	43	8	6	13	119	10	17	5	14	21	9	993
husbands	60	18	13	47	15	14	5	7	29	22	10	5	17	4	2	3	47	5	10	1	5	8	3	350
wives	73	18	17	58	24	21	8	9	33	23	10	7	18	4	3	3	48	5	10	1	5	8	3	409
single men	15	1	3	20	2	5	2	3	9	9	6	2	4	3	3	0	15	1	1	4	2	1	3	114
single women	11	0	8	9	7	6	1	3	8	5	3	0	0	0	0	1	11	1	0	0	0	2	0	77
boys	75	18	15	66	41	31	9	11	48	26	10	6	20	3	1	8	44	5	11	1	4	11	2	466
girls	66	23	13	65	36	22	8	12	33	27	7	10	20	3	1	7	49	4	6	2	8	9	2	433
widowers	2	1	1	2	4	2	0	2	2	1	0	1	1	0	0	0	0	0	1	0	0	0	0	23
widows	10	0	3	9	7	2	2	3	3	0	4	0	4	1	1	2	5	0	2	2	1	2	4	69
returned women	1	0	0	1	0	0	0	0	0	1	0	0	1	0	0	0	3	0	0	0	0	0	0	7
Servants																								
husbands	3	1	1	0	0	0	0	0	0	0	0	0	0	0	0	0	0	0	0	0	0	0	0	5
wives	3	1	1	0	0	0	0	0	0	0	0	0	0	0	0	0	0	0	0	0	0	0	0	5
single men	8	0	0	0	0	0	0	0	1	0	0	0	0	0	0	0	0	0	0	0	0	0	0	9
single women	3	0	0	0	0	0	0	0	0	0	0	0	0	0	0	0	1	0	0	0	0	0	0	4
widowers	1	0	0	0	0	0	0	0	0	0	0	0	0	0	0	0	0	0	0	0	0	0	0	1
Houses																								
number	41	15	13	39	24	15	7	8	24	18	9	3	16	3	2	3	44	5	7	2	4	6	4	312
persons per house	8	5.4	5.7	7.1	5.7	6.7	5	6.3	6.9	6.3	5.5	10	5.3	6	6	8	5.3	4.2	4.3	5.5	6.3	7	4.5	6.3

Table A.2 Residents per Household

Persons per house	Pukhtun							Stanadar		Laborers and Specialists														Totals
	MK	J	UK	KK	DK	MS	OK	Mi	Mu	P	T	Z	G	Ko	Da	Du	F	C	Jo	Kl	S	N	OL	
28	0	0	0	1	0	0	0	0	0	0	0	0	0	0	0	0	0	0	0	0	0	0	0	1
25	1	0	0	0	0	0	0	0	0	0	0	0	0	0	0	0	0	0	0	0	0	0	0	1
20	0	0	0	1	0	0	0	0	0	0	0	0	0	0	0	0	0	0	0	0	0	0	0	1
19	0	0	0	0	0	0	0	0	0	0	0	0	0	0	0	0	0	0	0	0	0	0	1	1
18	0	0	0	1	0	0	0	0	1	0	0	0	0	0	0	0	0	0	0	0	0	0	0	2
17	1	0	0	0	0	0	0	0	0	0	0	0	0	0	0	0	0	0	0	0	0	0	0	1
16	0	0	0	0	0	0	0	0	0	0	0	0	0	0	0	0	0	0	0	0	1	0	0	1
14	0	0	0	1	0	0	0	0	0	0	0	0	0	0	0	0	0	0	1	0	0	0	0	2
13	2	0	0	1	0	0	0	0	1	0	0	0	1	0	0	0	0	0	0	0	0	0	0	5
12	0	0	0	1	0	0	0	0	1	0	0	0	0	0	0	0	1	0	0	1	0	0	0	5
11	2	0	1	0	0	0	0	1	1	1	0	0	0	0	0	0	2	0	0	0	0	0	0	7
10	3	0	0	0	1	1	1	0	0	0	1	1	0	0	1	1	1	0	1	0	0	0	0	14
9	2	1	0	3	1	0	0	1	0	3	0	0	0	0	0	0	1	0	0	0	1	0	0	13
8	3	3	1	1	1	4	1	0	3	1	1	1	1	0	0	1	3	0	1	0	0	1	0	23
7	8	1	4	8	5	5	0	1	3	3	0	0	1	0	0	0	8	1	1	1	1	1	1	55
6	5	1	0	7	5	1	1	1	5	4	2	0	1	2	0	0	8	1	0	0	0	0	0	51
5	5	3	3	5	7	3	1	2	0	2	1	0	4	0	0	0	7	0	3	0	1	1	1	45
4	3	3	2	4	3	0	1	0	3	1	4	0	4	0	0	0	4	2	0	1	0	1	1	35
3	2	0	1	3	1	1	0	2	0	3	0	0	1	1	0	0	2	2	3	0	0	1	0	21
2	2	1	1	1	1	0	2	0	4	0	0	0	3	0	0	0	4	1	0	0	0	0	1	22
1	0	1	0	0	0	0	1	0	0	0	0	0	0	0	0	0	3	0	0	0	0	0	0	6
Total houses	41	15	13	39	24	15	7	8	24	18	9	3	16	3	2	3	44	5	7	2	4	6	4	312
Avg. persons per house	8	5.4	5.8	7.1	5.7	6.7	5	6.3	6.9	6.3	5.5	10.3	5.3	5.5	6	6	8	5.2	4.2	5.7	5.5	6.3	7	4.5

Table A.3 Rooms and House Ownership Data

	Pukhtun							Stanadar						Laborers and Specialists									
No. of Rooms	MK	J	UK	KK	DK	MS	OK	Mi	Mu	P	T	Z	G	Ko	Da	Du	F	C	Jo	Kl	S	N	OL
6 rooms	1	0	0	0	0	0	0	0	0	0	0	0	0	0	0	0	0	0	0	0	0	0	0
5 rooms	5	0	0	0	0	0	0	0	0	0	0	0	0	0	0	0	0	0	0	0	0	0	0
4 rooms	3	1	1	3	0	0	0	0	1	0	0	0	0	0	0	0	2	0	0	0	0	0	0
3 rooms	7	4	0	3	0	0	0	0	1	2	0	0	0	0	0	0	0	0	0	0	0	0	0
2 rooms	17	3	2	16	2	2	1	0	2	2	1	1	0	0	0	1	2	0	2	0	0	0	2
1 room	8	7	10	17	22	13	6	8	20	14	8	2	16	3	2	2	40	5	5	2	4	6	2
avg. rooms per house	2.6	1.9	1.4	1.8	1.1	1.1	1.1	1	1.3	1.3	1.1	1.3	1	1	1	1.3	1.2	1	1.3	1	1	1	1.5
avg. persons per room	3.1	2.8	4	3.9	5.7	6.1	4.5	6.3	5.4	4.9	5	7.8	5.3	6	6	6	4.4	4.2	4.4	5.5	6.3	6.8	2.8

Overall avg. number of rooms per house: 1.47
Overall avg. number of persons per room: 4.29

	Pukhtun							Stanadar						Laborers and Specialists										
House Ownership	MK	J	UK	KK	DK	MS	OK	Mi	Mu	P	T	Z	G	Ko	Da	Du	F	C	Jo	Kl	S	N	OL	Totals
Self-owned	41	15	12	39	24	15	7	3	18	3	0	2	0	0	1	2	1	2	1	0	2	1	0	189
Rented (ijara)	0	0	1	0	0	0	0	0	2	12	4	0	2	1	0	1	5	0	3	1	0	1	2	35
In return for service (kandari)	0	0	0	0	0	0	0	4	2	3	1	1	13	2	0	0	35	3	3	1	2	4	2	76
As Loan Guarantee (ganra)	0	0	0	0	0	0	0	1	1	0	0	0	1	0	1	0	2	0	0	0	0	0	0	6
Free gift	0	0	0	0	0	0	0	0	1	0	4	0	0	0	0	0	1	0	0	0	0	0	0	6
Totals	41	15	13	39	24	15	7	8	24	18	9	3	16	3	2	3	44	5	7	2	4	6	4	312

Table A.4 Neighborhoods (PULAO) and Wards (TəL)

	Pukhtun							Stanadar		Laborers and Specialists														Totals (tal)	Totals (palao)
	MK	J	UK	KK	DK	MS	OK	Mi	Mu	P	T	Z	G	Ko	Da	Du	F	C	Jo	Kl	S	N	OL		
KUZE PALAO																									
Qamar's tal	5	0	0	7	9	2	5	3	2	7	1	0	1	0	1	0	1	0	1	0	1	0	1	47	
Subidar's tal	2	0	7	11	5	0	2	0	0	2	1	0	0	3	0	1	3	0	4	1	2	1	2	47	119
Shalyar's tal	0	15	0	0	0	0	0	0	0	1	1	0	1	0	0	0	5	0	0	1	0	0	1	25	
COURT PALAO																									
Qasin's tal	9	0	0	0	7	1	0	4	9	1	3	1	0	0	0	0	10	1	2	0	0	1	0	49	
Arjuman's tal	5	0	0	6	1	10	0	1	2	2	1	0	2	0	0	0	10	0	0	0	0	1	0	41	102
Malik's tal	5	0	0	2	2	0	0	0	0	0	0	0	1	0	0	0	1	0	0	0	0	1	0	12	
BAR PALAO																									
Qalander's tal	3	0	6	13	0	2	0	0	11	5	0	2	11	0	1	2	14	4	0	0	1	2	0	77	
Other khans	12	0	0	0	0	0	0	0	0	0	2	0	0	0	0	0	0	0	0	0	0	0	0	14	91

Table A.5 Migrant Laborers Working Out of Shin Bagh in 1977

	Pukhtun							Stanadar			Laborer and Specialist														Totals
	MK	J	UK	KK	DK	MS	OK	Sb	Mi	Mu	P	T	Z	G	Ko	Da	Du	F	C	Jo	Kl	S	N	OL	
Karachi workers																									
15 years or more	3	3	0	7	0	1	0	0	0	1	0	0	0	0	0	0	0	0	0	0	0	0	0	0	15
10–15 yrs.	0	0	0	1	0	0	0	0	0	0	0	0	0	2	0	0	0	3	3	0	0	1	1	0	11
5–10 yrs.	3	3	5	2	1	0	0	0	0	4	1	0	3	0	0	0	0	2	3	0	0	2	1	2	32
1–5 yrs.	1	3	5	14	4	7	0	0	0	4	0	0	0	0	1	0	0	7	0	0	1	0	0	0	47
0–1 yr.	2	0	0	1	0	2	0	0	0	1	2	0	0	0	0	0	0	1	0	0	0	0	0	0	9
Mid-East workers																									
1–5 yrs. or more	2	1	0	6	4	2	3	2	0	0	0	0	0	0	1	0	0	1	0	1	1	0	0	0	24
0–1 yrs.	2	0	0	3	2	0	0	1	0	1	1	0	0	0	0	0	0	0	0	0	0	0	0	0	10
Swat workers																									
Total	1	1	0	0	0	0	0	0	0	0	0	0	0	0	0	1	1	3	7	0	0	0	0	1	15
NWFP Workers																									
Total	3	0	0	0	0	0	0	0	0	2	0	0	2	0	0	0	0	2	0	0	0	0	2	0	11
Pakistan workers																									
Total	0	0	0	0	0	0	0	0	2	0	0	0	0	0	0	0	0	2	0	0	0	0	0	0	4
Foreign																									
Total	0	0	0	0	0	0	1	1	0	0	0	0	0	0	0	0	0	0	0	0	0	0	1	0	3
Total migrants	17	11	10	34	14	12	4	4	2	13	4	0	5	2	2	1	1	21	13	1	2	3	5	3	184
Migrant husbands	7	0	4	9	9	5	2	0	2	4	1	0	2	1	1	0	0	1	0	0	0	0	0	0	48
Migrant bachelors	10	11	6	25	5	7	2	4	0	9	3	0	3	1	1	1	1	20	13	1	2	3	5	3	136

Table A.6 Migrant Laborers Living in Shin Bagh in 1977

	Pukhtun							Stanadar		Laborers and Specialists														Totals
	MK	J	UK	KK	DK	MS	OK	Mi	Mu	P	T	Z	G	Ko	Da	Du	F	C	Jo	Kl	S	N	OL	
Worked in Karachi																								
15 years or more	1	0	1	0	0	0	1	0	0	0	0	0	0	0	0	0	0	0	0	0	0	0	0	3
10–15 yrs.	2	3	0	0	0	0	0	0	0	0	0	0	0	0	0	0	1	0	0	0	0	0	0	6
5–10 yrs.	3	0	2	15	6	4	0	0	6	1	0	2	2	0	0	2	12	0	0	0	0	4	0	59
1–5 yrs.	8	0	2	7	3	3	0	1	8	0	0	0	2	0	1	0	5	0	0	0	0	0	0	40
0–1 yr.	0	0	0	0	0	0	0	0	0	0	0	0	0	0	0	0	0	0	0	0	0	0	0	0
Worked in Bombay																								
15 years or more	1	0	0	0	0	0	0	0	0	1	0	0	0	0	0	0	1	0	0	0	0	0	0	3
10–15 yrs.	1	0	0	0	1	0	0	1	0	0	0	0	0	0	0	0	1	0	0	0	0	0	0	4
5–10 yrs.	0	1	0	0	0	1	0	1	1	0	0	2	1	0	0	0	1	1	0	0	0	0	0	9
1–5 yrs.	2	1	0	2	1	0	0	0	1	0	0	0	0	0	0	0	1	0	0	0	0	0	0	8
0–1 yr.	0	0	0	0	0	0	1	0	0	0	0	0	0	0	0	0	0	0	0	0	0	0	0	1
Worked elsewhere																								
10 years or more	0	0	0	0	0	0	0	0	0	0	0	0	3	0	0	0	0	0	0	0	0	0	0	3
5–10 yrs.	2	0	0	0	0	0	0	0	0	0	0	0	0	0	0	0	0	0	1	0	0	0	0	3
1–5 yrs.	1	0	0	0	0	2	0	0	0	0	0	0	0	0	0	0	0	3	2	0	0	0	0	8
0–1 yr.	1	0	0	0	0	0	0	0	0	0	0	0	0	0	0	0	1	0	0	0	0	0	0	2
Totals	22	5	5	24	11	10	2	3	16	2	0	4	8	0	1	2	23	4	3	0	0	4	0	149

Table A.7 Landholding: dauftar and tseri

	Pukhtun							Stanadar		Laborers and Specialists														Total house-	Total land
	MK	J	UK	KK	DK	MS	OK	Mi	Mu	P	T	Z	G	Ko	Da	Du	F	C	Jo	Kl	S	N	OL	holds	(avg.)
Household dauftar																									
32–36 (paisa*)	3	0	0	2	0	0	0	0	0	0	0	0	0	0	0	0	0	0	0	0	0	0	0	5	170
28–32 "	2	0	1	1	0	0	0	0	0	0	0	0	0	0	0	0	0	0	0	0	0	0	0	4	120
24–28 "	5	0	0	0	0	0	0	0	0	0	0	0	0	0	0	0	0	0	0	0	0	0	0	5	130
16–24 "	1	2	0	3	0	2	1	0	0	0	0	0	0	0	0	0	0	0	0	0	0	0	0	9	180
12–16 "	4	2	0	7	2	0	1	0	0	0	0	0	0	0	0	0	0	0	0	0	0	0	0	16	224
8–12 "	10	4	5	7	2	0	0	0	0	0	0	0	0	0	0	0	0	0	0	0	0	0	0	28	280
4–8 "	6	1	5	11	2	5	4	0	0	0	0	0	0	0	0	0	0	0	0	0	0	0	0	34	204
2–4 "	6	5	0	3	17	7	0	0	0	0	0	0	0	0	0	0	0	0	0	0	0	0	0	38	114
1–2 "	0	0	1	5	0	0	0	0	0	0	0	0	0	0	0	0	0	0	0	0	0	0	0	6	9
0–1 "	0	0	0	0	0	0	0	0	0	3	3	0	3	0	0	0	0	0	0	0	0	0	0	9	4.5
Landlords	37	14	12	39	23	14	6	0	0	3	3	0	3	0	0	0	0	0	0	0	0	0	0	154	
Total paisa	522	129	111	409	111	91	58	0	0	1.5	1.5	0	1.5	0	0	0	0	0	0	0	0	0	0		1,435.5
Avg. paisa per landlord	12.7	8.6	8.6	10.4	4.6	4.7	9.6	0	0	.5	.5	0	.5	0	0	0	0	0	0	0	0	0	0		9.3
Household tseri																									
3 or more	7	0	0	0	0	0	0	0	4	0	0	0	0	0	0	0	0	0	0	0	0	0	0	11	33
2	6	0	0	0	0	0	0	0	6	1	0	1	0	0	0	0	0	0	0	0	0	0	0	14	28
1	11	0	1	11	4	0	4	4	9	0	0	0	1	1	1	0	0	0	0	0	1	0	0	48	48
0–1	2	0	0	0	0	3	0	0	0	0	0	0	0	0	0	0	0	0	0	0	0	0	0	5	2.5
Landlords	26	0	1	11	4	3	4	4	19	1	0	1	1	1	1	0	0	0	0	0	1	0	0	78	
Total tseri	45	0	1	11	1.5	4	4	4	33	2	0	2	1	1	1	0	0	0	0	0	1	0	0		111.5
Avg. tseri per landlord	1.7	0	1	1	.5	1	1	1	1.7	2	0	2	1	1	1	0	0	0	0	0	1	0	0		1.4

Note: Dauftar are reckoned in paisas and rupees (the same term used for money). One rupee is generally assumed to be about 10 acres or about 8,800 lbs. (100 mounds) of wheat. There are 48 paisa in a rupee and approximately 30 rupees in a village.

Table A.8 Landlords Renting Out Land

	Pukhtun							Stanadar						Laborers and Specialists												Land
	MK	J	UK	KK	DK	MS	OK	Mi	Mu	P	T	Z	G	Ko	Da	Du	F	C	Jo	KI	S	N	OL	Ren-tiers	rented out
Dauftar rented out																									
24 paisa	3	0	0	0	0	0	0	0	0	0	0	0	0	0	0	0	0	0	0	0	0	0	0	3	72
20–24	1	0	0	1	0	0	0	0	0	0	0	0	0	0	0	0	0	0	0	0	0	0	0	1	22
16–20	0	0	0	1	1	0	0	0	0	0	0	0	0	0	0	0	0	0	0	0	0	0	0	2	36
12–16	1	0	0	1	1	0	1	0	0	0	0	0	0	0	0	0	0	0	0	0	0	0	0	3	42
8–12	3	1	0	1	1	0	0	0	0	0	0	0	0	0	0	0	0	0	0	0	0	0	0	5	50
4–8	3	0	0	2	2	2	3	0	0	0	0	0	0	0	0	0	0	0	0	0	0	0	0	10	60
2–4	0	0	0	0	0	0	0	0	0	0	0	0	0	0	0	0	0	0	0	0	0	0	0	2	6
Rentiers	11	1	0	2	6	2	4	0	0	0	0	0	0	0	0	0	0	0	0	0	0	0	0	26	
Paisa rented	156	10	0	24	54	12	32	0	0	0	0	0	0	0	0	0	0	0	0	0	0	0	0		288
Avg. paisa rented out	14	10	0	12	9	6	8	0	0	0	0	0	0	0	0	0	0	0	0	0	0	0	0		11
Tseri rented out																									
3	7	0	0	0	0	0	0	0	0	0	0	0	0	0	0	0	0	0	0	0	0	0	0	7	21
2	3	0	0	0	0	0	0	0	1	0	0	1	0	0	0	0	0	0	0	0	0	0	0	5	10
1	2	0	0	1	1	0	0	0	0	0	1	1	0	0	0	0	0	0	0	0	0	0	0	6	6
0–1	2	0	0	0	0	0	0	0	1	1	1	0	0	0	0	0	0	0	0	0	0	0	0	5	2.5
Rentiers	14	0	0	1	1	0	0	0	2	1	2	2	0	0	0	0	0	0	0	0	0	0	0	23	
Tseri rented	30	0	0	1	1.5	0	0	0	3	0	0	2	0	0	0	0	0	0	0	0	0	0	0		39.5
Avg. tseri rented out	2.1	0	0	1	.5	0	0	0	1.5	0	0	1	0	0	0	0	0	0	0	0	0	0	0		1.7

Table A.9 Working as Tenant Farmers

	Pukhtun							Stanadar		Laborers and Specialists															Land
	MK	J	UK	KK	DK	MS	OK	Mi	Mu	P	T	Z	G	Ko	Da	Du	F	C	Jo	Kl	S	N	OL	Tenants Worked	Worked
Dauftar Worked as Tenant																									
24 paisa	0	0	0	1	0	0	0	0	0	0	0	0	0	0	0	0	0	0	0	0	0	0	0	1	24
20–24	0	0	0	0	0	0	0	0	0	0	0	0	0	0	0	0	0	0	1	0	0	0	0	1	22
16–20	0	0	0	0	0	0	0	0	0	1	0	0	0	0	0	0	1	0	0	0	0	0	0	2	36
12–15	1	0	0	0	0	0	0	0	0	0	0	0	0	0	0	0	0	0	0	0	0	0	0	1	14
8–12	0	0	0	1	0	1	0	0	0	0	0	0	0	0	0	0	0	0	0	0	0	0	0	2	20
4–8	0	1	0	2	1	2	0	0	1	1	0	0	2	0	0	0	0	0	0	0	0	0	0	10	60
2–4	0	0	2	3	6	1	0	0	0	0	0	0	0	0	0	0	1	0	0	0	0	0	1	14	42
Tenants	1	1	2	7	7	4	0	0	1	2	0	0	2	0	0	0	2	0	1	0	0	0	1	31	
Paisa renting	14	6	6	58	24	25	0	0	6	24	0	0	9	0	0	0	21	0	22	0	0	0	3		218
Avg. paisa per tenant	14	6	3	8.3	3.5	6.3	0	0	6	12	0	0	4.5	0	0	0	10.5	0	22	0	0	0	3		7
Tseri Worked as Tenant																									
3	0	0	0	0	0	0	0	0	1	0	0	0	0	0	0	0	0	0	0	0	0	0	0	1	3
2	0	0	0	0	0	0	0	0	2	0	0	0	0	0	0	0	0	0	0	0	0	0	0	2	4
1	4	1	0	2	0	3	0	0	0	0	0	0	0	0	0	6	0	0	0	0	0	0	0	16	16
Tenants	4	1	0	2	0	3	0	0	3	0	0	0	0	0	0	6	0	0	0	0	0	0	0	19	
Tseri renting	4	1	0	2	0	3	0	0	7	0	0	0	0	0	0	6	0	0	0	0	0	0	0		23
Avg. tseri per tenant	1	1	0	1	0	1	0	0	2.3	0	0	0	0	0	0	1	0	0	0	0	0	0	0		1.2

Table A.10 Livestock Owned

| | Pukhtun | | | | | | | Stanadar | | | | | | | | | | | | | | | | | Laborers and Specialists | Totals |
	MK	J	UK	KK	DK	MS	OK	Mi	Mu	P	T	Z	G	Ko	Da	Du	F	C	Jo	Kl	S	N	OL		
Female buffalo	24	3	11	32	8	13	0	3	9	2	0	1	12	0	0	0	5	0	1	1	0	1	2		129
Male buffalo	0	0	1	5	0	0	0	0	0	0	0	0	0	0	0	0	0	0	1	0	0	0	0		7
Cow	21	1	4	16	9	7	3	5	17	12	6	4	12	1	0	0	19	2	1	2	2	4	2		152
Bull	27	17	6	46	13	16	2	5	27	2	0	0	5	0	0	0	3	0	2	1	0	0	2		174
Totals	72	21	22	99	30	36	5	13	53	16	6	5	29	1	0	2	27	2	5	4	2	5	6		462
Other livestock																									
Goat	2	0	0	1	1	2	0	1	1	0	2	0	1	0	0	0	8	5	2	2	0	1	0		27
Sheep	3	0	0	39	4	13	0	32	0	2	0	0	7	0	0	0	17	0	3	4	0	0	0		124
Donkey	0	0	0	1	0	3	0	0	0	60	0	0	0	0	0	0	0	0	0	0	0	7	0		71
Horse	0	0	0	0	0	0	0	0	0	1	0	0	0	0	0	0	0	0	0	0	0	0	0		2
All livestock totals	77	21	22	140	35	54	5	46	54	79	8	5	38	1	0	2	52	7	10	8	2	6	13		686
Households without livestock	15	6	3	7	8	3	4	2	8	5	3	1	0	2	2	2	17	1	2	0	3	1	2		97
Location Animals *Gojal*	24	9	6	28	15	12	3	5	14	12	3	1	10	1	0	1	23	2	4	2	1	5	2		183
Kept House	2	0	4	4	1	0	0	1	2	1	3	1	6	0	0	0	4	2	1	0	0	0	0		32

Table A.11 Deaths, Widow Remarriages, Wives Returned, Wives Divorced

	Pukhtun							Stanadar									Laborers and Specialists							
	MK	J	UK	KK	DK	MS	OK	Mi	Mu	P	T	Z	G	Ko	Da	Du	F	C	Jo	Kl	S	N	OL	Totals
Children	64	12	16	45	19	33	12	6	17	15	4	7	12	1	1	0	54	11	9	0	5	6	0	338
Women in childbirth	2	0	1	3	0	2	0	2	0	0	1	0	0	0	0	0	0	0	1	0	2	0	0	14
Other	19	1	5	15	17	10	0	1	10	4	0	2	7	0	0	0	5	1	0	0	0	1	0	105
Totals	85	13	22	63	36	45	12	8	27	19	5	9	19	1	1	0	59	12	11	0	6	7	0	457
Widow remarriage	5	0	1	1	0	0	0	0	3	1	1	0	1	0	0	0	4	1	0	0	1	0	0	19
Wives returned to parents	4	0	0	0	0	0	1	0	0	0	0	0	0	0	0	1	1	0	0	0	0	2	0	9
Wives divorced	0	0	0	0	0	0	1	0	0	0	0	0	0	0	0	0	0	1	0	0	0	0	0	2

Appendix B
Attitude Test

During the course of my fieldwork, I gave a number of attitude tests to students of different ages in different schools. These tests were not given under the best of circumstances. For instance, in my first attempt with seventh graders in the local school the teacher, a religious man, interrupted me several times while I was asking the questions in order to make propaganda points for Islam. When I asked if a small lie was sometimes a good thing, he said "Muslim do not lie!" Nonetheless, 18 of the 44 boys responded yes. Besides interference from the teacher (never so overt after that class), I also found that boys who sat near one another tended to give exactly the same answers. Whether this was the result of collusion or simply similar views, I don't know.

There were other problems as well. I found that some questions got quite divergent responses when I changed the question form. For instance, when question 39 was changed from "If a man is poor, is he wise to flatter a rich man?" to "Will most poor people flatter the rich?" the number of yes responses jumped from 59 percent to 86 percent. I also reversed two questions when the responses I was getting seemed odd. I shifted "Is it better to be poor and honest than rich and dishonest?" (to which only 3 percent answered no) to the more impersonal "Would most people lie to become rich?" (to which 36 percent answered yes). In the other example, when I asked "Is it true that some men in this world are completely good?" only 26 percent said no (the rest were evidently thinking of Muhammad and the saintly tradition). But when the question was reversed and they were asked "Is it true that in this world every man commits some wrong?" 95 percent answered yes.

Below I give an English version of the test (table B.1). The odd numbered questions are adapted from Christie and Geis (1970) on Machiavellianism, with the assumption on my part that the Pukhtun would test out as highly Machiavellian (or "Mach"). The other questions were derived partly from the basic authoritarianism F-scale developed by Adorno, et al. (1950), and partly from the particular circumstances of Swat. The data were collected from boys in the seventh and tenth grades in the Durushkhela public school; from two classes at the local college in Matta; from the seventh and combined ninth and tenth grades of an elite private school run by Catholic missionaries in Sangota, where many of the wealthiest Swati families send their children; from eighth and ninth graders in the conservative neighboring valley of Dir; from seventh and tenth graders in Ayun in Chitral, north of Swat, where the boys are non-Pukhtun; and from Pukhtun college students in Karachi from all over the North-West Frontier Province. I also collected data from girls in the seventh grade of the only local public girl's school in Matta, and from seventh and tenth grade girls in the elite school at Sangota.

Table B.1 shows the results of the attitude test, with figures showing the number of students who gave the expected responses. In line 1, for example, we see that 17 of the 40 students in the local seventh grade gave the coded response (yes) to question 1. The percentage (43) is given below that result in italics. Question 4 is coded no, and 18 of 35 (or 51 percent) of the students in the local seventh grade answered no. The results are arranged in the order in which I administered the tests.

Asterisks next to the figures for questions 11 and 19 indicate a reversal of the form of the question, so the coded reply shifts, in later cases, from no to yes. See the list of questions for the form of the reversal. Blank spaces indicate that a particular question was not asked. These results are presented in raw form for the interested reader. I make no claims to having completed an analysis yet.

Response
Code   Question

yes   1. Is it dangerous to trust someone else completely? (After college A the question becomes "Do most people think . . .")

yes   2. Do men prefer the children of their favorite wife?

yes   3. Do liars and cheaters become rich? (After Ayun the question becomes "To become rich must a man lie and cheat?")

no   4. May science sometimes show our heartfelt beliefs to be wrong?

no   5. Do most men tell the truth even if the truth harms them?

yes   6. Are you ever attacked by a spirit? (Question omitted in Ayun and Karachi.)

yes   7. Do most people have cruelty in their hearts?

yes	8. Do you have trouble sleeping?
no	9. Is it true that most people will not steal? (After local 10th grades "if they get a chance" is added to the question.)
yes	10. Do you often have headaches?
no	11. Is it better to be poor and honest than rich and dishonest? (After college A the question was reversed to "Would most people lie to become rich?")
yes	12. If a woman does bad things should she be beaten? (In colleges A and B "makes mistakes in the house" was substituted for "does bad things.")
yes	13. Are most people easily tricked by a clever man?
yes	14. Some people say the end of the world is coming. Is this true?
yes	15. Is a small lie sometimes a good thing?
yes	16. When parents get old, do their children forget them?
yes	17. Do big men become big by force and lies?
yes	18. If children are disobedient, should they be beaten?
no	19. In this world, some men are completely good. Is this true? (After college A the statement was reversed to read "In this world, every man does some wrong.")
yes	20. If you have a worry, do you have trouble forgetting it?
no	21. Are most men brave?
no	22. Do you think your future will be good?
no	23. Are most people kind and generous?
no	24. If a man becomes rich, it is hard work and not fate which is the cause. Is this true?
yes	25. If a man loses his property, does he forget the death of his father?
yes	26. Is it foolish to educate a woman?
yes	27. Is it true that servants will not work hard unless carefully watched?
no	28. Is it good to forget an insult? (After college A the question was reversed to read "Is it true that most people never forget an insult?")
no	29. Are rich men usually honest and religious?
yes	30. Is it true that the best way to get ahead is to know important people?
yes	31. Should a man keep his thoughts and business secret?
no	32. Are most parents too cruel to their children?
yes	33. Is it a good idea to tell people what they want to hear, even if it is a lie?

yes	34. When you meet someone, do you know immediately if he or she is good or bad?
yes	35. Should an intelligent man make friends with the rich? (After college A the question was changed to read "Do most people think it wise . . .")
yes	36. Are most people jealous?
yes	37. Are most people today so interested in money that they don't care about religion?
yes	38. Is it true that what Pakistan really needs is a strong leader?
yes	39. Is a poor man wise to flatter the rich? (After college A the question was changed to read "Will most poor people . . .")
yes	40. There are only two kinds of people in the world: the weak and the strong. Is this true?

The 280 students who took these tests also gave me a great deal of information on their backgrounds, thoughts, and ideas for the future. They enjoyed taking the tests, and many commented to me that they found the questions extremely interesting. I hope to publish a complete analysis of the results at a later date. I also collected sociometric data on patterns of friendship and enmity in the high school samples, but this too needs further work.

Table B.1 Results of the Attitude Test

	Local				Ayun	Sangota				Dir	Matta	Karachi
	7th grade	10th grade	College A	College B	7th and 10th grades	Boys 10th grade	Girls 10th grade	Boys 7th grade	Girls 7th grade	8th and 9th grade	Girls 7th grade	College
1.	17–40 / 43	21–37 / 57	20–27 / 74	15–19 / 78	11–23 / 48	8–14 / 57	10–10 / 100	30–30 / 100	7–9 / 78	10–28 / 36	2–7 / 29	19–32 / 60
2.	27–38 / 71	36–37 / 97	23–27 / 85	14–19 / 74	20–25 / 80	14–14 / 100	9–11 / 82	29–30 / 97	7–9 / 78	28–28 / 100	7–7 / 100	21–28 / 75
3.	19–37 / 51	3–37 / 8	11–27 / 41	2–19 / 11	5–25 / 20	9–14 / 64	5–11 / 45	26–30 / 87	9–9 / 100	14–28 / 50	0–7 / 0	16–31 / 52
4.	18–35 / 51	11–36 / 31	10–27 / 37	6–18 / 33	13–25 / 52	6–14 / 43	2–11 / 18	24–28 / 86	7–9 / 77	15–28 / 54	6–6 / 100	13–30 / 43
5.	3–41 / 7	3–37 / 8	6–27 / 22	0–19 / 0	19–25 / 76	3–14 / 21	5–11 / 45	6–30 / 20	2–9 / 22	0–28 / 0	0–7 / 0	11–31 / 35
6.	11–41 / 27	14–37 / 38	15–27 / 56	7–19 / 37		6–14 / 43	1–10 / 10	15–30 / 50	2–9 / 22	8–28 / 29	1–7 / 14	
7.	25–37 / 68	30–37 / 81	16–26 / 62	7–19 / 37	15–25 / 60	12–14 / 86	9–10 / 90	26–30 / 87	8–9 / 89	5–28 / 18	7–7 / 100	15–31 / 48
8.	1–41 / 2	2–37 / 5	5–27 / 19	5–19 / 26	10–25 / 40	1–14 / 7	2–11 / 18	5–30 / 17	0–9 / 0	7–27 / 26	1–7 / 14	9–28 / 32
9.	3–41 / 7	6–37 / 16	13–27 / 48	13–19 / 68	3–24 / 13	1–14 / 7	0–11 / 0	2–30 / 13	1–9 / 11	26–28 / 93	0–7 / 0	4–30 / 13
10.	38–39 / 97	37–37 / 100	23–27 / 85	9–19 / 47	20–24 / 83	12–14 / 86	10–11 / 91	30–30 / 100	9–9 / 100	28–28 / 100	2–3 / 66	17–30 / 57
11.	1–40 / 3	3–37 / 8	0–26 / 0	*5–19 / 26	*2–25 / 8	*12–13 / 92	*11–11 / 100			0–28 / 0	0–7 / 0	*5–28 / 18
12.	37–41 / 90	36–37 / 97	13–26 / 50	5–19 / 26	25–25 / 100	12–14 / 86	9–11 / 82	29–30 / 97	4–9 / 44	27–28 / 96	6–6 / 100	16–27 / 59

Table B.1 (Continued)

	Local				Ayun			Sangota			Dir	Matta	Karachi
	7th grade	10th grade	College A	College B	7th and 10th grades	Boys 10th grade	Girls 10th grade	Boys 7th grade	Girls 7th grade	8th and 9th grades	Girls 7th grade	College
13.	26–40 / 65	10–37 / 27	12–27 / 44	7–19 / 37	4–24 / 17	4–14 / 29	8–11 / 73	25–29 / 86	5–9 / 56	15–28 / 54	6–7 / 86	13–28 / 46
14.	30–39 / 77	36–37 / 97	25–27 / 93	17–19 / 89	17–23 / 74	13–13 / 100	7–11 / 64	22–29 / 76	9–9 / 100	28–28 / 100	6–7 / 86	17–23 / 74
15.	18–41 / 44	19–37 / 51	23–27 / 85	16–19 / 84	8–24 / 33	12–14 / 86	10–11 / 91	27–30 / 90	8–9 / 89	18–28 / 64	4–7 / 57	22–30 / 73
16.	34–40 / 85	17–37 / 46	18–26 / 69	8–18 / 44	6–25 / 24	5–13 / 38	6–11 / 55	22–30 / 73	9–9 / 100	6–28 / 21	2–7 / 29	7–27 / 26
17.	12–41 / 29	3–37 / 8	2–26 / 8	3–19 / 16	6–25 / 24	5–14 / 36	1–11 / 9	29–30 / 97	6–8 / 75	24–28 / 86	4–7 / 57	11–30 / 37
18.	37–41 / 90	35–37 / 95	12–27 / 44	9–18 / 50	12–24 / 50	10–14 / 71	8–11 / 73	28–30 / 93	7–9 / 78	25–28 / 89	7–7 / 100	15–28 / 54
19.	7–41 / 17	7–37 / 19	1–27 / 4	*17–18 / 94	*23–25 / 92	*14–14 / 100	*11–11 / 100	*26–30 / 87	*9–9 / 100	*28–28 / 100	*5–5 / 100	*28–29 / 97
20.	32–41 / 78	26–36 / 73	23–27 / 85	9–18 / 50	17–25 / 68	7–14 / 50	3–11 / 27	16–30 / 53	5–8 / 63	24–28 / 86	7–7 / 100	15–26 / 58
21.	4–40 / 10	3–37 / 8	16–27 / 59	5–18 / 28	4–25 / 16	1–14 / 7	2–11 / 18	4–29 / 14	1–9 / 11	0–28 / 0	0–7 / 0	8–30 / 27
22.	17–41 / 41	10–37 / 27	5–25 / 20	7–18 / 39	0–24 / 0	0–14 / 0	9–11 / 82	12–28 / 43	4–8 / 50	0–28 / 0	3–7 / 43	9–29 / 31
23.	1–40 / 3	0–37 / 0	14–26 / 54	4–18 / 22	1–24 / 4	1–14 / 7	1–11 / 9	4–30 / 13	1–9 / 11	0–28 / 0	1–7 / 14	7–30 / 23
24.	12–38 / 32	14–37 / 38	22–27 / 81	6–18 / 33	12–25 / 48	9–14 / 64	0–11 / 0	10–28 / 36	6–9 / 66	2–28 / 7	4–7 / 57	17–26 / 65
25.	30–40 / 75	17–37 / 46	18–26 / 69	4–18 / 22	6–25 / 24	7–14 / 50	2–11 / 18	23–30 / 77	5–9 / 56	26–28 / 93	3–7 / 43	6–29 / 21

Item												
26.	3-29 / 10	0-7 / 0	10-28 / 36	1-9 / 11	9-29 / 31	0-10 / 0	0-13 / 0	9-25 / 36	8-19 / 50	6-27 / 22	10-37 / 27	26-41 / 63
27.	22-29 / 76	2-5 / 40	26-28 / 93	8-9 / 89	29-30 / 97	9-11 / 82	12-14 / 86	17-25 / 68	13-18 / 72	23-27 / 85	36-37 / 97	32-39 / 82
28.	*25-29 / 86	*1-5 / 20	*25-28 / 89	*3-9 / 33	*18-30 / 60	*9-11 / 82	*12-14 / 86	*9-25 / 36	*14-19 / 74	20-27 / 74	28-37 / 76	10-41 / 24
29.	14-27 / 52	0-7 / 0	19-28 / 68	6-9 / 66	19-30 / 63	9-11 / 82	12-14 / 86	11-24 / 46	13-18 / 72	24-27 / 88	17-33 / 51	13-37 / 35
30.	14-30 / 47	7-7 / 100	26-28 / 93	7-9 / 78	18-30 / 60	7-11 / 64	9-14 / 64	18-25 / 72	5-19 / 26	17-27 / 63	4-37 / 11	16-40 / 40
31.	23-30 / 77	6-6 / 100	27-28 / 96	7-9 / 78	30-30 / 100	7-11 / 64	9-14 / 64	24-25 / 96	7-18 / 39	14-27 / 52	35-37 / 95	39-39 / 100
32.	26-29 / 90	7-7 / 100	27-28 / 96	8-9 / 89	29-30 / 97	11-11 / 100	14-14 / 100	22-25 / 88	18-19 / 95	26-26 / 100	34-37 / 92	33-40 / 83
33.	13-28 / 46	5-5 / 100	19-28 / 68	9-9 / 100	25-30 / 83	8-11 / 73	8-14 / 57	17-25 / 68	3-18 / 17	4-26 / 15	16-36 / 44	20-39 / 51
34.	7-28 / 25	0-7 / 0	4-28 / 14	1-9 / 11	5-30 / 17	2-11 / 18	1-14 / 7	19-25 / 76	5-19 / 26	11-27 / 41	14-37 / 38	12-38 / 32
35.	7-30 / 23	5-7 / 71	7-28 / 25	8-9 / 89	22-30 / 73	3-11 / 27	8-14 / 57	20-25 / 80	5-19 / 26	4-27 / 15	15-37 / 41	25-39 / 64
36.	25-30 / 83	7-7 / 100	8-28 / 40	7-8 / 88	18-29 / 62	11-11 / 100	14-14 / 100	19-24 / 79	8-18 / 44	11-27 / 41	35-37 / 95	31-41 / 76
37.	21-29 / 72	4-6 / 67	2-28 / 7	9-9 / 100	20-29 / 69	9-11 / 82	5-14 / 36	6-24 / 25	1-18 / 5	6-27 / 22	6-37 / 16	13-39 / 33
38.	23-27 / 85	7-7 / 100	25-28 / 89	9-9 / 100	30-30 / 100	11-11 / 100	13-14 / 93	25-25 / 100	12-19 / 63	23-27 / 85	36-37 / 97	34-41 / 83
39.	23-29 / 79	7-7 / 100	21-28 / 75	8-9 / 89	29-30 / 97	11-11 / 100	13-14 / 93	25-25 / 100	10-18 / 56	12-27 / 44	21-37 / 57	28-39 / 72
40.	22-25 / 88	7-7 / 100	28-28 / 100	7-7 / 100	29-30 / 97	11-11 / 100	14-14 / 100	22-25 / 88	18-19 / 95	26-27 / 96	37-37 / 100	39-39 / 100
Mach Totals	288- / 591 / 49	61- / 132 / 46	288- / 560 / 51	117- / 170 / 69	402- / 567 / 71	131- / 218 / 60	156- / 279 / 56	227- / 492 / 46	243- / 369 / 66	239- / 534 / 45	271- / 735 / 37	336- / 790 / 43

Glossary

NOTE: Pukhto has many plural forms. For the sake of simplicity, I have used the English *s* after the Pukhto singular throughout the text except in words which are generally plural, such as *mamagan*.

Pukhto pronunciation is close enough to English that the reader should get an idea of the sounds of the words without my having to resort to a phonetic alphabet. Of course, this obscures the subtleties of the language, such as the consistent use of the "light" *l* in Pukhto, like the *l* in look and unlike the *l* in pull. I have also left out some rather more important elements, including the distinction between *t* (pronounced much like the English *t* except with the tongue touching the upper teeth) and *ṭ* (where tip of the tongue goes far back in the mouth). This distinction (which also holds true for *d* and *ḍ*) was one I could never hear properly, much to my chagrin, and therefore I have omitted it. My consolation is that my Pukhtun friends could never learn to distinguish between English *p* and *f*. I could, however, hear two different versions of *r*. The first *r* is produced by tapping the tongue just above the teeth, the second *ṛ* again has the tongue tap much farther back. Both are quite unlike the English *r*. Two sounds that may confuse the English reader are the *ə*, similar to the vowel sound in "but" and "ton," and the *x*, pronounced like *gh*, but without voicing.

It is perhaps appropriate to correct here a confusion about the name for the people themselves. I have called them Pukhtun, following Ahmed (1980). This is perhaps the closest equivalent in English script to the people's own pronunciation, which is *pəxtuń*, with a strong accent on the last syllable. The *u* in Pukhto is like the vowel sound in "boot." The British and the Indians called them Pathans, and later writers have used Pashtun, taking as standard a major dialect in which *x* is pronounced *sh*. The Yusufzai, however, are proud of their way of speaking, and claim their "hard" version is the correct one. Other writers, including myself, have used Pakhtun, but English readers tend to say the first syllable like the word "pack," giving it a very incorrect pronunciation.

adal-badal: barter
ashar: cooperative work group
bən: co-wife
badal: revenge
baraka: charismatic power
bedagh: passive homosexual
begherata: without honor

betək: a guest room attached to a house

braxikor: rent on land paid by a proportion of the crop

chəm: roadside villages inhabited by members of religious lineages

chamyar: a shoemaker

charas: hashish

dəla: a political alliance; traditionally, Swat was divided into two fluid *dəlas*

darzi: a tailor

dauftar: land held by the patrilineage

dekan: a sharecropper

deran: a compost pit

dolie: the bridal palanquin

dukan: a shop

dukandar: a shopkeeper

duma: dancer/prostitute; also the barber's wife

fakir: a landless laborer (no religious connotation)

ganṛa: property given as guarantee on a loan

ghəm: a funeral

ghəm-khadi: a reciprocal obligation between families to attend one another's funerals and weddings

gherat: honor; a feast or free gift

gojəl: cowshed

Gujar: an ethnic group of herdsmen and laborers

halak: a boy between the ages of seven and fifteen

hujera: a men's house

ijara: a set rent in cash or kind

imam: Koranic scholar who oversees the mosque

jabəi: a wasting disease of young children, supposedly caused by withdrawal of a beloved person or object

jalawan: a boatman

jang: warfare

jinai: a girl between the ages of seven and fifteen

jirga: a council of respected men

jola: a weaver

jora: a cash payment from the bride's family to the groom

junj: a cash payment to the groom from his own relatives and allies; also the procession carrying the *dolie*

kam: occupational group; may be synonymous with clan

kandari: a man who pays for his house with labor

kas: unirrigated land of poor quality

khadi: a wedding

kham: a lineage segment extending back five generations (an Arabic term not found in Swat)

khan: an elite man of the village

khel: a patrilineal group

Kohistani: an ethnic group of herdsmen and laborers

kolal: a potter

kurimar: a dependent who is fed by a khan and expected to fight for him in return

kushur: younger, junior

landap: a cotton carder

las niwa: a short prayer offered at a funeral

liff: the Moroccan Berber equivalent of Swati *dǝlas*

mahar: jewelry and land given the bride by her husband's family

malang: a dervish

malik: headman, war leader

mamagan: the people of one's matrilineage

marate: a slave

mas: overly proud

maund: a measure of weight, roughly a bushel

melma: a guest

melmastia: hospitality

mia: descendant of a prominent follower of a pir

minae: love

mirasi: a relationship of inheritance

mirat: without sons

misri: a mechanic

mullah: descendant of a Koranic scholar

murid: disciple of a religious teacher

mushur: elder, senior

nǝswar: local chewing tobacco

nai: a barber

nanawatia: refuge offered to guests

nang: honor, sacrifice for a friend

nasab: lineage tied to one's own by marriage

naukar: personal servant

nazar: the evil eye

newai: a bride

nif: a Kabyle term for honor, not used in Swat

nikanǝ: cognatic relatives up to the grandparents

omela: local market operating at fixed days of the week

paisa: in local dialect, a unit of land; in Pakistan, a unit of money, a small coin

palao: a village neighborhood; each village usually contains three *palaos*

paracha: a muleteer

pir: a holy man with baraka, often drawn from dervish or malang groups

Pukhtunwali: the Pukhtun code of conduct

purdah: seclusion of women

qalang: taxation

rupee: in local dialect, a unit of land (a village is said to have 30 *rupees* in its *dauftar*, each *rupee* yielding 100 *maunds* of wheat); in Pakistan, a rupee is the unit of paper money

səm: well-irrigated bottom land

sadar: shawl worn to maintain women's seclusion

sahibzada: descendant of a local religious ecstatic

sayyid: descendant of the Prophet Muhammad

shahkhel: leatherworker

soch: thoughts, worries

stanadar: a collective term referring to all descendants of holy men

swori: charity

təl: a village ward; each *palao* is divided into several *təl*, each with its own leading man or men

ta'ifa: Arabic term for the cult of a holy man

taliki: divorced

taliman: child considered to be good luck

tanga: horse-drawn cart

tarbur: patrilateral parallel cousin; also an enemy

tarburwali: the relationship of enmity and alliance prevailing between *tarbur*

tariqa: Sufic school

tseri: land not a part of the *dauftar*

umzoli: age-mates

wara: girl between the age of eighteen months and seven years

warukəi: boy between the age of eighteen months and seven years

wesh: periodic redistribution of land within and between villages

xapasa: an evil spirit that attacks sleepers

xpəl wuli: a family with whom one's own family regularly intermarries

zai: place

zakat: a religious donation

zurgar: a goldsmith

References

Adorno, T., E. Frenkel-Brunswik, D. Levinson, and N. Sanford. 1950. *The Authoritarian Personality*. New York: Harper and Row.

Ahmad, M. 1962. *Social Organization in Yusufzai Swat*. Lahore: Punjab University Press.

Ahmed, A. 1975. *Mataloona: Pukhto Proverbs*. Karachi: Oxford University Press.

—— 1976. *Millennium and Charisma Among Pathans*. London: Routledge and Kegan Paul.

—— 1980. *Pukhtun Economy and Society*. London: Routledge and Kegan Paul.

Ainsworth, M. 1967. *Infancy in Uganda: Infant Care and the Growth of Love*. Baltimore, Md.: Johns Hopkins University Press.

—— 1972. "Attachment and Dependency: A Comparison." In J. Gewirtz, ed., *Attachment and Dependency*. New York: Halsted Press.

Ammar, H. 1970. "The Aims and Methods of Socialization in Silwa." In J. Middleton, ed., *From Child to Adult*. Garden City, N.Y.: Natural History Press.

Arnold, M. and J. Gasson. 1968. "Feelings and Emotions as Dynamic Factors in Personality Integration." In M. Arnold, ed., *The Nature of Emotion*. Middlesex, England: Penguin Books.

Asad, T. 1972. "Market Model, Class Structure and Consent: A Reconsideration of Swat Political Organization," *Man* 7:74–94.

—— 1978. "Equality in Nomadic Social Systems?" *Critique of Anthropology* 11:57–65.

Aswad, B. 1970. "Social and Ecological Aspects in the Formation of Islam." In L. Sweet, ed., *Peoples and Cultures of the Middle East*, vol. 1. Garden City, N.Y.: Natural History Press.

Barnouw, V. 1973. *Culture and Personality*. Homewood, Ill.: Dorsey Press.

Barth, F. 1956. *Indus and Swat Kohistan*, Studies Honouring the Centennial of Universitets Etnografiske Museum, vol. 2. Oslo: Ferenede Trykkerier.

—— 1958. "Ecological Relationships of Ethnic Groups in Swat, North Pakistan," *American Anthropologist* 60:1079–1088.

—— 1959. "Segmentary Opposition and the Theory of Games: A Study of Pathan Organization," *Journal of the Royal Anthropological Institute* 89:5–21.

—— 1961. *Nomads of South Persia*. Boston: Little, Brown.

—— 1965. *Political Leadership among Swat Pathans*. London: Athalone Press.

—— 1969. "Pathan Identity and its Maintanance." In F. Barth, ed., *Ethnic Groups and Boundaries*. London: Allen and Unwin.

Becker, E. 1973. *The Denial of Death*. New York: Macmillan.

Beidelman, T. 1966. "The Ox and Nuer Sacrifice: Some Freudian Hypotheses About Nuer Symbolism," *Man* 1:453–67.

Bellew, H. 1864. *A General Report on the Yusufzais*. Lahore: Government Press. Reprinted 1977. Peshawar: Saeed Press.

Benedict, R. 1934. *Patterns of Culture*. Boston: Houghton Mifflin.

Black, J. 1972. "Tyranny as a Strategy for Survival in an 'Egalitarian' Society: Luri Facts Versus an Anthropological Mystique," *Man* 7:614–34.

Black-Michaud, J. 1975. *Cohesive Force*. New York: St. Martin's Press.

Bourdieu, P. 1974. "The Sentiment of Honour in Kabyle Society." In J. Peristiany, ed., *Honour and Shame*. Chicago: University of Chicago Press.

Bowlby, J. 1969. *Attachment*. New York: Basic Books.

—— 1973. *Separation: Anxiety and Anger*. New York: Basic Books.

Brain, R. 1971. "Friends and Twins in Bangwa." In M. Douglas and P. Kaberry, eds., *Man in Africa*. Garden City, N.Y.: Anchor Books.

—— 1976. *Friends and Lovers*. New York: Basic Books.

Brown, N. 1959. *Life Against Death: The Psychoanalytic Meaning of History*. New York: Random House.

Burlingham, D. and A. Freud. 1944. *Infants Without Families*. London: Allen and Unwin.

Burnes, A. 1834. *Travels Into Bokhara*, 3 vols. London: John Murray. Reprinted 1973. Karachi: Oxford University Press.

Campbell, J. 1963. *Mediterranean Countrymen*. The Hague: Mouton.

Cannon, W. 1927. "The James-Lange Theory of Emotion: A Critical Examination and an Alternative Theory," *American Journal of Psychology* 39:106–24.

Caroe, O. 1965. *The Pathans*. London: Macmillan.

Census of Pakistan 1972, 1975. *Swat*. Karachi: Printing Corporation of Pakistan.

Chavarria-Aguilar, O. 1962. *Pashto Instructor's Handbook*. Ann Arbor: University of Michigan Press.

Christie, R. and F. Geis. 1970. *Studies in Machiavellianism*. New York: Academic Press.

Cohen, A. 1969. "Political Anthropology: The Analysis of the Symbolism of Power Relations," *Man* 4:215–35.

Cohen, Y. 1961. "Patterns of Friendship." In Y. Cohen, ed., *Social Structure and Personality*. New York: Holt, Rinehart and Winston.

Cunnison, I. 1966. *Baggara Arabs*. Oxford: Oxford University Press, Clarendon Press.

Darwin, C. 1873. *The Expression of the Emotions in Man and Animals*. New York: Appleton Press.

Denich, B. 1974. "Sex and Power in the Balkans." In M. Rosaldo and L. Lamphere, eds., *Women, Culture and Society*. Stanford, Calif.: Stanford University Press.

Dentan, R. 1968. *The Semai, A Nonviolent People of Malaya*. New York: Holt, Rinehart and Winston.

Dewey, J. 1894. "The Theory of Emotion," *Psychological Review* 1:553–69.

Douglas, M. 1966. *Purity and Danger*. London: Routledge and Kegan Paul.

—— 1970. *Natural Symbols*. London: Routledge and Kegan Paul.

—— 1975. *Implicit Meanings*. London: Routledge and Kegan Paul.

Dover, K. 1978. *Greek Homosexuality*. London: Duckworth.

DuBois, C. 1961. *The People of Alor*, vol. 1. New York: Harper and Row.

Duffy, E. 1941. "An Explanation of 'Emotional' Phenomena Without the Use of the Concept 'Emotion'," *Journal of General Psychology* 25:283–93.

Durkheim, E. and M. Mauss. 1967. *Primitive Classification*. Chicago: University of Chicago Press.

Elphinstone, M. 1815. *An Account of the Kingdom of Caubul*, 2 vols. London: Longman. Reprinted 1972. Karachi: Oxford University Press.

Erikson, E. 1950. *Childhood and Society*. New York: Norton.

Evans-Pritchard, E. 1940. *The Nuer*. New York: Oxford University Press.

Fairbairn, W. 1954. *The Object-Relations Theory of the Personality*. New York: Basic Books.

Fernea, R. 1970. *Shaykh and Effendi*. Cambridge, Mass.: Harvard University Press.

Fortes, M. 1949. *The Web of Kinship Among the Tallensi*. London: Oxford University Press.

Fortune, R. 1939. "Arapesh Warfare," *American Anthropologist* 41:22–41.

Foster, G. 1967. "Peasant Society and the Image of Limited Good." In J. Potter, M. Diaz, and G. Foster, eds., *Peasant Society*. Boston: Little, Brown.

—— 1972. "The Anatomy of Envy: A Study in Symbolic Behavior," *Current Anthropology* 13:165–202.

Freed, S. and R. Freed. 1964. "Spirit Possession as Illness in a North Indian Village," *Ethnology* 3:152–71.

Freud, A. 1936. *The Ego and the Mechanisms of Defense*. London: Hogarth.

—— 1960. "A Discussion of Dr. John Bowlby's Paper," *The Psychoanalytic Study of the Child* 15:53–62.

Freud, S. 1911. "The Two Principles of Mental Functioning." In *The Complete Psychological works of Sigmund Freud*, vol. 12. London: Hogarth.

—— 1914. "On Narcissism: An Introduction." In *The Complete Psychological Works of Sigmund Freud*, vol. 14. London: Hogarth.

—— 1915. "Instincts and Their Vicissitudes." In *The Complete Psychological Works of Sigmund Freud*, vol. 14. London: Hogarth.

—— 1949. *An Outline of Psycho-Analysis*. London: Hogarth.

—— 1960. *The Ego and the Id*. New York: Norton.

—— 1961. *Beyond the Pleasure Principle*. New York: Norton.

Garrison, V. and C. Arensberg. 1976. "The Evil Eye: Envy or Risk of Seizure? Paranoia or Patronal Dependency?" In C. Maloney, ed., *The Evil Eye*. New York: Columbia University Press.

Gellner, E. 1969. *Saints of the Atlas*. London: Weidenfeld and Nicholson.

Goffman, E. 1959. *The Presentation of Self in Everyday Life*. Garden City, N.Y.: Doubleday.

Goldfrank, E. 1945. "Socialization, Personality and the Structure of Pueblo Society," *American Anthropologist* 47:516–39.

Gorer, G. 1967. *Himalayan Village*. New York: Basic Books.

Guntrip, H. 1973. *Psychoanalytic Theory, Therapy and the Self*. New York: Basic Books.

Hall, C. and G. Lindzey. 1957. *Theories of Personality*. New York: John Wiley.

Hammoudi, A. 1980. "Segmentarity, Social Stratification, Political Power and Sainthood: Reflections on Gellner's Thesis," *Economy and Society* 9:279–303.

Harris, M. 1968. *The Rise of Anthropological Theory*. New York: Crowell.

Hart, D. 1970. "Clan, Lineage, Local Community and the Feud in a

Riffian Tribe." In L. Sweet, ed., *Peoples and Cultures of the Middle East*, vol. 2. Garden City, N.Y.: Natural History Press.

Helson, R. and V. Mitchell. 1978. "Personality." In *Annual Review of Psychology*, vol. 29.

Hobbes, T. 1958. *Leviathan*. Indianapolis: Bobbs-Merrill.

Hsu, F. 1972. "Kinship and Ways of Life: An Exploration." In F. Hsu, ed., *Psychological Anthropology*. Cambridge, Mass.: Schenkman.

Jacobson, D. 1975. "Separate Spheres: Differential Modernization in Rural Central India." In H. Ullrich, ed., *Competition and Modernization in South Asia*. New Dehli: Abhinav.

Kakar, S. 1978. *The Inner World: A Psychoanalytic Study of Childhood and Society in India*. New Dehli: Oxford University Press.

Kardiner, A. 1939. *The Individual and His Society*. New York: Columbia University Press.

Khan, F. M. 1971. *Integrated Resource Survey and Development Potentials of Swat River Watershed*. Peshawar: Aerial Forest Inventory Project, Pakistan Forest Institute.

Khan, G. 1958. *The Pathans, a Sketch*. Peshawar: University Books.

Khattak K. 1963. *The Poems of Khushal Khan Khatak*, translated by E. Howell and O. Caroe. Peshawar: Peshawar University Press.

—— 1965. *Poems from the Diwan of Khushal Khan Khattack*, translated by D. Mackenzie. London: Allen and Unwin.

Klein, M. 1975. *Envy and Gratitude and Other Works*. New York: Dell.

Lange, C. and James, W. 1922. *The Emotions*. New York: Macmillan, Hafner Press.

Lasch, C. 1977. *Haven in a Heartless World*. New York: Basic Books.

Lazarus, R. 1966. *Psychological Stress and the Coping Process*. New York: McGraw-Hill.

Leacock, E. 1980. "Social Behavior, Biology and the Double Standard." In G. Barlow and J. Silverberg, eds., *Sociobiology: Beyond Nature/Nurture*. Boulder, Co.: Westview Press.

Leeper, R. 1948. "A Motivational Theory of Emotion to Replace 'Emotion as a Disorganized Response'," *Psychological Review* 55:5–21.

—— 1968. "The Motivational Theory of Emotion." In M. Arnold, ed., *The Nature of Emotion*. Middlesex, England: Penguin Books.

Levine, R. 1976. *Culture, Behavior and Personality*. Chicago: Aldine.

Lévi-Strauss, C. 1963. *Totemism*. Boston: Beacon Press.

—— 1967. "Structural Analysis in Linguistics and in Anthropology." In C. Lévi-Strauss, ed., *Structural Anthropology*, vol. 1. Garden City, N.Y.: Doubleday, Anchor Books.

—— 1976. "Reflections on the Atom of Kinship." In C. Lévi-Strauss, ed., *Structural Anthropology*, vol. 2. New York: Basic Books.

Lindholm, C. 1977. "The Segmentary Lineage System: Its Applicability to Pakistan's Political Structure." In A. Embree, ed., *Pakistan's Western Borderlands*. Durham, N.C.: Carolina Academic Press.

—— 1979. "Contemporary Politics in a Tribal Society: An Example from Swat District, NWFP, Pakistan," *Asian Survey* 19:485–505.

—— 1980. "Images of the Pathan: The Usefulness of Colonial Ethnography," *European Journal of Sociology* 21:350–60.

—— 1981a. "The Structure of Violence Among the Swat Pukhtun," *Ethnology* 20:147–56.

—— 1981b. "Leatherworkers and Love Potions," *American Ethnologist* 9:512–25.

—— in press. "The Evolution of Segmentary States: The Cases of Dir and Swat." In S. Pastner and L. Flomm, eds., *Current Anthropology in Pakistan*. Ithaca, N.Y.: Cornell University Press.

Lindholm, C. and C. Lindholm. 1979. "Marriage as Warfare," *Natural History* 88(8):11–21.

MacPherson, C. 1962. *The Political Theory of Possessive Individualism*. London: Oxford University Press.

Mahler, M. 1969. *On Human Symbiosis and the Vicissitudes of Individuation*, vol. 1. New York: International University Press.

Maloney, C. 1976. "Don't Say 'Pretty Baby' Lest You Zap it With Your Evil Eye—The Evil Eye in South Asia." In C. Maloney, ed., *The Evil Eye*. New York: Columbia University Press.

Marcuse, H. 1962. *Eros and Civilization*. New York: Random House, Vintage Books.

—— 1965. "The Ideology of Death." In H. Feifel, ed., *The Meaning of Death*. New York: McGraw-Hill.

Marx, E. 1967. *Bedouin of the Negev*. New York: Praeger.

Masson, C. 1842. *Narrative of Various Journeys in Balochistan, Afghanistan and the Panjab*, 3 vols. London: Bentley. Reprinted 1974. Karachi: Oxford University Press.

Mauss, M. 1967. *The Gift*, New York: Norton.

Mead, M. 1935. *Sex and Temperament*. New York: Morrow.

Meeker, M. 1980. "The Twilight of a South Asian Heroic Age: A Rereading of Barth's Study of Swat," *Man* 15:682–701.

Mernissi, F. 1975. *Beyond the Veil*. Cambridge, Mass.: Schenkman.

Minturn, L. and J. Hitchock. 1963. "The Rajputs of Khalapur, India." In B. Whiting, ed., *Six Cultures—Studies in Child Rearing*. New York: John Wiley.

Montagne, R. 1973. *The Berbers*. London: Frank Cass.

Murphy. R. 1979. *An Overture to Social Anthropology*. Englewood Cliffs, N. J.: Prentice-Hall.

Murphy, R. and L. Kasdan. 1959. "The Structure of Parallel Cousin Marriage," *American Anthropologist* 61:17–29.

Nevill, R. 1911. *Campaigns on the North-West Frontier*. No publisher given. Reprinted 1977. Lahore: Sang-e-Meel.

Newman, R. 1965. *Pathan Tribal Patterns*. Ridgewood, N. J.: Foreign Studies Institute.

Paul, R. 1978. "Instinctive Aggression in Man: The Semai Case," *The Journal of Psychological Anthropology* 1:65–79.

Paz, O. 1970. *Claude Lévi-Strauss*. Ithaca, N.Y.: Cornell University Press.

Pehrson, R. 1966. *The Social Organization of the Marri Baluch*. The Viking Fund Publications in Anthropology, 43. New York: Wenner-Gren Foundation.

Pennell, T. 1909. *Among the Wild Tribes of the Afghan Frontier*. London: Seely. Reprinted 1975. Karachi: Oxford University Press.

Peters, E. 1960. "The Proliferation of Segments in the Lineage of the Bedouin of Cyrenaica (Libya)," *Journal of the Royal Anthropological Institute* 90:29–53.

Piker, S. 1968. "Friendship to the Death in Rural Thai Society," *Human Organization* 27:200–4.

Pocock, D. 1962. "Notes on Jajmani Relationships," *Contributions to Indian Sociology* 6:78–95.

Rabinow, P. 1977. *Reflections on Fieldwork in Morocco*. Berkeley: University of California Press.

Radcliffe-Brown, A. 1924. "The Mother's Brother in South Africa," *South African Journal of Science* 21:542–55.

—— 1958. *Method in Social Anthropology*. Chicago: University of Chicago Press.

Rahman Baba. 1977. *Selections From Rahman Baba*, translated by J. Enevoldsen. Herning, Denmark: Poul Kristensen.

Reich, W. 1972. *Character Analysis*. New York: Farrar, Strauss and Giroux.

Reina, R. 1959. "Two Patterns of Friendship in A Guatemalan Community," *American Anthropologist* 61:44–50.

—— 1966. *The Law of the Saints: A Pokoman Pueblo and its Community Structure*. Indianapolis: Bobbs-Merrill.

Robarchek, C. 1977. "Frustration, Aggression and the Non-violent Semai," *American Ethnologist* 4:762–79.

Robertson-Smith. W. 1903. *Kinship and Marriage in Early Arabia*. Boston: Beacon Press.

Roheim, G. 1943. *The Origin and Function of Culture*. New York: Nervous and Mental Disease Monographs.

—— 1970. "The Psychoanalytic Interpretation of Culture." In W. Muensterberger, ed., *Man and His Culture*. New York: Taplinger.

Roland, A. 1980. "Psychoanalytic Perspectives on Personality Development in India," *The International Review of Psycho-Analysis* 7:73–88.

Rosenblatt, P. 1967. "Marital Residence and the Functions of Romantic Love," *Ethnology* 6:471–80.

Sahlins, M. 1961. "The Segmentary Lineage—An Organization of Predatory Expansion," *American Anthropologist* 63:332–45.

—— 1976. *Culture and Practical Reason*. Chicago: University of Chicago Press.

Salzman, P. 1978a. "Does Complementary Opposition Exist?" *American Anthropologist* 80:53–70.

—— 1978b. "Ideology and Change in Middle Eastern Tribal Societies," *Man* 13:618–37.

Schachter, S. and J. Singer. 1962. "Cognitive, Social and Physiological Determinants of Emotional State," *Psychological Review* 69:379–99.

Schomberg, R. 1935. *Between Oxus and Indus*. London: Hopkinson.

Scott, J. 1972. "Patron-Client Politics and Political Change in Southeast Asia," *American Political Science Review* 66:91–113.

Scott, J. and B. Kerkvliet. 1975. "How Traditional Rural Patrons Lose Legitimacy," *Cultures et Développement* 5:501–40.

Sillitoe, P. 1978. "Big Men and War in New Guinea," *Man* 13:252–71.

Smith, M. 1954. *Baba of Karo, a Woman of the Muslim Hausa*. London: Faber and Faber.

Spindler, G. 1980. "Introduction." In G. Spindler, ed., *The Making of Psychological Anthropology*. Berkeley: University of California Press.

Spooner, B. 1969. "Politics, Kinship and Ecology in South East Persia," *Ethnology* 8:139–52.

—— 1976. "The Evil Eye in the Middle East." In C. Maloney, ed., *The Evil Eye*. New York: Columbia University Press.

Stayton, M., M. Ainsworth and M. Main. 1973. "The Development of Separation Behavior in the First Year of Life: Protest, Following, and Greeting," *Developmental Psychology* 9:213–25.

Stein, A. 1929. *On Alexander's Track to the Indus*. London: Macmillan.

Strathern, M. 1972. *Women In Between*. London: Seminar Press.

Swidler, N. 1977. "Brahui Political Organization and the National State."

In A. Embree, ed., *Pakistan's Western Borderlands*. Durham, N.C.: Carolina Academic Press.

Titmuss, R. 1971. *The Gift Relationship*. London: Allen and Unwin.

Trimingham, J. 1971. *The Sufi Orders in Islam*. Oxford: Oxford University Press, Clarendon Press.

Turnbull, C. 1972. *The Mountain People*. New York: Simon and Schuster.

Turner, V. 1969. "Forms of Symbolic Action." In R. Spencer, ed., *Forms of Symbolic Action*. Seattle: University of Washington Press.

—— 1974. *Dramas, Fields and Metaphors: Symbolic Action in Human Society*. Ithaca, N.Y.: Cornell University Press.

—— 1977. *The Ritual Process*. Ithaca, N.Y.: Cornell University Press.

Wadud, A. 1962. *The Story of Swat as Told by the Founder*, translated by Ashruf Husain. Peshawar: Ferozsons.

Wallace, A. 1970. *Culture and Personality*. New York: Random House.

Warburton, R. 1900. *Eighteen Years in the Khyber*. London: Murray. Reprinted 1970. Karachi: Oxford University Press.

White, L. 1949. *The Science of Culture*. New York: Grove Press.

Wilson, E. 1978. *On Human Nature*. Cambridge, Mass.: Harvard University Press.

Winnicott, D. 1965. *The Maturation Processes and the Facilitating Environment*. New York: International University Press.

Wolf, E. 1951. "The Social Organization of Mecca and the Origins of Islam," *Southwestern Journal of Anthropology* 7:329–56.

—— 1966. "Kinship, Friendship, and Patron-Client Relations in Complex Societies." In M. Banton, ed., *The Social Anthropology of Complex Societies*. London: Travistock.

Zinoviev, A. 1979. *The Yawning Heights*. New York: Random House.

Index

Beidelman, T., 266
Bellew, H., 245; on disease, 4; on history, 33; on hospitality, xviii–xxix; on Pukhtun custom, 195, 210–11, 212; on social structure, 55, 205
Benedict, R., xxxi
Berbers, 79
birth, 163–68; abortion, 164, 224; couvade, 164, 167; fertility symbolism, 157, 183
Black, J., 90, 212
Black-Michaud, J.: on leadership, 78; on scarcity, 75, 89; on violence, 76, 77, 85, 210
blood, ideology of, 129
blood brother, 250
blood money, 69, 75, 77
bodyguard, 105–7
Bourdieu, P., 85, 210; on fighting, 77
Bowlby, J.: on behavior, xiii; on emotions, 263–66, 269
boys: appearance of, 15; behavior expected of, 174, 181–83; friendships among, 243; gangs of, 175–76, 183, 188, 202; training of, 170–74; see also children; family; infants
Brain, R.: on friendship, 253–54; on twins, 240–41
bravery, 204, 216–17, 238
bride price, 138–39; denied, 38; disputes over, 132; and dowry, 138; and endogamy, 143; as objectifying women, 147–48, 220–22; and professionals, 139n; and religious practitioners, 93, 95; see also marriage
British: as friends, 244–45; irrigation schemes of, 198; role in Dir of, 40, 86; role in Frontier of, 37–39; role in Swat of, 40–42, 52
Brown, N., 273; on instincts, 260–61
Buddhism, 32–33
buffalo, symbolism of, 157
Burlingham, D. and A. Freud, 264
Burnes, A., 245; on betrayal of in-laws, 195; on envy, 196; on the men's house, 16

Campbell, J., 253
Cannon, W., 255–56
Caroe, O., 245; on the Akhund of Swat, 39;

on Dir Nawab, 39; on leadership, 37; on marriage, 38, 113, 154; on Swati history, 32, 33
carpenters and smiths, 27, 98–99, 102, 103
Census of Pakistan, 6–7
charity, 116–17, 124, 125, 160, 236
Chavarria-Aguilar, O., xix
children: care of, 168–88; demands by, 170, 204; and evil eye, 197; and favoritism, 185; grooming of, 173; and parent's death, 128, 156; psychology of, 258–60, 262–66, 268–69; results of training of, 163, 188–207; rights of matrilineage over, 128–29; rights of patrilineage over, 128–29; and school, 176–78, 188, 204; and theft, 200–1; training of, 171, 174, 181–83, 185–86; see also boys; family; girls; infants
Chitral, 39
Christie, R. and F. Geis, 289
circumcision, 100, 120–21, 152, 152n, 219
clan, 70–74; see also agnates
class, xvii; awareness of, 49–50; and segmentary system, 91–92, 110–11
classification systems, 123
climate, 4, 7–8
cognatic descent: in Albania, 78; in Swat, 61, 129
cognition: abstract thought, 188, 205; and emotion, 249, 256, 264–65, 273
Cohen, A., 81
Cohen, Y., 251
compadrazgo, 250´
conversation: children's, 183–85; closure of, 179–81; curses and insults in, 158–59, 173, 175, 183; freedom of, 213, 215; gossip, 181, 189, 196, 271; greetings, 174, 212
cooperative work groups, 11, 104–5
cotton carder, 96, 98
court cases: mahar rights, 140; violence to mother, 130
culture: autonomy of, 255, 268, 273; and nature, 253
Culture and Personality school, xxxi, 162
Cunnison, I., 69

dancers: at circumcision, 152; as homosex-

feasts (*Continued*)
demonstrations, 213; at weddings, 132–33, 136–37
Fernea, R., 69, 90
ferryman, 96, 98
food: distribution of, 170, 173, 213, 220; for guest, 231; symbolism of, 166–67*n*; taboos regarding, 166–67; theft of by women, 201
Fortes, M., 126, 174
Fortune, R., xxxi
Foster, G., 198, 205
Frankfurt School, 250
Freed, S., and R. Freed, 151
Freud, A., 262, 269; on altruism, 266; on emotional structure, 267
Freud, S., 252, 254, 256, 260, 261; on the death instinct, 257, 258, 259; on the dualism of instinct, 257–58, 267; on the life instinct, 257; on the mother-child tie, 258
friendship: and altruism, 269; of boys, 244; of brothers, 243; cognitive theory of, 248–49; and domination, 242, 245; functionalist theories of, 228, 251; and guests, xxviii, 232, 236, 242; ideal of, xxviii, 226–27, 237–38, 240–47, 255, 273; and Islam, 240; and Zaman Khan, xv, xx, xxi, 246–47; psychoanalytic theory of, xxxi, 269, 273; and romance, 226–27; of sisters' sons, 142; and social structure, 242, 246, 271–73; of strangers, 242, 244–46; and trade, 250; and twins, 240–42; types of, 229, 245; various societies' concepts of, 253–54, 272; and women, 271–72; and worship, 225–27; *see also* altruism; guest; hospitality; refuge; romantic love; worship
funeral, 155–58; coffin likened to wedding palanquin, 131, 156; fasting and feasting, 157; men's silence at, 156–57, 160, 192; patterns of mourning, 126, 155–56; sacrifice at, 157–58; women's role at, 156, 219; *see also*, death

Gaffur, Abdul (Akhund of Swat), 38–39, 52, 94, 213
Gandhara, 32
Garrison, V. and C. Arensberg, 198

Gellner, E., 79
genealogy: Malik *khel*, 70–72; of poor people, 218; and vicinity, 70, 72–73, 78; Yusufzai, 70, 218
generosity, xxiv, 107, 120, 183, 227; celebration of at funerals, 158; and friendship, 241; and guests, 233; and honor, 237; as instrumental, 228; myths of, 227; shaming by, 115
Ghilji, Muhammad Shah, 37
gifts: between brothers and sisters, 126–27, 155; denigrated, 200, 202; to guests, 232, 235, 237; to host, 232
girls: appearance of, 15; behavior expected of, 127, 181; child care and, 127; friendships among, 272; gossip by, 181; play of, 130; work of, 168, 173; *see also* children; family; infants
Goldfrank, E., 188
goldsmith, 98, 99
Gorer, G., 272
Great Game, 38–39
greed, 198–202; rationality and, 248
Guatemalan Indians, 253
guest: affection for, 232, 236; and charity, 117; host's relation to, 84, 231–32, 235–36; powerlessness of, 237; refuge for, 234–36; rivalry over, 209, 228, 232; stranger as, xix, 229–31, 236; treatment of, xxi, 228–33; women's attitude toward, 232–33, 271; *see also* friendship; hospitality; refuge
guest house, *see hujera*
guest room, 22, 229
Gujar, 27, 96–98; as leader, 110
Guntrip, H.: on Freudian theory, 258, 261–62; on M. Klein, 260; on object relations, 262

Hall, C. and G. Lindzey, 162
Hammoudi, A., 213
Harris, H., 248
Hart, D.: on the *liff*, 79; on the segmentary system, 56; on vengeance, 69
Hausa, 253
Helson, R. and V. Mitchell, 249
Hindustani fanatics, 38
Hobbes, T., 210
homosexuality, male: and ambiguity, 123;

and boys, 174; causes of, 135–36, 148–49, 224–25; and friendship, 226–27; Greek, 224; and marriage, 135–36; and romance, 224–25; and sexual practices, 224; and transvestite dancers, 120, 224

honor: and economic exchange, 115, 117–18, 125, 137–38; and hospitality, 228, 232, 235; and land, 65; and Mohmand, 90; and poverty, 107; and refuge, 234; and self-sacrifice, 237, 240; and "state of nature," 210; and violence, 77, 84, 87, 189, 218; and women, 126, 132, 145, 191, 195, 200, 222, 223

hospitality, xxviii–xxi, 227–33, 268–73; charity as, xix; dimunition of, 229–31; economic function of, xix; and emotions, xxxi, 269, 273; enactment of, 231–32; and friendship, 237–38, 240; and Hindus, 213; instrumentality of, 228; myth of, 227; and potlatch, xxix, 228; and Pukhtunwali, 211; rate of, 270–71; refusal of, 235; and Scripture, xxx; and self-sacrifice, 232, 237; and social organization, 235–36, 268; as symbolic, xxx; and women, 232–33, 271; see also friendship; guest; refuge

hot and cold, symbolism of, 166–67, 183

household: construction of, 218; interior of, 16–21, 186; rental of, 107; theft within, 201

Hsu, F., 249, 268

hujera, 13, 16, 21–24, 173; as church, 225n; and clients, 23, 28; and funerals, 156–57; and groom, 134; and guests, 23, 228–29; performances in, 224; prostitutes in, 202, 220; rank displays in, 213–14, 216; servants in, 105

Huq, General Zia al', 51–52

Ibn Khaldun, 212

Ik, 272

infants, 168–70; abandonment of, 163; death rate of, 163; swaddling of, 168; training of, 170; wet nurse and, 100; see also boys; family; girls

inheritance, 62–63; and tarburwali, 128; and widow remarriage, 128; and women's rights, 62–63, 221

instinct, 252, 256–67, 273; death, 257–61; life, 257–60

Islam: equality in, 213; and funeral, 156; inheritance laws in, 62; and interest, 199; marriage exchanges in, 138–40; and mullahs, 93; orthodoxy in, 226; private property in, 50; and sin; 191, 226; women in, 145, 219–21; see also religious practitioners

Jacobson, D., 228

Jahanzeb, Miangul (Wali of Swat), 42, 46–48, 53

jajmani system, 100

jealousy, 196–98; among boys, 244; in the family, 130, 185–86, 220; in friendship, 242, 247; in Guatemala, 253; and guests, 236; insecurity and, 265, 269; and loss, 266; pride in exciting, 205; and sex, 267

jirga, 75, 79, 86

jora, see dowry

Kabyle, 85, 210

Kajju, Khan, 33

Kakar, S., 268

Kamal, mythical ancestor of Malik khel, 227

Kardiner, A., 162, 163

kham, 76, 89

Khan, Ajab, 107

Khan, Ayub, 42, 53

Khan, Dost Muhammad (king of Afghanistan), 195

Khan, Dost Muhammad (PPP candidate in Swat), 47, 51, 53

Khan, Feteh (prime minister of Afghanistan), 195

Khan, Feteh Muhammad (PPP candidate in Swat), 48, 51, 53–54; lawsuits against, 92

Khan, F. M.: on erosion, 8; on overpopulation, 6–8

Khan, G.: on child raising, 185–86, 189; on honor, 113; on hospitality, 232; on Pukhtun worldview, 55, 93; on theft, 118

Khan, Habibullah, 154

Khan, Muhammad Afzal, 53

Khan, Muhammad Alam, 53

Khan, Muhammad Qamar, xx

Khan, Muhammad Qawi, xvi, xix
Khan, Muhammad Zaman: appearance of, xiv, xvi; dependents and allies of, xix; family of, xv, 64, 151, 177; friendship with, xv, xx–xxi, 229, 246–47; history of, xviii, 64; and work, xviii, 64, 114
Khan, Nisar, 46–47, 53
Khan, Shad Muhammad, xix
Khan, Shahbaz, 154
Khan, Sher Azim, 223, 226
Khan, Umrah (leader of rebels in Jandul), 40–41
Khan, Umrah (Malik *khel* ancestor), 152
Khan, Yakub, 31
Khan, Zaman; *see* Khan, Muhammad Zaman
Khana, Qajira, xv, xvi, xix; and in-laws, 64, 151; and literacy, 177
khans, 21–23, 28; attitudes toward poor, 212–13; attitudes toward work, 103; egoism of, 206; and guests, 228; and land, 90–91; and leadership, 213; political strategies of, 51–53; rights of, 107–9, 171, 201–2; and romance, 223; and school, 176; and violence, 176, 201; *see also* laborers; leaders; Malik *khel*; patron-client relations; rank
Khattak, K.: on the family, 161, 193; on friendship, 240, 247; on greed, 199; on pride, 206; on secrecy, 196; on Swat, 1
Klein, M., 258, 260–61; on the death instinct, 259
Kohistan, 87
Kohistani, 33, 97, 98, 152
Kohnawal, 225
!Kung, 265
Kwakuitl, xxxi

laborers: and compulsory labor, 49, 104, 107, 109; image of, 109, 111–12; landless, 94, 96, 98, 103–4, 111; migration of, 9–10, 48, 193, 198–99; oppression of, 109; shortage of, 10, value system of, 110–11; *see also* economy; khans; patron-client relations; rank
land: affinal rights to, 151, 154; conflict over, 51, 63–64, 74, 112; and crops, 5–8; exile's rights to, 83; leasing of, 65, 103; lineage rights to, 64–66, 91; purchase of, 9, 99, 102, 107; and purdah, 222; redistribution of by PPP, 49; redistribution of by *wesh*, 33–34, 92; reduction of holdings, 91–92; rent on, 103; and revenge, 81; selling of, 65, 109–10, 199; sharecroppers, 103–4; and social structure, 56–57, 62–66, 69; and status, 90–91, 99, 109–10; and tenant's rights, 49–50; *tseri*, 34, 65–66, 86, 91, 102, 154; units of, 102; women's rights to, 126, 140, 191; *see also* agnates; social structure; *tarburwali*
Lange, C. and W. James, 255
Lasch, C., 272
Lazarus, R., 256
Leacock, E., 265
leaders: in boys' gangs, 176; bribes from, 206; land grants to, 91; limits of, 91–92, 206, 215–16; local, 79; among nomads, 89–90; among poor, 110; religious practitioners as, 39, 86; among sedentary agriculturalists, 89; and social structure, 78, 82, 213; and treachery, 193; types of, 87; in wars of expansion, 87; *see also* khans; rank; religious practitioners; warfare
leatherworker, 97, 98, 99, 102; as foster father, 100; symbolic role of, 121; wife of, 100
Leeper, R., 256
Lepcha, 272
Levine, R., 249
levirate, 111, 128, 222
Levi-Strauss, C., xxiv, xxvi, xxvii, 252; on emotion, 248
liff, 79
Lindholm, C., 34, 39, 43, 47, 52, 55, 84, 87, 120, 227, 244; and C. Lindholm, 60, 149
livestock, 6, 12; cooperative herding of, 104–5; pens for, 25; taboos regarding, 167
loans, 117–18; arranging of, 200; and banks, 117; and confidence games, 118; debtor's position, 116–17, 137–38; interest on, 199; intermediaries in, 118, 125; from patron, 216; services as, 124; women as mediators in, 155
Lodi Dynasty, 38
love, *see* romantic love
loyalty, 215–16, 238

MacPherson, C., 80
magic, 135, 167, 227
mahar, 140–41; and endogamy, 143; and friendship ideal, 242; negotiation of, 136; and polygamy, 141; reciprocal image of, 141, 148, 242; rights to, 140, 147–48, 191; and separation, 147; and women's individuality, 147; *see also* marriage
Mahler, M., 263, 264
Mahmat *khel:* and elections, 47, 50–51; leader killed, 45; relations with Malik *khel,* 154; party of, 45, 52–53
Mahmud of Ghazni, 33
Mali, Shaikh, 33, 35
Malik *khel:* age grading of, 214; feud within, 132; genealogy of, 70--72, 98, 152; history of, 27–28, 154; and land grants to affines, 154; marriage alliances of, 61, 144; origin myth of, 227; party of, 45, 47–48; pride of, 218; strength of, 28, 102, 154; weakness of, 91, 154; wedding prestations among, 136–37; *see also* khans
Maloney, C., 198
Marcuse, H., 260–61
Mardan, 198
marriage, 130–50, 111; age at, 131; anti-marriage symbolism, 120, 131, 156; and barter, 116, 142; bride's role in, 134–35, 137; brother and sister divided by, 129; brothers divided by, 120; contradictions of, 147–49; and educated women, 178; endogamy (FBD marriage), 126, 142–43; 143n, 154, 222; exchange at, 136–43, 148; exogamy, 93, 95, 98, 99–100, 139; and go-betweens, 100, 120; groom's role in, 134–35, 137–38; and impotence, 135, 224; and incest, 130; of merchants, 139n; pattern of, 61–62, 142–45; of poor, 97, 111; of professionals, 139n; refusal of, 131; and romance, 224; and separation, 129, 146–47; and shame, 129, 141; and sister exchange, 141–42; and wedding ceremony, 130–36; *see also* affines; bride price; divorce; family; *mahar*
Marri Baluch, 224
Marx, E., 69
Masson, C., 245; on mutilation, 161
Mauss, M., 237
Mead, M., xxxi, 162

mechanic, 96
mediator: Badshah as, 42; barber as, 120–22; bureaucracy as, 51, 96; dancer as, 118–20; and friendship, 241; *jirga* as, 75; leatherworker as, 121–22; levels of, 89; and loans, 117–18, 125; mother's brother as, 151; religious practitioner as, 38, 42, 86, 95–96, 121–23, 159, 227; symbolism of, 118–23; woman as, 155
Meeker, M., 34, 76
men: appearance of, 13–15, 220; behavior of, 174, 188–89; despair of, 192–93; politeness of, 202–3; rivalry of, 126, 243; stoicism of, 156, 191–92; *see also* agnates; family
men's house, *see* hujera
Mernissi, F., 148
Minturn, L. and J. Hitchcock, 171
Mohmand, 68
Montagnais, 265
Montagne, R., 79
mosque, 13, 23–24; equality in, 213; rank in, 214
muleteer, 25, 98–99, 102–3; upward mobility of, 110
mullah, 93; Pukhtun marriage with, 93, 132; *see also* religious practitioners
murder, 60, 67, 159, 191, 234; *see also* revenge; *tarburwali;* violence
Murphy, R., 262; and L. Kasdan, 56, 222

Nakrudin *khel,* 47–48
Naqshabandiyya sect, 94
National Assembly, 47, 51, 53–54
national character, studies of, 162
neighborhood (*palao*), 78, 82, 229
Nevill, R., 41, 245
Newman, R., 175, 192

object-relations, 262–66, 273
oil presser, 96, 98
orphan, 151

Pakistan, 42, 46–48, 53, 92; and martial law, 51–52
palao, see neighborhood
party system, 40, 79–82, 111; affines and, 143, 149, 152; and Berbers, 79; and bloc organization, 68, 79; and fragmentation,

party system (*Continued*)
92–93; history of in Shamizai/Sebujni,
45, 46–47, 50; individuals in, 79; patterning of, 79, 82; resilience of, 52; and
revenge, 80, 82, 87; stagnation of, 81;
third party manipulation in, 40, 74–75,
79–82; and warfare, 83; *see also* elections; political parties; social structure;
tarburwali
patron-client relations, 102–3, 107–12; absence of servility, 213; and Eid homage,
136; and employer-employee relations,
114; and feuds, 51, 75, 235; fluid allegiance in, 215; friendship in, 243; and
hospitality, 228, 231; and loyalty, 102,
216; and market economy, 8–9, 28,
48–49, 96, 110; ritualized, 100, 102; and
sexuality, 223; and warfare, 49; *see also*
economy; khans; laborers; rank
Paul, R., 273
Paz, O., 250
Pehrson, R., 224
Pennell, T.: on adultery, 219; on bride
price, 138; on dervishes, 122; on mother's
influence, 130; on sister exchange, 142
personality theory, 162
Peters, E., 69, 76
Piker, S., 253
Pir Baba, *see* Baba, Pir
Plato, 240
play, 15, 130; and ritual, 266–67
Pocock, D., 100
political parties: Jamaat i Ulema i Islam,
49–51; Muslim League, 48, 53; National
Awami Party, 47, 53; Pakistan National
Alliance, 51, 53–54; Pakistan People's
Party (PPP), 23, 47–51, 53, 107; *see also*
elections; party system
pollution, 97, 212–13
polygamy, 111, 191; and birth rate, 164;
and co-wives' relations, 60, 129; and endogamy (FBD marriage), 143, 143*n*; and
mahar, 141; pattern of, 146; statistics on,
144; *see also* family
population pressure, 6–8; in nomadic societies, 76; in sedentary societies, 76–77
possession, 149–51, 163–64
potter, 96, 98
pride, 205–6, 216–17; bearing and, xx,

217; in evil eye, 198; of women, 148,
175
prostitution, 139, 148, 220
Provincial Assembly, 47, 53–54
Pukhtunwali, 210, 238; function of, 237–38;
learning of, 174; public enactment of,
188–89; *see also* social structure;
worldview
punishment, 172–73, 183, 188, 261; for
breaking purdah, 204, 219–20
purdah, 111; and boys, 173; and educated
women, 178; for engaged couple, 136;
and fieldwork, xv–vi, xix, xxiii; girls in,
15, 175, 181; parameters of, 61, 74, 105;
punishment for breaking, 204, 219–20;
and romance, 223; and social structure,
145, 218–22, 238; and symbolism of
dancer, 120; *see also* women

Rabinow, P., 250
Radcliffe-Brown, A., 248
Rahman, Maulana Abdul, 54
Rahman Baba, *see* Baba, R.
rank: and conquest, 34–35; and friendship,
241; of laborers, 98–100; and land rights,
90–92, 101–2; and social structure,
213–15, 218; *see also*; khans; laborers;
leaders; patron-client relations
Rashid, Qais Abdur, 70
records, xxi
reference, terms of, 57–59
refuge, 233–35; and altruism, 269; and
army recruitment, 235; and Pukhtunwali,
211; and revenge, 234; and warfare, 84,
234–35; offered to women, 84, 127–28,
151, 234; refused women, 147–48; *see
also*; friendship; guest; hospitality
Reich, W., 266, 267; on punishment, 261
Reina, R., 253
religious practitioners: and *baraka*, 35, 39,
94; as beggars, 227; categories of, 35,
93–94; and charity, 117, 227; and class,
213; and elections, 37, 49–50, 54; as
guardians of goods, 85; *imams*, 49–50,
54, 93, 98, 99, 122, 156; incorporation
into Pukhtun, 154; as leaders, 38–39, 86,
92, 94–96; as mediators, 38, 42, 86,
95–96, 121–23, 159, 227; modern role
of, 49–50; *sahibzadas*, 27, 94; shrines of,

13, 95, 121, 226; and Sufism, 94, 121, 225–27; symbolism of, 121–23, 227; and *tseri* land, 34, 86; and unorthodoxy, 35, 225; and war, 35, 38–39, 86; and worship, 225–27; *see also* Allah; dervish; Islam; leaders; *mullah*; worship

research methods, xxii, xxiv–xix; constraints of, xxi–xxiv

respect, 237–38; for elders, 214–15; for husband's family, 151; for khans, 213–15; for women, 163, 214

revenge, 211, 237; and affines, 67, 80, 155; limits of, 76, 89; in nuclear family, 66–67; and poor, 75; and promiscuous woman, 60, 147; and refuge, 234; and ritual war, 83; and social structure, 68, 80, 87; in various societies, 69; and warfare, 83–84; and wife, 60, 67, 126, 159, 203, 219–20; *see also* agnates; murder; *tarburwali*; violence

Robarchek, C., 272

Robertson-Smith, W., 56

Roheim, G., 268

Roland, A., 268, 270n

romantic love: in anthropology, 250–51; and death, 121, 224; and friendship, 226, 238, 240; and homosexuality, 224; and purdah, 221; and sex, 226; and *shahkhel*, 121; stories of, 223–24; and strangers, 223; in United States, 272; women's role in, 223; and worship, 225; *see also* friendship; sex

Rosenblatt, P., 250–51

Sadullah (Mastan Mullah), 41, 94

Sahlins, M., 87, 244; on social structure, 69, 81

Salzman, P.: on complementary opposition, 80; on rank, 212; on Swat, 69, 79

Sangota school, 177

Saraktsani, 253

Schachter, S. and J. Singer, 256

Schomberg, R.: on the party system, 40; on treachery, 193

Scott, J., 49; and B. Kerkvliet, 49

self-image: of poor, 109–12; of Pukhtun, 109–12, 125, 192, 210–11, 242; of religious practitioners, 94; *see also* worldview

Semai, 272–73

separation, 259–60, 263, 265–68, 272–73

servant, 105; theft by, 201

sex: and antagonism, 145, 148, 160; and consummation of marriage, 134–35; and father's brother's daughter, 143; and friendship, 226–27; impotence, 100, 135, 148, 224; payment for, 137, 140, 242; and pleasure, 166; and promiscuity, 60, 100, 111, 120–22, 147, 195, 204, 225; and sadism, 148, 204; and seduction, 111, 223; taboos, 164, 166; talk about, 173, 220; theories of, 254, 257–58, 261, 265, 267; women's desire for, 166–67, 219, 223; *see also* romantic love

Shagufta, 177

Shah, Nadir, 37

shame: and conformity, 204; of customer, 115; and debt, 117–18; and funeral, 157; of groom, 134; of host, 237; of husband, 129, 141, 147, 151; of parents, 170, 172; and sexual deviance, 224; training by, 174, 181, 188; and weakness, 205–6, 236–37; of wife, 145–47; of women teachers, 178

Shamizai-Sebujni, 43–54

Shin Bagh, xvi, 7, 9–29

shoemaker, 96, 98

shopkeeper, 96, 98; and loans, 117

shops, 23–25

Sillitoe, P., 84

Singh, Ranjit, 37

slave, 105

smith, *see* carpenter

Smith, M., 253

social structure, xxvi–xxvii, 56, 69–93, 111; and class, 92, 110; and complementary opposition, xvii, 69, 78–80, 87; and dyads, 82, 116; and emotional structure, xxxi, 126, 249–50, 252, 268–73; and exchange, 114, 125; and expansion, 87, 244; fragmentation of, 34–35, 37–38, 52, 186; and friendship, 245–47, 251, 255, 268, 273; history of, 37–38, 52–54, 92, 212; and hospitality, 235–36, 273; and instrumentality, 81; models of, 67–69, 79, 87, 89; of nomads, 76–78, 89; pervasiveness of, xxx; and Pukhtunwali, 211–38; and scarcity, 76; of sedentary

social structure (*Continued*)
agriculturalists, 76–78; and triads, 40, 74–75, 78, 82, 86; unity in, 37–38, 51–52, 80, 86; women as contradiction in, 148, 159; and worldview, 188–89; *see also* agnates; family; land; party system; Pukhtunwali; *tarburwali*; violence
sociobiology, 264–65
Spindler, G., 248, 249
Spooner, B., 89, 98
Stayton, M., M. Ainsworth, and M. Main, 264
Stein, A., 32, 33
Strathern, M., 155
succubus, 270
suicide, 270
superego, 258–59, 266
Swat, xvi, 2–9; history of, 32–43, 46–54
Swidler, N., 90

tal, see ward
tailor, 96, 98
Tapirapé, 265
tarburwali, 57, 61, 66, 111, 193; and alliance, 61–62, 80; cases of, 56, 67, 67n, 74–75, 235; and distance, 142; and ecology, 78; and feud, 77, 82, 86–87; and inheritance, 128; and land, 74–75; and marriage with father's brother's daughter, 143, 143n; and mediation, 86, 89; and party system, 79, 82; and revenge, 74, 80, 82, 87, and social structure, 67–68, 76, 78, 80; in Swat, 90; and warfare, 82–83; 87; *see also* agnates; land; murder; party system; revenge; social structure; violence
taxation, 35, 38, 40, 45, 86; in Upper Swat, 90
teacher, 96
teknonymy, 214
temper: of children, 168–70; 188; of men, 169, 192
Thailand, 253–54
theft: as balancing of accounts, 64; and begging, 118; by children, 172, 183, 188, 200–1; from guest, 234; in household, 201; by professional thieves, 201; by servants, 201; by women, xviii, 126, 201
Titmuss, R., 207

Trimingham, J., 94
troubadors, 224
trust: absence of, 160, 268–69; in Erikson's theory, 263, 269; and friendship, 240–41, 254; and guest, 236
Turnbull, C., 272
Turner, V., 255; on emotions, 252–53; on power of the weak, 151
twins, as metaphors for friends, 240–43

United States, 272

violence: to animals, 203–4; of brothers, 62–63, 66–67; of brothers to sisters, 173; of children, 75, 172, 176, 186, 202; to children, 170, 171–72, 186, 203; of father and son, 66–67; of husband and wife, 66–67, 145, 148, 159, 189–91, 203; of men, 56, 57, 67n, 74–75, 202–3, 235; pleasure of, 171–72, 202; and poor, 75, 203; and scarcity, 76–78; of son to mother, 130; structure of, 56, 76–78, 82, 87–88; of women, 15–16, 191, 203; *see also* murder; revenge; social structure; *tarburwali*; warfare

Wadud, Miangul Abdul (Badshah of Swat), 41–46, 52, 86, 94–95; and class, 91; and dervishes, 122, 213; on the khans of Upper Swat, 43–45; on poverty, 8; on *tarburwali*, 56; on Yusufzai genealogy, 70
Wali of Swat, *see* Jahanzeb, Miangul
Wallace, A., 162, 249
Warburton, R.: on child training, 193; on friendship, 244, 245
ward (*tal*): exchange in, 136, 152; gangs of boys in, 175–76; hospitality in 228–29; property of, 25, 27; services in, 102; social structure of, 78–79, 82, 85
warfare, 31, 83–86; defensive, 37–41, 86; expansionist, 33–34, 87, 111, 201; and land pressure, 86; and marriage alliances, 61, 142; Pukhtun against religious lineage, 35; Pukhtun against tenants, 49; and refuge, 83–84, 86, 235; rewards of, 84–85; ritual, 83; suppression of, 47; and taking women, 141, 145; and treachery, 83–84, and village nucleation, 27; *see also* leaders; violence

weaver, 96–98

White, L., 248

Wilson, E., 264–65

Winnicott, D.: on anxiety, 262; on death, 258; on dualism, 263

Wolf, E., 89, 251

women: ambiguity of, 148–49, 155, 159, 243; appearance of, 13–15, 220; death rate of, 159; debasement of, 130, 148–49, 155, 159, 167, 220–22, 269; deference of, 173, 220; education of, 177–78; and hoarding, 200; individuality of, 141–42, 145, 147–48, 155, 221; men's ideal of, 145, 151, 189–91; and patrilineage, 126–27, 129, 145, 191, 222; as pawns, 129, 142, 220; power of, 129, 141, 147, 149, 200, 222; separation from husband of, 128–29, 146–48, 151, 234; and sex, 148, 167, 204, 219, 223; unity of, 189–91, 203, 271–72; work of, 19, 163, 189; see also affines; agnates; family; purdah

worldview, 112, 181, 207, 289–295; and abstract thought, 179; and conformity, 204–5; and egalitarianism, 55, 117–18, 122, 124, 183, 211–13, 218, 237–38, 242; and hoarding, 119–200; and independence, 114, 145, 205–7, 242; and insecurity, 189; and marriage, 129, 146–49, 155; and narcissism, 269; and poverty, 110–12, 212–13; and suspicion, 193–96; training for, 174, 181–83, 186–89; and weakness, 159–69; of women, 175, 189–91

worship, 225–27, 238, 240; see also friendship; religious practitioners

Yanomamo, 265

Yarkand, China, 198

Yusufzai: genealogy, 70; history, 33, 35–37

Zinoviev, A.: on science, xiii; on social structure, 55

Zorastrianism, 32

Zuni, xxi